Praise for Ernest Shackleton's
SOUTH

"Sir Ernest Shackleton's book adds another to those priceless records of high human quality, and the story that it tells, aside from its scientific value, will have many readers who will find its pages enthralling and deeply moving."

—*The New York Times*
January 1, 1920

"The story of the voyage that six men made in an open boat across eight hundred miles of the roughest water in the world, to bring relief to the twenty-two companions who remained on the island, rivals the best sea tale ever written."

—*Springfield Republican*
March 7, 1920

ABOUT THE AUTHOR

SIR ERNEST SHACKLETON, C.V.O. (1874–1922) is regarded as perhaps the greatest of all Antarctic explorers. He was a member of Captain Scott's 1901–1903 expedition to the South Pole, and in 1907 led his own expedition on the whaler *Nimrod,* coming within ninety-seven miles of the South Pole, the feat for which he was knighted. The events of that expedition are chronicled in his first book, *The Heart of the Antarctic.* He is considered one of England's greatest heroes for his actions during the ill-fated *Endurance* expedition, leading all of his men to safety after being marooned for two years on the polar ice. *South* is his recounting of this expedition. He died at the age of forty-seven during his final expedition, and was buried in the whaler's cemetery on South Georgia Island in the South Atlantic.

SOUTH

THE *ENDURANCE* EXPEDITION

BY

Sir Ernest Shackleton, C.V.O.

ILLUSTRATED

Photographs by Frank Hurley

A SIGNET BOOK

SIGNET
Published by New American Library, a division of
Penguin Putnam Inc., 375 Hudson Street,
New York, New York 10014, U.S.A.
Penguin Books Ltd, 27 Wrights Lane,
London W8 5TZ, England
Penguin Books Australia Ltd,
Ringwood, Victoria, Australia
Penguin Books Canada Ltd, 10 Alcorn Avenue,
Toronto, Ontario, Canada M4V 3B2
Penguin Books (N.Z.) Ltd, 182–190 Wairau Road,
Auckland 10, New Zealand

Penguin Books Ltd, Registered Offices:
Harmondsworth, Middlesex, England

Published by Signet, an imprint of New American Library,
a division of Penguin Putnam Inc.
First published by William Heinemann, London, 1919
Macmillan, New York, 1920

First Signet Printing, April 1999
10 9 8 7 6

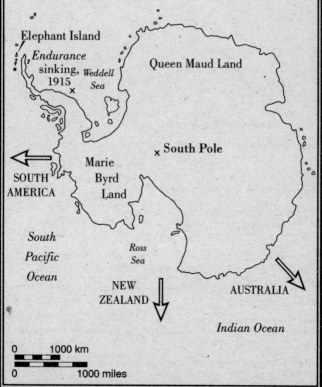

ANTARCTICA
SOUTH
The *Endurance* Expedition

AFRICA

South Georgia Island

South Atlantic Ocean

Elephant Island

Endurance sinking, 1915

Weddell Sea

Queen Maud Land

SOUTH AMERICA

× South Pole

Marie Byrd Land

South Pacific Ocean

Ross Sea

NEW ZEALAND

AUSTRALIA

Indian Ocean

0   1000 km

0   1000 miles

CONTENTS

INTRODUCTION

BRAVERY. Heroism. Fearlessness. Honor. We love to read about these larger-than-life human qualities that are invoked more often than not during life-and-death situations—while we are safe at home in a comfortable chair, or while we are commuting to or from work, or on vacation when we are least distracted by the rigors of daily life. For some reason, we cannot get enough of these accounts about disaster and survival, about those who have exposed themselves either willingly or accidentally to incredible dangers and risk, and about those who, even with fortune and chance against them, somehow survive despite unbeatable odds. What *is* it, after all, that compels the most daring and adventurous among us to risk our lives, to expose ourselves to the harshest conditions and confront the impossible? And what is it about these endeavors that so intrigues us? Why are these accounts so much fun to read?

At the turn of the last century, during what has been called the Heroic Age, the exploratory instinct peaked in what became a remarkable succession of almost suicidal expeditions. From the mid-nineteenth century on, the North and South Poles became the Holy Grail of explorers, along with the source of the Nile, the quest to summit the highest mountain in the world, and to plumb the bottom of the sea. It was still possible, then, to explore unexplored locations on Earth. In this century, when we felt we had explored Earth enough, we sought to visit the Moon and space. But just as America and Russia were engaged in a race to be the first to put a man into orbit, and then a flag on the moon, so were England and America racing to be the first to set foot on the poles. While America triumphed at the North Pole, England—a dying empire—failed to reach the South Pole first, losing out to Norway.

In modern times, outdoor enthusiasts of all kinds have the choice to equip themselves with sophisticated communication systems and navigational aids: global positioning system satellite trackers, emergency beacons, radar and sonar, Loran, and cell phones—which not only help to determine geographic location, but let others know where we are in case we need to be rescued. It is difficult to imagine the time when sophisticated technology did not exist. In 1914—the year when Sir Ernest Shackleton set out on his famous expedition—the telephone was not even forty years old and was still decades away from going cellular, Commercial radio was not to exist for another eight years. And only two years earlier, our mightiest modern example of hubris—the unsinkable H.M.S. *Titanic*—hit an iceberg and sank in two hours. The loss of life was incredible, shattering the confidence and conviction of a people who believed that life in the twentieth century would continue to improve as technological advancements were made.

Sir Ernest Shackleton was born on February 15, 1874, in County Kildare, Ireland. His family moved to Dublin and then to London, where his father became a doctor and where Ernest attended Dulwich College (P. G. Wodehouse, creator of Jeeves, is Dulwich's other famous alumnus). He left London to become a qualified master mariner in the merchant fleet. He was a member of Robert Falcon Scott's 1901–1903 Antarctic expedition. From 1907 to 1909, he led his own expedition on the whaler *Nimrod* and succeeded in getting as close as ninety-seven miles to the South Pole. Shackleton was knighted for his "Farthest South" efforts. While the Norwegian Roald Amundsen and the English Scott had reached the South Pole by 1912, Scott and his men perishing in the quest, Shackleton set out on the last great explorer's quest—to traverse and chart the mostly unexplored Antarctic continent on foot, something no one had done. As an experienced Antarctic explorer, Shackleton knew what he needed in the way of men and supplies, and spent years soliciting patrons for financial support to fund the expedition. He eventually purchased a 300-ton wooden barquentine, which he called *Endurance,* from a Norwegian shipyard. It was built to withstand the ice, rigged with sails, and outfitted with a coal-fired steam engine. He gathered other Antarctic veterans—scientists, sailors, a photographer, a cook, a navigator, and a carpenter. He also brought with him Canadian sled dogs and skis. Shackleton chose his crew wisely, for he knew from experience that each of them would be put to the ultimate test.

Endurance set sail from London on August 1, 1914, and almost never made it out of British waters. Britain mobilized for World War I on August 4, but the Admiralty gave Shackleton permission to proceed. *Endurance* arrived at the South Georgia Island whaling station, by way of Buenos Aires, on November 5. The ship then encountered heavy pack ice on December 7, and finally became trapped in the Weddell Sea, very near the Antarctic continent, on January 18, 1915. The ship drifted for ten months, encased in an ice floe, until it was crushed on October 26 and finally sank on November 21. After gathering supplies from the doomed *Endurance,* the crew set up camp on the ice. Their ice floe continued to drift northward and dangerously began to melt and break up. On April 9, 1916, Shackleton and his crew resolved to set out for Elephant Island in the three small lifeboats they had rescued from the ship. Three days later they became the first humans to set foot there. On April 24, Shackleton, along with five select men, headed for South Georgia— eight hundred miles away from Elephant Island. They set out in the *James Caird,* the largest of the lifeboats, and after encountering sixty-foot waves with little food and sleep, arrived back at South Georgia sixteen days later. But the whaling station they were hoping to reach was on the other side of the island. So they crossed the uncharted glaciers, crevasses, and mountainous interior of the island, and finally arrived at the whaling station, much to the astonishment of the workers there who had seen them off eighteen months earlier. The twenty-two men they left behind on Elephant Island survived, somehow, for another four months before they were eventually rescued.

Shackleton dictated the account of his expedition to a New Zealand journalist not long after his return. *South* was published by Heinemann in England in 1919, and then by Macmillan in the United States in 1920. It was an instant success. Included in *South* were the wonderful photographs of Frank Hurley, some of which are reproduced here from the original glass plate negatives taken by Hurley on the expedition. Shackleton did not live long after the publication of *South*. In 1921, he gathered together some of the men who had accompanied him on the *Endurance* voyage for what would become his final expedition on a ship called the *Quest*. Soon after the *Quest* arrived at South Georgia Island in January 1922, Shackleton suffered a massive heart attack and died. He was forty-seven years old. He was buried there, near Antarctica, with which his name is synonymous.

It is difficult to put the hardships of Shackleton's men into a contemporary perspective. The crew of the *Endurance* subsisted on meager rations, were constantly freezing and soaked to the bone, went without bathing for nearly a year, and wore their clothes until they were practically rags. They were forced to eat penguin and seal blubber—sometimes raw—and lived in a hut fashioned from two overturned rowboats for over four months. They traveled eight hundred miles over the open seas navigating by sextant and dead reckoning in little more than a large rowboat. They endured privation and hardships difficult to comprehend. Yet the entire crew survived, and they seemed to have remained in remarkably good spirits during their ordeal—an ordeal that is enough to make the reader of this incredible account hesitate to complain about ever being cold or hungry again.

South is certainly one of the most thrilling adventure stories ever written—as thrilling as the assault on Mt. Everest chronicled by Jon Krakauer in *Into Thin Air,* or the experience of the sailors who perish in Sebastian Junger's *The Perfect Storm.* But *South* is much more than a thrilling adventure story; more than the "safe risk" thrills of riding a rollercoaster or watching a terrifying horror movie. It is an affirmation of our inability to conquer nature and of our innate instinct to survive. Even eighty years after its initial publication, *South* provides us with an accurate perspective from which to judge our shrinking world. It is a window to a lost era of Victorian mores and Edwardian ideals, and an affirmation of the optimism that was quickly erased by the calamitous events of World War I—oblivious to these men who had left civilization behind. But more than anything, *South* is an invitation to explore the world, to seek and discover, to venture out into the unknown confident that even once we safely return to the comfort of our homes, the only thing on our minds is the next adventure.

—The Editors
New American Library
January 1999

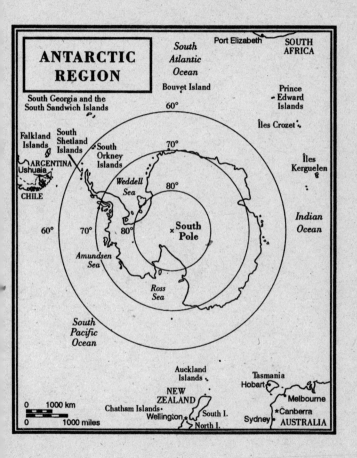

PREFACE

AFTER THE CONQUEST of the South Pole by Amundsen, who, by a narrow margin of days only, was in advance of the British Expedition under Scott, there remained but one great main object of Antarctic journeyings—the crossing of the South Polar continent from sea to sea.

When I returned from the *Nimrod* Expedition on which we had to turn back from our attempt to plant the British flag on the South Pole, being beaten by stress of circumstances within ninety-seven miles of our goal, my mind turned to the crossing of the continent, for I was morally certain that either Amundsen or Scott would reach the Pole on our own route or a parallel one. After hearing of the Norwegian success I began to make preparations to start a last great journey—so that the first crossing of the last continent should be achieved by a British Expedition.

We failed in this object, but the story of our attempt is the subject for the following pages, and I think that though failure in the actual accomplishment must be recorded, there are chapters in this book of high adventure, strenuous days, lonely nights, unique experiences, and, above all, records of unflinching determination, supreme loyalty, and generous self-sacrifice on the part of my men which, even in these days that have witnessed the sacrifices of nations and regardlessness of self on the part of individuals, still will be of interest to readers who now turn gladly from the red horror of war and the strain of the last five years to read, perhaps with more understanding minds, the tale of the White Warfare of the South. The struggles, the disappointments, and the endurance of this small party of Britishers, hidden away for nearly two years in the fastnesses of the Polar ice, striving to carry out the ordained task and ignorant of the crises through which the world was passing, make a story which is unique in the history of Antarctic exploration.

Owing to the loss of the *Endurance* and the disaster to the *Aurora,* certain documents relating mainly to the organization and preparation of the Expedition have been lost; but, anyhow, I had no intention of presenting a detailed account of the scheme of preparation, storing, and other necessary but, to the general reader, unimportant affairs, as since the beginning of this century every book on Antarctic exploration has dealt fully with this matter. I therefore briefly place before you the inception and organization of the Expedition, and insert here the copy of the program which I prepared in order to arouse the interest of the general public in the Expedition.

The Transcontinental Party.

"The first crossing of the Antarctic continent from sea to sea via the Pole, apart from its historic value, will be a journey of great scientific importance.

"The distance will be roughly 1800 miles, and the first half of this, from the Weddell Sea to the Pole, will be over unknown ground. Every step will be an advance in geographical science. It will be learned whether the great Victoria chain of mountains, which has been traced from the Ross Sea to the Pole, extends across the continent and thus links up (except for the ocean break) with the Andes of South America, and whether the great plateau around the Pole dips gradually towards the Weddell Sea.

"Continuous magnetic observations will be taken on the journey. The route will lead towards the Magnetic Pole, and the determination of the dip of the magnetic needle will be of importance in practical magnetism. The meteorological conditions will be carefully noted, and this should help to solve many of our weather problems.

"The glaciologist and geologist will study ice formations and the nature of the mountains, and this report will prove of great scientific interest.

Scientific Work by Other Parties

"While the Transcontinental party is carrying out, for the British Flag, the greatest Polar journey ever attempted, the other parties will be engaged in important scientific work.

"Two sledging parties will operate from the base on the Weddell Sea. One will travel westwards towards Graham Land, making observations, collecting geological specimens, and proving whether there are mountains in that region linked up with those found on the other side of the Pole.

"Another party will travel eastward toward Enderby Land, carrying out a similar program, and a third, remaining at the base, will study the fauna of the land and sea, and the meteorological conditions.

"From the Ross Sea base, on the other side of the Pole, another party will push southward and will probably await the arrival of the Transcontinental party at the top of the Beardmore Glacier, near Mount Buckley, where the first seams of coal were discovered in the Antarctic. This region is of great importance to the geologist, who will be enabled to read much of the history of the Antarctic in the rocks.

"Both the ships of the Expedition will be equipped for dredging, sounding, and every variety of hydrographical work. The Weddell Sea ship will endeavor to trace the unknown coastline of Graham Land, and from both the vessels, with their scientific staffs, important results may be expected.

"The several shore parties and the two ships will thus carry out geographical and scientific work on a scale and over an area never before attempted by any one Polar expedition.

"This will be the first use of the Weddell Sea as a base for exploration, and all the parties will open up vast stretches of unknown land. It is appropriate that this work should be carried out under the British Flag, since the whole of the area southward to the Pole is British territory. In July 1908, Letters Patent were issued under the Great Seal declaring that the Governor of the Falkland Islands should be the Governor of Graham Land (which forms the western side of the Weddell Sea), and another section of the same proclamation defines the area of British territory as 'situated in the South Atlantic Ocean to the south of the 50th parallel of south latitude, and lying between 20 degrees and 80 degrees west longitude.' Reference to a map will show that this includes the area in which the present Expedition will work.

How the Continent will be crossed.

"The Weddell Sea ship, with all the members of the Expedition operating from that base, will leave Buenos Aires in October 1914, and endeavor to land in November in latitude 78 degrees south.

"Should this be done, the Transcontinental party will set out on their 1800-mile journey at once, in the hope of accomplishing the march across the Pole and reaching the Ross Sea base in five months. Should the landing be made too late in the season, the party will go into winter quarters, lay out depots during the autumn and the following spring, and as early as possible in 1915 set out on the journey.

"The Transcontinental party will be led by Sir Ernest Shackleton, and will consist of six men. It will take 100 dogs with sledges, and two motor sledges with aerial propellers. The equipment will embody everything that the experience of the leader and his expert advisers can suggest. When this party has reached the area of the Pole, after covering 800 miles of unknown ground, it will strike due north towards the head of the Beardmore Glacier, and there it is hoped to meet the outcoming party from the Ross Sea. Both will join up and make for the Ross Sea base, where the previous Expedition had its winter quarters.

"In all, fourteen men will be landed by the *Endurance* on the Weddell Sea. Six will set out on the Transcontinental journey, three will go westward, three eastward, and two remain at the base carrying on the work already outlined.

"The *Aurora* will land six men at the Ross Sea base. They will lay down depots on the route of the Transcontinental party, and make a march south to assist that party, and to make geological and other observations as already described.

"Should the Transcontinental party succeed, as is hoped, in crossing during the first season, its return to civilization may be expected about April 1915. The other sections in April 1916.

The Ships of the Expedition.

"The two ships for the Expedition have now been selected.

"The *Endurance,* the ship which will take the Transcontinental party to the Weddell Sea, and will afterwards explore along an unknown coastline, is a new vessel, specially constructed for Polar work under the supervision of a committee of Polar explorers. She was built by Christensen, the famous Norwegian constructor of sealing vessels, at Sandefjord. She is barquentine rigged, and has triple expansion engines giving her a speed under steam of nine to ten knots. To enable her to stay longer at sea, she will carry oil fuel as well as coal. She is of about 350 tons, and built of selected pine, oak, and greenheart. This fine vessel, equipped, has cost the Expedition £14,000.

"The *Aurora,* the ship which will take out the Ross Sea party, has been bought from Dr. Mawson. She is similar in all respects to the *Terra Nova,* of Captain Scott's last Expedition. She had extensive alterations made by the Government authorities in Australia to fit her for Dr. Mawson's Expedition, and is now at Hobart, Tasmania, where the Ross Sea party will join her in October next."

* * *

I started the preparations in the middle of 1913, but no public announcement was made until January 13, 1914. For the last six months of 1913 I was engaged in the necessary preliminaries, solid mule work, showing nothing particular to interest the public, but essential for an Expedition that had to have a ship on each side of the Continent, with a land journey of eighteen hundred miles to be made, the first nine hundred miles to be across an absolutely unknown land mass.

On January 1, 1914, having received a promised financial support sufficient to warrant the announcement of the Expedition, I made it public.

The first result of this was a flood of applications from all classes of the community to join the adventure. I received nearly five thousand applications, and out of these were picked fifty-six men.

In March, to my great disappointment and anxiety, the promised financial help did not materialize, and I was now faced with the fact that I had contracted for a ship and stores, and had engaged the staff, and I was not in possession of funds to meet these liabilities. I immediately set about appealing for help, and met with generous response from all sides. I cannot here give the names of all who supported my application, but whilst taking this opportunity of thanking every one for their support, which came from parts as far apart as the interior of China, Japan, New Zealand, and Australia, I must particularly refer to the munificent donation of £24,000 from the late Sir James Caird, and to one of £10,000 from the British Government. I must also thank Mr. Dudley Docker, who enabled me to complete the purchase of the *Endurance,* and Miss Elizabeth Dawson Lambton, who since 1901 has always been a firm friend to Antarctic exploration, and who again, on this occasion, assisted largely. The Royal Geographical Society made a grant of £1000; and last, but by no means least, I take this opportunity of tendering my grateful thanks to Dame Janet Stancomb Wills, whose generosity enabled me to equip the *Endurance* efficiently, especially as regards boats (which boats were the means of our ultimate safety), and who not only, at the inception of the Expedition, gave financial help, but also continued it through the dark days when we were overdue, and funds were required to meet the need of the dependents of the Expedition.

The only return and privilege an explorer has in the way of acknowledgment for the help accorded him is to record on the discovered lands the names of those to whom the Expedition owes its being.

Owing to the exigencies of the war the publication of this book has been long delayed, and the detailed maps must come with the scientific monographs. I have the honor to place on the new land the names of the above and other generous donors to the Expedition. The two hundred miles of new coastline I have called Caird Coast. Also, as a more personal note, I named the three ship's boats, in which we ultimately escaped from the grip of the ice, after the three principal donors to the Expedition—the *James Caird,* the *Stancomb Wills,* and the *Dudley Docker.* The two last-named are still on the desolate sandy spit of Elephant Island, where under their shelter twenty-two of my comrades eked out a bare existence for four and a half months.

The *James Caird* is now in Liverpool, having been brought home from South Georgia after her adventurous voyage across the sub-Antarctic ocean.

Most of the Public Schools of England and Scotland helped the Expedition to purchase the dog teams, and I named a dog after each school that helped. But apart from these particular donations I again thank the many people who assisted us.

So the equipment and organization went on. I purchased the *Aurora* from Sir Douglas Mawson, and arranged for

Mackintosh to go to Australia and take charge of her, there
sending sledges, equipment, and most of the stores from this
side, but depending somewhat on the sympathy and help
of Australia and New Zealand for coal and certain other
necessities, knowing that previously these two countries had
always generously supported the exploration of what one
might call their hinterland.

Towards the end of July all was ready, when suddenly the
war clouds darkened over Europe.

It had been arranged for the *Endurance* to proceed to
Cowes, to be inspected by His Majesty on the Monday of
Cowes week. But on Friday I received a message to say that
the King would not be able to go to Cowes. My readers will
remember how suddenly came the menace of war. Naturally
both my comrades and I were greatly exercised as to the prob-
able outcome of the danger threatening the peace of the world.

We sailed from London on Friday, August 1, 1914, and
anchored off Southend all Saturday. On Sunday afternoon I
took the ship off Margate, growing hourly more anxious as
the ever-increasing rumors spread; and on Monday morning
I went ashore and read in the morning paper the order for
general mobilization.

I immediately went on board and mustered all hands and
told them that I proposed to send a telegram to the Admiralty offering the ships, stores, and, if they agreed, our own
services to the country in the event of war breaking out. All
hands immediately agreed, and I sent off a telegram in
which everything was placed at the disposal of the Admiralty. We only asked that, in the event of the declaration of
war, the Expedition might be considered as a single unit, so
as to preserve its homogeneity. There were enough trained
and experienced men amongst us to man a destroyer. Within
an hour I received a laconic wire from the Admiralty saying
"Proceed." Within two hours a longer wire came from Mr.
Winston Churchill, in which we were thanked for our offer,

and saying that the authorities desired that the Expedition, which had the full sanction and support of the Scientific and Geographical Societies, should go on.

So, according to these definite instructions, the *Endurance* sailed to Plymouth. On Tuesday the King sent for me and handed me the Union Jack to carry on the Expedition. That night, at midnight, war broke out. On the following Saturday, August 8, the *Endurance* sailed from Plymouth, obeying the direct orders of the Admiralty. I make particular reference to this phase of the Expedition as I am aware that there was a certain amount of criticism of the Expedition having left the country, and regarding this I wish further to add that the preparation of the Expedition had been proceeding for over a year, and large sums of money had been spent. We offered to give the Expedition up without even consulting the donors of this money, and but a few thought that the war would last through these five years and involve the whole world. The Expedition was not going on a peaceful cruise to the South Sea Islands, but to a most dangerous, difficult, and strenuous work that has nearly always involved a certain percentage of loss of life. Finally, when the Expedition did return, practically the whole of those members who had come unscathed through the dangers of the Antarctic took their places in the wider field of battle, and the percentage of casualties amongst the members of this Expedition is high.

The voyage out to Buenos Aires was uneventful, and on October 26 we sailed from that port for South Georgia, the most southerly outpost of the British Empire. Here, for a month, we were engaged in final preparation. The last we heard of the war was when we left Buenos Aires. Then the Russian Steam-Roller was advancing. According to many the war would be over within six months. And so we left, not without regret that we could not take our place there, but secure in the knowledge that we were taking part in a strenuous campaign for the credit of our country.

Apart from private individuals and societies I here acknowledge most gratefully the assistance rendered by the Dominion Government of New Zealand and the Commonwealth Government of Australia at the start of the Ross Sea section of the Expedition; and to the people of New Zealand and the Dominion Government I tender my most grateful thanks for their continued help, which was invaluable during the dark days before the relief of the Ross Sea Party.

Mr. James Allen (acting Premier), the late Mr. McNab (Minister of Marine), Mr. Leonard Tripp, Mr. Mabin, and Mr. Toogood, and many others have laid me under a debt of gratitude that can never be repaid.

This is also the opportunity for me to thank the Uruguayan Government for their generous assistance in placing the government trawler, *Instituto de Pesca,* for the second attempt at the relief of my men on Elephant Island.

Finally, it was the Chilean Government that was directly responsible for the rescue of my comrades. This southern Republic was unwearied in its efforts to make a successful rescue, and the gratitude of our whole party is due to them. I especially mention the sympathetic attitude of Admiral Muñoz Hurtado, head of the Chilean Navy, and Captain Luis Pardo, who commanded the *Yelcho* on our last and successful venture.

Sir Daniel Gooch came with us as far as South Georgia. I owe him my special thanks for his help with the dogs, and we all regretted losing his cheery presence when we sailed for the South.

SOUTH

THE STORY OF SHACKLETON'S LAST EXPEDITION 1914–1917

CHAPTER I

INTO THE WEDDELL SEA

I HAD DECIDED to leave South Georgia about December 5, and in the intervals of final preparation scanned again the plans for the voyage to winter quarters. What welcome was the Weddell Sea preparing for us? The whaling captains at South Georgia were generously ready to share with me their knowledge of the waters in which they pursued their trade, and, while confirming earlier information as to the extreme severity of the ice conditions in this sector of the Antarctic, they were able to give advice that was worth attention.

It will be convenient to state here briefly some of the considerations that weighed with me at that time and in the weeks that followed. I knew that the ice had come far north that season, and, after listening to the suggestions of the whaling captains, had decided to steer to the South Sandwich Group, round Ultima Thule, and work as far to the eastward as the fifteenth meridian west longitude before pushing south. The whalers emphasized the difficulty of getting through the ice in the neighborhood of the South Sandwich Group. They told me they had often seen the floes come right up to the group in the summertime, and they thought the Expedition would have to push through heavy pack in order to reach the Weddell Sea. Probably the best time to get into the Weddell Sea would be the end of February or the beginning of March. The whalers had gone right round the South Sandwich Group and they were familiar with the conditions. The predictions they made had induced me to take the deck-load of coal, for if we had to fight our way through to Coats' Land we would need every ton of fuel the ship could carry.

I hoped that by first moving to the east as far as the fifteenth meridian west we would be able to go south through looser ice, pick up Coats' Land and finally reach Vahsel Bay, where Filchner made his attempt at landing in 1912. Two considerations were occupying my mind at this juncture. I was anxious for certain reasons to winter the *Endurance* in the Weddell Sea, but the difficulty of finding a safe harbor might be very great. If no safe harbor could be found, the ship must winter at South Georgia. It seemed to me hopeless now to think of making the journey across the continent in the first summer, as the season was far advanced and the ice conditions were likely to prove unfavorable. In view of the possibility of wintering the ship in the ice, we took extra clothing from the stores at the various stations in South Georgia.

The other question that was giving me anxious thought was the size of the shore party. If the ship had to go out during the winter, or if she broke away from winter quarters, it would be preferable to have only a small, carefully selected party of men ashore after the hut had been built and the stores landed. These men could proceed to lay out depots by man-haulage and make short journeys with the dogs, training them for the long early march in the following spring. The majority of the scientific men would live aboard the ship, where they could do their work under good conditions. They would be able to make short journeys if required, using the *Endurance* as a base. All these plans were based on an expectation that the finding of winter quarters was likely to be difficult. If a really safe base could be established on the continent, I would adhere to the original program of sending one party to the south, one to the west round the head of the Weddell Sea towards Graham Land, and one to the east towards Enderby Land.

We had worked out details of distances, courses, stores required, and so forth. Our sledging ration, the result of experience as well as close study, was perfect. The dogs gave promise, after training, of being able to cover fifteen to twenty miles a day with loaded sledges. The transcontinental journey, at this rate, should be completed in 120 days unless some unforeseen obstacle intervened. We longed keenly for the day when we could begin this march, the last great adventure in the history of South Polar exploration, but a knowledge of the obstacles that lay between us and our starting point served as a curb on impatience. Everything depended upon the landing. If we could land at Filchner's base there was no reason why a band of experienced men should not winter there in safety. But the Weddell Sea was notoriously inhospitable, and already we knew that its sternest face was turned towards us. All the conditions in the Weddell Sea are unfavorable from the navigator's point of view. The winds are comparatively light, and consequently new ice can form even in the summertime. The absence of strong winds has the additional effect of allowing the ice to accumulate in masses, undisturbed. Then great quantities of ice sweep along the coast from the east under the influence of the prevailing current, and fill up the bight of the Weddell Sea as they move north in a great semicircle. Some of this ice doubtless describes almost a complete circle, and is held up eventually, in bad seasons, against the South Sandwich Islands. The strong currents, pressing the ice masses against the coasts, create heavier pressure than is found in any other part of the Antarctic. This pressure must be at least as severe as the pressure experienced in the congested North Polar basin, and I am inclined to think that a comparison would be to the advantage of the Arctic. All these considerations naturally had a bearing upon our immediate problem, the penetration of the pack and the finding of a safe harbor on the continental coast.

The day of departure arrived. I gave the order to heave anchor at 8:45 a.m. on December 5, 1914, and the clanking

of the windlass broke for us the last link with civilization.
The morning was dull and overcast, with occasional gusts
of snow and sleet, but hearts were light aboard the *Endurance.* The long days of preparation were over and the adventure lay ahead.

We had hoped that some steamer from the north would
bring news of the war and perhaps letters from home before
our departure. A ship did arrive on the evening of the 4th,
but she carried no letters, and nothing useful in the way of
information could be gleaned from her. The captain and
crew were all stoutly pro-German, and the "news" they had
to give took the unsatisfying form of accounts of British and
French reverses. We would have been glad to have had the
latest tidings from a friendlier source. A year and a half later
we were to learn that the *Harpoon,* the steamer which tends
the Grytviken station, had arrived with mail for us not more
than two hours after the *Endurance* had proceeded down the
coast.

The bows of the *Endurance* were turned to the south, and
the good ship dipped to the southwesterly swell. Misty rain
fell during the forenoon, but the weather cleared later in the
day, and we had a good view of the coast of South Georgia
as we moved under steam and sail to the southeast. The
course was laid to carry us clear of the island and then south
of South Thule, Sandwich Group. The wind freshened during the day, and all square sail was set, with the foresail
reefed in order to give the lookout a clear view ahead; for
we did not wish to risk contact with a "growler," one of
those treacherous fragments of ice that float with surface
awash. The ship was very steady in the quarterly sea, but
certainly did not look as neat and trim as she had done when
leaving the shores of England four months earlier. We had
filled up with coal at Grytviken, and this extra fuel was
stored on deck, where it impeded movement considerably.
The carpenter had built a false deck, extending from the

poopdeck to the chartroom. We had also taken aboard a ton of whale meat for the dogs. The big chunks of meat were hung up in the rigging, out of reach but not out of sight of the dogs, and as the *Endurance* rolled and pitched, they watched with wolfish eyes for a windfall.

I was greatly pleased with the dogs, which were tethered about the ship in the most comfortable positions we could find for them. They were in excellent condition, and I felt that the Expedition had the right tractive-power. They were big sturdy animals, chosen for endurance and strength, and if they were as keen to pull our sledges as they were now to fight one another all would be well. The men in charge of the dogs were doing their work enthusiastically, and the eagerness they showed to study the natures and habits of their charges gave promise of efficient handling and good work later on.

During December 6 the *Endurance* made good progress on a southeasterly course. The northerly breeze had freshened during the night and had brought up a high following sea. The weather was hazy, and we passed two bergs, several growlers, and numerous lumps of ice. Staff and crew were settling down to the routine. Bird life was plentiful, and we noticed Cape pigeons, whalebirds, terns, mollymauks, nellies, sooty and wandering albatrosses in the neighborhood of the ship. The course was laid for the passage between Sanders Island and Candlemas Volcano. December 7 brought the first check. At six o'clock that morning the sea, which had been green in color all the previous day, changed suddenly to a deep indigo. The ship was behaving well in a rough sea, and some members of the scientific staff were transferring to the bunkers the coal we had stowed on deck. Sanders Island and Candlemas were sighted early in the afternoon, and the *Endurance* passed between them at 6 p.m. Worsley's observations indicated that Sanders Island was, roughly, three miles east and five miles north of the charted

position. Large numbers of bergs, mostly tabular in form,
lay to the west of the islands, and we noticed that many of
them were yellow with *diatoms*. One berg had large patches
of red-brown soil down its sides. The presence of so many
bergs was ominous, and immediately after passing between
the islands we encountered stream-ice. All sail was taken in
and we proceeded slowly under steam. Two hours later, fifteen miles northeast of Sanders Island, the *Endurance* was
confronted by a belt of heavy pack-ice, half a mile broad
and extending north and south. There was clear water beyond, but the heavy southwesterly swell made the pack impenetrable in our neighborhood. This was disconcerting.
The noon latitude had been 57° 26′ S., and I had not expected to find pack-ice nearly so far north, though the whalers had reported pack right up to South Thule.

The situation became dangerous that night. We pushed
into the pack in the hope of reaching open water beyond,
and found ourselves after dark in a pool which was growing
smaller and smaller. The ice was grinding around the ship
in the heavy swell, and I watched with some anxiety for any
indication of a change of wind to the east, since a breeze
from that quarter would have driven us towards the land.
Worsley and I were on deck all night, dodging the pack. At
3 a.m. we ran south, taking advantage of some openings that
had appeared, but met heavy rafted pack-ice, evidently old;
some of it had been subjected to severe pressure. Then we
steamed northwest and saw open water to the northeast. I
put the *Endurance*'s head for the opening, and, steaming at
full speed, we got clear. Then we went east in the hope of
getting better ice, and five hours later, after some dodging,
we rounded the pack and were able to set sail once more.
This initial tussle with the pack had been exciting at times.
Pieces of ice and bergs of all sizes were heaving and jostling
against each other in the heavy southwesterly swell. In spite
of all our care the *Endurance* struck large lumps stem on,

but the engines were stopped in time and no harm was done. The scene and sounds throughout the day were very fine. The swell was dashing against the sides of huge bergs and leaping right to the top of their icy cliffs. Sanders Island lay to the south, with a few rocky faces peering through the misty swirling clouds that swathed it most of the time, the booming of the sea running into ice caverns, the swishing break of the swell on the loose pack, and the graceful bowing and undulating of the inner pack to the steeply rolling swell, which here was robbed of its break by the masses of ice to windward.

We skirted the northern edge of the pack in clear weather with a light southwesterly breeze and an overcast sky. The bergs were numerous. During the morning of December 9 an easterly breeze brought hazy weather with snow, and at 4:30 p.m. we encountered the edge of pack-ice in lat. 58° 27′ S., long. 22° 08′ W. It was one-year-old ice interspersed with older pack, all heavily snow-covered and lying west-southwest to east-northeast. We entered the pack at 5 p.m., but could not make progress, and cleared it again at 7:40 p.m. Then we steered east-northeast and spent the rest of the night rounding the pack. During the day we had seen adelie and ringed penguins, also several humpback and finner whales. An ice-blink to the westward indicated the presence of pack in that direction. After rounding the pack we steered S. 40° E., and at noon on the 10th had reached lat. 58° 28′ S., long. 20° 28′ W. Observations showed the compass variation to be 1½° less than the chart recorded. I kept the *Endurance* on the course till midnight, when we entered loose open ice about ninety miles southeast of our noon position. This ice proved to fringe the pack, and progress became slow. There was a long easterly swell with a light northerly breeze, and the weather was clear and fine. Numerous bergs lay outside the pack.

The *Endurance* steamed through loose open ice till 8 a.m.

on the 11th, when we entered the pack in lat. 59° 46′ S.,
long. 18° 22′ W. We could have gone farther east, but the
pack extended far in that direction, and an effort to circle it
might have involved a lot of northing. I did not wish to lose
the benefit of the original southing. The extra miles would
not have mattered to a ship with larger coal capacity than
the *Endurance* possessed, but we could not afford to sacrifice miles unnecessarily. The pack was loose and did not
present great difficulties at this stage. The foresail was set
in order to take advantage of the northerly breeze. The ship
was in contact with the ice occasionally and received some
heavy blows. Once or twice she was brought up all standing
against solid pieces, but no harm was done. The chief concern was to protect the propeller and rudder. If a collision
seemed to be inevitable the officer in charge would order
"slow" or "half speed" with the engines, and put the helm
over so as to strike the floe a glancing blow. Then the helm
would be put over towards the ice with the object of throwing the propeller clear of it, and the ship would forge ahead
again. Worsley, Wild, and I, with three officers, kept three
watches while we were working through the pack, so that
we had two officers on deck all the time. The carpenter had
rigged a six-foot wooden semaphore on the bridge to enable
the navigating officer to give the seamen or scientists at the
wheel the direction and the exact amount of helm required.
This device saved time as well as the effort of shouting. We
were pushing through this loose pack all day, and the view
from the crow's nest gave no promise of improved conditions ahead. A Weddell seal and a crab-eater seal were noticed on the floes, but we did not pause to secure fresh meat.
It was important that we should make progress towards our
goal as rapidly as possible, and there was reason to fear that
we should have plenty of time to spare later on if the ice
conditions continued to increase in severity.

On the morning of December 12 we were working

through loose pack which later became thick in places. The sky was overcast and light snow was falling. I had all square sail set at 7 a.m. in order to take advantage of the northerly breeze, but it had to come in again five hours later when the wind hauled round to the west. The noon position was lat. 60° 26′ S., long. 17° 58′ W., and the run for the twenty-four hours had been only 33 miles. The ice was still badly congested, and we were pushing through narrow leads and occasional openings with the floes often close abeam on either side. Antarctic, snow and stormy petrels, fulmars, white-rumped terns, and adelies were around us. The quaint little penguins found the ship a cause of much apparent excitement and provided a lot of amusement aboard. One of the standing jokes was that all the adelies on the floe seemed to know Clark, and when he was at the wheel rushed along as fast as their legs could carry them, yelling out "Clark! Clark!" and apparently very indignant and perturbed that he never waited for them or even answered them.

We found several good leads to the south in the evening, and continued to work southward throughout the night and the following day. The pack extended in all directions as far as the eye could reach. The noon observation showed the run for the twenty-four hours to be 54 miles, a satisfactory result under the conditions. Wild shot a young Ross seal on the floe, and we maneuvered the ship alongside. Hudson jumped down, bent a line on to the seal, and the pair of them were hauled up. The seal was 4 ft. 9 in. long and weighed about ninety pounds. He was a young male and proved very good eating, but when dressed and minus the blubber made little more than a square meal for our twenty-eight men, with a few scraps for our breakfast and tea. The stomach contained only *amphipods* about an inch long, allied to those found in the whales at Grytviken.

The conditions became harder on December 14. There was a misty haze, and occasional falls of snow. A few bergs were in sight. The pack was denser than it had been on the previous days. Older ice was intermingled with the young ice, and our progress became slower. The propeller received several blows in the early morning, but no damage was done. A platform was rigged under the jib boom in order that Hurley might secure some motion pictures of the ship breaking through the ice. The young ice did not present difficulties to the *Endurance,* which was able to smash a way through, but the lumps of older ice were more formidable obstacles, and conning the ship was a task requiring close attention. The most careful navigation could not prevent an occasional bump against ice too thick to be broken or pushed aside. The southerly breeze strengthened to a moderate southwesterly gale during the afternoon, and at 8 p.m. we hove to, stern against a floe, it being impossible to proceed without serious risk of damage to rudder or propeller. I was interested to notice that, although we had been steaming through the pack for three days, the northwesterly swell still held with us. It added to the difficulties of navigation in the lanes, since the ice was constantly in movement.

The *Endurance* remained against the floe for the next twenty-four hours, when the gale moderated. The pack extended to the horizon in all directions and was broken by innumerable narrow lanes. Many bergs were in sight, and they appeared to be traveling through the pack in a southwesterly direction under the current influence. Probably the pack itself was moving northeast with the gale. Clark put down a net in search of specimens, and at two fathoms it was carried southwest by the current and fouled the propeller. He lost the net, two leads, and a line. Ten bergs drove to the south through the pack during the twenty-four hours. The noon position was lat. 61° 31′ S., long. 18° 12′ W. The gale had moderated at 8 p.m., and we made five miles to the south before midnight and then stopped at the end of a long lead, waiting till the weather cleared. It was during this short run that the captain, with semaphore hard-a-port, shouted to the scientist at the wheel: "Why in Paradise don't you port!" The answer came in indignant tones: "I am blowing my nose."

The *Endurance* made some progress on the following day. Long leads of open water ran towards the southwest, and the ship smashed at full speed through occasional areas of young ice till brought up with a heavy thud against a section of older floe. Worsley was out on the jib-boom end for a few minutes while Wild was conning the ship, and he came back with a glowing account of a novel sensation. The boom was swinging high and low and from side to side, while the massive bows of the ship smashed through the ice, splitting it across, piling it mass on mass and then shouldering it aside. The air temperature was 37° Fahr., pleasantly warm, and the water temperature 29° Fahr. We continued to advance through fine long leads till 4 a.m. on December 17, when the ice became difficult again. Very large floes of six-months-old ice lay close together. Some of these floes presented a square mile of unbroken surface, and among them were patches of thin ice and several floes of heavy old ice. Many bergs were in sight, and the course became devious. The ship was blocked at one point by a wedge-shaped piece of floe, but we put the ice anchor through it, towed it astern, and proceeded through the gap. Steering under these conditions required muscle as well as nerve. There was a clatter aft during the afternoon, and Hussey, who was at the wheel, explained that "The wheel spun round and threw me over the top of it!" The noon position was lat. 62° 13' S., long. 18° 53' W., and the run for the preceding twenty-four hours had been 32 miles in a southwesterly direction. We saw three blue whales during the day and one emperor penguin, a 58-lb. bird, which was added to the larder.

The morning of December 18 found the *Endurance* proceeding amongst large floes with thin ice between them. The leads were few. There was a northerly breeze with occasional snow flurries. We secured three crab-eater seals—two cows and a bull. The bull was a fine specimen, nearly white all over and 9 ft. 3 in. long; he weighed 600 lb. Shortly before noon further progress was barred by heavy pack, and we put an ice anchor on the floe and banked the fires. I had been prepared for evil conditions in the Weddell Sea, but had hoped that in December and January, at any rate, the pack would be loose, even if no open water was to be found. What we were actually encountering was fairly dense pack of a very obstinate character. Pack-ice might be described as a gigantic and interminable jigsaw puzzle devised by Nature. The parts of the puzzle in loose pack have floated slightly apart and become disarranged; at numerous places they have pressed together again; as the pack gets closer the congested areas grow larger and the parts are jammed harder till finally it becomes "close pack," when the whole of the jigsaw puzzle becomes jammed to such an extent that with care and labor it can be traversed in every direction on foot. Where the parts do not fit closely there is, of course, open water, which freezes over in a few hours after giving off volumes of "frost-smoke." In obedience to renewed pressure this young ice "rafts," so forming double thicknesses of a toffee-like consistency. Again the opposing edges of heavy floes rear up in slow and almost silent conflict, till high "hedge-rows" are formed round each part of the puzzle. At the junction of several floes chaotic areas of piled-up blocks and masses of ice are formed. Sometimes 5-ft. to 6-ft. piles of evenly shaped blocks of ice are seen so neatly laid that it seems impossible for them to be Nature's work. Again, a winding canyon may be traversed between icy walls 6 ft. to 10 ft. high, or a dome may be formed that under renewed pressure bursts upward like a volcano. All through the winter the drifting pack changes—grows by freezing, thickens by rafting, and corrugates by pressure. If, finally, in its drift it impinges on a coast, such as the western shore of the Weddell Sea, terrific pressure is set up and an inferno of ice blocks, ridges, and hedgerows results, extending possibly for 150 or 200 miles off shore. Sections of pressure ice may drift away subsequently and become embedded in new ice.

I have given this brief explanation here in order that the reader may understand the nature of the ice through which we pushed our way for many hundreds of miles. Another point that may require to be explained was the delay caused by wind while we were in the pack. When a strong breeze or moderate gale was blowing the ship could not safely work through any except young ice, up to about two feet in thickness. As ice of that nature never extended for more than a mile or so, it followed that in a gale in the pack we had always to lie to. The ship was 3 ft. 3 in. down by the stern, and while this saved the propeller and rudder a good deal, it made the *Endurance* practically unmanageable in close pack when the wind attained a force of six miles an hour from ahead, since the air currents had such a big surface forward to act upon. The pressure of wind on bows and the yards of the foremast would cause the bows to fall away, and in these conditions the ship could not be steered into the narrow lanes and leads through which we had to thread our way. The falling away of the bows, moreover, would tend to bring the stern against the ice, compelling us to stop the engines in order to save the propeller. Then the ship would become unmanageable and drift away, with the possibility of getting excessive sternway on her and so damaging rudder or propeller, the Achilles heel of a ship in pack-ice.

While we were waiting for the weather to moderate and the ice to open, I had the Lucas sounding-machine rigged over the rudder-trunk and found the depth to be 2810 fathoms. The bottom sample was lost, owing to the line parting 60 fathoms from the end. During the afternoon three adelie penguins approached the ship across the floe while Hussey was discoursing sweet music on the banjo. The solemn-looking little birds appeared to appreciate "It's a Long Way to Tipperary," but they fled in horror when Hussey treated them to a little of the music that comes from Scotland. The shouts of laughter from the ship added to their dismay, and they made off as fast as their short legs would carry them. The pack opened slightly at 6:15 p.m., and we proceeded through lanes for three hours before being forced to anchor to a floe for the night. We fired a Hjort mark harpoon, No. 171, into a blue whale on this day.

The conditions did not improve during December 19. A fresh to strong northerly breeze brought haze and snow, and after proceeding for two hours the *Endurance* was stopped again by heavy floes. It was impossible to maneuver the ship in the ice owing to the strong wind, which kept the floes in movement and caused lanes to open and close with dangerous rapidity. The noon observation showed that we had made six miles to the southeast in the previous twenty-four hours. All hands were engaged during the day in rubbing shoots off our potatoes, which were found to be sprouting freely. We remained moored to a floe over the following day, the wind not having moderated; indeed, it freshened to a gale in the afternoon, and the members of the staff and crew took advantage of the pause to enjoy a vigorously contested game of soccer on the level surface of the floe alongside the ship. Twelve bergs were in sight at this time. The noon position was lat. 62° 42′ S., long. 17° 54′ W., showing that we had drifted about six miles in a northeasterly direction.

Monday, December 21, was beautifully fine, with a gentle west-northwesterly breeze. We made a start at 3 a.m. and proceeded through the pack in a southwesterly direction. At noon we had gained seven miles almost due east, the northerly drift of the pack having continued while the ship was apparently moving to the south. Petrels of several species, penguins, and seals were plentiful, and we saw four small

blue whales. At noon we entered a long lead to the southward and passed around and between nine splendid bergs.
One mighty specimen was shaped like the Rock of Gibraltar
but with steeper cliffs, and another had a natural dock that
would have contained the *Aquitania*. A spur of ice closed
the entrance to the huge blue pool. Hurley brought out his
motion-picture camera in order to make a record of these
bergs. Fine long leads running east and southeast among
bergs were found during the afternoon, but at midnight the
ship was stopped by small, heavy ice floes, tightly packed
against an unbroken plain of ice. The outlook from the masthead was not encouraging. The big floe was at least 15 miles
long and 10 miles wide. The edge could not be seen at the
widest part, and the area of the floe must have been not less
than 150 square miles. It appeared to be formed of year-old
ice, not very thick and with very few hummocks or ridges
in it. We thought it must have been formed at sea in very
calm weather and drifted up from the southeast. I have never
seen such a large area of unbroken ice in the Ross Sea.

We waited with banked fires for the strong easterly breeze
to moderate or the pack to open. At 6:30 p.m. on December
22 some lanes opened and we were able to move towards the
south again. The following morning found us working
slowly through the pack and the noon observation gave us a
gain of 19 miles S. 41° W. for the seventeen and a half hours
under steam. Many year-old adelies, three crab eaters, six sea
leopards, one Weddell and two blue whales were seen. The
air temperature, which had been down to 25° Fahr. on December 21, had risen to 34° Fahr. While we were working
along leads to the southward in the afternoon, we counted
fifteen bergs. Three of these were table-topped, and one was
about 70 ft. high and 5 miles long. Evidently it had come
from a barrier edge. The ice became heavier but slightly
more open, and we had a calm night with fine long leads of
open water. The water was so still that new ice was forming

on the leads. We had a run of 70 miles to our credit at noon on December 24, the position being lat. 64° 32′ S., long. 17° 17′ W. All the dogs except eight had been named. I do not know who had been responsible for some of the names, which seemed to represent a variety of tastes. They were as follows: Rugby, Upton, Bristol, Millhill, Songster, Sandy, Mack, Mercury, Wolf, Amundsen, Hercules, Hackenschmidt, Samson, Sammy, Skipper, Caruso, Sub, Ulysses, Spotty, Bosun, Slobbers, Sadie, Sue, Sally, Jasper, Tim, Sweep, Martin, Splitlip, Luke, Saint, Satan, Chips, Stumps, Snapper, Painful, Bob, Snowball, Jerry, Judge, Sooty, Rufus, Sidelights, Simeon, Swanker, Chirgwin, Steamer, Peter, Fluffy, Steward, Slippery, Elliott, Roy, Noel, Shakespeare, Jamie, Bummer, Smuts, Lupoid, Spider, and Sailor. Some of the names, it will be noticed, had a descriptive flavor.

Heavy floes held up the ship from midnight till 6 a.m. on December 25, Christmas Day. Then they opened a little and we made progress till 11:30 a.m., when the leads closed again. We had encountered good leads and workable ice during the early part of the night, and the noon observation showed that our run for the twenty-four hours was the best since we entered the pack a fortnight earlier. We had made 71 miles S. 4° W. The ice held us up till the evening, and then we were able to follow some leads for a couple of hours before the tightly packed floes and the increasing wind compelled a stop. The celebration of Christmas was not forgotten. Grog was served at midnight to all on deck. There was grog again at breakfast, for the benefit of those who had been in their bunks at midnight. Lees had decorated the wardroom with flags and had a little Christmas present for each of us. Some of us had presents from home to open. Later there was a really splendid dinner, consisting of turtle soup, whitebait, jugged hare, Christmas pudding, mince pies, dates, figs and crystallized fruits, with rum and stout as drinks. In the evening everybody joined in a "sing-song."

Hussey had made a one-stringed violin, on which, in the words of Worsley, he "discoursed quite painlessly." The wind was increasing to a moderate southeasterly gale and no advance could be made, so we were able to settle down to the enjoyments of the evening.

The weather was still bad on December 26 and 27, and the *Endurance* remained anchored to a floe. The noon position on the 26th was lat. 65° 43′ S., long. 17° 36′ W. We made another sounding on this day with the Lucas machine and found bottom at 2819 fathoms. The specimen brought up was a terrigenous blue mud (glacial deposit) with some *radiolaria*. Every one took turns at the work of heaving in, two men working together in ten-minute spells.

Sunday, December 27, was a quiet day aboard. The southerly gale was blowing the snow in clouds off the floe and the temperature had fallen to 23° Fahr. The dogs were having an uncomfortable time in their deck quarters. The wind had moderated by the following morning, but it was squally with snow flurries, and I did not order a start till 11 p.m. The pack was still close, but the ice was softer and more easily broken. During the pause the carpenter had rigged a small stage over the stern. A man was stationed there to watch the propeller and prevent it striking heavy ice, and the arrangement proved very valuable. It saved the rudder as well as the propeller from many blows.

The high winds that had prevailed for four and a half days gave way to the gentle southerly breeze in the evening of December 29. Owing to the drift we were actually eleven miles farther north than we had been on December 25. But we made fairly good progress on the 30th in fine, clear weather. The ship followed a long lead to the southeast during the afternoon and evening, and at 11 p.m. we crossed the Antarctic Circle. An examination of the horizon disclosed considerable breaks in the vast circle of pack-ice, interspersed with bergs of different sizes. Leads could be traced

in various directions, but I looked in vain for an indication
of open water. The sun did not set that night, and as it was
concealed behind a bank of clouds we had a glow of crimson and gold to the southward, with delicate pale green re-
flections in the water of the lanes to the southeast.

The ship had a serious encounter with the ice on the
morning of December 31. We were stopped first by floes
closing around us, and then about noon the *Endurance* got
jammed between two floes heading east-northeast. The pressure heeled the ship over six degrees while we were getting
an ice-anchor on to the floe in order to heave astern and thus
assist the engines, which were running at full speed. The
effort was successful. Immediately afterwards, at the spot
where the *Endurance* had been held, slabs of ice 50 ft. by
15 ft. and 4 ft. thick were forced ten and twelve feet up on
the lee floe at an angle of 45 degrees. The pressure was
severe, and we were not sorry to have the ship out of its
reach. The noon position was lat. 66° 47' S., long. 15° 52'
W., and the run for the preceding twenty-four hours was 51
miles S. 29° E.

"Since noon the character of the pack has improved,"
wrote Worsley on this day. "Though the leads are short, the
floes are rotten and easily broken through if a good place is
selected with care and judgment. In many cases we find
large sheets of young ice through which the ship cuts for a
mile or two miles at a stretch. I have been conning and
working the ship from the crow's nest and find it much the
best place, as from there one can see ahead and work out
the course beforehand, and can also guard the rudder and
propeller, the most vulnerable parts of a ship in the ice. At
midnight, as I was sitting in the 'tub,' I heard a clamorous
noise down on the deck, with ringing of bells, and realized
that it was the New Year." Worsley came down from his
lofty seat and met Wild, Hudson, and myself on the bridge,
where we shook hands and wished one another a happy and

successful New Year. Since entering the pack on December 11 we had come 480 miles through loose and close pack-ice. We had pushed and fought the little ship through, and she stood the test well, though the propeller had received some shrewd blows against hard ice and the vessel had been driven against the floe until she had fairly mounted up on it and slid back rolling heavily from side to side. The rolling had been more frequently caused by the operation of cracking through thickish young ice, where the crack had taken a sinuous course. The ship, in attempting to follow it, struck first one bilge and then the other, causing her to roll six or seven degrees. Our advance through the pack had been in a S. 10° E. direction, and I estimated that the total steaming distance had exceeded 700 miles. The first 100 miles had been through loose pack, but the greatest hindrances had been three moderate southwesterly gales, two lasting for three days each and one for four and a half days. The last 250 miles had been through close pack alternating with fine long leads and stretches of open water.

During the weeks we spent maneuvering to the south through the tortuous mazes of the pack it was necessary often to split floes by driving the ship against them. This form of attack was effective against ice up to three feet in thickness, and the process is interesting enough to be worth describing briefly. When the way was barred by a floe of moderate thickness we would drive the ship at half speed against it, stopping the engines just before the impact. At the first blow the *Endurance* would cut a V-shaped nick in the face of the floe, the slope of her cutwater often causing her bows to rise till nearly clear of the water, when she would slide backwards, rolling slightly. Watching carefully that loose lumps of ice did not damage the propeller, we would reverse the engines and back the ship off 200 to 300 yds. She would then be driven full speed into the V, taking care to hit the center accurately. The operation would be repeated until a short dock was cut, into which the ship, acting as a large wedge, was driven. At about the fourth attempt, if it was to succeed at all, the floe would yield. A black, sinuous line, as though pen-drawn on white paper, would appear ahead, broadening as the eye traced it back to the ship. Presently it would be broad enough to receive her, and we would forge ahead. Under the bows and alongside, great slabs of ice were being turned over and slid back on the floe, or driven down and under the ice or ship. In this way the *Endurance* would split a 2-ft. to 3-ft. floe a square mile in extent. Occasionally the floe, although cracked across, would be so held by other floes that it would refuse to open wide, and so gradually would bring the ship to a standstill. We would then go astern for some distance and again drive her full speed into the crack, till finally the floe would yield to the repeated onslaughts.

CHAPTER II

NEW LAND

THE FIRST DAY of the New Year (January 1, 1915) was cloudy, with a gentle northerly breeze and occasional snow squalls. The condition of the pack improved in the evening, and after 8 p.m. we forged ahead rapidly through brittle young ice, easily broken by the ship. A few hours later a moderate gale came up from the east, with continuous snow. After 4 a.m. on the 2nd we got into thick old pack ice, showing signs of heavy pressure. It was much hummocked, but large areas of open water and long leads to the southwest continued until noon. The position then was lat. 69° 49′ S., long. 15° 42′ W., and the run for the twenty-four hours had been 124 miles S. 3° W. This was cheering.

The heavy pack blocked the way south after midday. It would have been almost impossible to have pushed the ship into the ice, and in any case the gale would have made such a proceeding highly dangerous. So we dodged along to the west and north, looking for a suitable opening towards the south. The good run had given me hope of sighting the land on the following day, and the delay was annoying. I was growing anxious to reach land on account of the dogs, which had not been able to get exercise for four weeks, and were becoming run down. We passed at least two hundred bergs during the day, and we noticed also large masses of hummocky bay ice and ice foot. One floe of bay ice had black earth upon it, apparently basaltic in origin, and there was a large berg with a broad band of yellowish brown right through it. The stain may have been volcanic dust. Many of the bergs had quaint shapes. There was one that exactly resembled a large two-funnel liner, complete in silhouette except for smoke. Later in the day we found an opening in the pack and made 9 miles to the southwest, but at 2 a.m. on January 3 the lead ended in hummocky ice, impossible to penetrate. A moderate easterly gale had come up with snow-squalls, and we could not get a clear view in any direction. The hummocky ice did not offer a suitable anchorage for the ship, and we were compelled to dodge up and down for ten hours before we were able to make fast to a small floe under the lee of a berg 120 ft. high. The berg broke the wind and saved us drifting fast to leeward. The position was 69° 59′ S., long. 17° 31′ W. We made a move again at 7 p.m., when we took in the ice anchor and proceeded south, and at 10 p.m. we passed a small berg that the ship had nearly touched twelve hours previously. Obviously we were not making much headway. Several of the bergs passed during this day were of solid blue ice, indicating true glacier origin.

By midnight of the 3rd we had made 11 miles to the south, and then came to a full stop in weather so thick with snow that we could not learn if the leads and lanes were worth entering. The ice was hummocky, but, fortunately, the gale was decreasing, and after we had scanned all the leads and pools within our reach we turned back to the northeast. Two sperm and two large blue whales were sighted, the first we had seen for 260 miles. We saw also petrels, numerous ade-lies, emperors, crab eaters, and sea leopards. The clearer weather of the morning showed us that the pack was solid and impassable from the southeast to the southwest, and at 10 a.m. on the 4th we again passed within five yards of the small berg that we had passed twice on the previous day. We had been steaming and dodging about over an area of twenty square miles for fifty hours, trying to find an opening to the south, southeast, or southwest, but all the leads ran north, northeast, or northwest. It was as though the spirits of the Antarctic were pointing us to the backward track—the track we were determined not to follow. Our desire was to make easting as well as southing so as to reach the land, if possible, east of Ross's farthest south and well east of Coats' Land. This was more important as the prevailing winds appeared to be to easterly, and every mile of easting would count. In the afternoon we went west in some open water, and by 4 p.m. we were making west-southwest with more water opening up ahead. The sun was shining brightly, over three degrees high at midnight, and we were able to maintain this direction in fine weather till the following noon. The position then was lat. 70° 28' S., long. 20° 16' W., and the run had been 62 miles S. 62° W. At 8 a.m. there had been open water from north round by west to southwest, but impenetrable pack to the south and east. At 3 p.m. the way to the southwest and west-northwest was absolutely blocked, and as we experienced a set to the west, I did not feel justified in burning more of the reduced stock of coal to go west or north. I took the ship back over our course for four miles, to a point where some looser pack gave faint promise of a way through; but, after battling for three hours with very heavy hummocked ice and making four miles to the south, we were brought up by huge blocks and floes of very old pack. Further effort seemed useless at that time, and I gave the order to bank fires after we had moored the *Endurance* to a solid floe. The weather was clear, and some enthusiastic soccer players had a game on the floe until, about midnight, Worsley dropped through a hole in rotten ice while retrieving the ball. He had to be retrieved himself.

Solid pack still barred the way to the south on the following morning (January 6). There was some open water north of the floe, but as the day was calm and I did not wish to use coal in a possibly vain search for an opening to the southward, I kept the ship moored to the floe. This pause in good weather gave an opportunity to exercise the dogs, which were taken on to the floe by the men in charge of them. The excitement of the animals was intense. Several

managed to get into the water, and the muzzles they were
wearing did not prevent some hot fights. Two dogs which
had contrived to slip their muzzles fought themselves into
an icy pool and were hauled out still locked in a grapple.
However, men and dogs enjoyed the exercise. A sounding
gave a depth of 2400 fathoms, with a blue mud bottom. The
wind freshened from the west early the next morning, and
we started to skirt the northern edge of the solid pack in an
easterly direction under sail. We had cleared the close pack
by noon, but the outlook to the south gave small promise of
useful progress, and I was anxious now to make easting. We
went northeast under sail, and after making thirty-nine miles
passed a peculiar berg that we had been abreast of sixty
hours earlier. Killer whales were becoming active around
us, and I had to exercise caution in allowing any one to
leave the ship. These beasts have a habit of locating a resting
seal by looking over the edge of a floe and then striking
through the ice from below in search of a meal; they would
not distinguish between seal and man.

The noon position on January 8 was lat. 70° 0′ S., long.
19° 09′ W. We had made 66 miles in a northeasterly direction during the preceding twenty-four hours. The course
during the afternoon was east-southeast through loose pack
and open water, with deep hummocky floes to the south.
Several leads to the south came in view, but we held on the
easterly course. The floes were becoming looser, and there
were indications of open water ahead. The ship passed not
fewer than five hundred bergs that day, some of them very
large. A dark water-sky extended from east to south-southeast on the following morning, and the *Endurance,* working
through loose pack at half speed, reached open water just
before noon. A rampart berg 150 ft. high and a quarter of a
mile long lay at the edge of the loose pack, and we sailed
over a projecting foot of this berg into rolling ocean, stretching to the horizon. The sea extended from a little to the west

of south, round by east to north-northeast, and its welcome promise was supported by a deep water-sky to the south. I laid a course south by east in an endeavor to get south and east of Ross's farthest south (lat. 71° 30′ S.).

We kept the open water for a hundred miles, passing many bergs but encountering no pack. Two very large whales, probably blue whales, came up close to the ship, and we saw spouts in all directions. Open water inside the pack in that latitude might have the appeal of sanctuary to the whales, which are harried by man farther north. The run southward in blue water, with a path clear ahead and the miles falling away behind us, was a joyful experience after the long struggle through the ice lanes. But, like other good things, our spell of free movement had to end. The *Endurance* encountered the ice again at 1 a.m. on the 10th. Loose pack stretched to east and south, with open water to the west and a good water-sky. It consisted partly of heavy hummocky ice showing evidence of great pressure, but contained also many thick, flat floes evidently formed in some sheltered bay and never subjected to pressure or to much motion. The swirl of the ship's wash brought diatomaceous scum from the sides of this ice. The water became thick with *diatoms* at 9 a.m., and I ordered a cast to be made. No bottom was found at 210 fathoms. The *Endurance* continued to advance southward through loose pack that morning. We saw the spouts of numerous whales and noticed some hundreds of crab eaters lying on the floes. White-rumped terns, Antarctic petrels and snow petrels were numerous, and there was a colony of adelies on a low berg. A few killer whales, with their characteristic high dorsal fin, also came in view. The noon position was lat. 72° 02′ S., long. 16° 07′ W., and the run for the twenty-four hours had been 136 miles S. 6° E.

We were now in the vicinity of the land discovered by Dr. W. S. Bruce, leader of the *Scotia* Expedition, in 1904, and named by him Coats' Land. Dr. Bruce encountered an ice

barrier in lat. 72° 18′ S., long. 10° W., stretching from northeast to southwest. He followed the barrier edge to the southwest for 150 miles and reached lat. 74° 1′ S., long. 22° W.
He saw no naked rock, but his description of rising slopes
of snow and ice, with shoaling water off the barrier wall,
indicated clearly the presence of land. It was up those
slopes, at a point as far south as possible, that I planned to
begin the march across the Antarctic continent. All hands
were watching now for the coast described by Dr. Bruce,
and at 5 p.m. the lookout reported an appearance of land to
the south-southeast. We could see a gentle snow slope rising
to a height of about one thousand feet. It seemed to be an
island or a peninsula with a sound on its south side, and the
position of its most northerly point was about 72° 34′ S.,
16° 40′ W. The *Endurance* was passing through heavy loose
pack, and shortly before midnight she broke into a lead of
open sea along a barrier edge. A sounding within one cable's length of the barrier edge gave no bottom with 210
fathoms of line. The barrier was 70 ft. high, with cliffs of
about 40 ft. The *Scotia* must have passed this point when
pushing to Bruce's farthest south on March 6, 1904, and I
knew from the narrative of that voyage, as well as from our
own observation, that the coast trended away to the southwest. The lead of open water continued along the barrier
edge, and we pushed forward without delay.

An easterly breeze brought cloud and falls of snow during
the morning of January 11. The barrier trended southwest
by south, and we skirted it for fifty miles until 11 a.m. The
cliffs in the morning were 20 ft. high, and by noon they had
increased to 110 and 115 ft. The brow apparently rose 20 to
30 ft. higher. We were forced away from the barrier once for
three hours by a line of very heavy pack-ice. Otherwise
there was open water along the edge, with high loose pack
to the west and northwest. We noticed a seal bobbing up and
down in an apparent effort to swallow a long silvery fish

that projected at least eighteen inches from its mouth. The noon position was lat. 73° 13′ S., long. 20° 43′ W., and a sounding then gave 155 fathoms at a distance of a mile from the barrier. The bottom consisted of large igneous pebbles. The weather then became thick, and I held away to the westward, where the sky had given indications of open water, until 7 p.m., when we laid the ship alongside a floe in loose pack. Heavy snow was falling, and I was anxious lest the westerly wind should bring the pack hard against the coast and jam the ship. The *Nimrod* had a narrow escape from a misadventure of this kind in the Ross Sea early in 1908.

We made a start again at 5 a.m. the next morning (January 12) in overcast weather with mist and snow-showers, and four hours later broke through loose pack-ice into open water. The view was obscured, but we proceeded to the southeast and had gained 24 miles by noon, when three soundings in lat. 74° 4′ S., long. 22° 48′ W. gave 95, 128, and 103 fathoms, with a bottom of sand, pebbles, and mud. Clark got a good haul of biological specimens in the dredge. The *Endurance* was now close to what appeared to be the barrier, with a heavy pack-ice foot containing numerous bergs frozen in and possibly aground. The solid ice turned away towards the northwest, and we followed the edge for 48 miles N. 60° W. to clear it.

Now we were beyond the point reached by the *Scotia*, and the land underlying the ice sheet we were skirting was new. The northerly trend was unexpected, and I began to suspect that we were really rounding a huge ice tongue attached to the true barrier edge and extending northward. Events confirmed this suspicion. We skirted the pack all night, steering northwest; then went west by north till 4 a.m. and round to southwest. The course at 8 a.m. on the 13th was south-southwest. The barrier at midnight was low and distant, and at 8 a.m. there was merely a narrow ice foot about two hundred yards across separating it from the open

water. By noon there was only an occasional shelf of ice
foot. The barrier in one place came with an easy sweep to
the sea. We could have landed stores there without difficulty. We made a sounding 400 ft. off the barrier but got no
bottom at 676 fathoms. At 4 p.m., still following the barrier
to the southwest, we reached a corner and found it receding
abruptly to the southeast. Our way was blocked by very
heavy pack, and after spending two hours in a vain search
for an opening, we moored the *Endurance* to a floe and
banked fires. During that day we passed two schools of
seals, swimming fast to the northwest and north-northeast.
The animals swam in close order, rising and blowing like
porpoises, and we wondered if there was any significance in
their journey northward at that time of the year. Several
young emperor penguins had been captured and brought
aboard on the previous day. Two of them were still alive
when the *Endurance* was brought alongside the floe. They
promptly hopped on to the ice, turned round, bowed grace-
fully three times, and retired to the far side of the floe. There
is something curiously human about the manners and movements of these birds. I was concerned about the dogs. They
were losing condition and some of them appeared to be ailing. One dog had to be shot on the 12th.

We did not move the ship on the 14th. A breeze came
from the east in the evening, and under its influence the pack
began to work off shore. Before midnight the close ice that
had barred our way had opened and left a lane along the
foot of the barrier. I decided to wait for the morning, not
wishing to risk getting caught between the barrier and the
pack in the event of the wind changing. A sounding gave
1357 fathoms, with a bottom of glacial mud. The noon observation showed the position to be lat. 74° 09′ S., long. 27°
16′ W. We cast off at 6 a.m. on the 15th in hazy weather
with a northeasterly breeze, and proceeded along the barrier
in open water. The course was southeast for sixteen miles,

then south-southeast. We now had solid pack to windward, and at 3 p.m. we passed a bight probably ten miles deep and running to the northeast. A similar bight appeared at 6 p.m. These deep cuts strengthened the impression we had already formed that for several days we had been rounding a great mass of ice, at least fifty miles across, stretching out from the coast and possibly destined to float away at some time in the future. The soundings—roughly, 200 fathoms at the landward side and 1300 fathoms at the seaward side— suggested that this mighty projection was afloat. Seals were plentiful. We saw large numbers on the pack and several on low parts of the barrier, where the slope was easy. The ship passed through large schools of seals swimming from the barrier to the pack off shore. The animals were splashing and blowing around the *Endurance,* and Hurley made a record of this unusual sight with the motion-picture camera.

The barrier now stretched to the southwest again. Sail was set to a fresh easterly breeze, but at 7 p.m. it had to be furled, the *Endurance* being held up by pack-ice against the barrier for an hour. We took advantage of the pause to sound and got 268 fathoms with glacial mud and pebbles. Then a small lane appeared ahead. We pushed through at full speed, and by 8:30 p.m. the *Endurance* was moving southward with sails set in a fine expanse of open water. We continued to skirt the barrier in clear weather. I was watching for possible landing places, though as a matter of fact I had no intention of landing north of Vahsel Bay, in Luitpold Land, except under pressure of necessity. Every mile gained towards the south meant a mile less sledging when the time came for the overland journey.

Shortly before midnight on the 15th we came abreast of the northern edge of a great glacier or overflow from the inland ice, projecting beyond the barrier into the sea. It was 400 or 500 ft. high, and at its edge was a large mass of thick bay ice. The bay formed by the northern edge of this glacier

would have made an excellent landing place. A flat ice foot
nearly three feet above sea level looked like a natural quay.
From this ice foot a snow slope rose to the top of the barrier.
The bay was protected from the southeasterly wind and was
open only to the northerly wind, which is rare in those latitudes. A sounding gave 80 fathoms, indicating that the glacier was aground. I named the place Glacier Bay, and had
reason later to remember it with regret.

The *Endurance* steamed along the front of this ice flow
for about seventeen miles. The glacier showed huge crevasses and high pressure ridges, and appeared to run back to
ice-covered slopes or hills 1000 or 2000 ft. high. Some bays
in its front were filled with smooth ice, dotted with seals and
penguins. At 4 a.m. on the 16th we reached the edge of another huge glacial overflow from the ice sheet. The ice appeared to be coming over low hills and was heavily broken.
The cliff face was 250 to 350 ft. high, and the ice surface
two miles inland was probably 2000 ft. high. The cliff front
showed a tide mark of about 6 ft., proving that it was not
afloat. We steamed along the front of this tremendous glacier
for 40 miles and then, at 8:30 a.m., we were held up by solid
pack-ice, which appeared to be held by stranded bergs. The
depth, two cables off the barrier cliff, was 134 fathoms. No
further advance was possible that day, but the noon observation, which gave the position as lat. 76° 27′ S., long. 28° 51′
W., showed that we had gained 124 miles to the southwest
during the preceding twenty-four hours. The afternoon was
not without incident. The bergs in the neighborhood were
very large, several being over 200 ft. high, and some of them
were firmly aground, showing tide marks. A barrier berg
bearing northwest appeared to be about 25 miles long. We
pushed the ship against a small banded berg, from which
Wordie secured several large lumps of biotite granite. While
the *Endurance* was being held slow ahead against the berg a
loud crack was heard, and the geologist had to scramble

aboard at once. The bands on this berg were particularly well defined; they were due to morainic action in the parent glacier. Later in the day the easterly wind increased to a gale. Fragments of floe drifted past at about two knots, and the pack to leeward began to break up fast. A low berg of shallow draught drove down into the grinding pack and, smashing against two larger stranded bergs, pushed them off the bank. The three went away together pell-mell. We took shelter under the lee of a large stranded berg.

A blizzard from the east-northeast prevented us leaving the shelter of the berg on the following day (Sunday, January 17). The weather was clear, but the gale drove dense clouds of snow off the land and obscured the coastline most of the time. "The land, seen when the air is clear, appears higher than we thought it yesterday; probably it rises to 3000 ft. above the head of the glacier. Caird Coast, as I have named it, connects Coats' Land, discovered by Bruce in 1904, with Luitpold Land, discovered by Filchner in 1912. The northern part is similar in character to Coats' Land. It is fronted by an undulating barrier, the van of a mighty ice sheet that is being forced outward from the high interior of the Antarctic Continent and apparently is sweeping over low hills, plains, and shallow seas as the great Arctic ice sheet once pressed over Northern Europe. The barrier surface, seen from the sea, is of a faint golden brown color. It terminates usually in cliffs ranging from 10 to 300 ft. in height, but in a very few places sweeps down level with the sea. The cliffs are of dazzling whiteness, with wonderful blue shadows. Far inland higher slopes can be seen, appearing like dim blue or faint golden fleecy clouds. These distant slopes have increased in nearness and clearness as we have come to the southwest, while the barrier cliffs here are higher and apparently firmer. We are now close to the junction with Luitpold Land. At this southern end of the Caird Coast the ice sheet, undulating over the hidden and imprisoned land, is bursting down a steep slope in tremendous glaciers, bristling with ridges and spikes of ice and seamed by thousands of crevasses. Along the whole length of the coast we have seen no bare land or rock. Not as much as a solitary nunatak has appeared to relieve the surface of ice and snow. But the upward sweep of the ice slopes towards the horizon and the ridges, terraces, and crevasses that appear as the ice approaches the sea tell of the hills and valleys that lie below."

The *Endurance* lay under the lee of the stranded berg until 7 a.m. on January 18. The gale had moderated by that time, and we proceeded under sail to the southwest through a lane that had opened along the glacier front. We skirted the glacier till 9:30 a.m., when it ended in two bays, open to the northwest but sheltered by stranded bergs to the west. The coast beyond trended south-southwest with a gentle land slope. "The pack now forces us to go west 14 miles, when we break through a long line of heavy brash mixed with large lumps and 'growlers.' We do this under the fore topsail only, the engines being stopped to protect the propeller. This takes us into open water, where we make S. 50°W. for 24 miles. Then we again encounter pack which forces us to the northwest for 10 miles, when we are brought up by heavy snow lumps, brash, and large, loose floes. The character of the pack shows change. The floes are very thick and are covered by deep snow. The brash between the floes is so thick and heavy that we cannot push through without a great expenditure of power, and then for a short distance only. We therefore lie to for a while to see if the pack opens at all when this northeast wind ceases."

Our position on the morning of the 19th was lat. 76° 34′ S., long. 31° 30′ W. The weather was good, but no advance could be made. The ice had closed around the ship during the night, and no water could be seen in any direction from the deck. A few lanes were in sight from the masthead. We sounded in 312 fathoms, finding mud, sand, and pebbles.

The land showed faintly to the east. We waited for the conditions to improve, and the scientists took the opportunity to dredge for biological and geological specimens. During the night a moderate northeasterly gale sprang up, and a survey of the position on the 20th showed that the ship was firmly beset. The ice was packed heavily and firmly all round the *Endurance* in every direction as far as the eye could reach from the masthead. There was nothing to be done till the conditions changed, and we waited through that day and the succeeding days with increasing anxiety. The east-northeasterly gale that had forced us to take shelter behind the stranded berg on the 16th had veered into the bight of the Weddell Sea, and the ship was now drifting southwest with the floes which had enclosed it. A slight movement of the ice round the ship caused the rudder to become dangerously jammed on the 21st, and we had to cut away the ice with ice chisels, heavy pieces of iron with 6-ft. wooden hafts. We kept steam up in readiness for a move if the opportunity offered, and the engines running full speed ahead helped to clear the rudder. Land was in sight to the east and south about sixteen miles distant on the 22nd. The land ice seemed to be faced with ice cliffs at most points, but here and there slopes ran down to sea level. Large crevassed areas in terraces parallel with the coast showed where the ice was moving down over foothills. The inland ice appeared for the most part to be undulating, smooth, and easy to march over, but many crevasses might have been concealed from us by the surface snow or by the absence of shadows. I thought that the land probably rose to a height of 5000 ft. forty or fifty miles inland. The accurate estimation of heights and distances in the Antarctic is always difficult, owing to the clear air, the confusing monotony of coloring, and the deceptive effect of mirage and refraction. The land appeared to increase in height to the southward, where we saw a line of land or barrier that must have been seventy miles, and possibly was even more distant.

Sunday, January 24, was a clear sunny day, with gentle easterly and southerly breezes. No open water could be seen from the masthead, but there was a slight water-sky to the west and northwest. "This is the first time for ten days that the wind has varied from northeast and east, and on five of these days it has risen to a gale. Evidently the ice has become firmly packed in this quarter, and we must wait patiently till a southerly gale occurs or currents open the ice. We are drifting slowly. The position today was 76° 49′ S., 33° 51′ W. Worsley and James, working on the floe with a Kew magnetometer, found the variation to be six degrees west." Just before midnight a crack developed in the ice five yards wide and a mile long, fifty yards ahead of the ship. The crack had widened to a quarter of a mile by 10 a.m. on the 25th, and for three hours we tried to force the ship into this opening with engines at full speed ahead and all sails set. The sole effect was to wash some ice away astern and clear the rudder, and after convincing myself that the ship was firmly held I abandoned the attempt. Later in the day Crean and two other men were over the side on a stage chipping at a large piece of ice that had got under the ship and appeared to be impeding her movement. The ice broke away suddenly, shot upward and overturned, pinning Crean between the stage and the haft of the heavy 11-ft. iron pincher. He was in danger for a few moments, but we got him clear, suffering merely from a few bad bruises. The thick iron bar had been bent against him to an angle of 45 degrees.

The days that followed were uneventful. Moderate breezes from the east and southwest had no apparent effect upon the ice, and the ship remained firmly held. On the 27th, the tenth day of inactivity, I decided to let the fires out. We had been burning half a ton of coal a day to keep steam in the boilers, and as the bunkers now contained only 67 tons, representing thirty-three days' steaming, we could not afford to continue this expenditure of fuel. Land still showed to the east and south when the horizon was clear. The biologist was securing some interesting specimens with the hand dredge at various depths. A sounding on the 26th gave 360 fathoms, and another on the 29th 449 fathoms. The drift was to the west, and an observation on the 31st (Sunday) showed that the ship had made eight miles during the week. James and Hudson rigged the wireless in the hope of hearing the monthly message from the Falkland Islands. This message would be due about 3:20 a.m. on the following morning, but James was doubtful about hearing anything with our small apparatus at a distance of 1630 miles from the dispatching station. We heard nothing, as a matter of fact, and later efforts were similarly unsuccessful. The conditions would have been difficult even for a station of high power.

We were accumulating gradually a stock of seal meat during these days of waiting. Fresh meat for the dogs was needed, and seal steaks and liver made a very welcome change from the ship's rations aboard the *Endurance*. Four crab eaters and three Weddells, over a ton of meat for dog and man, fell to our guns on February 2, and all hands were occupied most of the day getting the carcasses back to the ship over the rough ice. We rigged three sledges for man haulage and brought the seals about two miles, the sledging parties being guided among the ridges and pools by semaphore from the crow's nest. Two more seals were sighted on the far side of a big pool, but I did not allow them to be pursued. Some of the ice was in a treacherous condition, with thin films hiding cracks and pools, and I did not wish to risk an accident.

A crack about four miles long opened in the floe to the stern of the ship on the 3rd. The narrow lane in front was still open, but the prevailing light breezes did not seem likely to produce any useful movement in the ice. Early on the morning of the 5th a northeasterly gale sprang up, bringing overcast skies and thick snow. Soon the pack was open-

ing and closing without much loosening effect. At noon the
ship gave a sudden start and heeled over three degrees. Immediately afterwards, a crack ran from the bows to the lead
ahead and another to the lead astern. I thought it might be
possible to reeve the ship through one of these leads towards
open water, but we could see no water through the thick
snow, and before steam was raised, and while the view was
still obscured, the pack closed again. The northerly gale had
given place to light westerly breezes on the 6th. The pack
seemed to be more solid than ever. It stretched almost unbroken to the horizon in every direction, and the situation
was made worse by very low temperatures in succeeding
days. The temperature was down to zero on the night of the
7th and was two degrees below zero on the 8th. This cold
spell in midsummer was most unfortunate from our point of
view, since it cemented the pack and tightened the grip of
the ice upon the ship. The slow drift to the southwest continued, and we caught occasional glimpses of distant uplands
on the eastern horizon. The position on the 7th was lat. 76°
57′ S., long. 35° 7′ W. Soundings on the 6th and 8th found
glacial mud at 530 and 529 fathoms.

The *Endurance* was lying in a pool covered by young ice
on the 9th. The solid floes had loosened their grip on the
ship itself, but they were packed tightly all around. The
weather was foggy. We felt a slight northerly swell coming
through the pack, and the movement gave rise to hope that
there was open water near to us. At 11 a.m. a long crack
developed in the pack, running east and west as far as we
could see through the fog, and I ordered steam to be raised
in the hope of being able to break a way into this lead. The
effort failed. We could break the young ice in the pool, but
the pack defied us. The attempt was renewed on the 11th, a
fine clear day with blue sky. The temperature was still low,
−2° Fahr. at midnight. After breaking through some young
ice the *Endurance* became jammed against soft floe. The

engines running full speed astern produced no effect until
all hands joined in "sallying" ship. The dog kennels amidships made it necessary for the people to gather aft, where
they rushed from side to side in a mass in the confined space
around the wheel. This was a ludicrous affair, the men falling over one another amid shouts of laughter without producing much effect on the ship. She remained fast, while all
hands jumped at the word of command, but finally slid off
when the men were stamping hard at the double. We were
now in a position to take advantage of any opening that
might appear. The ice was firm around us, and as there
seemed small chance of making a move that day, I had the
motor crawler and warper put out on the floe for a trial run.
The motor worked most successfully, running at about six
miles an hour over slabs and ridges of ice hidden by a foot
or two of soft snow. The surface was worse than we would
expect to face on land or barrier ice. The motor warped itself
back on a 500-fathom steel wire and was taken aboard
again. "From the masthead the mirage is continually giving
us false alarms. Everything wears an aspect of unreality.
Icebergs hang upside down in the sky; the land appears as
layers of silvery or golden cloud. Cloud banks look like
land, icebergs masquerade as islands or nunataks, and the
distant barrier to the south is thrown into view, although it
really is outside our range of vision. Worst of all is the deceptive appearance of open water, caused by the refraction
of distant water, or by the sun shining at an angle on a field
of smooth snow or the face of ice cliffs below the horizon."

The second half of February produced no important
change in our situation. Early in the morning of the 14th I
ordered a good head of steam on the engines and sent all
hands on to the floe with ice chisels, prickers, saws, and
picks. We worked all day and throughout most of the next
day in a strenuous effort to get the ship into the lead ahead.
The men cut away the young ice before the bows and pulled

it aside with great energy. After twenty-four hours' labor we
had got the ship a third of the way to the lead. But about 400
yds. of heavy ice, including old rafted pack, still separated
the *Endurance* from the water, and reluctantly I had to admit
that further effort was useless. Every opening we made froze
up again quickly owing to the unseasonably low temperature.
The young ice was elastic and prevented the ship delivering
a strong, splitting blow to the floe, while at the same time it
held the older ice against any movement. The abandonment
of the attack was a great disappointment to all hands. The
men had worked long hours without thought of rest, and they
deserved success. But the task was beyond our powers. I had
not abandoned hope of getting clear, but was counting now
on the possibility of having to spend a winter in the inhospitable arms of the pack. The sun, which had been above the
horizon for two months, set at midnight on the 17th, and,
although it would not disappear until April, its slanting rays
warned us of the approach of winter. Pools and leads appeared occasionally, but they froze over very quickly.

   We continued to accumulate a supply of seal meat and
blubber, and the excursions across the floes to shoot and
bring in the seals provided welcome exercise for all hands.
Three crab-eater cows shot on the 21st were not accompanied
by a bull, and blood was to be seen about the hole from which
they had crawled. We surmised that the bull had become the
prey of one of the killer whales. These aggressive creatures
were to be seen often in the lanes and pools, and we were
always distrustful of their ability or willingness to discrimi-
nate between seal and man. A lizard-like head would show
while the killer gazed along the floe with wicked eyes. Then
the brute would dive, to come up a few moments later, perhaps, under some unfortunate seal reposing on the ice. Worsley examined a spot where a killer had smashed a hole 8 ft.
by 12 ft. in 12½ in. of hard ice, covered by 2½ in. of snow.
Big blocks of ice had been tossed on to the floe surface. Wor-

die, engaged in measuring the thickness of young ice, went through to his waist one day just as a killer rose to blow in the adjacent lead. His companions pulled him out hurriedly.

On the 22nd the *Endurance* reached the farthest south point of her drift, touching the 77th parallel of latitude in long. 35° W. The summer had gone; indeed the summer had scarcely been with us at all. The temperatures were low day and night, and the pack was freezing solidly around the ship. The thermometer recorded 10° below zero Fahr. at 2 a.m. on the 22nd. Some hours earlier we had watched a wonderful golden mist to the southward, where the rays of the declining sun shone through vapor rising from the ice. All normal standards of perspective vanish under such conditions, and the low ridges of the pack, with mist lying between them, gave the illusion of a wilderness of mountain peaks like the Bernese Oberland. I could not doubt now that the *Endurance* was confined for the winter. Gentle breezes from the east, south, and southwest did not disturb the hardening floes. The seals were disappearing and the birds were leaving us. The land showed still in fair weather on the distant horizon, but it was beyond our reach now, and regrets for havens that lay behind us were vain. "We must wait for the spring, which may bring us better fortune. If I had guessed a month ago that the ice would grip us here, I would have established our base at one of the landing places at the great glacier. But there seemed no reason to anticipate then that the fates would prove unkind. This calm weather with intense cold in a summer month is surely exceptional. My chief anxiety is the drift. Where will the vagrant winds and currents carry the ship during the long winter months that are ahead of us? We will go west, no doubt, but how far? And will it be possible to break out of the pack early in the spring and reach Vahsel Bay or some other suitable landing place? These are momentous questions for us."

On February 24 we ceased to observe ship routine, and

the *Endurance* became a winter station. All hands were on
duty during the day and slept at night, except a watchman
who looked after the dogs and watched for any sign of movement in the ice. We cleared a space of 10 ft. by 20 ft. round
the rudder and propeller, sawing through ice 2 ft. thick, and
lifting the blocks with a pair of tongs made by the carpenter.
Crean used the blocks to make an ice house for the dog
Sally, which had added a little litter of pups to the strength
of the expedition. Seals appeared occasionally, and we killed
all that came within our reach. They represented fuel as well
as food for men and dogs. Orders were given for the after-
hold to be cleared and the stores checked, so that we might
know exactly how we stood for a siege by an Antarctic winter. The dogs went off the ship on the following day. Their
kennels were placed on the floe along the length of a wire
rope to which the leashes were fastened. The dogs seemed
heartily glad to leave the ship, and yelped loudly and joy-
ously as they were moved to their new quarters. We had
begun the training of teams, and already there was keen ri-
valry between the drivers. The flat floes and frozen leads in
the neighborhood of the ship made excellent training
grounds. Hockey and soccer on the floe were our chief recre-
ations, and all hands joined in many a strenuous game.

Worsley took a party to the floe on the 26th and started
building a line of igloos and "dogloos" round the ship.
These little buildings were constructed, Eskimo fashion, of
big blocks of ice, with thin sheets for the roofs. Boards or
frozen sealskins were placed over all, snow was piled on top
and pressed into the joints, and then water was thrown over
the structures to make everything firm. The ice was packed
down flat inside and covered with snow for the dogs, which
preferred, however, to sleep outside except when the
weather was extraordinarily severe. The tethering of the
dogs was a simple matter. The end of a chain was buried
about eight inches in the snow, some fragments of ice were

pressed around it, and a little water poured over all. The icy breath of the Antarctic cemented it in a few moments. Four dogs which had been ailing were shot. Some of the dogs were suffering badly from worms, and the remedies at our disposal, unfortunately, were not effective. All the fit dogs were being exercised in the sledges, and they took to the work with enthusiasm. Sometimes their eagerness to be off and away produced laughable results, but the drivers learned to be alert. The wireless apparatus was still rigged, but we listened in vain for the Saturday night time signals from New Year Island, ordered for our benefit by the Argentine Government. On Sunday the 28th, Hudson waited at 2 a.m. for the Port Stanley monthly signals, but could hear nothing. Evidently the distances were too great for our small plant.

CHAPTER III

WINTER MONTHS

THE MONTH OF March opened with a severe northeasterly gale. Five Weddells and two crab eaters were shot on the floe during the morning of March 1, and the wind, with fine drifting snow, sprang up while the carcasses were being brought in by sledging parties. The men were compelled to abandon some of the blubber and meat, and they had a struggle to get back to the ship over the rough ice in the teeth of the storm. This gale continued until the 3rd, and all hands were employed clearing out the 'tween decks, which was to be converted into a living and dining room for officers and scientists. The carpenter erected in this room the stove that had been intended for use in the shore hut, and the quarters were made very snug. The dogs appeared indifferent to the blizzard. They emerged occasionally from the drift to shake themselves and bark, but were content most of the time to lie, curled into tight balls, under the snow. One of the old dogs, Saint, died on the night of the 2nd, and the doctors reported that the cause of death was appendicitis.

When the gale cleared we found that the pack had been driven in from the northeast and was now more firmly consolidated than before. A new berg, probably fifteen miles in length, had appeared on the northern horizon. The bergs within our circle of vision had all become familiar objects, and we had names for some of them. Apparently they were all drifting with the pack. The sighting of a new berg was of more than passing interest, since in that comparatively shallow sea it would be possible for a big berg to become stranded. Then the island of ice would be a center of tremendous pressure and disturbance amid the drifting pack. We had seen something already of the smashing effect of a contest between berg and floe, and had no wish to have the helpless *Endurance* involved in such a battle of giants. During the 3rd the seal meat and blubber was restowed on hummocks around the ship. The frozen masses had been sinking into the floe. Ice, though hard and solid to the touch, is never firm against heavy weights. An article left on the floe for any length of time is likely to sink into the surface ice. Then the salt water will percolate through and the article will become frozen into the body of the floe.

Clear weather followed the gale, and we had a series of mock suns and parhelia. Minus temperatures were the rule, 21° below zero Fahr. being recorded on the 6th. We made mattresses for the dogs by stuffing sacks with straw and rubbish, and most of the animals were glad to receive this furnishing in their kennels. Some of them had suffered through the snow melting with the heat of their bodies and then freezing solid. The scientific members of the expedition were all busy by this time. The meteorologist had got his recording station, containing anemometer, barograph, and thermograph, rigged over the stern. The geologist was making the best of what to him was an unhappy situation, but was not altogether without material. The pebbles found in the penguins were often of considerable interest, and some fragments of rock were brought up from the sea floor with the sounding lead and the drag net. On the 7th Wordie and Worsley found some small pebbles, a piece of moss, a perfect bivalve shell, and some dust on a berg fragment, and brought their treasure trove proudly to the ship. Clark was using the drag net frequently in the leads and secured good hauls of *plankton,* with occasional specimens of greater scientific interest. Seals were not plentiful, but our store of meat and blubber grew gradually. All hands ate seal meat with relish and would not have cared to become dependent on the ship's tinned meat. We preferred the crab eater to the

Weddell, which is a very sluggish beast. The crab eater seemed cleaner and healthier. The killer whales were still with us. On the 8th we examined a spot where the floe ice had been smashed up by a blow from beneath, delivered presumably by a large whale in search of a breathing place. The force that had been exercised was astonishing. Slabs of ice 3 ft. thick, and weighing tons, had been tented upwards over a circular area with a diameter of about 25 ft., and cracks radiated outwards for more than 20 ft.

The quarters in the 'tween decks were completed by the 10th, and the men took possession of the cubicles that had been built. The largest cubicle contained Macklin, McIlroy, Hurley, and Hussey and it was named "The Billabong." Clark and Wordie lived opposite in a room called "Auld Reekie." Next came the abode of "The Nuts" or engineers, followed by "The Sailors' Rest," inhabited by Cheetham and McNeish. "The Anchorage" and "The Fumarole" were on the other side. The new quarters became known as "The Ritz," and meals were served there instead of in the ward-room. Breakfast was at 9 a.m., lunch at 1 p.m., tea at 4 p.m., and dinner at 6 p.m. Wild, Marston, Crean, and Worsley established themselves in cubicles in the wardroom, and by the middle of the month all hands had settled down to the winter routine. I lived alone aft.

Worsley, Hurley, and Wordie made a journey to a big berg, called by us the Rampart Berg, on the 11th. The distance out was 7½ miles, and the party covered a total distance of about 17 miles. Hurley took some photographs and Wordie came back rejoicing with a little dust and some moss. "Within a radius of one mile round the berg there is thin young ice, strong enough to march over with care," wrote Worsley. "The area of dangerous pressure, as regards a ship, does *not* seem to extend for more than a quarter of a mile from the berg. Here there are cracks and constant slight movement, which becomes exciting to the traveler when he feels a piece of ice gradually upending beneath his feet. Close to the berg the pressure makes all sorts of quaint noises. We heard tapping as from a hammer, grunts, groans and squeaks, electric trams running, birds singing, kettles boiling noisily, and an occasional swish as a large piece of ice, released from pressure, suddenly jumped or turned over. We noticed all sorts of quaint effects, such as huge bubbles or domes of ice, 40 ft. across and 4 or 5 ft. high. Large sinuous pancake sheets were spread over the floe in places, and in one spot we counted five such sheets, each about 2½ in. thick, imbricated under one another. They look as though made of barley sugar and are very slippery." The noon position on the 14th was lat. 76° 54′ S., long. 36° 10′ W. The land was visible faintly to the southeast, distant about 36 miles. A few small leads could be seen from the ship, but the ice was firm in our neighborhood. The drift of the *Endurance* was still towards the northwest.

I had the boilers blown down on the 15th, and the consumption of 2 cwt. of coal per day to keep the boilers from freezing then ceased. The bunkers still contained 52 tons of coal, and the daily consumption in the stoves was about 2½ cwt. There would not be much coal left for steaming purposes in the spring, but I anticipated eking out the supply with blubber.

A moderate gale from the northeast on the 17th brought fine, penetrating snow. The weather cleared in the evening, and a beautiful crimson sunset held our eyes. At the same time the ice cliffs of the land were thrown up in the sky by mirage, with an apparent reflection in open water, though the land itself could not be seen definitely. The effect was repeated in an exaggerated form on the following day, when the ice cliffs were thrown up above the horizon in double and treble parallel lines, some inverted. The mirage was due probably to lanes of open water near the land. The water would be about 30° warmer than the air and would cause warmed strata to ascend. A sounding gave 606 fathoms, with a bottom of glacial mud. Six days later, on the 24th, the depth was 419 fathoms. We were drifting steadily, and the constant movement, coupled with the appearance of lanes near the land, convinced me that we must stay by the ship till she got clear. I had considered the possibility of making a landing across the ice in the spring, but the hazards of such an undertaking would be too great.

The training of the dogs in sledge teams was making progress. The orders used by the drivers were "Mush" (Go on), "Gee" (Right), "Haw" (Left), and "Whoa" (Stop). These are the words that the Canadian drivers long ago adopted, borrowing them originally from England. There were many fights at first, until the dogs learned their positions and their duties, but as days passed drivers and teams became efficient. Each team had its leader, and efficiency depended largely on the willingness and ability of this dog to punish skulking and disobedience. We learned not to interfere unless the disciplinary measures threatened to have a fatal termination. The drivers could sit on the sledge and jog along at ease if they chose. But the prevailing minus temperatures made riding unpopular, and the men preferred usually to run or walk alongside the teams. We were still losing dogs through sickness, due to stomach and intestinal worms.

Dredging for specimens at various depths was one of the duties during these days. The dredge and several hundred fathoms of wire line made a heavy load, far beyond the unaided strength of the scientists. On the 23rd, for example, we put down a 2-ft. dredge and 650 fathoms of wire. The dredge was hove in four hours later and brought much glacial mud, several pebbles and rock fragments, three sponges, some worms, *brachiopods,* and *foraminiferæ.* The mud was troublesome. It was heavy to lift, and as it froze rapidly when brought to the surface, the recovery of the specimens embedded in it was difficult. A haul made on the 26th brought a prize for the geologist in the form of a lump of sandstone weighing 75 lb., a piece of fossiliferous limestone, a fragment of striated shale, sandstone grit, and some pebbles. Hauling in the dredge by hand was severe work, and on the 24th we used the Girling tractor motor, which brought in 500 fathoms of line in thirty minutes, including stops. One stop was due to water having run over the friction gear and frozen. It was a day or two later that we heard a great yell from the floe and found Clark dancing about and shouting Scottish war cries. He had secured his first complete specimen of an Antarctic fish, apparently a new species.

Mirages were frequent. Barrier cliffs appeared all around us on the 29th, even in places where we knew there was deep water. "Bergs and pack are thrown up in the sky and distorted into the most fantastic shapes. They climb, trembling, upwards, spreading out into long lines at different levels, then contract and fall down, leaving nothing but an uncertain, wavering smudge which comes and goes. Presently the smudge swells and grows, taking shape until it presents the perfect inverted reflection of a berg on the horizon, the shadow hovering over the substance. More smudges appear at different points on the horizon. These spread out into long lines till they meet, and are girdled by lines of shining snow cliffs, laved at their bases by waters of illusion in which they appear to be faithfully reflected. So the shadows come and go silently, melting away finally as the sun declines to the west. We seem to be drifting helplessly in a strange world of unreality. It is reassuring to feel the ship beneath one's feet and to look down at the familiar line of kennels and igloos on the solid floe." The floe was not so solid as it appeared. We had reminders occasionally that the greedy sea was very close, and that the floe was but a treacherous friend, which might open suddenly beneath us. Towards the end of the month I had our store of seal meat and blubber brought aboard. The depth as recorded by a sounding on the last day of March was 256 fathoms. The continuous shoaling from 606 fathoms in a drift of 39 miles N. 26° W. in thirty days was interesting. The sea shoaled as we went north, either to east or to west, and the fact suggested that the contour lines ran east and west, roughly. Our total drift between January 19, when the ship was frozen in, and March 31, a period of seventy-one days, had been 95 miles in a N. 80° W. direction. The icebergs around us had not changed their relative positions.

The sun sank lower in the sky, the temperatures became lower, and the *Endurance* felt the grip of the icy hand of winter. Two northeasterly gales in the early part of April assisted to consolidate the pack. The young ice was thickening rapidly, and though leads were visible occasionally from the ship, no opening of a considerable size appeared in our neighborhood. In the early morning of April 1 we listened again for the wireless signals from Port Stanley. The crew had lashed three 20-ft. rickers to the mastheads in order to increase the spread of our aerials, but still we failed to hear anything. The rickers had to come down subsequently, since we found that the gear could not carry the accumulating weight of rime. Soundings proved that the sea continued to shoal as the *Endurance* drifted to the northwest. The depth on April 2 was 262 fathoms, with a bottom of glacial mud. Four weeks later a sounding gave 172 fathoms. The presence of grit in the bottom samples towards the end of the month suggested that we were approaching land again.

The month was not uneventful. During the night of the 3rd we heard the ice grinding to the eastward, and in the morning we saw that young ice was rafted 8 to 10 ft. high in places. This was the first murmur of the danger that was to reach menacing proportions in later months. The ice was heard grinding and creaking during the 4th and the ship vibrated slightly. The movement of the floe was sufficiently pronounced to interfere with the magnetic work. I gave orders that accumulations of snow, ice, and rubbish alongside the *Endurance* should be shoveled away, so that in case of pressure there would be no weight against the topsides to check the ship rising above the ice. All hands were busy with pick and shovel during the day, and moved many tons of material. Again, on the 9th, there were signs of pressure. Young ice was piled up to a height of 11 ft. astern of the ship, and the old floe was cracked in places. The movement was not serious, but I realized that it might be the beginning of trouble for the Expedition. We brought certain stores aboard and provided space on deck for the dogs in case they had to be removed from the floe at short notice. We had run a 500-fathom steel wire round the ship, snow huts, and kennels, with a loop out to the lead ahead, where the dredge was used. This wire was supported on ice pillars, and it served as a guide in bad weather when the view was obscured by driving snow and a man might have lost himself altogether. I had this wire cut in five places, since otherwise it might have been dragged across our section of the floe with damaging effect in the event of the ice splitting suddenly.

The dogs had been divided into six teams of nine dogs each. Wild, Crean, Macklin, McIlroy, Marston, and Hurley each had charge of a team, and were fully responsible for the exercising, training, and feeding of their own dogs. They called in one of the surgeons when an animal was sick. We were still losing some dogs through worms, and it was unfortunate that the doctors had not the proper remedies. Worm powders were to have been provided by the expert Canadian dog driver I had engaged before sailing for the south, and when this man did not join the Expedition the matter was overlooked. We had fifty-four dogs and eight pups early in April, but several were ailing, and the number of mature dogs was reduced to fifty by the end of the month. Our store of seal meat amounted now to about 5000 lb., and I calculated that we had enough meat and blubber to feed the dogs for ninety days without trenching upon the sledging rations. The teams were working well, often with heavy loads. The biggest dog was Hercules, who tipped the beam at 86 lb. Samson was 11 lb. lighter, but he justified his name one day by starting off at a smart pace with a sledge carrying 200 lb. of blubber and a driver.

A new berg that was going to give us some cause for anxiety made its appearance on the 14th. It was a big berg, and we noticed as it lay on the northwest horizon that it had a hummocky, crevassed appearance at the east end. During the day this berg increased its apparent altitude and changed its bearing slightly. Evidently it was aground and was holding its position against the drifting pack. A sounding at 11 a.m. gave 197 fathoms, with a hard stony or rocky bottom. During the next twenty-four hours the *Endurance* moved steadily towards the crevassed berg, which doubled its altitude in that time. We could see from the masthead that the pack was piling and rafting against the mass of ice, and it was easy to imagine what would be the fate of the ship if she entered the area of disturbance. She would be crushed like an eggshell amid the shattering masses.

Worsley was in the crow's nest on the evening of the 15th, watching for signs of land to the westward, and he reported an interesting phenomenon. The sun set amid a glow of prismatic colors on a line of clouds just above the horizon. A minute later Worsley saw a golden glow, which expanded as he watched it, and presently the sun appeared again and rose a semi-diameter clear above the western horizon. He hailed Crean, who from a position on the floe 90 ft. below the crow's nest also saw the reborn sun. A quarter of an hour later from the deck Worsley saw the sun set a second time. This strange phenomenon was due to mirage or refraction. We attributed it to an ice crack to the westward, where the band of open water had heated a stratum of air.

The drift of the pack was not constant, and during the

succeeding days the crevassed berg alternately advanced and receded as the *Endurance* moved with the floe. On Sunday, April 18, it was only seven miles distant from the ship. "It is a large berg, about three-quarters of a mile long on the side presented to us and probably well over 200 ft. high. It is heavily crevassed, as though it once formed the sérac portion of a glacier. Two specially wide and deep chasms across it from southeast to northwest give it the appearance of having broken its back on the shoal ground. Huge masses of pressure ice are piled against its cliffs to a height of about 60 ft., showing the stupendous force that is being brought to bear upon it by the drifting pack. The berg must be very firmly aground. We swing the arrow on the current meter frequently and watch with keen attention to see where it will come to rest. Will it point straight for the berg, showing that our drift is in that direction? It swings slowly round. It points to the northeast end of the berg, then shifts slowly to the center and seems to stop; but it moves again and swings 20 degrees clear of our enemy to the southwest. . . . We notice that two familiar bergs, the Rampart Berg and the Peak Berg, have moved away from the ship. Probably they also have grounded or dragged on the shoal." A strong drift to the westward during the night of the 18th relieved our anxiety by carrying the *Endurance* to the lee of the crevassed berg, which passed out of our range of vision before the end of the month.

We said good-bye to the sun on May 1 and entered the period of twilight that would be followed by the darkness of midwinter. The sun by the aid of refraction just cleared the horizon at noon and set shortly before 2 p.m. A fine aurora in the evening was dimmed by the full moon, which had risen on April 27 and would not set again until May 6. The disappearance of the sun is apt to be a depressing event in the polar regions, where the long months of darkness involve mental as well as physical strain. But the *Endurance*'s company refused to abandon their customary cheerfulness, and a concert in the evening made the Ritz a scene of noisy merriment, in strange contrast with the cold, silent world that lay outside. "One feels our helplessness as the long winter night closes upon us. By this time, if fortune had smiled upon the Expedition, we would have been comfortably and securely established in a shore base, with depots laid to the south and plans made for the long march in the spring and summer. Where will we make a landing now? It is not easy to forecast the future. The ice may open in the spring, but by that time we will be far to the northwest. I do not think we shall be able to work back to Vahsel Bay. There are possible landing places on the western coast of the Weddell Sea, but can we reach any suitable spot early enough to attempt the overland journey next year? Time alone will tell. I do not think any member of the Expedition is disheartened by our disappointment. All hands are cheery and busy, will do their best when the time for action comes. In the meantime we must wait."

The ship's position on Sunday, May 2, was lat. 75° 23′ S., long. 42° 14′ W. The temperature at noon was 5° below zero Fahr., and the sky was overcast. A seal was sighted from the masthead at lunch time, and five men, with two dog teams, set off after the prize. They had an uncomfortable journey outward in the dim, diffused light, which cast no shadows and so gave no warning of irregularities in the white surface. It is a strange sensation to be running along on apparently smooth snow and to fall suddenly into an unseen hollow, or bump against a ridge. "After going out three miles to the eastward," wrote Worsley in describing this seal hunt, "we range up and down but find nothing, until from a hummock I fancy I see something apparently a mile away, but probably little more than half that distance. I ran for it, found the seal, and with a shout brought up the others at the double. The seal was a big Weddell, over 10 ft. long and weighing more than 800 lb. But Soldier, one of the team leaders, went for its throat without a moment's hesitation, and we had to beat off the dogs before we could shoot the seal. We caught five or six gallons of blood in a tin for the dogs, and let the teams have a drink of fresh blood from the seal. The light was worse than ever on our return, and we arrived back in the dark. Sir Ernest met us with a lantern and guided us into the lead astern and thence to the ship." This was the first seal we had secured since March 19, and the meat and blubber made a welcome addition to the stores.

Three emperor penguins made their appearance in a lead west of the ship on May 3. They pushed their heads through the young ice while two of the men were standing by the lead. The men imitated the emperor's call and walked slowly, penguin fashion, away from the lead. The birds in succession made a magnificent leap 3 ft. clear from the water on to the young ice. Thence they tobogganed to the bank and followed the men away from the lead. Their retreat was soon cut off by a line of men. "We walk up to them, talking loudly and assuming a threatening aspect. Notwithstanding our bad manners, the three birds turn towards us, bowing ceremoniously. Then, after a closer inspection, they conclude that we are undesirable acquaintances and make off across the floe. We head them off and finally shepherd them close to the ship, where the frenzied barking of the dogs so frightens them that they make a determined effort to break through the line. We seize them. One bird of philosophic mien goes quietly, led by one flipper. The others show fight, but all are imprisoned in an igloo for the night. . . . In the afternoon we see five emperors in the western lead and capture one. Kerr and Cheetham fight a valiant action with two large birds. Kerr rushes at one, seizes it, and is promptly knocked down by the angered penguin, which jumps on his chest before retiring. Cheetham comes to Kerr's assistance, and between them they seize another penguin, bind his bill and lead him, muttering muffled protests, to the ship like an inebriated old man between two policemen. He weighs 85 lb., or 5 lb. less than the heaviest emperor captured previously. Kerr and Cheetham insist that he is nothing to the big fellow who escaped them." This penguin's stomach proved to be filled with freshly caught fish up to 10 in. long. Some of the fish were of a coastal or littoral variety. Two more emperors were captured on the following day, and, while Wordie was leading one of them towards the ship, Wild came along with his team. The dogs, uncontrollable in a moment, made a frantic rush for the bird, and were almost upon him when their harness caught upon an ice pylon, which they had tried to pass on both sides at once. The result was a seething tangle of dogs, traces, and men, and an overturned sledge, while the penguin, three yards away, nonchalantly and indifferently surveyed the disturbance. He had never seen anything of the kind before and had no idea at all that the strange disorder might concern him. Several cracks had opened in the neighborhood of the ship, and the emperor penguins, fat and glossy of plumage, were appearing in considerable numbers. We secured nine of them on May 6, an important addition to our supply of fresh food.

The sun, which had made "positively his last appearance" seven days earlier, surprised us by lifting more than half its disk above the horizon on May 8. A glow on the northern horizon resolved itself into the sun at 11 a.m. that day. A quarter of an hour later the unseasonable visitor disappeared again, only to rise again at 11:40 a.m., set at 1 p.m., rise at 1:10 p.m., and set lingeringly at 1:20 p.m. These curious phenomena were due to refraction, which amounted to 2° 37' at 1:20 p.m. The temperature was 15° below Fahr., and we calculated that the refraction was 2° above normal. In other words, the sun was visible 120 miles farther south than the refraction tables gave it any right to be. The navigating officer naturally was aggrieved. He had informed all hands on May 1 that they would not see the sun again for seventy days, and now had to endure the jeers of friends who affected to believe that his observations were inaccurate by a few degrees.

The *Endurance* was drifting north-northeast under the influence of a succession of westerly and southwesterly breezes. The ship's head, at the same time, swung gradually to the left, indicating that the floe in which she was held was turning. During the night of the 14th a very pronounced swing occurred, and when daylight came at noon on the 15th we observed a large lead running from the northwest horizon towards the ship till it struck the western lead, circling ahead of the ship, then continuing to the south-southeast. A lead astern connected with this new lead on either side of the *Endurance,* thus separating our floe completely from the main body of the pack. A blizzard from the southeast swept down during the 16th. At 1 p.m. the blizzard lulled for five minutes; then the wind jumped round to the opposite quarter and the barometer rose suddenly. The center of a cyclonic movement had passed over us, and the compass recorded an extraordinarily rapid swing of the floe. I could see nothing through the mist and snow, and I thought it possible that a magnetic storm or a patch of local magnetic attraction had caused the compass, and not the floe, to swing. Our floe was now about 2½ miles long north and south and 3 miles wide east and west.

The month of May passed with few incidents of importance. Hurley, our handy man, installed our small electric-lighting plant and placed lights for occasional use in the observatory, the meteorological station, and various other points. We could not afford to use the electric lamps freely. Hurley also rigged two powerful lights on poles projecting from the ship to port and starboard. These lamps would illuminate the "dogloos" brilliantly on the darkest winter's day

and would be invaluable in the event of the floe breaking
during the dark days of winter. We could imagine what it
would mean to get fifty dogs aboard without lights while the
floe was breaking and rafting under our feet. May 24, Empire Day, was celebrated with the singing of patriotic songs
in the Ritz, where all hands joined in wishing a speedy victory for the British arms. We could not know how the war
was progressing, but we hoped that the Germans had already
been driven from France and that the Russian armies had
put the seal on the Allies' success. The war was a constant
subject of discussion aboard the *Endurance,* and many campaigns were fought on the map during the long months of
drifting. The moon in the latter part of May was sweeping
continuously through our starlit sky in great high circles.
The weather generally was good, with constant minus temperatures. The log on May 27 recorded: "Brilliantly fine
clear weather with bright moonlight throughout. The
moon's rays are wonderfully strong, making midnight seem
as light as an ordinary overcast midday in temperate climes.
The great clearness of the atmosphere probably accounts for
our having eight hours of twilight with a beautiful soft
golden glow to the northward. A little rime and glazed frost
are found aloft. The temperature is − 20° Fahr. A few wisps
of cirrus cloud are seen and a little frost-smoke shows in
one or two directions, but the cracks and leads near the ship
appear to have frozen over again."

Crean had started to take the pups out for runs, and it was
very amusing to see them in their rolling canter just managing to keep abreast by the sledge and occasionally cocking
an eye with an appealing look in the hope of being taken
aboard for a ride. As an addition to the foster father, Crean,
the pups had adopted Amundsen. They tyrannized over him
most unmercifully. It was a common sight to see him, the
biggest dog in the pack, sitting out in the cold with an air of
philosophic resignation while a corpulent pup occupied the

entrance of his dogloo. The intruder was generally the pup Nelson, who just showed his forepaws and face, and one was fairly sure to find Nelly, Roger, and Toby coiled up comfortably behind him. At hoosh time Crean had to stand by Amundsen's food, since otherwise the pups would eat the big dog's ration while he stood back to give them fair play. Sometimes their consciences would smite them and they would drag round a seal's head, half a penguin, or a large lump of frozen meat or blubber to Amundsen's kennel for rent. It was interesting to watch the big dog play with them, seizing them by throat or neck in what appeared to be a fierce fashion, while really quite gentle with them, and all the time teaching them how to hold their own in the world and putting them up to all the tricks of dog life.

The drift of the *Endurance* in the grip of the pack continued without incident of importance through June. Pressure was reported occasionally, but the ice in the immediate vicinity of the ship remained firm. The light was now very bad except in the period when the friendly moon was above the horizon. A faint twilight round about noon of each day reminded us of the sun, and assisted us in the important work of exercising the dogs. The care of the teams was our heaviest responsibility in those days. The movement of the floes was beyond all human control, and there was nothing to be gained by allowing one's mind to struggle with the problems of the future, though it was hard to avoid anxiety at times. The conditioning and training of the dogs seemed essential, whatever fate might be in store for us, and the teams were taken out by their drivers whenever the weather permitted. Rivalries arose, as might have been expected, and on the 15th of the month a great race, the "Antarctic Derby," took place. It was a notable event. The betting had been heavy, and every man aboard the ship stood to win or lose on the results of the contest. Some money had been staked, but the wagers that thrilled were those involving stores of chocolate and cigarettes. The course had been laid off from Khyber Pass, at the eastern end of the old lead ahead of the ship, to a point clear of the jib boom, a distance of about 700 yds. Five teams went out in the dim noon twilight, with a zero temperature and an aurora flickering faintly to the southward. The starting signal was to be given by the flashing of a light on the meteorological station. I was appointed starter, Worsley was judge, and James was timekeeper. The bos'n, with a straw hat added to his usual Antarctic attire, stood on a box near the winning post, and was assisted by a couple of shady characters to shout the odds, which were displayed on a board hung around his neck—6 to 4 on Wild, "evens" on Crean, 2 to 1 against Hurley, 6 to 1 against Macklin, and 8 to 1 against McIlroy. Canvas handkerchiefs fluttered from an improvised grandstand, and the pups, which had never seen such strange happenings before, sat round and howled with excitement. The spectators could not see far in the dim light, but they heard the shouts of the drivers as the teams approached and greeted the victory of the favorite with a roar of cheering that must have sounded strange indeed to any seals or penguins that happened to be in our neighborhood. Wild's time was 2 min. 16 sec., or at the rate of 10½ miles per hour for the course.

We celebrated Midwinter's Day on the 22nd. The twilight extended over a period of about six hours that day, and there was a good light at noon from the moon, and also a northern glow with wisps of beautiful pink cloud along the horizon. A sounding gave 262 fathoms with a mud bottom. No land was in sight from the masthead, although our range of vision extended probably a full degree to the westward. The day was observed as a holiday, necessary work only being undertaken, and, after the best dinner the cook could provide, all hands gathered in the Ritz, where speeches, songs, and toasts occupied the evening. After supper at midnight we

sang "God Save the King" and wished each other all success in the days of sunshine and effort that lay ahead. At
this time the *Endurance* was making an unusually rapid drift
to the north under the influence of a fresh southerly to
southwesterly breeze. We traveled 39 miles to the north in
five days before a breeze that only once attained the force
of a gale and then for no more than an hour. The absence of
strong winds, in comparison with the almost unceasing winter blizzards of the Ross Sea, was a feature of the Weddell
Sea that impressed itself upon me during the winter months.

Another race took place a few days after the "Derby."
The two crack teams, driven by Hurley and Wild, met in a
race from Khyber Pass. Wild's team, pulling 910 lb., or 130
lb. per dog, covered the 700 yds. in 2 min. 9 sec., or at the
rate of 11.1 miles per hour. Hurley's team, with the same
load, did the run in 2 min. 16 sec. The race was awarded by
the judge to Hurley owing to Wild failing to "weigh in"
correctly. I happened to be a part of the load on his sledge,
and a skid over some new drift within fifty yards of the
winning post resulted in my being left on the snow. It should
be said in justice to the dogs that this accident, while justify-
ing the disqualification, could not have made any material
difference in the time.

The approach of the returning sun was indicated by beautiful sunrise glows on the horizon in the early days of July.
We had nine hours' twilight on the 10th, and the northern
sky, low to the horizon, was tinted with gold for about seven
hours. Numerous cracks and leads extended in all directions
to within 300 yds. of the ship. Thin wavering black lines
close to the northern horizon were probably distant leads
refracted into the sky. Sounds of moderate pressure came
to our ears occasionally, but the ship was not involved. At
midnight on the 11th a crack in the lead ahead of the *Endurance* opened out rapidly, and by 2 a.m. was over 200 yds.
wide in places with an area of open water to the southwest.

Sounds of pressure were heard along this lead, which soon closed to a width of about 30 yds. and then froze over. The temperature at that time was −23° Fahr.

The most severe blizzard we had experienced in the Weddell Sea swept down upon the *Endurance* on the evening of the 13th, and by breakfast time on the following morning the kennels to the windward, or southern side of the ship were buried under 5 ft. of drift. I gave orders that no man should venture beyond the kennels. The ship was invisible at a distance of fifty yards, and it was impossible to preserve one's sense of direction in the raging wind and suffocating drift. To walk against the gale was out of the question. Face and eyes became snowed up within two minutes, and serious frostbites would have been the penalty of perseverance. The dogs stayed in their kennels for the most part, the "old stagers" putting out a paw occasionally in order to keep open a breathing hole. By evening the gale had attained a force of 60 or 70 miles an hour, and the ship was trembling under the attack. But we were snug enough in our quarters aboard until the morning of the 14th, when all hands turned out to shovel the snow from deck and kennels. The wind was still keen and searching, with a temperature of something like −30° Fahr., and it was necessary for us to be on guard against frostbite. At least 100 tons of snow were piled against the bows and port side, where the weight of the drift had forced the floe downward. The lead ahead had opened out during the night, cracked the pack from north to south and frozen over again, adding 300 yds. to the distance between the ship and "Khyber Pass." The breakdown gang had completed its work by lunchtime. The gale was then decreasing and the three-days-old moon showed as a red crescent on the northern horizon. The temperature during the blizzard had ranged from −21° to −33.5° Fahr. It is usual for the temperature to rise during a blizzard, and the failure to produce any *Föhn* effect of this nature suggested an absence of high land for at least 200 miles to the south and southwest. The weather did not clear until the 16th. We saw then that the appearance of the surrounding pack had been altered completely by the blizzard. The "island" floe containing the *Endurance* still stood fast, but cracks and masses of ice thrown up by pressure could be seen in all directions. An area of open water was visible on the horizon to the north, with a water indication in the northern sky.

The ice pressure, which was indicated by distant rumblings and the appearance of formidable ridges, was increasingly a cause of anxiety. The areas of disturbance were gradually approaching the ship. During July 21 we could hear the grinding and crashing of the working floes to the southwest and west and could see cracks opening, working, and closing ahead. "The ice is rafting up to a height of 10 or 15 ft. in places, the opposing floes are moving against one another at the rate of about 200 yds. per hour. The noise resembles the roar of heavy, distant surf. Standing on the stirring ice one can imagine it is disturbed by the breathing and tossing of a mighty giant below." Early on the afternoon of the 22nd a 2-ft. crack, running southwest and northeast for a distance of about two miles, approached to within 35 yds. of the port quarter. I had all the sledges brought aboard and set a special watch in case it became necessary to get the dogs off the floe in a hurry. This crack was the result of heavy pressure 300 yds. away on the port bow, where huge blocks of ice were piled up in wild and threatening confusion. The pressure at that point was enormous. Blocks weighing many tons were raised 15 ft. above the level of the floe. I arranged to divide the night watches with Worsley and Wild, and none of us had much rest. The ship was shaken by heavy bumps, and we were on the alert to see that no dogs had fallen into cracks. The morning light showed that our island had been reduced considerably during the night. Our long months of rest and safety seemed to be at an end, and a period of stress had begun.

During the following day I had a store of sledging provisions, oil, matches, and other essentials placed on the upper deck handy to the starboard quarter boat, so as to be in readiness for a sudden emergency. The ice was grinding and working steadily to the southward, and in the evening some large cracks appeared on the port quarter, while a crack alongside opened out to 15 yds. The blizzard seemed to have set the ice in strong movement towards the north, and the southwesterly and west-southwesterly winds that prevailed two days out of three maintained the drift. I hoped that this would continue unchecked, since our chance of getting clear of the pack early in the spring appeared to depend upon our making a good northing. Soundings at this time gave depths of from 186 to 190 fathoms, with a glacial mud bottom. No land was in sight. The light was improving. A great deal of ice pressure was heard and observed in all directions during the 25th, much of it close to the port quarter of the ship. On the starboard bow huge blocks of ice, weighing many tons and 5 ft. in thickness, were pushed up on the old floe to a height of 15 to 20 ft. The floe that held the *Endurance* was swung to and fro by the pressure during the day, but came back to the old bearing before midnight. "The ice for miles around is much looser. There are numerous cracks and short leads to the northeast and southeast. Ridges are being forced up in all directions, and there is a water-sky to the southeast. It would be a relief to be able to make some effort on our own behalf; but we can do nothing until the ice releases our ship. If the floes continue to loosen, we may break out within the next few weeks and resume the fight. In the meantime the pressure continues, and it is hard to foresee the outcome. Just before noon today (July 26) the top of the sun appeared by refraction for one minute, seventy-nine days after our last sunset. A few minutes earlier a small patch of the sun had been thrown up on one of the black streaks above the horizon. All hands are cheered by the indi-

cation that the end of the winter darkness is near . . . Clark
finds that with returning daylight the *diatoms* are again appearing. His nets and line are stained a pale yellow, and
much of the newly formed ice has also a faint brown or
yellow tinge. The *diatoms* cannot multiply without light,
and the ice formed since February can be distinguished in
the pressure ridges by its clear blue color. The older masses
of ice are of a dark earthy brown, dull yellow, or reddish
brown."

The breakup of our floe came suddenly on Sunday, August 1, just one year after the *Endurance* left the South-West
Indian Docks on the voyage to the Far South. The position
was lat. 72° 26′ S., long. 48° 10′ W. The morning brought a
moderate southwesterly gale with heavy snow, and at 8
a.m., after some warning movements of the ice, the floe
cracked 40 yds. off the starboard bow. Two hours later the
floe began to break up all round us under pressure and the
ship listed over 10 degrees to starboard. I had the dogs and
sledges brought aboard at once and the gangway hoisted.
The animals behaved well. They came aboard eagerly as
though realizing their danger, and were placed in their quarters on deck without a single fight occurring. The pressure
was cracking the floe rapidly, rafting it close to the ship
and forcing masses of ice beneath the keel. Presently the
Endurance listed heavily to port against the gale, and at the
same time was forced ahead, astern, and sideways several
times by the grinding floes. She received one or two hard
nips, but resisted them without as much as a creak. It looked
at one stage as if the ship was to be made the plaything of
successive floes, and I was relieved when she came to a
standstill with a large piece of our old "dock" under the
starboard bilge. I had the boats cleared away ready for lowering, got up some additional stores, and set a double watch.
All hands were warned to stand by, get what sleep they
could, and have their warmest clothing at hand. Around us

lay the ruins of "Dog Town" amid the debris of pressure ridges. Some of the little dwellings had been crushed flat beneath blocks of ice; others had been swallowed and pulverized when the ice opened beneath them and closed again. It was a sad sight, but my chief concern just then was the safety of the rudder, which was being attacked viciously by the ice. We managed to pole away a large lump that had become jammed between the rudder and the stern post, but I could see that damage had been done, though a close examination was not possible that day.

After the ship had come to a standstill in her new position very heavy pressure was set up. Some of the trenails were started and beams buckled slightly under the terrific stresses. But the *Endurance* had been built to withstand the attacks of the ice, and she lifted bravely as the floes drove beneath her. The effects of the pressure around us were awe-inspiring. Mighty blocks of ice, gripped between meeting floes, rose slowly till they jumped like cherry-stones squeezed between thumb and finger. The pressure of millions of tons of moving ice was crushing and smashing inexorably. If the ship was once gripped firmly her fate would be sealed.

The gale from the southwest blew all night and moderated during the afternoon of the 2nd to a stiff breeze. The pressure had almost ceased. Apparently the gale had driven the southern pack down upon us, causing congestion in our area; the pressure had stopped when the whole of the pack got into motion. The gale had given us some northing, but it had dealt the *Endurance* what might prove to be a severe blow. The rudder had been driven hard over to starboard and the blade partially torn away from the rudder head. Heavy masses of ice were still jammed against the stern, and it was impossible to ascertain the extent of the damage at that time. I felt that it would be impossible in any case to effect repairs in the moving pack. The ship lay steady all night, and the sole sign of continuing pressure was an occasional slight rumbling shock. We rigged shelters and kennels for the dogs inboard.

The weather on August 3 was overcast and misty. We had nine hours of twilight, with good light at noon. There was no land in sight for ten miles from the masthead. The pack as far as the eye could reach was in a condition of chaos, much rafted and consolidated, with very large pressure ridges in all directions. At 9 p.m. a rough altitude of Canopus gave the latitude as 71° 55′ 17″ S. The drift, therefore, had been about 37 miles to the north in three days. Four of the poorest dogs were shot this day. They were suffering severely from worms, and we could not afford to keep sick dogs under the changed conditions. The sun showed through the clouds on the northern horizon for an hour on the 4th. There was no open water to be seen from aloft in any direction. We saw from the masthead to west-southwest an appearance of barrier, land, or a very long iceberg, about 20 odd miles away, but the horizon clouded over before we could determine its nature. We tried twice to make a sounding that day, but failed on each occasion. The Kelvin machine gave no bottom at the full length of the line, 370 fathoms. After much labor we made a hole in the ice near the stern post large enough for the Lucas machine with a 32-lb. lead; but this appeared to be too light. The machine stopped at 452 fathoms, leaving us in doubt as to whether bottom had been reached. Then in heaving up we lost the lead, the thin wire cutting its way into the ice and snapping. All hands and the carpenter were busy this day making and placing kennels on the upper deck, and by nightfall all the dogs were comfortably housed, ready for any weather. The sun showed through the clouds above the northern horizon for nearly an hour.

The remaining days of August were comparatively uneventful. The ice around the ship froze firm again and little

movement occurred in our neighborhood. The training of
the dogs, including the puppies, proceeded actively, and
provided exercise as well as occupation. The drift to the
northwest continued steadily. We had bad luck with soundings, the weather interfering at times and the gear breaking
on several occasions, but a big increase in the depth showed
that we had passed over the edge of the Weddell Sea plateau.
A sounding of about 1700 fathoms on August 10 agreed
fairly well with Filchner's 1924 fathoms, 130 miles east of
our then position. An observation at noon of the 8th had
given us lat. 71° 23' S., long. 49° 13' W. Minus temperatures
prevailed still, but the daylight was increasing. We captured
a few emperor penguins which were making their way to
the southwest. Ten penguins taken on the 19th were all in
poor condition, and their stomachs contained nothing but
stones and a few cuttlefish beaks. A sounding on the 17th
gave 1676 fathoms, 10 miles west of the charted position of
Morell Land. No land could be seen from the masthead, and
I decided that Morell Land must be added to the long list of
Antarctic islands and continental coasts that on close investigation have resolved themselves into icebergs. On clear
days we could get an extended view in all directions from
the masthead, and the line of the pack was broken only by
familiar bergs. About one hundred bergs were in view on a
fine day, and they seemed practically the same as when they
started their drift with us nearly seven months earlier. The
scientists wished to inspect some of the neighboring bergs
at close quarters, but sledge traveling outside the well-trod-
den area immediately around the ship proved difficult and
occasionally dangerous. On August 20, for example, Worsley, Hurley, and Greenstreet started off for the Rampart
Berg and got on to a lead of young ice that undulated peril-
ously beneath their feet. A quick turn saved them.

A wonderful mirage of the *fata Morgana* type was visible
on August 20. The day was clear and bright, with a blue sky

overhead and some rime aloft. "The distant pack is thrown up into towering barrier-like cliffs, which are reflected in blue lakes and lanes of water at their base. Great white and golden cities of Oriental appearance at close intervals along these cliff tops indicate distant bergs, some not previously known to us. Floating above these are wavering violet and creamy lines of still more remote bergs and pack. The lines rise and fall, tremble, dissipate, and reappear in an endless transformation scene. The southern pack and bergs, catching the sun's rays, are golden, but to the north the ice masses are purple. Here the bergs assume changing forms, first a castle, then a balloon just clear of the horizon, that changes swiftly into an immense mushroom, a mosque, or a cathedral. The principal characteristic is the vertical lengthening of the object, a small pressure ridge being given the appearance of a line of battlements or towering cliffs. The mirage is produced by refraction and is intensified by the columns of comparatively warm air rising from several cracks and leads that have opened eight to twenty miles away north and south." We noticed this day that a considerable change had taken place in our position relative to the Rampart Berg. It appeared that a big lead had opened and that there had been some differential movement of the pack. The opening movement might presage renewed pressure. A few hours later the dog teams, returning from exercise, crossed a narrow crack that had appeared ahead of the ship. This crack opened quickly to 60 ft. and would have given us trouble if the dogs had been left on the wrong side. It closed on the 25th and pressure followed in its neighborhood.

On August 24 we were two miles north of the latitude of Morell's farthest south, and over 10° of longitude, or more than 200 miles, west of his position. From the masthead no land could be seen within twenty miles, and no land of over 500 ft. altitude could have escaped observation on our side of long. 52° W. A sounding of 1900 fathoms on August 25

was further evidence of the nonexistence of New South
Greenland. There was some movement of the ice near the
ship during the concluding days of the month. All hands
were called out in the night of August 26, sounds of pressure
having been followed by the cracking of the ice alongside
the ship, but the trouble did not develop immediately. Late
on the night of the 31st the ice began to work ahead of
the ship and along the port side. Creaking and groaning of
timbers, accompanied by loud snapping sounds fore and aft,
told their story of strain. The pressure continued during the
following day, beams and deck planks occasionally buckling to the strain. The ponderous floes were grinding against
each other under the influence of wind and current, and our
ship seemed to occupy for the time being an undesirable
position near the center of the disturbance; but she resisted
staunchly and showed no sign of water in the bilges, although she had not been pumped out for six months. The
pack extended to the horizon in every direction. I calculated
that we were 250 miles from the nearest known land to the
westward, and more than 500 miles from the nearest outpost
of civilization, Wilhelmina Bay. I hoped we would not have
to undertake a march across the moving ice fields. The *Endurance* we knew to be stout and true; but no ship ever built
by man could live if taken fairly in the grip of the floes and
prevented from rising to the surface of the grinding ice.
These were anxious days. In the early morning of September
2 the ship jumped and shook to the accompaniment of
cracks and groans, and some of the men who had been in
the berths hurried on deck. The pressure eased a little later
in the day, when the ice on the port side broke away from
the ship to just abaft the main rigging. The *Endurance* was
still held aft and at the rudder, and a large mass of ice could
be seen adhering to the port bow, rising to within three feet
of the surface. I wondered if this ice had got its grip by
piercing the sheathing.

CHAPTER IV

LOSS OF THE *ENDURANCE*

THE ICE DID NOT trouble us again seriously until the end of September, though during the whole month the floes were seldom entirely without movement. The roar of pressure would come to us across the otherwise silent ice fields, and bring with it a threat and a warning. Watching from the crow's nest, we could see sometimes the formation of pressure ridges. The sunshine glittered on newly riven ice surfaces as the masses of shattered floe rose and fell away from the line of pressure. The area of disturbance would advance towards us, recede, and advance again. The routine of work and play on the *Endurance* proceeded steadily. Our plans and preparations for any contingency that might arise during the approaching summer had been made, but there seemed always plenty to do in and about our prisoned ship. Runs with the dogs and vigorous games of hockey and soccer on the rough snow-covered floe kept all hands in good fettle. The record of one or two of these September days will indicate the nature of our life and our surroundings:

"*September* 4.—Temperature, −14.1° Fahr. Light easterly breeze, blue sky, and stratus clouds. During forenoon notice a distinct terracotta or biscuit color in the stratus clouds to the north. This traveled from east to west and could conceivably have come from some of the Graham Land volcanoes, now about 300 miles distant to the northwest. The upper current of air probably would come from that direction. Heavy rime. Pack unbroken and unchanged as far as visible. No land for 22 miles. No animal life observed."

"*September* 7.—Temperature, −10.8° Fahr. Moderate

easterly to southerly winds, overcast and misty, with light snow till midnight, when weather cleared. Blue sky and fine clear weather to noon. Much rime aloft. Thick fresh snow on ship and floe that glistens brilliantly in the morning sunlight. Little clouds of faint violet-colored mist rise from the lower and brinier portions of the pack, which stretches unbroken to the horizon. Very great refraction all round. A tabular berg about fifty feet high ten miles west is a good index of the amount of refraction. On ordinary days it shows from the masthead, clear-cut against the sky; with much refraction, the pack beyond at the back of it lifts up into view; today a broad expanse of miles of pack is seen above it. Numerous other bergs generally seen in silhouette are, at first sight, lost, but after a closer scrutiny they appear as large lumps or dark masses well below the horizon. Refraction generally results in too big an altitude when observing the sun for position, but today the horizon is thrown up so much that the altitude is about 12' too small. No land visible for twenty miles. No animal life observed. Lower Clark's tow net with 566 fathoms wire, and hoist it up at two and a half miles an hour by walking across the floe with the wire. Result rather meager— jellyfish and some fish larvae. Exercise dogs in sledge teams. The young dogs, under Crean's care, pull as well, though not so strongly, as the best team in the pack. Hercules for the last fortnight or more has constituted himself leader of the orchestra. Two or three times in the twenty-four hours he starts a howl—a deep, melodious howl—and in about thirty seconds he has the whole pack in full song, the great deep, booming, harmonious song of the half-wolf pack."

By the middle of September we were running short of fresh meat for the dogs. The seals and penguins seemed to have abandoned our neighborhood altogether. Nearly five months had passed since we killed a seal, and penguins had been seen seldom. Clark, who was using his trawl as often as possible, reported that there was a marked absence of *plankton* in the sea, and we assumed that the seals and the penguins had gone in search of their accustomed food. The men got an emperor on the 23rd. The dogs, which were having their sledging exercise, became wildly excited when the penguin, which had risen in a crack, was driven ashore, and the best efforts of the drivers failed to save it alive. On the following day Wild, Hurley, Macklin, and McIlroy took their teams to the Stained Berg, about seven miles west of the ship, and on their way back got a female crab eater, which they killed, skinned, and left to be picked up later. They ascended to the top of the berg, which lay in about lat. 69° 30′ S., long. 51° W., and from an elevation of 110 ft. could see no land. Samples of the discolored ice from the berg proved to contain dust with black gritty particles or sandgrains. Another seal, a bull Weddell, was secured on the 26th. The return of seal life was opportune, since we had nearly finished the winter supply of dog biscuit and wished to be able to feed the dogs on meat. The seals meant a supply of blubber, moreover, to supplement our small remaining stock of coal when the time came to get up steam again. We initiated a daylight-saving system on this day by putting forward the clock one hour. "This is really pandering to the base but universal passion that men, and especially seafarers, have for getting up late, otherwise we would be honest and make our routine earlier instead of flogging the clock."

During the concluding days of September the roar of the pressure grew louder, and I could see that the area of disturbance was rapidly approaching the ship. Stupendous forces were at work and the fields of firm ice around the *Endurance* were being diminished steadily. September 30 was a bad day. It began well, for we got two penguins and five seals during the morning. Three other seals were seen. But at 3 p.m. cracks that had opened during the night alongside the ship commenced to work in a lateral direction. The ship sustained terrific pressure on the port side forward, the heaviest shocks

being under the forerigging. It was the worst squeeze we had
experienced. The decks shuddered and jumped, beams
arched, and stanchions buckled and shook. I ordered all
hands to stand by in readiness for whatever emergency might
arise. Even the dogs seemed to feel the tense anxiety of the
moment. But the ship resisted valiantly, and just when it appeared that the limit of her strength was being reached the
huge floe that was pressing down upon us cracked across and
so gave relief. "The behavior of our ship in the ice has been
magnificent," wrote Worsley. "Since we have been beset her
staunchness and endurance have been almost past belief
again and again. She has been nipped with a million-ton
pressure and risen nobly, falling clear of the water out on the
ice. She has been thrown to and fro like a shuttlecock a dozen
times. She has been strained, her beams arched upwards, by
the fearful pressure; her very sides opened and closed again
as she was actually bent and curved along her length, groaning like a living thing. It will be sad if such a brave little craft
should be finally crushed in the remorseless, slowly stran-
gling grip of the Weddell pack after ten months of the bravest
and most gallant fight ever put up by a ship."

The *Endurance* deserved all that could be said in praise
of her. Shipwrights had never done sounder or better work;
but how long could she continue the fight under such conditions? We were drifting into the congested area of the western Weddell Sea, the worst portion of the worst sea in the
world, where the pack, forced on irresistibly by wind and
current, impinges on the western shore and is driven up in
huge corrugated ridges and chaotic fields of pressure. The
vital question for us was whether or not the ice would open
sufficiently to release us, or at least give us a chance of
release, before the drift carried us into the most dangerous
area. There was no answer to be got from the silent bergs
and the grinding floes, and we faced the month of October
with anxious hearts.

The leads in the pack appeared to have opened out a little on October 1, but not sufficiently to be workable even if we had been able to release the *Endurance* from the floe. The day was calm, cloudy and misty in the forenoon and clearer in the afternoon, when we observed well-defined parhelia. The ship was subjected to slight pressure at intervals. Two bull crab eaters climbed on to the floe close to the ship and were shot by Wild. They were both big animals in prime condition, and I felt that there was no more need for anxiety as to the supply of fresh meat for the dogs. Seal liver made a welcome change in our own menu. The two bulls were marked, like many of their kinds, with long parallel scars about three inches apart, evidently the work of the killers. A bull we killed on the following day had four parallel scars, sixteen inches long, on each side of its body; they were fairly deep and one flipper had been nearly torn away. The creature must have escaped from the jaws of a killer by a very small margin. Evidently life beneath the pack is not always monotonous. We noticed that several of the bergs in the neighborhood of the ship were changing their relative positions more than they had done for months past. The floes were moving.

Our position on Sunday, October 3, was lat. 69° 14′ S., long. 51° 8′ W. During the night the floe holding the ship aft cracked in several places, and this appeared to have eased the strain on the rudder. The forenoon was misty, with falls of snow, but the weather cleared later in the day and we could see that the pack was breaking. New leads had appeared, while several old leads had closed. Pressure ridges had risen along some of the cracks. The thickness of the season's ice, now about 230 days old, was 4 ft. 5 in. under 7 or 8 in. of snow. This ice had been slightly thicker in the early part of September, and I assumed that some melting had begun below. Clark had recorded plus temperatures at depths of 150 and 200 fathoms in the concluding days of

September. The ice obviously had attained its maximum thickness by direct freezing, and the heavier older floes had been created by the consolidation of pressure ice and the overlapping of floes under strain. The air temperatures were still low, $-24.5°$ Fahr. being recorded on October 4.

The movement of the ice was increasing. Frost-smoke from opening cracks was showing in all directions during October 6. It had the appearance in one place of a great prairie fire, rising from the surface and getting higher as it drifted off before the wind in heavy, dark, rolling masses. At another point there was the appearance of a train running before the wind, the smoke rising from the locomotive straight upwards; and the smoke columns elsewhere gave the effect of warships steaming in line ahead. During the following day the leads and cracks opened to such an extent that if the *Endurance* could have been forced forward for thirty yards we could have proceeded for two or three miles; but the effort did not promise any really useful result. The conditions did not change materially during the rest of that week. The position on Sunday, October 10, was lat. 69° 21′ S., long. 50° 34′ W. A thaw made things uncomfortable for us that day. The temperature had risen from $-10°$ Fahr. to $+29.8°$ Fahr., the highest we had experienced since January, and the ship got dripping wet between decks. The upper deck was clear of ice and snow and the cabins became unpleasantly messy. The dogs, who hated wet, had a most unhappy air. Undoubtedly one grows to like familiar conditions. We had lived long in temperatures that would have seemed distressingly low in civilized life, and now we were made uncomfortable by a degree of warmth that would have left the unaccustomed human being still shivering. The thaw was an indication that winter was over, and we began preparations for reoccupying the cabins on the main deck. I had the shelter house round the stern pulled down on the 11th and made other preparations for working the ship as soon as she got clear. The carpenter had built a wheelhouse over the wheel aft as shelter in cold and heavy weather. The ice was still loosening and no land was visible for twenty miles.

The temperature remained relatively high for several days. All hands moved to their summer quarters in the upper cabins on the 12th, to the accompaniment of much noise and laughter. Spring was in the air, and if there were no green growing things to gladden our eyes, there were at least many seals, penguins, and even whales disporting themselves in the leads. The time for renewed action was coming, and though our situation was grave enough, we were facing the future hopefully. The dogs were kept in a state of uproar by the sight of so much game. They became almost frenzied when a solemn-looking emperor penguin inspected them gravely from some point of vantage on the floe and gave utterance to an apparently derisive "Knark!" At 7 p.m. on the 13th the ship broke free of the floe on which she had rested to starboard sufficiently to come upright. The rudder freed itself, but the propeller was found to be athwartship, having been forced into that position by the floe some time after August 1. The water was very clear and we could see the rudder, which appeared to have suffered only a slight twist to port at the water line. It moved quite freely. The propeller, as far as we could see, was intact, but it could not be moved by the hand gear, probably owing to a film of ice in the stern gland and sleeve. I did not think it advisable to attempt to deal with it at that stage. The ship had not been pumped for eight months, but there was no water and not much ice in the bilges. Meals were served again in the wardroom that day.

The southwesterly breeze freshened to a gale on the 14th, and the temperature fell from $+31°$ Fahr. to $-1°$ Fahr. At midnight the ship came free from the floe and drifted rapidly astern. Her head fell off before the wind until she lay nearly at right angles across the narrow lead. This was a dangerous position for rudder and propeller. The spanker was set, but the weight of the wind on the ship gradually forced the floes open until the *Endurance* swung right round and drove 100 yds. along the lead. Then the ice closed and at 3 a.m. we were fast again. The wind died down during the day and the pack opened for five or six miles to the north. It was still loose on the following morning, and I had the boiler pumped up with the intention of attempting to clear the propeller; but one of the manholes developed a leak, the packing being perished by cold or loosened by contraction, and the boiler had to be emptied out again.

The pack was rather closer on Sunday the 17th. Topsails and headsails were set in the afternoon, and with a moderate northeasterly breeze we tried to force the ship ahead out of the lead; but she was held fast. Later that day heavy pressure developed. The two floes between which the *Endurance* was lying began to close and the ship was subjected to a series of tremendously heavy strains. In the engine room, the weakest point, loud groans, crashes, and hammering sounds were heard. The iron plates on the floor buckled up and overrode with loud clangs. Meanwhile the floes were grinding off each other's projecting points and throwing up pressure ridges. The ship stood the strain well for nearly an hour and then, to my great relief, began to rise with heavy jerks and jars. She lifted ten inches forward and three feet four inches aft, at the same time heeling six degrees to port. The ice was getting below us and the immediate danger had passed. The position was lat. 69° 19′ S., long. 50° 40′ W.

The next attack of the ice came on the afternoon of October 18th. The two floes began to move laterally, exerting great pressure on the ship. Suddenly the floe on the port side cracked and huge pieces of ice shot up from under the port bilge. Within a few seconds the ship heeled over until she had a list of thirty degrees to port, being held under the starboard bilge by the opposing floe. The lee boats were now almost resting on the floe. The midship dog kennels broke away and crashed down on to the lee kennels, and the howls and barks of the frightened dogs assisted to create a perfect pandemonium. Everything movable on deck and below fell to the lee side, and for a few minutes it looked as if the *Endurance* would be thrown upon her beam ends. Order was soon restored. I had all fires put out and battens nailed on the deck to give the dogs a foothold and enable people to get about. Then the crew lashed all the movable gear. If the ship had heeled any farther it would have been necessary to release the lee boats and pull them clear, and Worsley was watching to give the alarm. Hurley meanwhile descended to the floe and took some photographs of the ship in her unusual position. Dinner in the wardroom that evening was a curious affair. Most of the diners had to sit on the deck, their feet against battens and their plates on their knees. At 8 p.m. the floes opened, and within a few minutes the *Endurance* was nearly upright again. Orders were given for the ice to be chipped clear of the rudder. The men poled the blocks out of the way when they had been detached from the floe with the long ice chisels, and we were able to haul the ship's stern into a clear berth. Then the boiler was pumped up. This work was completed early in the morning of October 19, and during that day the engineer lit fires and got up steam very slowly, in order to economize fuel and avoid any strain on the chilled boilers by unequal heating. The crew cut up all loose lumber, boxes, etc., and put them in the bunkers for fuel. The day was overcast, with occasional snowfalls, the temperature $+12°$ Fahr. The ice in our neighborhood was quiet, but in the distance pressure was at work. The wind freshened in the evening, and we ran a wire mooring astern. The barometer at 11 p.m. stood at 28.96, the lowest since the gales of July. An uproar among the dogs attracted attention late in the afternoon, and we found a

25-ft. whale cruising up and down in our pool. It pushed its head up once in characteristic killer fashion, but we judged from its small curved dorsal fin that it was a specimen of *Balænoptera acutorostrata,* not *Orca gladiator.*

A strong southwesterly wind was blowing on October 20 and the pack was working. The *Endurance* was imprisoned securely in the pool, but our chance might come at any time. Watches were set so as to be ready for working ship. Wild and Hudson, Greenstreet and Cheetham, Worsley and Crean, took the deck watches, and the Chief Engineer and Second Engineer kept watch and watch with three of the A.B.'s for stokers. The staff and the forward hands, with the exception of the cook, the carpenter and his mate, were on "watch and watch"—that is, four hours on deck and four hours below, or off duty. The carpenter was busy making a light punt, which might prove useful in the navigation of lanes and channels. At 11 a.m. we gave the engines a gentle trial turn astern. Everything worked well after eight months of frozen inactivity, except that the bilge pump and the discharge proved to be frozen up; they were cleared with some little difficulty. The engineer reported that to get steam he had used one ton of coal, with wood ashes and blubber. The fires required to keep the boiler warm consumed one and a quarter to one and a half hundred weight of coal per day. We had about fifty tons of coal remaining in the bunkers.

October 21 and 22 were days of low temperature, which caused the open leads to freeze over. The pack was working, and ever and anon the roar of pressure came to our ears. We waited for the next move of the gigantic forces arrayed against us. The 23rd brought a strong northwesterly wind, and the movement of the floes and pressure ridges became more formidable. Then on Sunday, October 24, there came what for the *Endurance* was the beginning of the end. The position was lat. 69° 11′ S., long. 51° 5′ W. We had now twenty-two and a half hours of daylight, and throughout the day we watched the threatening advance of the floes. At 6:45 p.m. the ship sustained heavy pressure in a dangerous position. The attack of the ice is illustrated roughly in the ap-

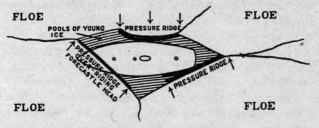

pended diagram. The shaded portions represent the pool, covered with new ice that afforded no support to the ship, and the arrows indicate the direction of the pressure exercised by the thick floes and pressure ridges. The onslaught was all but irresistible. The *Endurance* groaned and quivered as her starboard quarter was forced against the floe, twisting the stern post and starting the heads and ends of planking. The ice had lateral as well as forward movement, and the ship was twisted and actually bent by the stresses. She began to leak dangerously at once.

I had the pumps rigged, got up steam, and started the bilge pumps at 8 p.m. The pressure by that time had relaxed. The ship was making water rapidly aft, and the carpenter set to work to make a coffer dam astern of the engines. All hands worked, watch and watch, throughout the night, pumping ship and helping the carpenter. By morning the leak was being kept in check. The carpenter and his assistants caulked the coffer dam with strips of blankets and nailed strips over the seams wherever possible. The main or hand pump was frozen up and could not be used at once. After it had been knocked out Worsley, Greenstreet, and Hudson went down in the bunkers and cleared the ice from the bilges. "This is not a pleasant job," wrote Worsley. "We

have to dig a hole down through the coal while the beams
and timbers groan and crack all around us like pistol shots.
The darkness is almost complete, and we mess about in the
wet with half-frozen hands and try to keep the coal from
slipping back into the bilges. The men on deck pour buckets
of boiling water from the galley down the pipe as we prod
and hammer from below, and at last we get the pump clear,
cover up the bilges to keep the coal out, and rush on deck,
very thankful to find ourselves safe again in the open air."

Monday, October 25, dawned cloudy and misty, with a
minus temperature and a strong southeasterly breeze. All
hands were pumping at intervals and assisting the carpenter
with the coffer dam. The leak was being kept under fairly
easily, but the outlook was bad. Heavy pressure ridges were
forming in all directions, and though the immediate pressure
upon the ship was not severe, I realized that the respite
would not be prolonged. The pack within our range of vision was being subjected to enormous compression, such as
might be caused by cyclonic winds, opposing ocean currents, or constriction in a channel of some description. The
pressure ridges, massive and threatening, testified to the
overwhelming nature of the forces that were at work. Huge
blocks of ice, weighing many tons, were lifted into the air
and tossed aside as other masses rose beneath them. We
were helpless intruders in a strange world, our lives dependent upon the play of grim elementary forces that made a
mock of our puny efforts. I scarcely dared hope now that
the *Endurance* would live, and throughout that anxious day
I reviewed again the plans made long before for the sledging
journey that we must make in the event of our having to
take to the ice. We were ready, as far as forethought could
make us, for every contingency. Stores, dogs, sledges, and
equipment were ready to be moved from the ship at a moment's notice.

The following day brought bright clear weather, with a

blue sky. The sunshine was inspiriting. The roar of pressure could be heard all around us. New ridges were rising, and I could see as the day wore on that the lines of major disturbance were drawing nearer to the ship. The *Endurance* suffered some strains at intervals. Listening below, I could hear the creaking and groaning of her timbers, the pistol-like cracks that told of the starting of a trenail or plank, and the faint, indefinable whispers of our ship's distress. Overhead the sun shone serenely; occasional fleecy clouds drifted before the southerly breeze, and the light glinted and sparkled on the million facets of the new pressure ridges. The day passed slowly. At 7 p.m. very heavy pressure developed, with twisting strains that racked the ship fore and aft. The butts of planking were opened four and five inches on the starboard side, and at the same time we could see from the bridge that the ship was bending like a bow under titanic pressure. Almost like a living creature, she resisted the forces that would crush her; but it was a one-sided battle. Millions of tons of ice pressed inexorably upon the little ship that had dared the challenge of the Antarctic. The *Endurance* was now leaking badly, and at 9 p.m. I gave the order to lower boats, gear, provisions, and sledges to the floe, and move them to the flat ice a little way from the ship. The working of the ice closed the leaks slightly at midnight, but all hands were pumping all night. A strange occurrence was the sudden appearance of eight emperor penguins from a crack 100 yds. away at the moment when the pressure upon the ship was at its climax. They walked a little way towards us, halted, and after a few ordinary calls proceeded to utter weird cries that sounded like a dirge for the ship. None of us had ever before heard the emperors utter any other than the most simple calls or cries, and the effect of this concerted effort was almost startling.

Then came a fateful day—Wednesday, October 27. The position was lat. 69° 5′ S., long. 51° 30′ W. The temperature was −8.5° Fahr., a gentle southerly breeze was blowing and the sun shone in a clear sky. "After long months of ceaseless anxiety and strain, after times when hope beat high and times when the outlook was black indeed, the end of the *Endurance* has come. But though we have been compelled to abandon the ship, which is crushed beyond all hope of ever being righted, we are alive and well, and we have stores and equipment for the task that lies before us. The task is to reach land with all the members of the Expedition. It is hard to write what I feel. To a sailor his ship is more than a floating home, and in the *Endurance* I had centered ambitions, hopes, and desires. Now, straining and groaning, her timbers cracking and her wounds gaping, she is slowly giving up her sentient life at the very outset of her career. She is crushed and abandoned after drifting more than 570 miles in a northwesterly direction during the 281 days since she became locked in the ice. The distance from the point where she became beset to the place where she now rests mortally hurt in the grip of the floes is 573 miles, but the total drift through all observed positions has been 1186 miles, and probably we actually covered more than 1500 miles. We are now 346 miles from Paulet Island, the nearest point where there is any possibility of finding food and shelter. A small hut built there by the Swedish expedition in 1902 is filled with stores left by the Argentine relief ship. I know all about those stores, for I purchased them in London on behalf of the Argentine Government when they asked me to equip the relief expedition. The distance to the nearest barrier west of us is about 180 miles, but a party going there would still be about 360 miles from Paulet Island and there would be no means of sustaining life on the barrier. We could not take from here food enough for the whole journey; the weight would be too great.

"This morning, our last on the ship, the weather was clear, with a gentle south-southeasterly to south-southwesterly breeze. From the crow's nest there was no sign of land of any sort. The pressure was increasing steadily, and the passing hours brought no relief or respite for the ship. The attack of the ice reached its climax at 4 p.m. The ship was hove stern up by the pressure, and the driving floe, moving laterally across the stern, split the rudder and tore out the rudder post and stern post. Then, while we watched, the ice loosened and the *Endurance* sank a little. The decks were breaking upwards and the water was pouring in below. Again the pressure began, and at 5 p.m. I ordered all hands on to the ice. The twisting, grinding floes were working their will at last on the ship. It was a sickening sensation to feel the decks breaking up under one's feet, the great beams bending and then snapping with a noise like heavy gunfire. The water was overmastering the pumps, and to avoid an explosion when it reached the boilers I had to give orders for the fires to be drawn and the steam let down. The plans for abandoning the ship in case of emergency had been made well in advance, and men and dogs descended to the floe and made their way to the comparative safety of an unbroken portion of the floe without a hitch. Just before leaving, I looked down the engine room skylight as I stood on the quivering deck, and saw the engines dropping sideways as the stays and bed plates gave way. I cannot describe the impression of relentless destruction that was forced upon me as I looked down and around. The floes, with the force of millions of tons of moving ice behind them, were simply annihilating the ship."

Essential supplies had been placed on the floe about 100 yds. from the ship, and there we set about making a camp for the night. But about 7 p.m., after the tents were up, the ice we were occupying became involved in the pressure and started to split and smash beneath our feet. I had the camp moved to a bigger floe about 200 yds. away, just beyond the bow of the ship. Boats, stores, and camp equipment had to be conveyed across a working pressure ridge. The movement of the ice was so slow that it did not interfere much with our short trek, but the weight of the ridge had caused the floes to sink on either side and there were pools of water there. A pioneer party with picks and shovels had to build a snow causeway before we could get all our possessions across. By 8 p.m. the camp had been pitched again. We had two pole tents and three hoop tents. I took charge of the small pole tent, No. 1, with Hudson, Hurley, and James as companions; Wild had the small hoop tent, No. 2, with Wordie, McNeish, and McIlroy. These hoop tents are very easily shifted and set up. The eight forward hands had the large hoop tent, No. 3; Crean had charge of No. 4 hoop tent with Hussey, Marston, and Cheetham; and Worsley had the other pole tent, No. 5, with Greenstreet, Lees, Clark, Kerr, Rickenson, Macklin, and Blackborrow, the last named being the youngest of the forward hands.

"Tonight the temperatures had dropped to $-16°$ Fahr., and most of the men are cold and uncomfortable. After the tents had been pitched I mustered all hands and explained the position to them briefly and, I hope, clearly. I have told them the distance to the Barrier and the distance to Paulet Island, and have stated that I propose to try to march with equipment across the ice in the direction of Paulet Island. I thanked the men for the steadiness and good *morale* they have shown in these trying circumstances, and told them I had no doubt that, provided they continued to work their utmost and to trust me, we will all reach safety in the end. Then we had supper, which the cook had prepared at the big blubber stove, and after a watch had been set all hands except the watch turned in." For myself, I could not sleep. The destruction and abandonment of the ship was no sudden shock. The disaster had been looming ahead for many months, and I had studied my plans for all contingencies a hundred times. But the thoughts that came to me as I walked up and down in the darkness were not particularly cheerful. The task now was to secure the safety of the party, and to that I must bend my energies and mental power and apply every bit of knowledge that experience of the Antarctic had given me. The task was likely to be long and strenuous, and an ordered mind and a clear program were essential if we were to come through without loss of life. A man must shape himself to a new mark directly the old one goes to ground.

At midnight I was pacing the ice, listening to the grinding floe and to the groans and crashes that told of the death agony of the *Endurance,* when I noticed suddenly a crack running across our floe right through the camp. The alarm whistle brought all hands tumbling out, and we moved the tents and stores lying on what was now the smaller portion of the floe to the larger portion. Nothing more could be done at that moment, and the men turned in again; but there was little sleep. Each time I came to the end of my beat on the floe I could just see in the darkness the uprearing piles of pressure ice, which toppled over and narrowed still further the little floating island we occupied. I did not notice at the time that my tent, which had been on the wrong side of the crack, had not been erected again. Hudson and James had managed to squeeze themselves into other tents, and Hurley had wrapped himself in the canvas of No. 1 tent. I discovered this about 5 a.m. All night long the electric light gleamed from the stern of the dying *Endurance.* Hussey had left this light switched on when he took a last observation, and, like a lamp in a cottage window, it braved the night until in the early morning the *Endurance* received a particularly violent squeeze. There was a sound of rending beams and the light disappeared. The connection had been cut.

Morning came in chill and cheerless. All hands were stiff and weary after their first disturbed night on the floe. Just at daybreak I went over to the *Endurance* with Wild and Hurley, in order to retrieve some tins of petrol that could be used to boil up milk for the rest of the men. The ship presented a painful spectacle of chaos and wreck. The jib boom and bowsprit had snapped off during the night and now lay at right angles to the ship, with the chains, martingale, and bobstay dragging them as the vessel quivered and moved in the grinding pack. The ice had driven over the forecastle and she was well down by the head. We secured two tins of petrol with some difficulty, and postponed the further examination of the ship until after breakfast. Jumping across cracks with the tins, we soon reached camp, and built a fireplace out of the triangular watertight tanks we had ripped from the lifeboat. This we had done in order to make more room. Then we pierced a petrol tin in half a dozen places with an ice axe and set fire to it. The petrol blazed fiercely under the five-gallon drum we used as a cooker, and the hot milk was ready in quick time. Then we three ministering angels went round the tents with the life-giving drink, and were surprised and a trifle chagrined at the matter-of-fact manner in which some of the men accepted this contribution to their comfort. They did not quite understand what work we had done for them in the early dawn, and I heard Wild say, "If any of you gentlemen would like your boots cleaned just put them outside!" This was his gentle way of reminding them that a little thanks will go a long way on such occasions.

The cook prepared breakfast, which consisted of biscuit and hoosh, at 8 a.m., and I then went over to the *Endurance* again and made a fuller examination of the wreck. Only six of the cabins had not been pierced by floes and blocks of ice. Every one of the starboard cabins had been crushed. The whole of the after part of the ship had been crushed concertina fashion. The forecastle and the Ritz were submerged, and the wardroom was three-quarters full of ice. The starboard side of the wardroom had come away. The

motor engine forward had been driven through the galley.
Petrol cases that had been stacked on the foredeck had been
driven by the floe through the wall into the wardroom and
had carried before them a large picture. Curiously enough,
the glass of this picture had not been cracked, whereas in
the immediate neighborhood I saw heavy iron davits that
had been twisted and bent like the ironwork of a wrecked
train. The ship was being crushed remorselessly.

Under a dull, overcast sky I returned to camp and examined our situation. The floe occupied by the camp was still
subject to pressure, and I thought it wise to move to a larger
and apparently stronger floe about 200 yds. away, off the
starboard bow of the ship. This camp was to become known
as Dump Camp, owing to the amount of stuff that was
thrown away there. We could not afford to carry unnecessary gear, and a drastic sorting of equipment took place. I
decided to issue a complete new set of Burberrys and under-
clothing to each man, and also a supply of new socks. The
camp was transferred to the larger floe quickly, and I began
there to direct the preparations for the long journey across
the floes to Paulet Island or Snow Hill.

Hurley meanwhile had rigged his motion-picture camera
and was getting pictures of the *Endurance* in her death
throes. While he was engaged thus, the ice, driving against
the standing rigging and the fore-, main- and mizzenmasts,
snapped the shrouds. The foretop and topgallant mast came
down with a run and hung in wreckage on the foremast,
with the foreyard vertical. The mainmast followed immediately, snapping off about 10 ft. above the main deck. The
crow's nest fell within 10 ft. of where Hurley stood turning
the handle of his camera, but he did not stop the machine,
and so secured a unique, though sad, picture.

The issue of clothing was quickly accomplished. Sleeping
bags were required also. We had eighteen fur bags, and it
was necessary, therefore, to issue ten of the Jaeger woollen

bags in order to provide for the twenty-eight men of the
party. The woollen bags were lighter and less warm than the
reindeer bags, and so each man who received one of them
was allowed also a reindeer skin to lie upon. It seemed fair
to distribute the fur bags by lot, but some of us older hands
did not join in the lottery. We thought we could do quite as
well with the Jaegers as with the furs. With quick dispatch
the clothing was apportioned, and then we turned one of the
boats on its side and supported it with two broken oars to
make a lee for the galley. The cook got the blubber stove
going, and a little later, when I was sitting round the corner
of the stove, I heard one man say, "Cook, I like my tea
strong." Another joined in, "Cook, I like mine weak." It
was pleasant to know that their minds were untroubled, but
I thought the time opportune to mention that the tea would
be the same for all hands and that we would be fortunate if
two months later we had any tea at all. It occurred to me at
the time that the incident had psychological interest. Here
were men, their home crushed, the camp pitched on the unstable floes, and their chance of reaching safety apparently
remote, calmly attending to the details of existence and giving their attention to such trifles as the strength of a brew of
tea.

   During the afternoon the work continued. Every now and
then we heard a noise like heavy guns or distant thunder,
caused by the floes grinding together. "The pressure caused
by the congestion in this area of the pack is producing a
scene of absolute chaos. The floes grind stupendously,
throw up great ridges, and shatter one another mercilessly.
The ridges, or hedgerows, marking the pressure lines that
border the fast diminishing pieces of smooth floe ice, are
enormous. The ice moves majestically, irresistibly. Human
effort is not futile, but man fights against the giant forces of
Nature in a spirit of humility. One has a sense of depen-
dence on the higher Power. Today two seals, a Weddell and

a crab eater, came close to the camp and were shot. Four others were chased back into the water, for their presence disturbed the dog teams, and this meant floggings and trouble with the harness. The arrangement of the tents has been completed and their internal management settled. Each tent has a mess orderly, the duty being taken in turn on an alphabetical rota. The orderly takes the hoosh pots of his tent to the galley, gets all the hoosh he is allowed, and, after the meal, cleans the vessels with snow and stores them in sledge or boat ready for a possible move."

"*October* 29.—We passed a quiet night, although the pressure was grinding around us. Our floe is a heavy one and it withstood the blows it received. There is a light wind from the northwest to north northwest, and the weather is fine. We are twenty-eight men with forty-nine dogs, including Sue's and Sallie's five grownup pups. All hands this morning were busy preparing gear, fitting boats on sledges, and building up and strengthening the sledges to carry the boats. . . . The main motor sledge, with a little fitting from the carpenter, carried our largest boat admirably. For the next boat four ordinary sledges were lashed together, but we were dubious as to the strength of this contrivance, and as a matter of fact it broke down quickly under strain. . . . The ship is still afloat, with the spurs of the pack driven through her and holding her up. The forecastle head is under water, the decks are burst up by the pressure, the wreckage lies around in dismal confusion, but over all the blue ensign flies still.

"This afternoon Sallie's three youngest pups, Sue's Sirius, and Mrs. Chippy, the carpenter's cat, have to be shot. We could not undertake the maintenance of weaklings under the new conditions. Macklin, Crean, and the carpenter seemed to feel the loss of their friends rather badly. We propose making a short trial journey tomorrow, starting with two of the boats and the ten sledges. The number of dog

teams has been increased to seven, Greenstreet taking
charge of the new additional team, consisting of Snapper
and Sallie's four oldest pups. We have ten working sledges
to relay with five teams. Wild's and Hurley's teams will
haul the cutter with the assistance of four men. The whaler
and the other boats will follow, and the men who are hauling
them will be able to help with the cutter at the rough places.
We cannot hope to make rapid progress, but each mile
counts. Crean this afternoon has a bad attack of snow blindness."

The weather on the morning of October 30 was overcast
and misty, with occasional falls of snow. A moderate northeasterly breeze was blowing. We were still living on extra
food, brought from the ship when we abandoned her, and
the sledging and boating rations were intact. These rations
would provide for twenty-eight men for fifty-six days on
full rations, but we could count on getting enough seal and
penguin meat to at least double this time. We could even, if
progress proved too difficult and too injurious to the boats,
which we must guard as our ultimate means of salvation,
camp on the nearest heavy floe, scour the neighboring pack
for penguins and seals, and await the outward drift of the
pack to open and navigable water. "This plan would avoid
the grave dangers we are now incurring of getting entangled
in impassable pressure ridges and possibly irretrievably
damaging the boats, which are bound to suffer in rough ice;
it would also minimize the peril of the ice splitting under
us, as it did twice during the night at our first camp. Yet I
feel sure that it is the right thing to attempt a march, since
if we can make five or seven miles a day to the northwest
our chance of reaching safety in the months to come will
be increased greatly. There is a psychological aspect to the
question also. It will be much better for the men in general
to feel that, even though progress is slow, they are on their
way to land than it will be simply to sit down and wait for

the tardy northwesterly drift to take us out of this cruel waste of ice. We will make an attempt to move. The issue is beyond my power either to predict or to control."

That afternoon Wild and I went out in the mist and snow to find a road to the northeast. After many devious turnings to avoid the heavier pressure ridges, we pioneered a way for at least a mile and a half and then returned by a rather better route to the camp. The pressure now was rapid in movement and our floe was suffering from the shakes and jerks of the ice. At 3 p.m., after lunch, we got under way, leaving Dump Camp a mass of debris. The order was that personal gear must not exceed two pounds per man, and this meant that nothing but bare necessities was to be taken on the march. We could not afford to cumber ourselves with unnecessary weight. Holes had been dug in the snow for the reception of private letters and little personal trifles, the Lares and Penates of the members of the Expedition, and into the privacy of these white graves were consigned much of sentimental value and not a little of intrinsic worth. I rather grudged the two pounds allowance per man, owing to my keen anxiety to keep weights at a minimum, but some personal belongings could fairly be regarded as indispensable. The journey might be a long one, and there was a possibility of a winter in improvised quarters on an inhospitable coast at the other end. A man under such conditions needs something to occupy his thoughts, some tangible memento of his home and people beyond the seas. So sovereigns were thrown away and photographs were kept. I tore the fly-leaf out of the Bible that Queen Alexandra had given to the ship, with her own writing in it, and also the wonderful page of Job containing the verse:

> *Out of whose womb came the ice?*
> *And the hoary frost of Heaven, who hath gendered it?*
> *The waters are hid as with a stone,*
> *And the face of the deep is frozen.*

The other Bible, which Queen Alexandra had given for the use of the shore party, was down below in the lower hold in one of the cases when the ship received her death blow. Suitcases were thrown away; these were retrieved later as material for making boots, and some of them, marked "solid leather," proved, to our disappointment, to contain a large percentage of cardboard. The manufacturer would have had difficulty in convincing us at the time that the deception was anything short of criminal.

The pioneer sledge party, consisting of Wordie, Hussey, Hudson, and myself, carrying picks and shovels, started to break a road through the pressure ridges for the sledges carrying the boats. The boats, with their gear and the sledges beneath them, weighed each more than a ton. The cutter was smaller than the whaler, but weighed more and was a much more strongly built boat. The whaler was mounted on the sledge part of the Girling tractor forward and two sledges amidships and aft. These sledges were strengthened with cross timbers and shortened oars fore and aft. The cutter was mounted on the aero sledge. The sledges were the point of weakness. It appeared almost hopeless to prevent them smashing under their heavy loads when traveling over rough pressure ice which stretched ahead of us for probably 300 miles. After the pioneer sledge had started the seven dog teams got off. They took their sledges forward for half a mile, then went back for the other sledges. Worsley took charge of the two boats, with fifteen men hauling, and these also had to be relayed. It was heavy work for dogs and men, but there were intervals of comparative rest on the backward journey, after the first portion of the load had been taken forward. We passed over two opening cracks, through which killers were pushing their ugly snouts, and by 5 p.m. had covered a mile in a north-northwesterly direction. The condition of the ice ahead was chaotic, for since the morning increased pressure had developed and the pack was moving

and crushing in all directions. So I gave the order to pitch
camp for the night on flat ice, which, unfortunately, proved
to be young and salty. The older pack was too rough and too
deeply laden with snow to offer a suitable camping ground.
Although we had gained only one mile in a direct line, the
necessary deviations made the distance traveled at least two
miles, and the relays brought the distance marched up to six
miles. Some of the dog teams had covered at least ten miles.
I set the watch from 6 p.m. to 7 a.m., one hour for each man
in each tent in rotation.

   During the night snow fell heavily, and the floor cloths of
the tents got wet through, as the temperature had risen to
+ 25° Fahr. One of the things we hoped for in those days
was a temperature in the neighborhood of zero, for then the
snow surface would be hard, we would not be troubled by
damp, and our gear would not become covered in soft snow.
The killers were blowing all night, and a crack appeared
about 20 ft. from the camp at 2 a.m. The ice below us was
quite thin enough for the killers to break through if they
took a fancy to do so, but there was no other camping
ground within our reach and we had to take the risk. When
morning came the snow was falling so heavily that we could
not see more than a few score yards ahead, and I decided
not to strike camp. A path over the shattered floes would be
hard to find, and to get the boats into a position of peril
might be disastrous. Rickenson and Worsley started back
for Dump Camp at 7 a.m. to get some wood and blubber for
the fire, and an hour later we had hoosh, with one biscuit
each. At 10 a.m. Hurley and Hudson left for the old camp
in order to bring some additional dog pemmican, since there
were no seals to be found near us. Then, as the weather
cleared, Worsley and I made a prospect to the west and tried
to find a practicable road. A large floe offered a fairly good
road for at least another mile to the northwest, and we went
back prepared for another move. The weather cleared a lit-

tle, and after lunch we struck camp. I took Rickenson, Kerr, Wordie, and Hudson as a breakdown gang to pioneer a path among the pressure ridges. Five dog teams followed. Wild's and Hurley's teams were hitched on to the cutter and they started off in splendid style. They needed to be helped only once; indeed fourteen dogs did as well or even better than eighteen men. The ice was moving beneath and around us as we worked towards the big floe, and where this floe met the smaller ones there was a mass of pressed-up ice, still in motion, with water between the ridges. But it is wonderful what a dozen men can do with picks and shovels. We could cut a road through a pressure ridge about 14 ft. high in ten minutes and leave a smooth, or comparatively smooth, path for the sledges and teams.

CHAPTER V

• OCEAN CAMP

IN SPITE OF the wet, deep snow and the halts occasioned by thus having to cut our road through the pressure ridges, we managed to march the best part of a mile towards our goal, though the relays and the deviations again made the actual distance traveled nearer six miles. As I could see that the men were all exhausted I gave the order to pitch the tents under the lee of the two boats, which afforded some slight protection from the wet snow now threatening to cover everything. While so engaged one of the sailors discovered a small pool of water, caused by the snow having thawed, on a sail which was lying in one of the boats. There was not much—just a sip each; but, as one man wrote in his diary, "One has seen and tasted cleaner, but seldom more opportunely found water."

Next day broke cold and still with the same wet snow; and in the clearing light I could see that with the present loose surface, and considering how little result we had to show for all our strenuous efforts of the past four days, it would be impossible to proceed for any great distance. Taking into account also the possibility of leads opening close to us, and so of our being able to row northwest to where we might find land, I decided to find a more solid floe and there camp until conditions were more favorable for us to make a second attempt to escape from our icy prison. To this end we moved our tents and all our gear to a thick, heavy old floe about one and a half miles from the wreck and there made our camp. We called this "Ocean Camp." It was with the utmost difficulty that we shifted our two boats. The surface was terrible—like nothing that any of us had ever seen around us before. We were sinking at times up to our hips, and everywhere the snow was two feet deep.

I decided to conserve our valuable sledging rations, which would be so necessary for the inevitable boat journey, as much as possible, and to subsist almost entirely on seals and penguins.

A party was sent back to Dump Camp, near the ship, to collect as much clothing, tobacco, etc., as they could find. The heavy snow which had fallen in the last few days, combined with the thawing and consequent sinking of the surface, resulted in the total disappearance of a good many of the things left behind at this dump. The remainder of the men made themselves as comfortable as possible under the circumstances at Ocean Camp. This floating lump of ice, about a mile square at first but later splitting into smaller and smaller fragments, was to be our home for nearly two months. During these two months we made frequent visits to the vicinity of the ship and retrieved much valuable clothing and food and some few articles of personal value which in our lighthearted optimism we had thought to leave miles behind us on our dash across the moving ice to safety.

The collection of food was now the all-important consideration. As we were to subsist almost entirely on seals and penguins, which were to provide fuel as well as food, some form of blubber stove was a necessity. This was eventually very ingeniously contrived from the ship's steel ash shoot, as our first attempt with a large iron oil drum did not prove eminently successful. We could only cook seal or penguin hooshes or stews on this stove, and so uncertain was its action that the food was either burnt or only partially cooked; and, hungry though we were, half-raw seal meat was not very appetizing. On one occasion a wonderful stew made from seal meat, with two or three tins of Irish stew that had been salved from the ship, fell into the fire through the bottom of the oil drum that we used as a saucepan becoming burnt out on account of the sudden intense heat of the fire below. We lunched that day on one biscuit and a quarter of a tin of bully beef each, frozen hard.

This new stove, which was to last us during our stay at Ocean Camp, was a great success. Two large holes were punched, with much labor and few tools, opposite one another at the wider or top end of the shoot. Into one of these an oil drum was fixed, to be used as the fireplace, the other hole serving to hold our saucepan. Alongside this another hole was punched to enable two saucepans to be boiled at a time; and farther along still a chimney made from biscuit tins completed a very efficient, if not a very elegant, stove. Later on the cook found that he could bake a sort of flat bannock or scone on this stove, but he was seriously hampered for want of yeast or baking powder.

An attempt was next made to erect some sort of a galley to protect the cook against the inclemencies of the weather. The party which I had sent back under Wild to the ship returned with, amongst other things, the wheelhouse practically complete. This, with the addition of some sails and tarpaulins stretched on spars, made a very comfortable storehouse and galley. Pieces of planking from the deck were lashed across some spars stuck upright into the snow, and this, with the ship's binnacle, formed an excellent lookout from which to look for seals and penguins. On this platform, too, a mast was erected from which flew the King's flag and the Royal Clyde Yacht Club burgee.

I made a strict inventory of all the food in our possession, weights being roughly determined with a simple balance made from a piece of wood and some string, the counterweight being a 60-lb. box of provisions.

The dog teams went off to the wreck early each morning under Wild, and the men made every effort to rescue as much as possible from the ship. This was an extremely difficult task as the whole of the deck forward was under a foot of water on the port side, and nearly three feet on the starboard side. However, they managed to collect large quantities of wood and ropes and some few cases of provisions. Although the galley was under water, Bakewell managed to secure three or four saucepans, which later proved invaluable acquisitions. Quite a number of boxes of flour, etc., had been stowed in a cabin in the hold, and these we had been unable to get out before we left the ship. Having, therefore, determined as nearly as possible that portion of the deck immediately above these cases, we proceeded to cut a hole with large ice chisels through the 3-in. planking of which it was formed. As the ship at this spot was under 5 ft. of water and ice, it was not an easy job. However, we succeeded in making the hole sufficiently large to allow of some few cases to come floating up. These were greeted with great satisfaction, and later on, as we warmed to our work, other cases, whose upward progress was assisted with a boat-hook, were greeted with either cheers or groans according to whether they contained farinaceous food or merely luxuries such as jellies. For each man by now had a good idea of the calorific value and nutritive and sustaining qualities of the various foods. It had a personal interest for us all. In this way we added to our scanty stock between two and three tons of provisions, about half of which was farinaceous food, such as flour and peas, of which we were so short. This sounds a great deal, but at one pound per day it would only last twenty-eight men for three months. Previous to this I had reduced the food allowance to nine and a half ounces per man per day. Now, however, it could be increased, and "this afternoon, for the first time for ten days, we knew what it was to be really satisfied."

I had the sledges packed in readiness with the special sledging rations in case of a sudden move, and with the other food, allowing also for prospective seals and penguins, I calculated a dietary to give the utmost possible variety and yet to use our precious stock of flour in the most economical manner. All seals and penguins that appeared anywhere within the vicinity of the camp were killed to provide food and fuel. The dog pemmican we also added to our own larder, feeding the dogs on the seals which we caught, after removing such portions as were necessary for our own needs. We were rather short of crockery, but small pieces of venesta wood served admirably as plates for seal steaks; stews and liquids of all sorts were served in the aluminum sledging mugs, of which each man had one. Later on jelly tins and biscuit-tin lids were pressed into service.

Monotony in the meals, even considering the circumstances in which we found ourselves, was what I was striving to avoid, so our little stock of luxuries, such as fish paste, tinned herrings, etc., was carefully husbanded and so distributed as to last as long as possible. My efforts were not in vain, as one man states in his diary: "It must be admitted that we are feeding very well indeed, considering our position. Each meal consists of one course and a beverage. The dried vegetables, if any, all go into the same pot as the meat, and every dish is a sort of hash or stew, be it ham or seal meat or half and half. The fact that we only have two pots available places restrictions upon the number of things that can be cooked at one time, but in spite of the limitation of facilities, we always seem to manage to get just enough. The milk powder and sugar are necessarily boiled with the tea or cocoa.

"We are, of course, very short of the farinaceous element in our diet, and consequently have a mild craving for more of it. Bread is out of the question, and as we are husbanding the remaining cases of our biscuits for our prospective boat journey, we are eking out the supply of flour by making bannocks, of which we have from three to four each day. These bannocks are made from flour, fat, water, salt, and a little baking powder, the dough being rolled out into flat rounds and baked in about ten minutes on a hot sheet of iron over the fire. Each bannock weighs about one and a half to two ounces, and we are indeed lucky to be able to produce them."

A few boxes of army biscuits soaked with sea water were distributed at one meal. They were in such a state that they would not have been looked at a second time under ordinary circumstances, but to us on a floating lump of ice, over three hundred miles from land, and that quite hypothetical, and with the unplumbed sea beneath us, they were luxuries indeed. Wild's tent made a pudding of theirs with some dripping.

Although keeping in mind the necessity for strict economy with our scanty store of food, I knew how important it was to keep the men cheerful, and that the depression occasioned by our surroundings and our precarious position could to some extent be alleviated by increasing the rations, at least until we were more accustomed to our new mode of life. That this was successful is shown in their diaries. "Day by day goes by much the same as one another. We work; we talk; we eat. Ah, how we eat! No longer on short rations, we are a trifle more exacting than we were when we first commenced our 'simple life,' but by comparison with home standards we are positive barbarians, and our gastronomic rapacity knows no bounds.

"All is eaten that comes to each tent, and everything is most carefully and accurately divided into as many equal portions as there are men in the tent. One member then closes his eyes or turns his head away and calls out the names at random, as the cook for the day points to each portion, saying at the same time, 'Whose?'

"Partiality, however unintentional it may be, is thus entirely obviated and every one feels satisfied that all is fair, even though one may look a little enviously at the next man's helping, which differs in some especially appreciated detail from one's own. We break the Tenth Commandment energetically, but as we are all in the same boat in this respect, no one says a word. We understand each other's feelings quite sympathetically.

"It is just like schooldays over again, and very jolly it is too, for the time being!"

Later on, as the prospect of wintering in the pack became more apparent, the rations had to be considerably reduced. By that time, however, everybody had become more accustomed to the idea and took it quite as a matter of course.

Our meals now consisted in the main of a fairly generous helping of seal or penguin, either boiled or fried. As one man wrote: "We are now having enough to eat, but not by any means too much, and every one is always hungry enough to eat every scrap he can get. Meals are invariably taken very seriously, and little talking is done till the hoosh is finished."

Our tents made somewhat cramped quarters, especially during mealtimes. "Living in a tent without any furniture requires a little getting used to. For our meals we have to sit on the floor, and it is surprising how awkward it is to eat in such a position; it is better by far to kneel and sit back on one's heels, as do the Japanese." Each man took it in turn to be the tent "cook" for one day, and one writes:

"The word 'cook' is at present rather a misnomer, for whilst we have a permanent galley no cooking need be done in the tent.

"Really, all that the tent cook has to do is to take his two hoosh pots over to the galley and convey the hoosh and the beverage to the tent, clearing up after each meal and washing up the two pots and the mugs. There are no spoons, etc., to wash, for we each keep our own spoon and pocketknife in our pockets. We just lick them as clean as possible and replace them in our pockets after each meal.

"Our spoons are one of our indispensable possessions

here. To lose one's spoon would be almost as serious as it is for an edentate person to lose his set of false teeth."

During all this time the supply of seals and penguins, if not inexhaustible, was always sufficient for our needs.

Seal and penguin hunting was our daily occupation, and parties were sent out in different directions to search among the hummocks and the pressure ridges for them. When one was found a signal was hoisted, usually in the form of a scarf or a sock on a pole, and an answering signal was hoisted at the camp.

Then Wild went out with a dog team to shoot and bring in the game. To feed ourselves and the dogs at least one seal a day was required. The seals were mostly crab eaters, and emperor penguins were the general rule. On November 5, however, an adelie was caught, and this was the cause of much discussion, as the following extract shows: "The man on watch from 3 a.m. to 4 a m. caught an adelie penguin. This is the first of its kind that we have seen since January last, and it may mean a lot. It may signify that there is land somewhere near us, or else that great leads are opening up, but it is impossible to form more than a mere conjecture at present."

No skuas, Antarctic petrels, or sea leopards were seen during our two months' stay at Ocean Camp.

In addition to the daily hunt for food, our time was passed in reading the few books that we had managed to save from the ship. The greatest treasure in the library was a portion of the "Encyclopedia Britannica." This was being continually used to settle the inevitable arguments that would arise. The sailors were discovered one day engaged in a very heated discussion on the subject of *Money and Exchange*. They finally came to the conclusion that the Encyclopedia, since it did not coincide with their views, must be wrong.

"For descriptions of every American town that ever has been, is, or ever will be, and for full and complete biograph-

ies of every American statesman since the time of George
Washington and long before, the Encyclopedia would be
hard to beat. Owing to our shortage of matches we have
been driven to use it for purposes other than the purely liter-
ary ones though; and one genius having discovered that the
paper used for its pages had been impregnated with saltpe-
tre, we can now thoroughly recommend it as a very efficient
pipe lighter."

We also possessed a few books on Antarctic exploration,
a copy of Browning and one of "The Ancient Mariner." On
reading the latter, we sympathized with him and wondered
what he had done with the albatross; it would have made a
very welcome addition to our larder.

The two subjects of most interest to us were our rate of
drift and the weather. Worsley took observations of the sun
whenever possible, and his results showed conclusively that
the drift of our floe was almost entirely dependent upon the
winds and not much affected by currents. Our hope, of
course, was to drift northwards to the edge of the pack and
then, when the ice was loose enough, to take to the boats
and row to the nearest land. We started off in fine style,
drifting north about twenty miles in two or three days in
a howling southwesterly blizzard. Gradually, however, we
slowed up, as successive observations showed, until we
began to drift back to the south. An increasing northeasterly
wind, which commenced on November 7 and lasted for
twelve days, damped our spirits for a time, until we found
that we had only drifted back to the south three miles, so
that we were now seventeen miles to the good. This tended
to reassure us in our theories that the ice of the Weddell Sea
was drifting round in a clockwise direction, and that if we
could stay on our piece long enough we must eventually be
taken up to the north, where lay the open sea and the path
to comparative safety.

The ice was not moving fast enough to be noticeable. In

fact, the only way in which we could prove that we were moving at all was by noting the changes of relative positions of the bergs around us, and, more definitely, by fixing our absolute latitude and longitude by observations of the sun. Otherwise, as far as actual visible drift was concerned, we might have been on dry land.

For the next few days we made good progress, drifting seven miles to the north on November 24 and another seven miles in the next forty-eight hours. We were all very pleased to know that although the wind was mainly southwest all this time, yet we had made very little easting. The land lay to the west, so had we drifted to the east we should have been taken right away to the center of the entrance to the Weddell Sea, and our chances of finally reaching land would have been considerably lessened.

Our average rate of drift was slow, and many and varied were the calculations as to when we should reach the pack edge. On December 12, 1915, one man wrote: "Once across the Antarctic Circle, it will seem as if we are practically halfway home again; and it is just possible that with favorable winds we may cross the circle before the New Year. A drift of only three miles a day would do it, and we have often done that and more for periods of three or four weeks.

"We are now only 250 miles from Paulet Island, but too much to the east of it. We are approaching the latitudes in which we were at this time last year, on our way down. The ship left South Georgia just a year and a week ago, and reached this latitude four or five miles to the eastward of our present position on January 3, 1915, crossing the circle on New Year's Eve."

Thus, after a year's incessant battle with the ice, we had returned, by many strange turns of fortune's wheel, to almost identically the same latitude that we had left with such high hopes and aspirations twelve months previously; but under what different conditions now! Our ship crushed and lost, and we ourselves drifting on a piece of ice at the mercy of the winds. However, in spite of occasional setbacks due to unfavorable winds, our drift was in the main very satisfactory, and this went a long way towards keeping the men cheerful.

As the drift was mostly affected by the winds, the weather was closely watched by all, and Hussey, the meteorologist, was called upon to make forecasts every four hours, and sometimes more frequently than that. A meteorological screen, containing thermometers and a barograph, had been erected on a post frozen into the ice, and observations were taken every four hours. When we first left the ship the weather was cold and miserable, and altogether as unpropitious as it could possibly have been for our attempted march. Our first few days at Ocean Camp were passed under much the same conditions. At nights the temperature dropped to zero, with blinding snow and drift. One-hour watches were instituted, all hands taking their turn, and in such weather this job was no sinecure. The watchman had to be continually on the alert for cracks in the ice, or any sudden changes in the ice conditions, and also had to keep his eye on the dogs, who often became restless, fretful, and quarrelsome in the early hours of the morning. At the end of his hour he was very glad to crawl back into the comparative warmth of his frozen sleeping bag.

On November 6 a dull, overcast day developed into a howling blizzard from the southwest, with snow and low drift. Only those who were compelled left the shelter of their tent. Deep drifts formed everywhere, burying sledges and provisions to a depth of two feet, and the snow piling up round the tents threatened to burst the thin fabric. The fine drift found its way in through the ventilator of the tent, which was accordingly plugged up with a spare rock.

This lasted for two days, when one man wrote: "The blizzard continued through the morning, but cleared towards noon, and it was a beautiful evening; but we would far rather have the screeching blizzard with its searching drift and cold damp wind, for we drifted about eleven miles to the north during the night."

For four days the fine weather continued, with gloriously warm, bright sun, but cold when standing still or in the shade. The temperature usually dropped below zero, but every opportunity was taken during these fine, sunny days to partially dry our sleeping bags and other gear, which had become sodden through our body heat having thawed the snow which had drifted in on to them during the blizzard. The bright sun seemed to put new heart into all.

The next day brought a northeasterly wind with the very high temperature of 27° Fahr.—only 5° below freezing. "These high temperatures do not always represent the warmth which might be assumed from the thermometrical readings. They usually bring dull, overcast skies, with a raw, muggy, moisture-laden wind. The winds from the south, though colder, are nearly always coincident with sunny days and clear blue skies."

The temperature still continued to rise, reaching 33° Fahr. on November 14. The thaw consequent upon these high temperatures was having a disastrous effect upon the surface of our camp. "The surface is awful!—not slushy, but elusive. You step out gingerly. All is well for a few paces, then your foot suddenly sinks a couple of feet until it comes to a hard layer. You wade along in this way step by step, like a mudlark at Portsmouth Hard, hoping gradually to regain the surface. Soon you do, only to repeat the exasperating performance *ad lib.,* to the accompaniment of all the expletives that you can bring to bear on the subject. What actually happens is that the warm air melts the surface sufficiently to cause drops of water to trickle down slightly, where, on meeting colder layers of snow, they freeze again, forming a honeycomb of icy nodules instead of the soft, powdery, granular snow that we are accustomed to."

These high temperatures persisted for some days, and when, as occasionally happened, the sky was clear and the sun was shining it was unbearably hot. Five men who were sent to fetch some gear from the vicinity of the ship with a sledge marched in nothing but trousers and singlet, and even then were very hot; in fact they were afraid of getting sunstroke, so let down flaps from their caps to cover their necks. Their sleeves were rolled up over their elbows, and their arms were red and sunburnt in consequence. The temperature on this occasion was 26° Fahr., or 6° below freezing. For five or six days more the sun continued, and most of our clothes and sleeping·bags were now comparatively dry. A wretched day with rainy sleet set in on November 21, but one could put up with this discomfort as the wind was now from the south.

The wind veered later to the west, and the sun came out at 9 p.m. For at this time, near the end of November, we had the midnight sun. "A thrice-blessed southerly wind" soon arrived to cheer us all, occasioning the following remarks in one of the diaries: "Today is the most beautiful day we have had in the Antarctic—a clear sky, a gentle, warm breeze from the south, and the most brilliant sunshine. We all took advantage of it to strike tents, clean out, and generally dry and air ground sheets and sleeping bags."

I was up early—4 a.m.—to keep watch, and the sight was indeed magnificent. Spread out before one was an extensive panorama of ice fields, intersected here and there by small broken leads, and dotted with numerous noble bergs, partly bathed in sunshine and partly tinged with the grey shadows of an overcast sky.

As one watched one observed a distinct line of demarcation between the sunshine and the shade, and this line gradually approached nearer and nearer, lighting up the hummocky relief of the ice field bit by bit, until at last it reached us, and threw the whole camp into a blaze of glorious sunshine which lasted nearly all day.

"This afternoon we were treated to one or two showers of hail-like snow. Yesterday we also had a rare form of snow, or, rather, precipitation of ice spicules, exactly like little hairs, about a third of an inch long.

"The warmth in the tents at lunchtime was so great that we had all the side flaps up for ventilation, but it is a treat to get warm occasionally, and one can put up with a little stuffy atmosphere now and again for the sake of it. The wind has gone to the best quarter this evening, the southeast, and is freshening."

On these fine, clear, sunny days wonderful mirage effects could be observed, just as occur over the desert. Huge bergs were apparently resting on nothing, with a distinct gap between their bases and the horizon; others were curiously distorted into all sorts of weird and fantastic shapes, appearing to be many times their proper height. Added to this, the pure glistening white of the snow and ice made a picture which it is impossible adequately to describe.

Later on, the freshening southwesterly wind brought mild, overcast weather, probably due to the opening up of the pack in that direction.

I had already made arrangements for a quick move in case of a sudden breakup of the ice. Emergency orders were issued; each man had his post allotted and his duty detailed; and the whole was so organized that in less than five minutes from the sounding of the alarm on my whistle, tents were struck, gear and provisions packed, and the whole party was ready to move off. I now took a final survey of the men to note their condition, both mental and physical. For our time at Ocean Camp had not been one of unalloyed bliss. The loss of the ship meant more to us than we could ever put into words. After we had settled at Ocean Camp she still remained nipped by the ice, only her stern showing and her bows overridden and buried by the relentless pack. The tangled mass of ropes, rigging, and spars made the scene even more desolate and depressing.

It was with a feeling almost of relief that the end came. "*November* 21, 1915.—This evening, as we were lying in our tents we heard the Boss call out, 'She's going, boys!' We were out in a second and up on the lookout station and other points of vantage, and, sure enough, there was our poor ship a mile and a half away struggling in her death agony. She went down bows first, her stern raised in the air. She then gave one quick dive and the ice closed over her forever. It gave one a sickening sensation to see it, for, mastless and useless as she was, she seemed to be a link with the outer world. Without her our destitution seems more emphasized, our desolation more complete. The loss of the ship sent a slight wave of depression over the camp. No one said much, but we cannot be blamed for feeling it in a sentimental way. It seemed as if the moment of severance from many cherished associations, many happy moments, even stirring incidents, had come as she silently upended to find a last resting place beneath the ice on which we now stand. When one knows every little nook and corner of one's ship as we did, and has helped her time and again in the fight that she made so well, the actual parting was not without its pathos, quite apart from one's own desolation, and I doubt if there was one amongst us who did not feel some personal emotion when Sir Ernest, standing on the top of the lookout, said somewhat sadly and quietly, 'She's gone, boys.'

"It must, however, be said that we did not give way to depression for long, for soon every one was as cheery as usual. Laughter rang out from the tents, and even the Boss had a passage-at-arms with the storekeeper over the inadequacy of the sausage ration, insisting that there should be two each 'because they were such little ones,' instead of the one and a half that the latter proposed."

The psychological effect of a slight increase in the rations soon neutralized any tendency to downheartedness, but with the high temperatures surface thaw set in, and our bags and clothes were soaked and sodden. Our boots squelched as we walked, and we lived in a state of perpetual wet feet. At nights, before the temperature had fallen, clouds of steam could be seen rising from our soaking bags and boots. During the night, as it grew colder, this all condensed as rime on the inside of the tent, and showered down upon us if one happened to touch the side inadvertently. One had to be careful how one walked, too, as often only a thin crust of ice and snow covered a hole in the floe, through which many an unwary member went in up to his waist. These perpetual soakings, however, seemed to have had little lasting effect, or perhaps it was not apparent owing to the excitement of the prospect of an early release.

A northwesterly wind on December 7 and 8 retarded our progress somewhat, but I had reason to believe that it would help to open the ice and form leads through which we might escape to open water. So I ordered a practice launching of the boats and stowage of food and stores in them. This was very satisfactory. We cut a slipway from our floe into a lead which ran alongside, and the boats took the water "like a bird," as one sailor remarked. Our hopes were high in anticipation of an early release. A blizzard sprang up, increasing the next day and burying tents and packing cases in the drift. On December 12 it had moderated somewhat and veered to the southeast, and the next day the blizzard had ceased, but a good steady wind from south and southwest continued to blow us north.

"*December* 15, 1915.—The continuance of southerly winds is exceeding our best hopes, and raising our spirits in proportion. Prospects could not be brighter than they are just now. The environs of our floe are continually changing. Some days we are almost surrounded by small open leads, preventing us from crossing over to the adjacent floes." After two more days our fortune changed, and a strong northeasterly wind brought "a beastly cold, windy day" and drove us back three and a quarter miles. Soon, however, the wind once more veered to the south and southwest. These high temperatures, combined with the strong changeable winds that we had had of late, led me to conclude that the ice all around us was rotting and breaking up and that the moment of our deliverance from the icy maw of the Antarctic was at hand.

On December 20, after discussing the question with Wild, I informed all hands that I intended to try and make a march to the west to reduce the distance between us and Paulet Island. A buzz of pleasurable anticipation went round the camp, and every one was anxious to get on the move. So the next day I set off with Wild, Crean, and Hurley, with dog teams, to the westward to survey the route. After traveling about seven miles we mounted a small berg, and there as far as we could see stretched a series of immense flat floes from half a mile to a mile across, separated from each other by pressure ridges which seemed easily negotiable with pick and shovel. The only place that appeared likely to be formidable was a very much cracked-up area between the old floe that we were on and the first of the series of young flat floes about half a mile away.

December 22 was therefore kept as Christmas Day, and most of our small remaining stock of luxuries was consumed at the Christmas feast. We could not carry it all with us, so for the last time for eight months we had a really good meal—as much as we could eat. Anchovies in oil, baked beans, and jugged hare made a glorious mixture such as we have not dreamed of since our schooldays. Everybody was working at high pressure, packing and repacking sledges and stowing what provisions we were going to take with us in the various sacks and boxes. As I looked round at the eager faces of the men I could not but hope that this time the fates would be kinder to us than in our last attempts to march across the ice to safety.

CHAPTER VI

THE MARCH BETWEEN

WITH THE EXCEPTION of the night watchman we turned in at 11 p.m., and at 3 a.m. on December 23 all hands were roused for the purpose of sledging the two boats, the *James Caird* and the *Dudley Docker,* over the dangerously cracked portion to the first of the young floes, whilst the surface still held its night crust. A thick sea-fog came up from the west, so we started off finally at 4:30 a.m., after a drink of hot coffee.

Practically all hands had to be harnessed to each boat in succession, and by dint of much careful manipulation and tortuous courses amongst the broken ice we got both safely over the danger zone.

We then returned to Ocean Camp for the tents and the rest of the sledges, and pitched camp by the boats about one and a quarter miles off. On the way back a big seal was caught which provided fresh food for ourselves and for the dogs. On arrival at the camp a supper of cold tinned mutton and tea was served, and everybody turned in at 2 p.m. It was my intention to sleep by day and march by night, so as to take advantage of the slightly lower temperatures and consequent harder surfaces.

At 8 p.m. the men were roused, and after a meal of cold mutton and tea, the march was resumed. A large open lead brought us to a halt at 11 p.m., whereupon we camped and turned in without a meal. Fortunately just at this time the weather was fine and warm. Several men slept out in the open at the beginning of the march. One night, however, a slight snow shower came on, succeeded immediately by a lowering of the temperature. Worsley, who had hung up his trousers and socks on a boat, found them iced up and stiff; and it was quite a painful process for him to dress quickly that morning. I was anxious, now that we had started, that we should make every effort to extricate ourselves, and this temporary check so early was rather annoying. So that afternoon Wild and I skied out to the crack and found that it had closed up again. We marked out the track with small flags as we returned. Each day, after all hands had turned in, Wild and I would go ahead for two miles or so to reconnoiter the next day's route, marking it with pieces of wood, tins, and small flags. We had to pick the road which, though it might be somewhat devious, was flattest and had least hummocks. Pressure ridges had to be skirted, and where this was not possible the best place to make a bridge of ice blocks across the lead or over the ridge had to be found and marked. It was the duty of the dog drivers to thus prepare the track for those who were toiling behind with the heavy boats. These boats were hauled in relays, about sixty yards at a time. I did not wish them to be separated by too great a distance in case the ice should crack between them, and we should be unable to reach the one that was in rear. Every twenty yards or so they had to stop for a rest and to take breath, and it was a welcome sight to them to see the canvas screen go up on some oars, which denoted the fact that the cook had started preparing a meal, and that a temporary halt, at any rate, was going to be made. Thus the ground had to be traversed three times by the boat-hauling party. The dog sledges all made two, and some of them three, relays. The dogs were wonderful. Without them we could never have transported half the food and gear that we did.

We turned in at 7 p.m. that night, and at 1 a.m. next day, the 25th, and the third day of our march, a breakfast of sledging ration was served. By 2 a.m. we were on the march again. We wished one another a merry Christmas, and our thoughts went back to those at home. We wondered, too,

that day, as we sat down to our "lunch" of stale, thin bannock and a mug of thin cocoa, what they were having at
home.

All hands were very cheerful. The prospect of a relief
from the monotony of life on the floe raised all our spirits.
One man wrote in his diary: "It's a hard, rough, jolly life,
this marching and camping; no washing of self or dishes, no
undressing, no changing of clothes. We have our food anyhow, and always impregnated with blubber smoke; sleeping
almost on the bare snow and working as hard as the human
physique is capable of doing on a minimum of food."

We marched on, with one halt at 6 a.m., till half-past
eleven. After a supper of seal steaks and tea we turned in.
The surface now was pretty bad. High temperatures during
the day made the upper layers of snow very soft, and the
thin crust which formed at night was not sufficient to support a man. Consequently, at each step we went in over our
knees in the soft wet snow. Sometimes a man would step
into a hole in the ice which was hidden by the covering of
snow, and be pulled up with a jerk by his harness. The sun
was very hot and many were suffering from cracked lips.

Two seals were killed today. Wild and McIlroy, who went
out to secure them, had rather an exciting time on some very
loose, rotten ice, three killer whales in a lead a few yards
away poking up their ugly heads as if in anticipation of a
feast.

Next day, December 26, we started off again at 1 a.m.
"The surface was much better than it has been for the last
few days, and this is the principal thing that matters. The
route, however, lay over very hummocky floes, and required
much work with pick and shovel to make it passable for the
boat sledges. These are handled in relays by eighteen men
under Worsley. It is killing work on soft surfaces."

At 5 a.m. we were brought up by a wide open lead after
an unsatisfactorily short march. While we waited, a meal of

tea and two small bannocks was served, but as 10 a.m. came and there were no signs of the lead closing we all turned in.

It snowed a little during the day and those who were sleeping outside got their sleeping bags pretty wet.

At 9:30 p.m. that night we were off again. I was, as usual, pioneering in front, followed by the cook and his mate pulling a small sledge with the stove and all the cooking gear on. These two, black as two Mohawk Minstrels with the blubber soot, were dubbed "Potash and Perlmutter." Next come the dog teams, who soon overtake the cook, and the two boats bring up the rear. Were it not for these cumbrous boats we should get along at a great rate, but we dare not abandon them on any account. As it is we left one boat, the *Stancomb Wills,* behind at Ocean Camp, and the remaining two will barely accommodate the whole party when we leave the floe.

We did a good march of one and a half miles that night before we halted for "lunch" at 1 a.m., and then on for another mile, when at 5 a.m. we camped by a little sloping berg.

Blackie, one of Wild's dogs, fell lame and could neither pull nor keep up with the party even when relieved of his harness, so had to be shot.

Nine p.m. that night, the 27th, saw us on the march again. The first 200 yds. took us about five hours to cross, owing to the amount of breaking down of pressure ridges and filling in of leads that was required. The surface, too, was now very soft, so our progress was slow and tiring. We managed to get another three-quarters of a mile before lunch, and a further mile due west over a very hummocky floe before we camped at 5:30 a.m. Greenstreet and Macklin killed and brought in a huge Weddell seal weighing about 800 lb., and two emperor penguins made a welcome addition to our larder.

I climbed a small tilted berg near by. The country immediately ahead was much broken up. Great open leads inter-sected the floes at all angles, and it all looked very unpromising, Wild and I went out prospecting as usual, but it seemed too broken to travel over.

"*December* 29.—After a further reconnaissance the ice ahead proved quite unnegotiable, so at 8:30 p.m. last night, to the intense disappointment of all, instead of forging ahead, we had to retire half a mile so as to get on a stronger floe, and by 10 p.m. we had camped and all hands turned in again. The extra sleep was much needed, however disheart-ening the check may be."

During the night a crack formed right across the floe, so we hurriedly shifted to a strong old floe about a mile and a half to the east of our present position. The ice all around us was now too broken and soft to sledge over, and yet there was not sufficient open water to allow us to launch the boats with any degree of safety. We had been on the march for seven days; rations were short and the men were weak. They were worn out with the hard pulling over soft surfaces, and our stock of sledging food was very small. We had marched seven and a half miles in a direct line and at this rate it would take us over three hundred days to reach the land away to the west. As we only had food for forty-two days there was no alternative, therefore, but to camp once more on the floe and to possess our souls with what patience we could till conditions should appear more favorable for a re-newal of the attempt to escape. To this end, we stacked our surplus provisions, the reserve sledging rations being kept lashed on the sledges, and brought what gear we could from our but lately deserted Ocean Camp.

Our new home, which we were to occupy for nearly three and a half months, we called "Patience Camp."

CHAPTER VII

PATIENCE CAMP

THE APATHY WHICH seemed to take possession of some of the men at the frustration of their hopes was soon dispelled. Parties were sent out daily in different directions to look for seals and penguins. We had left, other than reserve sledging rations, about 110 lb. of pemmican, including the dog pemmican, and 300 lb. of flour. In addition there was a little tea, sugar, dried vegetables, and suet. I sent Hurley and Macklin to Ocean Camp to bring back the food that we had had to leave there. They returned with quite a good load, including 130 lb. of dry milk, about 50 lb. each of dog pemmican and jam, and a few tins of potted meats. When they were about a mile and a half away their voices were quite audible to us at Ocean Camp, so still was the air.

We were, of course, very short of the farinaceous element in our diet. The flour would last ten weeks. After that our sledging rations would last us less than three months. Our meals had to consist mainly of seal and penguin; and though this was valuable as an anti-scorbutic, so much so that not a single case of scurvy occurred amongst the party, yet it was a badly adjusted diet, and we felt rather weak and enervated in consequence.

"The cook deserves much praise for the way he has stuck to his job through all this severe blizzard. His galley consists of nothing but a few boxes arranged as a table, with a canvas screen erected around them on four oars and the two blubber stoves within. The protection afforded by the screen is only partial, and the eddies drive the pungent blubber smoke in all directions." After a few days we were able to build him an igloo of ice blocks with a tarpaulin over the top as a roof.

"Our rations are just sufficient to keep us alive, but we all feel that we could eat twice as much as we get. An average day's food at present consists of ½ lb. of seal with ¾ pint of tea for breakfast, a 4-oz. bannock with milk for lunch, and ¾ pint of seal stew for supper. That is barely enough, even doing very little work as we are, for of course we are completely destitute of bread or potatoes or anything of that sort. Some seem to feel it more than others and are continually talking of food; but most of us find that the continual conversation about food only whets an appetite that cannot be satisfied. Our craving for bread and butter is very real, not because we cannot get it, but because the system feels the need of it."

Owing to this shortage of food and the fact that we needed all that we could get for ourselves, I had to order all the dogs except two teams to be shot. It was the worst job that we had had throughout the Expedition, and we felt their loss keenly.

I had to be continually rearranging the weekly menu. The possible number of permutations of seal meat were decidedly limited. The fact that the men did not know what was coming gave them a sort of mental speculation, and the slightest variation was of great value.

"We caught an adelie today (January 26) and another whale was seen at close quarters, but no seals.

"We are now very short of blubber, and in consequence one stove has to be shut down. We only get one hot beverage a day, the tea at breakfast. For the rest we have iced water. Sometimes we are short even of this, so we take a few chips of ice in a tobacco tin to bed with us. In the morning there is about a spoonful of water in the tin, and one has to lie very still all night so as not to spill it."

To provide some variety in the food, I commenced to use the sledging ration at half strength twice a week.

The ice between us and Ocean Camp, now only about

five miles away and actually to the southwest of us, was very broken, but I decided to send Macklin and Hurley back with their dogs to see if there was any more food that could be added to our scanty stock. I gave them written instructions to take no undue risk or cross any wide-open leads, and said that they were to return by midday the next day. Although they both fell through the thin ice up to their waists more than once, they managed to reach the camp. They found the surface soft and sunk about two feet. Ocean Camp, they said, "looked like a village that had been razed to the ground and deserted by its inhabitants." The floorboards forming the old tent bottoms had prevented the sun from thawing the snow directly underneath them, and were in consequence raised about two feet above the level of the surrounding floe.

The storehouse next the galley had taken on a list of several degrees to starboard, and pools of water had formed everywhere.

They collected what food they could find and packed a few books in a venesta sledging case, returning to Patience Camp by about 8 p.m. I was pleased at their quick return, and as their report seemed to show that the road was favorable, on February 2 I sent back eighteen men under Wild to bring all the remainder of the food and the third boat, the *Stancomb Wills*. They started off at 1 a.m., towing the empty boat sledge on which the *James Caird* had rested, and reached Ocean Camp about 3:30 a.m.

"We stayed about three hours at the Camp, mounting the boat on the sledge, collecting eatables, clothing, and books. We left at 6 a.m., arriving back at Patience Camp with the boat at 12:30 p.m., taking exactly three times as long to return with the boat as it did to pull in the empty sledge to fetch it. On the return journey we had numerous halts while the pioneer party of four were busy breaking down pressure ridges and filling in open cracks with ice blocks, as the leads were opening up. The sun had softened the surface a good deal, and in places it was terribly hard pulling. Every one was a bit exhausted by the time we got back, as we are not now in good training and are on short rations. Every now and then the heavy sledge broke through the ice altogether and was practically afloat. We had an awful job to extricate it, exhausted as we were. The longest distance which we managed to make without stopping for leads or pressure ridges was about three-quarters of a mile.

"About a mile from Patience Camp we had a welcome surprise. Sir Ernest and Hussey sledged out to meet us with dixies of hot tea, well wrapped up to keep them warm.

"One or two of the men left behind had cut a moderately good track for us into the camp, and they harnessed themselves up with us, and we got in in fine style.

"One excellent result of our trip was the recovery of two cases of lentils weighing 42 lb. each."

The next day I sent Macklin and Crean back to make a further selection of the gear, but they found that several leads had opened up during the night, and they had to return when within a mile and a half of their destination. We were never able to reach Ocean Camp again. Still, there was very little left there that would have been of use to us.

By the middle of February the blubber question was a serious one. I had all the discarded seals' heads and flippers dug up and stripped of every vestige of blubber. Meat was very short too. We still had our three months' supply of sledging food practically untouched; we were only to use this as a last resort. We had a small supply of dog pemmican, the dogs that were left being fed on those parts of the seals that we could not use. This dog pemmican we fried in suet with a little flour and made excellent bannocks.

Our meat supply was now very low indeed; we were reduced to just a few scraps. Fortunately, however, we caught two seals and four emperor penguins, and next day forty

adelies. We had now only forty days' food left, and the lack
of blubber was being keenly felt. All our suet was used up,
so we used seal blubber to fry the meat in. Once we were
used to its fishy taste we enjoyed it; in fact, like Oliver
Twist, we wanted more.

On Leap Year day, February 29, we held a special celebration, more to cheer the men up than for anything else. Some
of the cynics of the party held that it was to celebrate their
escape from woman's wiles for another four years. The last
of our cocoa was used today. Henceforth water, with an occasional drink of weak milk, is to be our only beverage.
Three lumps of sugar were now issued to each man daily.

One night one of the dogs broke loose and played havoc
with our precious stock of bannocks. He ate four and half
of a fifth before he could be stopped. The remaining half,
with the marks of the dog's teeth on it, I gave to Worsley,
who divided it up amongst his seven tentmates; they each
received about half a square inch.

Lees, who was in charge of the food and responsible for
its safekeeping, wrote in his diary: "The shorter the provisions the more there is to do in the commissariat department, contriving to eke out our slender stores as the weeks
pass by. No housewife ever had more to do than we have in
making a little go a long way.

"Writing about the bannock that Peter bit makes one wish
now that one could have many a meal that one has given to
the dog at home. When one is hungry, fastidiousness goes
to the winds and one is only too glad to eat up any scraps,
regardless of their antecedents. One is almost ashamed to
write of all the tidbits one has picked up here, but it is
enough to say that when the cook upset some pemmican on
to an old sooty cloth and threw it outside his galley, one
man subsequently made a point of acquiring it and scraping
off the palatable but dirty compound." Another man
searched for over an hour in the snow where he had dropped

a piece of cheese some days before, in the hopes of finding a few crumbs. He was rewarded by coming across a piece as big as his thumbnail, and considered it well worth the trouble.

By this time blubber was a regular article of our diet—either raw, boiled, or fried. "It is remarkable how our appetites have changed in this respect. Until quite recently almost the thought of it was nauseating. Now, however, we positively demand it. The thick black oil which is rendered down from it, rather like train oil in appearance and cod liver oil in taste, we drink with avidity."

We had now about enough farinaceous food for two meals all round, and sufficient seal to last for a month. Our forty days' reserve sledging rations, packed on the sledges, we wished to keep till the last.

But, as one man philosophically remarked in his diary: "It will do us all good to be hungry like this, for we will appreciate so much more the good things when we get home."

Seals and penguins now seemed to studiously avoid us, and on taking stock of our provisions on March 21 I found that we had only sufficient meat to last us for ten days, and the blubber would not last that time even, so one biscuit had to be our midday meal.

Our meals were now practically all seal meat, with one biscuit at midday; and I calculated that at this rate, allowing for a certain number of seals and penguins being caught, we could last for nearly six months. We were all very weak though, and as soon as it appeared likely that we should leave our floe and take to the boats I should have to considerably increase the ration. One day a huge sea leopard climbed on to the floe and attacked one of the men. Wild, hearing the shouting, ran out and shot it. When it was cut up we found in its stomach several undigested fish. These we fried in some of its blubber, and so had our only "fresh" fish meal during the whole of our drift on the ice.

"As fuel is so scarce we have had to resort to melting ice for drinking water in tins against our bodies, and we treat the tins of dog pemmican for breakfast similarly by keeping them in our sleeping bags all night.

"The last two teams of dogs were shot today (April 2), the carcasses being dressed for food. We had some of the dog meat cooked, and it was not at all bad—just like beef, but, of course, very tough."

On April 5 we killed two seals, and this, with the sea leopard of a few days before, enabled us to slightly increase our ration. Everybody now felt much happier; such is the psychological effect of hunger appeased.

On cold days a few strips of raw blubber were served out to all hands, and it is wonderful how it fortified us against the cold.

Our stock of forty days' sledging rations remained practically untouched, but once in the boats they were used at full strength.

When we first settled down at Patience Camp the weather was very mild. New Year's Eve, however, was foggy and overcast, with some snow, and next day, though the temperature rose to 38° Fahr., it was "abominably cold and wet underfoot." As a rule, during the first half of January the weather was comparatively warm, so much so that we could dispense with our mitts and work outside for quite long periods with bare hands. Up till the 13th it was exasperatingly warm and calm. This meant that our drift northwards, which was almost entirely dependent on the wind, was checked. A light southerly breeze on the 16th raised all our hopes, and as the temperature was dropping we were looking forward to a period of favorable winds and a long drift north.

On the 18th it had developed into a howling southwesterly gale, rising next day to a regular blizzard with much drift. No one left the shelter of his tent except to feed the dogs, fetch the meals from the galley for his tent, or when his turn as watchman came round. For six days this lasted, when the drift subsided somewhat, though the southerly wind continued, and we were able to get a glimpse of the sun. This showed us to have drifted 84 miles north in six days, the longest drift we had made. For weeks we had remained on the 67th parallel, and it seemed as though some obstruction was preventing us from passing it. By this amazing leap, however, we had crossed the Antarctic Circle, and were now 146 miles from the nearest land to the west of us—Snow Hill—and 357 miles from the South Orkneys, the first land directly to the north of us.

As if to make up for this, an equally strong northeasterly wind sprang up next day, and not only stopped our northward drift but set us back three miles to the south. As usual, high temperatures and wet fog accompanied these northerly winds, though the fog disappeared on the afternoon of January 25, and we had the unusual spectacle of bright hot sun with a northeasterly wind. It was as hot a day as we had ever had. The temperature was 36° Fahr. in the shade and nearly 80° Fahr. inside the tents. This had an awful effect on the surface, covering it with pools and making it very treacherous to walk upon. Ten days of northerly winds rather damped our spirits, but a strong southerly wind on February 4, backing later to southeast, carried us north again. High temperatures and northerly winds soon succeeded this, so that our average rate of northerly drift was about a mile a day in February. Throughout the month the diaries record alternately "a wet day, overcast and mild," and "bright and cold with light southerly winds." The wind was now the vital factor with us and the one topic of any real interest.

The beginning of March brought cold, damp, calm weather, with much wet snow and overcast skies. The effect of the weather on our mental state was very marked. All hands felt much more cheerful on a bright sunny day, and looked forward with much more hope to the future, than when it was dull and overcast. This had a much greater effect than an increase in rations.

A southeasterly gale on the 13th lasting for five days sent us twenty miles north, and from now our good fortune, as far as the wind was concerned, never left us for any length of time. On the 20th we experienced the worst blizzard we had had up to that time, though worse were to come after landing on Elephant Island. Thick snow fell, making it impossible to see the camp from thirty yards off. To go outside for a moment entailed getting covered all over with fine powdery snow, which required a great deal of brushing off before one could enter again.

As the blizzard eased up, the temperature dropped and it became bitterly cold. In our weak condition, with torn, greasy clothes, we felt these sudden variations in temperature much more than we otherwise would have done. A calm, clear, magnificently warm day followed, and next day came a strong southerly blizzard. Drifts four feet deep covered everything, and we had to be continually digging up our scanty stock of meat to prevent its being lost altogether. We had taken advantage of the previous fine day to attempt to thaw out our blankets, which were frozen stiff and could be held out like pieces of sheet iron; but on this day, and for the next two or three also, it was impossible to do anything but get right inside one's frozen sleeping bag to try and get warm. Too cold to read or sew, we had to keep our hands well inside, and pass the time in conversation with each other.

"The temperature was not strikingly low as temperatures go down here, but the terrific winds penetrate the flimsy fabric of our fragile tents and create so much draught that it is impossible to keep warm within. At supper last night our drinking water froze over in the tin in the tent before we could drink it. It is curious how thirsty we all are."

Two days of brilliant warm sunshine succeeded these cold

times, and on March 29 we experienced, to us, the most
amazing weather. It began to rain hard, and it was the first
rain that we had seen since we left South Georgia sixteen
months ago. We regarded it as our first touch with civilization, and many of the men longed for the rain and fogs of
London.

Strong south winds with dull, overcast skies and occasional high temperatures were now our lot till April 7, when
the mist lifted and we could make out what appeared to be
land to the north.

Although the general drift of our ice floe had indicated to
us that we must eventually drift north, our progress in that
direction was not by any means uninterrupted. We were at
the mercy of the wind, and could no more control our drift
than we could control the weather.

A long spell of calm, still weather at the beginning of
January caused us some anxiety by keeping us at about the
latitude that we were in at the beginning of December.
Towards the end of January, however, a long drift of eighty-
four miles in a blizzard cheered us all up. This soon stopped
and we began a slight drift to the east. Our general drift now
slowed up considerably, and by February 22 we were still
eighty miles from Paulet Island, which now was our objective. There was a hut there and some stores which had been
taken down by the ship which went to the rescue of Nordenskjöld's Expedition in 1904, and whose fitting out and
equipment I had charge of. We remarked amongst ourselves
what a strange turn of fate it would be if the very cases of
provisions which I had ordered and sent out so many years
before were now to support us during the coming winter.
But this was not to be. March 5 found us about forty miles
south of the longitude of Paulet Island, but well to the east
of it; and as the ice was still too much broken up to sledge
over, it appeared as if we should be carried past it. By March
17 we were exactly on a level with Paulet Island but sixty
miles to the east. It might have been six hundred for all the

chance that we had of reaching it by sledging across the broken sea ice in its present condition.

Our thoughts now turned to the Danger Islands, thirty-five miles away. "It seems that we are likely to drift up and down this coast from southwest to northeast and back again for some time yet before we finally clear the point of Joinville Island; until we do we cannot hope for much opening up, as the ice must be very congested against the southeast coast of the island, otherwise our failure to respond to the recent southeasterly gale cannot be well accounted for. In support of this there has been some very heavy pressure on the northeast side of our floe, one immense block being upended to a height of 25 ft. We saw a Dominican gull fly over today, the first we have seen since leaving South Georgia; it is another sign of our proximity to land. We cut steps in this 25-ft. slab, and it makes a fine lookout. When the weather clears we confidently expect to see land."

A heavy blizzard obscured our view till March 23. " 'Land in sight' was reported this morning. We were skeptical, but this afternoon it showed up unmistakably to the west, and there can be no further doubt about it. It is Joinville Island, and its serrated mountain ranges, all snow-clad, are just visible on the horizon. This barren, inhospitable-looking land would be a haven of refuge to us if we could but reach it. It would be ridiculous to make the attempt though, with the ice all broken up as it is. It is too loose and broken to march over, yet not open enough to be able to launch the boats." For the next two or three days we saw ourselves slowly drifting past the land, longing to reach it yet prevented from doing so by the ice between, and towards the end of March we saw Mount Haddington fade away into the distance.

Our hopes were now centered on Elephant Island or Clarence Island, which lay 100 miles almost due north of us.

If we failed to reach either of them we might try for South Georgia, but our chances of reaching it would be very small.

CHAPTER VIII

ESCAPE FROM THE ICE

On April 7 at daylight the long-desired peak of Clarence Island came into view, bearing nearly north from our camp. At first it had the appearance of a huge berg, but with the growing light we could see plainly the black lines of scree and the high, precipitous cliffs of the island, which were miraged up to some extent. The dark rocks in the white snow were a pleasant sight. So long had our eyes looked on icebergs that apparently grew or dwindled according to the angles at which the shadows were cast by the sun; so often had we discovered rocky islands and brought in sight the peaks of Joinville Land, only to find them, after some change of wind or temperature, floating away as nebulous cloud or ordinary berg, that not until Worsley, Wild, and Hurley had unanimously confirmed my observation was I satisfied that I was really looking at Clarence Island. The land was still more than sixty miles away, but it had to our eyes something of the appearance of home, since we expected to find there our first solid footing after all the long months of drifting on the unstable ice. We had adjusted ourselves to the life on the floe, but our hopes had been fixed all the time on some possible landing place. As one hope failed to materialize, our anticipations fed themselves on another. Our drifting home had no rudder to guide it, no sail to give it speed. We were dependent upon the caprice of wind and current; we went whither those irresponsible forces listed. The longing to feel solid earth under our feet filled our hearts.

In the full daylight Clarence Island ceased to look like land and had the appearance of a berg not more than eight or ten miles away, so deceptive are distances in the clear air of the Antarctic. The sharp white peaks of Elephant Island showed to the west of north a little later in the day. "I have stopped issuing sugar now, and our meals consist of seal meat and blubber only, with 7 ozs. of dried milk per day for the party," I wrote. "Each man receives a pinch of salt, and the milk is boiled up to make hot drinks for all hands. The diet suits us, since we cannot get much exercise on the floe and the blubber supplies heat. Fried slices of blubber seem to our taste to resemble crisp bacon. It certainly is no hardship to eat it, though persons living under civilized conditions probably would shudder at it. The hardship would come if we were unable to get it." I think that the palate of the human animal can adjust itself to anything. Some creatures will die before accepting a strange diet if deprived of their natural food. The yaks of the Himalayan uplands must feed from the growing grass, scanty and dry though it may be, and would starve even if allowed the best oats and corn. "We still have the dark water-sky of the last week with us to the southwest and west, round to the northeast. We are leaving all the bergs to the west and there are few within our range of vision now. The swell is more marked today, and I feel sure we are at the verge of the floe ice. One strong gale followed by a calm would scatter the pack, I think, and then we could push through. I have been thinking much of our prospects. The appearance of Clarence Island after our long drift seems, somehow, to convey an ultimatum. The island is the last outpost of the south and our final chance of a landing place. Beyond it lies the broad Atlantic. Our little boats may be compelled any day now to sail unsheltered over the open sea with a thousand leagues of ocean separating them from the land to the north and east. It seems vital that we shall land on Clarence Island or its neighbor, Elephant Island. The latter island has an attraction for us, although as far as I know nobody has ever landed there. Its

name suggests the presence of the plump and succulent sea
elephant. We have an increasing desire in any case to get
firm ground under our feet. The floe has been a good friend
to us, but it is reaching the end of its journey, and it is liable
at any time now to break up and fling us into the unplumbed
sea."

A little later, after reviewing the whole situation in the
light of our circumstances, I made up my mind that we
should try to reach Deception Island. The relative positions
of Clarence, Elephant, and Deception Islands can be seen
on the chart. The two islands first named lay comparatively
near to us and were separated by some eighty miles of water
from Prince George Island, which was about 150 miles away
from our camp on the berg. From this island a chain of similar islands extends westward, terminating in Deception Island. The channels separating these desolate patches of rock
and ice are from ten to fifteen miles wide. But we knew
from the Admiralty sailing directions that there were stores
for the use of shipwrecked mariners on Deception Island,
and it was possible that the summer whalers had not yet
deserted its harbor. Also we had learned from our scanty
records that a small church had been erected there for the
benefit of the transient whalers. The existence of this building would mean to us a supply of timber, from which, if dire
necessity urged us, we could construct a reasonably seaworthy boat. We had discussed this point during our drift on the
floe. Two of our boats were fairly strong, but the third, the
James Caird, was light, although a little longer than the others. All of them were small for the navigation of these notoriously stormy seas, and they would be heavily loaded, so a
voyage in open water would be a serious undertaking. I fear
that the carpenter's fingers were already itching to convert
pews into topsides and decks. In any case, the worst that
could befall us when we had reached Deception Island
would be a wait until the whalers returned about the middle
of November.

Another bit of information gathered from the records of the west side of the Weddell Sea related to Prince George Island. The Admiralty "Sailing Directions," referring to the South Shetlands, mentioned a cave on this island. None of us had seen that cave or could say if it was large or small, wet or dry; but as we drifted on our floe and later, when navigating the treacherous leads and making our uneasy night camps, that cave seemed to my fancy to be a palace which in contrast would dim the splendors of Versailles.

The swell increased that night and the movement of the ice became more pronounced. Occasionally a neighboring floe would hammer against the ice on which we were camped, and the lesson of these blows was plain to read. We must get solid ground under our feet quickly. When the vibration ceased after a heavy surge, my thoughts flew round to the problem ahead. If the party had not numbered more than six men a solution would not have been so hard to find; but obviously the transportation of the whole party to a place of safety, with the limited means at our disposal, was going to be a matter of extreme difficulty. There were twenty-eight men on our floating cake of ice, which was steadily dwindling under the influence of wind, weather, charging floes, and heavy swell. I confess that I felt the burden of responsibility sit heavily on my shoulders; but, on the other hand, I was stimulated and cheered by the attitude of the men. Loneliness is the penalty of leadership, but the man who has to make the decisions is assisted greatly if he feels that there is no uncertainty in the minds of those who follow him, and that his orders will be carried out confidently and in expectation of success.

The sun was shining in the blue sky on the following morning (April 8). Clarence Island showed clearly on the horizon, and Elephant Island could also be distinguished. The single snow-clad peak of Clarence Island stood up as a beacon of safety, though the most optimistic imagination could not make an easy path of the ice and ocean that separated us from that giant, white and austere. "The pack was much looser this morning, and the long rolling swell from the northeast is more pronounced than it was yesterday. The floes rise and fall with the surge of the sea. We evidently are drifting with the surface current, for all the heavier masses of floe, bergs, and hummocks are being left behind. There has been some discussion in the camp as to the advisability of making one of the bergs our home for the time being and drifting with it to the west. The idea is not sound. I cannot be sure that the berg would drift in the right direction. If it did move west and carried us into the open water, what would be our fate when we tried to launch the boats down the steep sides of the berg in the sea swell after the surrounding floes had left us? One must reckon, too, the chance of the berg splitting or even overturning during our stay. It is not possible to gauge the condition of a big mass of ice by surface appearance. The ice may have a fault, and when the wind, current, and swell set up strains and tensions, the line of weakness may reveal itself suddenly and disastrously. No, I do not like the idea of drifting on a berg. We must stay on our floe till conditions improve and then make another attempt to advance towards the land."

At 6:30 p.m. a particularly heavy shock went through our floe. The watchman and other members of the party made an immediate inspection and found a crack right under the *James Caird* and between the other two boats and the main camp. Within five minutes the boats were over the crack and close to the tents. The trouble was not caused by a blow from another floe. We could see that the piece of ice we occupied had slewed and now presented its long axis towards the oncoming swell. The floe, therefore, was pitching in the manner of a ship, and it had cracked across when the swell lifted the center, leaving the two ends comparatively unsupported. We were now on a triangular raft of ice, the three sides measuring, roughly, 90, 100, and 120 yds. Night came down dull and overcast, and before midnight the wind had freshened from the west. We could see that the pack was opening under the influence of wind, wave, and current, and I felt that the time for launching the boats was near at hand. Indeed, it was obvious that even if the conditions were unfavorable for a start during the coming day, we could not safely stay on the floe many hours longer. The movement of the ice in the swell was increasing, and the floe might split right under our camp. We had made preparations for quick action if anything of the kind occurred. Our case would be desperate if the ice broke into small pieces not large enough to support our party and not loose enough to permit the use of the boats.

The following day was Sunday (April 9), but it proved no day of rest for us. Many of the important events of our Expedition occurred on Sundays, and this particular day was to see our forced departure from the floe on which we had lived for nearly six months, and the start of our journeyings in the boats. "This has been an eventful day. The morning was fine, though somewhat overcast by stratus and cumulus clouds; moderate south-southwesterly and southeasterly breezes. We hoped that with this wind the ice would drift nearer to Clarence Island. At 7 a.m. lanes of water and leads could be seen on the horizon to the west. The ice separating us from the lanes was loose, but did not appear to be workable for the boats. The long swell from the northwest was coming in more freely than on the previous day and was driving the floes together in the utmost confusion. The loose brash between the masses of ice was being churned to mud-like consistency, and no boat could have lived in the channels that opened and closed around us. Our own floe was suffering in the general disturbance, and after breakfast I ordered the tents to be struck and everything prepared for an immediate start when the boats could be launched." I

had decided to take the *James Caird* myself, with Wild and
eleven men. This was the largest of our boats, and in addition to her human complement she carried the major portion
of the stores. Worsley had charge of the *Dudley Docker* with
nine men, and Hudson and Crean were the senior men on
the *Stancomb Wills*.

Soon after breakfast the ice closed again. We were standing by, with our preparations as complete as they could be
made, when at 11 a.m. our floe suddenly split right across
under the boats. We rushed our gear on to the larger of the
two pieces and watched with strained attention for the next
development. The crack had cut through the site of my tent.
I stood on the edge of the new fracture, and, looking across
the widening channel of water, could see the spot where for
many months my head and shoulders had rested when I was
in my sleeping bag. The depression formed by my body and
legs was on our side of the crack. The ice had sunk under
my weight during the months of waiting in the tent, and I
had many times put snow under the bag to fill the hollow.
The lines of stratification showed clearly the different layers
of snow. How fragile and precarious had been our resting
place! Yet usage had dulled our sense of danger. The floe
had become our home, and during the early months of the
drift we had almost ceased to realize that it was but a sheet
of ice floating on unfathomed seas. Now our home was
being shattered under our feet, and we had a sense of loss
and incompleteness hard to describe.

The fragments of our floe came together again a little
later, and we had our lunch of seal meat, all hands eating
their fill. I thought that a good meal would be the best possible preparation for the journey that now seemed imminent,
and as we would not be able to take all our meat with us
when we finally moved, we could regard every pound eaten
as a pound rescued. The call to action came at 1 p.m. The
pack opened well and the channels became navigable. The

conditions were not all one could have desired, but it was best not to wait any longer. The *Dudley Docker* and the *Stancomb Wills* were launched quickly. Stores were thrown in, and the two boats were pulled clear of the immediate floes towards a pool of open water three miles broad, in which floated a lone and mighty berg. The *James Caird* was the last boat to leave, heavily loaded with stores and odds and ends of camp equipment. Many things regarded by us as essentials at that time were to be discarded a little later as the pressure of the primitive became more severe. Man can sustain life with very scanty means. The trappings of civilization are soon cast aside in the face of stern realities, and given the barest opportunity of winning food and shelter, man can live and even find his laughter ringing true.

The three boats were a mile away from our floe home at 2 p.m. We had made our way through the channels and had entered the big pool when we saw a rush of foam-clad water and tossing ice approaching us, like the tidal bore of a river. The pack was being impelled to the east by a tide-rip, and two huge masses of ice were driving down upon us on converging courses. The *James Caird* was leading. Starboarding the helm and bending strongly to the oars, we managed to get clear. The two other boats followed us, though from their position astern at first they had not realized the immediate danger. The *Stancomb Wills* was the last boat and she was very nearly caught, but by great exertion she was kept just ahead of the driving ice. It was an unusual and startling experience. The effect of tidal action on ice is not often as marked as it was that day. The advancing ice, accompanied by a large wave, appeared to be traveling at about three knots, and if we had not succeeded in pulling clear we would certainly have been swamped.

We pulled hard for an hour to windward of the berg that lay in the open water. The swell was crashing on its perpendicular sides and throwing spray to a height of sixty feet.

Evidently there was an ice foot at the east end, for the swell broke before it reached the berg face and flung its white spray on to the blue ice wall. We might have paused to have admired the spectacle under other conditions; but night was coming on apace, and we needed a camping place. As we steered northwest, still amid the ice floes, the *Dudley Docker* got jammed between two masses while attempting to make a short cut. The old adage about a short cut being the longest way round is often as true in the Antarctic as it is in the peaceful countryside. The *James Caird* got a line aboard the *Dudley Docker,* and after some hauling the boat was brought clear of the ice again. We hastened forward in the twilight in search of a flat, old floe, and presently found a fairly large piece rocking in the swell. It was not an ideal camping place by any means, but darkness had overtaken us. We hauled the boats up, and by 8 p.m. had the tents pitched and the blubber stove burning cheerily. Soon all hands were well fed and happy in their tents, and snatches of song came to me as I wrote up my log.

Some intangible feeling of uneasiness made me leave my tent about 11 p.m. that night and glance around the quiet camp. The stars between the snow flurries showed that the floe had swung round and was end on to the swell, a position exposing it to sudden strains. I started to walk across the floe in order to warn the watchman to look carefully for cracks, and as I was passing the men's tent the floe lifted on the crest of a swell and cracked right under my feet. The men were in one of the dome-shaped tents, and it began to stretch apart as the ice opened. A muffled sound, suggestive of suffocation, came from beneath the stretching tent. I rushed forward, helped some emerging men from under the canvas, and called out, "Are you all right?" "There are two in the water," somebody answered. The crack had widened to about four feet, and as I threw myself down at the edge, I saw a whitish object floating in the water. It was a sleeping bag with a man inside. I was able to grasp it, and with a heave lifted man and bag on to the floe. A few seconds later the ice edges came together again with tremendous force. Fortunately, there had been but one man in the water, or the incident might have been a tragedy. The rescued bag contained Holness, who was wet down to the waist but otherwise unscathed. The crack was now opening again. The *James Caird* and my tent were on one side of the opening and the remaining two boats and the rest of the camp on the other side. With two or three men to help me I struck my tent; then all hands manned the painter and rushed the *James Caird* across the opening crack. We held to the rope while, one by one, the men left on our side of the floe jumped the channel or scrambled over by means of the boat. Finally I was left alone. The night had swallowed all the others and the rapid movement of the ice forced me to let go the painter. For a moment I felt that my piece of rocking floe was the loneliest place in the world. Peering into the darkness, I could just see the dark figures on the other floe. I hailed Wild, ordering him to launch the *Stancomb Wills,* but I need not have troubled. His quick brain had anticipated the order and already the boat was being manned and hauled to the ice edge. Two or three minutes later she reached me, and I was ferried across to the camp.

We were now on a piece of flat ice about 200 ft. long and 100 ft. wide. There was no more sleep for any of us that night. The killers were blowing in the lanes around, and we waited for daylight and watched for signs of another crack in the ice. The hours passed with laggard feet as we stood huddled together or walked to and fro in the effort to keep some warmth in our bodies. We lit the blubber stove at 3 a.m., and with pipes going and a cup of hot milk for each man, we were able to discover some bright spots in our outlook. At any rate, we were on the move at last, and if dangers and difficulties loomed ahead we could meet and overcome them. No longer were we drifting helplessly at the mercy of wind and current.

The first glimmerings of dawn came at 6 a.m., and I waited anxiously for the full daylight. The swell was growing, and at times our ice was surrounded closely by similar pieces. At 6:30 a.m. we had hot hoosh, and then stood by waiting for the pack to open. Our chance came at 8, when we launched the boats, loaded them, and started to make our way through the lanes in a northerly direction. The *James Caird* was in the lead, with the *Stancomb Wills* next and the *Dudley Docker* bringing up the rear. In order to make the boats more seaworthy we had left some of our shovels, picks, and dried vegetables on the floe, and for a long time we could see the abandoned stores forming a dark spot on the ice. The boats were still heavily loaded. We got out of the lanes and entered a stretch of open water at 11 a.m. A strong easterly breeze was blowing, but the fringe of pack lying outside protected us from the full force of the swell, just as the coral reef of a tropical island checks the rollers of the Pacific. Our way was across the open sea, and soon after noon we swung round the north end of the pack and laid a course to the westward, the *James Caird* still in the lead. Immediately our deeply laden boats began to make heavy weather. They shipped sprays, which, freezing as they fell, covered men and gear with ice, and soon it was clear that we could not safely proceed. I put the *James Caird* round and ran for the shelter of the pack again, the other boats following. Back inside the outer line of ice the sea was not breaking. This was at 3 p.m., and all hands were tired and cold. A big floeberg resting peacefully ahead caught my eye, and half an hour later we had hauled up the boats and pitched camp for the night. It was a fine, big, blue berg with an attractively solid appearance, and from our camp we could get a good view of the surrounding sea and ice. The highest point was about 15 ft. above sea level. After a hot meal all hands, except the watchman, turned in. Every one was in need of rest after the troubles of the previous night and the unaccustomed strain of the last thirty-six hours at the oars. The berg appeared well able to withstand the battering of the sea, and too deep and massive to be seriously affected by the swell; but it was not as safe as it looked. About midnight the watchman called me and showed me that the heavy northwesterly swell was undermining the ice. A great piece had broken off within eight feet of my tent. We made what inspection was possible in the darkness, and found that on the westward side of the berg the thick snow covering was yielding rapidly to the attacks of the sea. An ice foot had formed just under the surface of the water. I decided that there was no immediate danger and did not call the men. The northwesterly wind strengthened during the night.

The morning of April 11 was overcast and misty. There was a haze on the horizon, and daylight showed that the pack had closed round our berg, making it impossible in the heavy swell to launch the boats. We could see no sign of the water. Numerous whales and killers were blowing between the floes, and Cape pigeons, petrels, and fulmars were circling round our berg. The scene from our camp as the daylight brightened was magnificent beyond description, though I must admit that we viewed it with anxiety. Heaving hills of pack and floe were sweeping towards us in long undulations, later to be broken here and there by the dark lines that indicated open water. As each swell lifted around our rapidly dissolving berg it drove floe ice on to the ice foot, shearing off more of the top snow covering and reducing the size of our camp. When the floes retreated to attack again the water swirled over the ice foot, which was rapidly increasing in width. The launching of the boats under such conditions would be difficult. Time after time, so often that a track was formed, Worsley, Wild, and I climbed to the

highest point of the berg and stared out to the horizon in
search of a break in the pack. After long hours had dragged
past, far away on the lift of the swell there appeared a dark
break in the tossing field of ice. Aeons seemed to pass, so
slowly it approached. I noticed enviously the calm, peaceful
attitudes of two seals which lolled lazily on a rocking floe.
They were at home and had no reason for worry or cause
for fear. If they thought at all, I suppose they counted it an
ideal day for a joyous journey on the tumbling ice. To us it
was a day that seemed likely to lead to no more days. I do
not think I had ever before felt the anxiety that belongs to
leadership quite so keenly. When I looked down at the camp
to rest my eyes from the strain of watching the wide white
expanse broken by that one black ribbon of open water, I
could see that my companions were waiting with more than
ordinary interest to learn what I thought about it all. After
one particularly heavy collision somebody shouted sharply,
"She has cracked in the middle." I jumped off the lookout
station and ran to the place the men were examining. There
was a crack, but investigation showed it to be a mere surface
break in the snow with no indication of a split in the berg
itself. The carpenter mentioned calmly that earlier in the day
he had actually gone adrift on a fragment of ice. He was
standing near the edge of our camping ground when the ice
under his feet parted from the parent mass. A quick jump
over the widening gap saved him.

The hours dragged on. One of the anxieties in my mind
was the possibility that we would be driven by the current
through the eighty-mile gap between Clarence Island and
Prince George Island into the open Atlantic; but slowly
the open water came nearer, and at noon it had almost
reached us. A long lane, narrow but navigable, stretched
out to the southwest horizon. Our chance came a little
later. We rushed our boats over the edge of the reeling
berg and swung them clear of the ice foot as it rose beneath

them. The *James Caird* was nearly capsized by a blow from below as the berg rolled away, but she got into deep water. We flung stores and gear aboard and within a few minutes were away. The *James Caird* and *Dudley Docker* had good sails and with a favorable breeze could make progress along the lane, with the rolling fields of ice on either side. The swell was heavy and spray was breaking over the ice floes. An attempt to set a little rag of sail on the *Stancomb Wills* resulted in serious delay. The area of sail was too small to be of much assistance, and while the men were engaged in this work the boat drifted down towards the ice floe, where her position was likely to be perilous. Seeing her plight, I sent the *Dudley Docker* back for her and tied the *James Caird* up to a piece of ice. The *Dudley Docker* had to tow the *Stancomb Wills,* and the delay cost us two hours of valuable daylight. When I had the three boats together again we continued down the lane, and soon saw a wider stretch of water to the west; it appeared to offer us release from the grip of the pack. At the head of an ice tongue that nearly closed the gap through which we might enter the open space was a wave-worn berg shaped like some curious antediluvian monster, an icy Cerberus guarding the way. It had head and eyes and rolled so heavily that it almost overturned. Its sides dipped deep in the sea, and as it rose again the water seemed to be streaming from its eyes, as though it were weeping at our escape from the clutch of the floes. This may seem fanciful to the reader, but the impression was real to us at the time. People living under civilized conditions, surrounded by Nature's varied forms of life and by all the familiar work of their own hands, may scarcely realize how quickly the mind, influenced by the eyes, responds to the unusual and weaves about it curious imaginings like the firelight fancies of our childhood days. We had lived long amid the ice, and we half-unconsciously strove to see resemblances to human faces and living forms in the fantastic contours and massively uncouth shapes of berg and floe.

At dusk we made fast to a heavy floe, each boat having its painter fastened to a separate hummock in order to avoid collisions in the swell. We landed the blubber stove, boiled some water in order to provide hot milk, and served cold rations. I also landed the dome tents and stripped the coverings from the hoops. Our experience of the previous day in the open sea had shown us that the tents must be packed tightly. The spray had dashed over the bows and turned to ice on the cloth, which had soon grown dangerously heavy. Other articles of our scanty equipment had to go that night. We were carrying only the things that had seemed essential, but we stripped now to the barest limit of safety. We had hoped for a quiet night, but presently we were forced to cast off, since pieces of loose ice began to work round the floe. Drift ice is always attracted to the lee side of a heavy floe, where it bumps and presses under the influence of the current. I had determined not to risk a repetition of the last night's experience and so had not pulled the boats up. We spent the hours of darkness keeping an offing from the main line of pack under the lee of the smaller pieces. Constant rain and snow squalls blotted out the stars and soaked us through, and at times it was only by shouting to each other that we managed to keep the boats together. There was no sleep for anybody owing to the severe cold, and we dare not pull fast enough to keep ourselves warm since we were unable to see more than a few yards ahead. Occasionally the ghostly shadows of silver, snow, and fulmar petrels flashed close to us, and all around we could hear the killers blowing, their short, sharp hisses sounding like sudden escapes of steam. The killers were a source of anxiety, for a boat could easily have been capsized by one of them coming up to blow. They would throw aside in a nonchalant fashion pieces of ice much bigger than our boats when they rose to the surface, and we had an uneasy feeling that the white bottoms of the boats would look like ice from below. Shipwrecked mariners drifting in the Antarctic seas would be things not dreamed of in the killers' philosophy, and might appear on closer examination to be tasty substitutes for seal and penguin. We certainly regarded the killers with misgivings.

Early in the morning of April 12 the weather improved and the wind dropped. Dawn came with a clear sky, cold and fearless. I looked around at the faces of my companions in the *James Caird* and saw pinched and drawn features. The strain was beginning to tell. Wild sat at the rudder with the same calm, confident expression that he would have worn under happier conditions; his steel-blue eyes looked out to the day ahead. All the people, though evidently suffering, were doing their best to be cheerful, and the prospect of a hot breakfast was inspiriting. I told all the boats that immediately we could find a suitable floe the cooker would be started and hot milk and Bovril would soon fix everybody up. Away we rowed to the westward through open pack, floes of all shapes and sizes on every side of us, and every man not engaged in pulling looking eagerly for a suitable camping place. I could gauge the desire for food of the different members by the eagerness they displayed in pointing out to me the floes they considered exactly suited to our purpose. The temperature was about 10° Fahr., and the Burberry suits of the rowers crackled as the men bent to the oars. I noticed little fragments of ice and frost falling from arms and bodies. At eight o'clock a decent floe appeared ahead and we pulled up to it. The galley was landed, and soon the welcome steam rose from the cooking food as the blubber stove flared and smoked. Never did a cook work under more anxious scrutiny. Worsley, Crean, and I stayed in our respective boats to keep them steady and prevent collisions with the floe, since the swell was still running strong, but the other men were able to stretch their cramped limbs and run to and fro "in the kitchen," as somebody put it.

The sun was now rising gloriously. The Burberry suits were drying and the ice was melting off our beards. The steaming food gave us new vigor, and within three-quarters of an hour we were off again to the west with all sails set. We had given an additional sail to the *Stancomb Wills* and she was able to keep up pretty well. We could see that we were on the true pack edge, with the blue, rolling sea just outside the fringe of ice to the north. White-capped waves vied with the glittering floes in the setting of blue water, and countless seals basked and rolled on every piece of ice big enough to form a raft.

We had been making westward with oars and sails since April 9, and fair easterly winds had prevailed. Hopes were running high as to the noon observation for position. The optimists thought that we had done sixty miles towards our goal, and the most cautious guess gave us at least thirty miles. The bright sunshine and the brilliant scene around us may have influenced our anticipations. As noon approached I saw Worsley, as navigating officer, balancing himself on the gunwale of the *Dudley Docker* with his arm around the mast, ready to snap the sun. He got his observation and we waited eagerly while he worked out the sight. Then the *Dudley Docker* ranged up alongside the *James Caird* and I jumped into Worsley's boat in order to see the result. It was a grievous disappointment. Instead of making a good run to the westward we had made a big drift to the southeast. We were actually thirty miles to the east of the position we had occupied when we left the floe on the 9th. It has been noted by sealers operating in this area that there are often heavy sets to the east in the Belgica Straits, and no doubt it was one of these sets that we had experienced. The originating cause would be a northwesterly gale off Cape Horn, producing the swell that had already caused us so much trouble. After a whispered consultation with Worsley and Wild I announced that we had not made as much progress as we expected, but I did not inform the hands of our retrograde movement.

The question of our course now demanded further consideration. Deception Island seemed to be beyond our reach. The wind was foul for Elephant Island, and as the sea was clear to the southwest, I discussed with Worsley and Wild the advisability of proceeding to Hope Bay on the mainland of the Antarctic Continent, now only eighty miles distant. Elephant Island was the nearest land, but it lay outside the main body of pack, and even if the wind had been fair we would have hesitated at that particular time to face the high sea that was running in the open. We laid a course roughly for Hope Bay, and the boats moved on again. I gave Worsley a line for a berg ahead and told him, if possible, to make fast before darkness set in. This was about three o'clock in the afternoon. We had set sail, and as the *Stancomb Wills* could not keep up with the other two boats I took her in tow, not being anxious to repeat the experience of the day we left the reeling berg. The *Dudley Docker* went ahead, but came beating down towards us at dusk. Worsley had been close to the berg, and he reported that it was unapproachable. It was rolling in the swell and displaying an ugly ice foot. The news was bad. In the failing light we turned towards a line of pack, and found it so tossed and churned by the sea that no fragment remained big enough to give us an anchorage and shelter. Two miles away we could see a larger piece of ice, and to it we managed, after some trouble, to secure the boats. I brought my boat bow on to the floe, whilst Howe, with the painter in his hand, stood ready to jump. Standing up to watch our chance, while the oars were held ready to back the moment Howe had made his leap, I could see that there would be no possibility of getting the galley ashore that night. Howe just managed to get a footing on the edge of the floe, and then made the painter fast to a hummock. The other two boats were fastened alongside the *James*

Caird. They could not lie astern of us in a line, since cakes of ice came drifting round the floe and gathering under its lee. As it was we spent the next two hours poling off the drifting ice that surged towards us. The blubber stove could not be used, so we started the Primus lamps. There was a rough, choppy sea, and the *Dudley Docker* could not get her Primus under way, something being adrift. The men in that boat had to wait until the cook on the *James Caird* had boiled up the first pot of milk.

The boats were bumping so heavily that I had to slack away the painter of the *Stancomb Wills* and put her astern. Much ice was coming round the floe and had to be poled off. Then the *Dudley Docker,* being the heavier boat, began to damage the *James Caird,* and I slacked the *Dudley Docker* away. The *James Caird* remained moored to the ice, with the *Dudley Docker* and the *Stancomb Wills* in line behind her. The darkness had become complete, and we strained our eyes to see the fragments of ice that threatened us. Presently we thought we saw a great berg bearing down upon us, its form outlined against the sky, but this startling spectacle resolved itself into a low-lying cloud in front of the rising moon. The moon appeared in a clear sky. The wind shifted to the southeast as the light improved and drove the boats broadside on towards the jagged edge of the floe. We had to cut the painter of the *James Caird* and pole her off, thus losing much valuable rope. There was no time to cast off. Then we pushed away from the floe, and all night long we lay in the open, freezing sea, the *Dudley Docker* now ahead, the *James Caird* astern of her, and the *Stancomb Wills* third in the line. The boats were attached to one another by their painters. Most of the time the *Dudley Docker* kept the *James Caird* and the *Stancomb Wills* up to the swell, and the men who were rowing were in better pass than those in the other boats, waiting inactive for the dawn. The temperature was down to 4° below zero, and a film of ice formed on the surface of the sea. When we were not on watch we lay in each other's arms for warmth. Our frozen suits thawed where our bodies met, and as the slightest movement exposed these comparatively warm spots to the biting air, we clung motionless, whispering each to his companion our hopes and thoughts. Occasionally from an almost clear sky came snow showers, falling silently on the sea and laying a thin shroud of white over our bodies and our boats.

The dawn of April 13 came clear and bright, with occasional passing clouds. Most of the men were now looking seriously worn and strained. Their lips were cracked and their eyes and eyelids showed red in their salt-encrusted faces. The beards even of the younger men might have been those of patriarchs, for the frost and the salt spray had made them white. I called the *Dudley Docker* alongside and found that the condition of the people there was no better than in the *James Caird*. Obviously we must make land quickly, and I decided to run for Elephant Island. The wind had shifted fair for that rocky isle, then about one hundred miles away, and the pack that separated us from Hope Bay had closed up during the night from the south. At 6 a.m. we made a distribution of stores among the three boats, in view of the possibility of their being separated. The preparation of a hot breakfast was out of the question. The breeze was strong and the sea was running high in the loose pack around us. We had a cold meal, and I gave orders that all hands might eat as much as they pleased, this concession being due partly to a realization that we would have to jettison some of our stores when we reached open sea in order to lighten the boats. I hoped, moreover, that a full meal of cold rations would compensate to some extent for the lack of warm food and shelter. Unfortunately, some of the men were unable to take advantage of the extra food owing to seasickness. Poor fellows, it was bad enough to be huddled in the deeply laden, spray-swept boats, frostbitten and half frozen, without having the pangs of seasickness added to the list of their woes. But some smiles were caused even then by the plight of one man, who had a habit of accumulating bits of food against the day of starvation that he seemed always to think was at hand, and who was condemned now to watch impotently while hungry comrades with undisturbed stomachs made biscuits, rations, and sugar disappear with extraordinary rapidity.

We ran before the wind through the loose pack, a man in the bow of each boat trying to pole off with a broken oar the lumps of ice that could not be avoided. I regarded speed as essential. Sometimes collisions were not averted. The *James Caird* was in the lead, where she bore the brunt of the encounters with lurking fragments, and she was holed above the waterline by a sharp spur of ice, but this mishap did not stay us. Later the wind became stronger and we had to reef sails, so as not to strike the ice too heavily. The *Dudley Docker* came next to the *James Caird* and the *Stancomb Wills* followed. I had given orders that the boats should keep 30 or 40 yds. apart, so as to reduce the danger of a collision if one boat was checked by the ice. The pack was thinning, and we came to occasional open areas where thin ice had formed during the night. When we encountered this new ice we had to shake the reef out of the sails in order to force a way through. Outside of the pack the wind must have been of hurricane force. Thousands of small dead fish were to be seen, killed probably by a cold current and the heavy weather. They floated in the water and lay on the ice, where they had been cast by the waves. The petrels and skua-gulls were swooping down and picking them up like sardines off toast.

We made our way through the lanes till at noon we were suddenly spewed out of the pack into the open ocean. Dark blue and sapphire green ran the seas. Our sails were soon

up, and with a fair wind we moved over the waves like three
Viking ships on the quest of a lost Atlantis. With the sheets
well out and the sun shining bright above, we enjoyed for a
few hours a sense of the freedom and magic of the sea,
compensating us for pain and trouble in the days that had
passed. At last we were free from the ice, in water that our
boats could navigate. Thoughts of home, stifled by the dead-
ening weight of anxious days and nights, came to birth once
more, and the difficulties that had still to be overcome dwindled in fancy almost to nothing.

During the afternoon we had to take a second reef in the
sails, for the wind freshened and the deeply laden boats
were shipping much water and steering badly in the rising
sea. I had laid the course for Elephant Island and we were
making good progress. The *Dudley Docker* ran down to me
at dusk and Worsley suggested that we should stand on all
night; but already the *Stancomb Wills* was barely discernible
among the rollers in the gathering dusk, and I decided that
it would be safer to heave to and wait for the daylight. It
would never have done for the boats to have become separated from one another during the night. The party must be
kept together, and, moreover, I thought it possible that we
might overrun our goal in the darkness and not be able to
return. So we made a sea anchor of oars and hove to, the
Dudley Docker in the lead, since she had the longest painter.
The *James Caird* swung astern of the *Dudley Docker* and
the *Stancomb Wills* again had the third place. We ate a cold
meal and did what little we could to make things comfortable for the hours of darkness. Rest was not for us. During
the greater part of the night the sprays broke over the boats
and froze in masses of ice, especially at the stern and bows.
This ice had to be broken away in order to prevent the boats
growing too heavy. The temperature was below zero and the
wind penetrated our clothes and chilled us almost unbearably. I doubted if all the men would survive that night. One

of our troubles was lack of water. We had emerged so suddenly from the pack into the open sea that we had not had
time to take aboard ice for melting in the cookers, and without ice we could not have hot food. The *Dudley Docker* had
one lump of ice weighing about ten pounds, and this was
shared out among all hands. We sucked small pieces and got
a little relief from thirst engendered by the salt spray, but at
the same time we reduced our bodily heat. The condition of
most of the men was pitiable. All of us had swollen mouths
and we could hardly touch the food. I longed intensely for
the dawn. I called out to the other boats at intervals during
the night, asking how things were with them. The men always managed to reply cheerfully. One of the people on the
Stancomb Wills shouted, "We are doing all right, but I
would like some dry mits." The jest brought a smile to
cracked lips. He might as well have asked for the moon. The
only dry things aboard the boats were swollen mouths and
burning tongues. Thirst is one of the troubles that confront
the traveler in polar regions. Ice may be plentiful on every
hand, but it does not become drinkable until it is melted,
and the amount that may be dissolved in the mouth is limited. We had been thirsty during the days of heavy pulling
in the pack, and our condition was aggravated quickly by
the salt spray. Our sleeping bags would have given us some
warmth, but they were not within our reach. They were
packed under the tents in the bows, where a mail-like coat-
ing of ice enclosed them, and we were so cramped that we
could not pull them out.

At last daylight came, and with the dawn the weather
cleared and the wind fell to a gentle southwesterly breeze.
A magnificent sunrise heralded in what we hoped would be
our last day in the boats. Rose pink in the growing light, the
lofty peak of Clarence Island told of the coming glory of
the sun. The sky grew blue above us and the crests of the
waves sparkled cheerfully. As soon as it was light enough

we chipped and scraped the ice off the bows and sterns. The rudders had been unshipped during the night in order to avoid the painters catching them. We cast off our ice anchor and pulled the oars aboard. They had grown during the night to the thickness of telegraph poles while rising and falling in the freezing seas, and had to be chipped clear before they could be brought inboard.

We were dreadfully thirsty now. We found that we could get momentary relief by chewing pieces of raw seal meat and swallowing the blood, but thirst came back with redoubled force owing to the saltness of the flesh. I gave orders, therefore, that meat was to be served out only at stated intervals during the day or when thirst seemed to threaten the reason of any particular individual. In the full daylight Elephant Island showed cold and severe in the north-northwest. The island was on the bearings that Worsley had laid down, and I congratulated him on the accuracy of his navigation under difficult circumstances, with two days' dead reckoning while following a devious course through the pack-ice and after drifting during two nights at the mercy of wind and waves. The *Stancomb Wills* came up and McIlroy reported that Blackborrow's feet were very badly frostbitten. This was unfortunate, but nothing could be done. Most of the people were frostbitten to some extend, and it was interesting to notice that the "old timers," Wild, Crean, Hurley, and I, were all right. Apparently we were acclimatized to ordinary Antarctic temperature, though we learned later that we were not immune.

All day, with a gentle breeze on our port bow, we sailed and pulled through a clear sea. We would have given all the tea in China for a lump of ice to melt into water, but no ice was within our reach. Three bergs were in sight and we pulled towards them, hoping that a train of brash would be floating on the sea to leeward; but they were hard and blue, devoid of any sign of cleavage, and the swell that surged

around them as they rose and fell made it impossible for us
to approach closely. The wind was gradually hauling ahead,
and as the day wore on the rays of the sun beat fiercely down
from a cloudless sky on pain-racked men. Progress was
slow, but gradually Elephant Island came nearer. Always
while I attended to the other boats, signalling and ordering,
Wild sat at the tiller of the *James Caird*. He seemed un-
moved by fatigue and unshaken by privation. About four
o'clock in the afternoon a stiff breeze came up ahead and,
blowing against the current, soon produced a choppy sea.
During the next hour of hard pulling we seemed to make no
progress at all. The *James Caird* and the *Dudley Docker* had
been towing the *Stancomb Wills* in turn, but my boat now
took the *Stancomb Wills* in tow permanently, as the *James
Caird* could carry more sail than the *Dudley Docker* in the
freshening wind.

We were making up for the southeast side of Elephant
Island, the wind being between northwest and west. The
boats, held as close to the wind as possible, moved slowly,
and when darkness set in our goal was still some miles
away. A heavy sea was running. We soon lost sight of the
Stancomb Wills, astern of the *James Caird* at the length of
the painter, but occasionally the white gleam of broken
water revealed her presence. When the darkness was complete I sat in the stern with my hand on the painter, so that
I might know if the other boat broke away, and I kept that
position during the night. The rope grew heavy with the ice
as the unseen seas surged past us and our little craft tossed
to the motion of the waters. Just at dusk I had told the men
on the *Stancomb Wills* that if their boat broke away during
the night and they were unable to pull against the wind, they
could run for the east side of Clarence Island and await our
coming there. Even though we could not land on Elephant
Island, it would not do to have the third boat adrift.

It was a stern night. The men, except the watch, crouched

and huddled in the bottom of the boat, getting what little warmth they could from the soaking sleeping bags and each other's bodies. Harder and harder blew the wind and fiercer and fiercer grew the sea. The boat plunged heavily through the squalls and came up to the wind, the sail shaking in the stiffest gusts. Every now and then, as the night wore on, the moon would shine down through a rift in the driving clouds, and in the momentary light I could see the ghostly faces of men, sitting up to trim the boat as she heeled over to the wind. When the moon was hidden its presence was revealed still by the light reflected on the streaming glaciers of the island. The temperature had fallen very low, and it seemed that the general discomfort of our situation could scarcely have been increased; but the land looming ahead was a beacon of safety, and I think we were all buoyed up by the hope that the coming day would see the end of our immediate troubles. At least we would get firm land under our feet. While the painter of the *Stancomb Wills* tightened and drooped under my hand, my thoughts were busy with plans for the future.

Towards midnight the wind shifted to the southwest, and this change enabled us to bear up closer to the island. A little later the *Dudley Docker* ran down to the *James Caird,* and Worsley shouted a suggestion that he should go ahead and search for a landing place. His boat had the heels of the *James Caird,* with the *Stancomb Wills* in tow. I told him he could try, but he must not lose sight of the *James Caird.* Just as he left me a heavy snow squall came down, and in the darkness the boats parted. I saw the *Dudley Docker* no more. This separation caused me some anxiety during the remaining hours of the night. A cross sea was running and I could not feel sure that all was well with the missing boat. The waves could not be seen in the darkness, though the direction and force of the wind could be felt, and under such conditions, in an open boat, disaster might overtake the most experienced navigator. I flashed our compass lamp on the sail in the hope that the signal would be visible on board the *Dudley Docker,* but could see no reply. We strained our eyes to windward in the darkness in the hope of catching a return signal and repeated our flashes at intervals.

My anxiety, as a matter of fact, was groundless. I will quote Worsley's own account of what happened to the *Dudley Docker*: "About midnight we lost sight of the *James Caird* with the *Stancomb Wills* in tow, but not long after saw the light of the *James Caird*'s compass lamp, which Sir Ernest was flashing on their sail as a guide to us. We answered by lighting our candle under the tent and letting the light shine through. At the same time we got the direction of the wind and how we were hauling from my little pocket compass, the boat's compass being smashed. With this candle our poor fellows lit their pipes, their only solace, as our raging thirst prevented us from eating anything. By this time we had got into a bad tide rip, which, combined with the heavy, lumpy sea, made it almost impossible to keep the *Dudley Docker* from swamping. As it was we shipped several bad seas over the stern as well as abeam and over the bows, although we were 'on a wind.' Lees, who owned himself to be a rotten oarsman, made good here by strenuous baling, in which he was well seconded by Cheetham. Greenstreet, a splendid fellow, relieved me at the tiller and helped generally. He and Macklin were my right and left bowers as stroke-oars throughout. McLeod and Cheetham were two good sailors and oars, the former a typical old deep-sea salt and growler, the latter a pirate to his fingertips. In the height of the gale that night Cheetham was buying matches from me for bottles of champagne, one bottle per match (too cheap; I should have charged him two bottles). The champagne is to be paid when he opens his 'pub' in Hull and I am able to call that way. . . . We had now had one hundred and eight hours of toil, tumbling, freezing, and soaking, with little or no sleep. I think Sir Ernest, Wild, Greenstreet, and I could say that we had no sleep at all. Although it was sixteen months since we had been in a rough sea, only four men were actually seasick, but several others were off color.

"The temperature was 20° below freezing point; fortunately, we were spared the bitterly low temperature of the previous night. Greenstreet's right foot got badly frostbitten, but Lees restored it by holding it in his sweater against his stomach. Other men had minor frostbites, due principally to the fact that their clothes were soaked through with salt water. . . . We were close to the land as the morning approached, but could see nothing of it through the snow and spindrift. My eyes began to fail me. Constant peering to windward, watching for seas to strike us, appeared to have given me a cold in the eyes. I could not see or judge distance properly, and found myself falling asleep momentarily at the tiller. At 3 a.m. Greenstreet relieved me there. I was so cramped from long hours, cold, and wet, in the constrained position one was forced to assume on top of the gear and stores at the tiller, that the other men had to pull me amidships and straighten me out like a jack-knife, first rubbing my thighs, groin, and stomach.

"At daylight we found ourselves close alongside the land, but the weather was so thick that we could not see where to make for a landing. Having taken the tiller again after an hour's rest under the shelter (save the mark!) of the dripping tent, I ran the *Dudley Docker* off before the gale, following the coast around to the north. This course for the first hour was fairly risky, the heavy sea before which we were running threatening to swamp the boat, but by 8 a.m. we had obtained a slight lee from the land. Then I was able to keep her very close in, along a glacier front, with the object of picking up lumps of fresh water ice as we sailed through them. Our thirst was intense. We soon had some ice aboard, and for the next hour and a half we sucked and chewed fragments of ice with greedy relish.

"All this time we were coasting along beneath towering rocky cliffs and sheer glacier faces, which offered not the slightest possibility of landing anywhere. At 9:30 a.m. we spied a narrow, rocky beach at the base of some very high crags and cliff, and made for it. To our joy, we sighted the *James Caird* and the *Stancomb Wills* sailing into the same haven just ahead of us. We were so delighted that we gave three cheers, which were not heard aboard the other boats owing to the roar of the surf. However, we soon joined them and were able to exchange experiences on the beach."

Our experiences on the *James Caird* had been similar, although we had not been able to keep up to windward as well as the *Dudley Docker* had done. This was fortunate as events proved, for the *James Caird* and *Stancomb Wills* went to leeward of the big bight the *Dudley Docker* entered and from which she had to turn out with the sea astern. We thus avoided the risk of having the *Stancomb Wills* swamped in the following sea. The weather was very thick in the morning. Indeed at 7 a.m. we were right under the cliffs, which plunged sheer into the sea, before we saw them. We followed the coast towards the north, and ever the precipitous cliffs and glacier faces presented themselves to our searching eyes. The sea broke heavily against these walls and a landing would have been impossible under any conditions. We picked up pieces of ice and sucked them eagerly. At 9 a.m. at the northwest end of the island we saw a narrow beach at the foot of the cliffs. Outside lay a fringe of rocks heavily beaten by the surf but with a narrow channel showing as a break in the foaming water. I decided that we must face the hazards of this unattractive landing place. Two days and nights without drink or hot food had played havoc with most of the men, and we could not assume that any safer haven lay within our reach. The *Stancomb Wills* was the lighter and handier boat—and I called her alongside with the intention of taking her through the gap first and ascertaining the possibilities of a landing before the *James Caird* made the venture. I was just climbing into the *Stancomb Wills* when I saw the *Dudley Docker* coming up astern under sail. The sight took a great load off my mind.

Rowing carefully and avoiding the blind rollers which showed where sunken rocks lay, we brought the *Stancomb Wills* towards the opening in the reef. Then, with a few strong strokes we shot through on the top of a swell and ran the boat on to a stony beach. The next swell lifted her a little farther. This was the first landing ever made on Elephant Island, and a thought came to me that the honor should belong to the youngest member of the Expedition, so I told Blackborrow to jump over. He seemed to be in a state almost of coma, and in order to avoid delay I helped him, perhaps a little roughly, over the side of the boat. He promptly sat down in the surf and did not move. Then I suddenly realized what I had forgotten, that both his feet were frostbitten badly. Some of us jumped over and pulled him into a dry place. It was a rather rough experience for Blackborrow, but, anyhow, he is now able to say that he was the first man to sit on Elephant Island. Possibly at the time he would have been willing to forgo any distinction of the kind. We landed the cook with his blubber stove, a supply of fuel and some packets of dried milk, and also several of the men. Then the rest of us pulled out again to pilot the other boats through the channel. The *James Caird* was too heavy to be beached directly, so after landing most of the men from the *Dudley Docker* and the *Stancomb Wills* I superintended the transhipment of the *James Caird*'s gear outside the reef. Then we all made the passage, and within a few minutes the three boats were aground. A curious spectacle met my eyes when I landed the second time. Some of the men were reeling about the beach as if they had found an unlimited supply of alcoholic liquor on the desolate shore. They were laughing uproariously, picking up stones

and letting handfuls of pebbles trickle between their fingers
like misers gloating over hoarded gold. The smiles and
laughter, which caused cracked lips to bleed afresh, and the
gleeful exclamations at the sight of two live seals on the
beach made me think for a moment of that glittering hour
of childhood when the door is open at last and the Christmas
tree in all its wonder bursts upon the vision. I remember that
Wild, who always rose superior to fortune, bad and good,
came ashore as I was looking at the men and stood beside
me as easy and unconcerned as if he had stepped out of his
car for a stroll in the Park.

Soon half a dozen of us had the stores ashore. Our
strength was nearly exhausted and it was heavy work carrying our goods over the rough pebbles and rocks to the foot
of the cliff, but we dare not leave anything within reach of
the tide. We had to wade knee deep in the icy water in order
to lift the gear from the boats. When the work was done we
pulled the three boats a little higher on the beach and turned
gratefully to enjoy the hot drink that the cook had prepared.
Those of us who were comparatively fit had to wait until the
weaker members of the party had been supplied; but every
man had his pannikin of hot milk in the end, and never did
anything taste better. Seal steak and blubber followed, for
the seals that had been careless enough to await our arrival
on the beach had already given up their lives. There was no
rest for the cook. The blubber stove flared and sputtered
fiercely as he cooked, not one meal, but many meals, which
merged into a day-long bout of eating. We drank water and
ate seal meat until every man had reached the limit of his
capacity.

The tents were pitched with oars for supports, and by 3
p.m. our camp was in order. The original framework of the
tents had been cast adrift on one of the floes in order to save
weight. Most of the men turned in early for a safe and glorious sleep, to be broken only by the call to take a turn on

watch. The chief duty of the watchman was to keep the blubber stove alight, and each man on duty appeared to find it necessary to cook himself a meal during his watch, and a supper before he turned in again.

Wild, Worsley, and Hurley accompanied me on an inspection of our beach before getting into the tents. I almost wished then that I had postponed the examination until after sleep, but the sense of caution that the uncertainties of polar travel implant in one's mind had made me uneasy. The outlook we found to be anything but cheering. Obvious signs showed that at spring tides the little beach would be covered by the water right up to the foot of the cliffs. In a strong northeasterly gale, such as we might expect to experience at any time, the waves would pound over the scant barrier of the reef and break against the sheer sides of the rocky wall behind us. Well-marked terraces showed the effect of other gales, and right at the back of the beach was a small bit of wreckage not more than three feet long, rounded by the constant chafing it had endured. Obviously we must find some better resting place. I decided not to share with the men the knowledge of the uncertainties of our situation until they had enjoyed the full sweetness of rest untroubled by the thought that at any minute they might be called to face peril again. The threat of the sea had been our portion during many, many days, and a respite meant much to weary bodies and jaded minds.

The accompanying plan will indicate our exact position more clearly than I can describe it. The cliffs at the back of the beach were inaccessible except at two points where there were steep snow slopes. We were not worried now about food, for, apart from our own rations, there were seals on the beach and we could see others in the water outside the reef. Every now and then one of the animals would rise in the shallows and crawl up on the beach, which evidently was a recognized place of resort for its kind. A small rocky

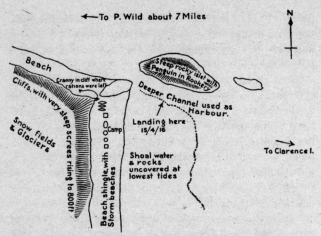

ROUGH SKETCH MAP OF LANDING PLACE AND FIRST CAMP AT
C. VALENTINE, ELEPHANT ISLAND

island which protected us to some extent from the northwesterly wind carried a ringed penguin rookery. These birds
were of migratory habit and might be expected to leave us
before the winter set in fully, but in the meantime they were
within our reach. These attractions, however, were overridden by the fact that the beach was open to the attack of wind
and sea from the northeast and east. Easterly gales are more
prevalent than western in that area of the Antarctic during
the winter. Before turning in that night I studied the whole
position and weighed every chance of getting the boats and
our stores into a place of safety out of reach of the water.
We ourselves might have clambered a little way up the snow
slopes, but we could not have taken the boats with us. The
interior of the island was quite inaccessible. We climbed up
one of the slopes and found ourselves stopped soon by overhanging cliffs. The rocks behind the camp were much
weathered, and we noticed the sharp, unworn boulders that

had fallen from above. Clearly there was a danger from overhead if we camped at the back of the beach. We must move on. With that thought in mind I reached my tent and fell asleep on the rubbly ground, which gave a comforting sense of stability. The fairy princess who would not rest on her seven downy mattresses because a pea lay underneath the pile might not have understood the pleasure we all derived from the irregularities of the stones, which could not possibly break beneath us or drift away; the very searching lumps were sweet reminders of our safety.

Early next morning (April 15) all hands were astir. The sun soon shone brightly and we spread out our wet gear to dry, till the beach looked like a particularly disreputable gipsy camp. The boots and clothing had suffered considerably during our travels. I had decided to send Wild along the coast in the *Stancomb Wills* to look for a new camping ground, and he and I discussed the details of the journey while eating our breakfast of hot seal steak and blubber. The camp I wished to find was one where the party could live for weeks or even months in safety, without danger from sea or wind in the heaviest winter gale. Wild was to proceed westwards along the coast and was to take with him four of the fittest men, Marston, Crean, Vincent, and McCarthy. If he did not return before dark we were to light a flare, which would serve him as a guide to the entrance of the channel. The *Stancomb Wills* pushed off at 11 a.m. and quickly passed out of sight around the island. Then Hurley and I walked along the beach towards the west, climbing through a gap between the cliff and a great detached pillar of basalt. The narrow strip of beach was cumbered with masses of rock that had fallen from the cliffs. We struggled along for two miles or more in the search for a place where we could get the boats ashore and make a permanent camp in the event of Wild's search proving fruitless, but after three hours' vain toil we had to turn back. We had found on the far side of the pillar of basalt a crevice in the rocks beyond the reach of all but the heaviest gales. Rounded pebbles showed that the seas reached the spot on occasions. Here I decided to depot ten cases of Bovril sledging ration in case of our having to move away quickly. We could come back for the food at a later date if opportunity offered.

Returning to the camp, we found the men resting or attending to their gear. Clark had tried angling in the shallows off the rocks and had secured one or two small fish. The day passed quietly. Rusty needles were rubbed bright on the rocks and clothes were mended and darned. A feeling of tiredness—due, I suppose, to reaction after the strain of the preceding days—overtook us, but the rising tide, coming farther up the beach than it had done on the day before, forced us to labor at the boats, which we hauled slowly to a higher ledge. We found it necessary to move our makeshift camp nearer the cliff. I portioned out the available ground for the tents, the galley, and other purposes, as every foot was of value. When night arrived the *Stancomb Wills* was still away, so I had a blubber flare lit at the head of the channel.

About 8 p.m. we heard a hail in the distance. We could see nothing, but soon like a pale ghost out of the darkness came the boat, the faces of the men showing white in the glare of the fire. Wild ran her on the beach with the swell, and within a couple of minutes we had dragged her to a place of safety. I was waiting Wild's report with keen anxiety, and my relief was great when he told me that he had discovered a sandy spit seven miles to the west, about 200 yds. long, running out at right angles to the coast and terminating at the seaward end in a mass of rock. A long snow slope joined the spit at the shore end, and it seemed possible that a "dugout" could be made in the snow. The spit, in any case, would be a great improvement on our narrow beach. Wild added that the place he described was the only possible camping ground he had seen. Beyond, to the west and south-west, lay a frowning line of cliffs and glaciers, sheer to the water's edge. He thought that in very heavy gales either from the southwest or east the spit would be spray blown, but that the seas would not actually break over it. The boats could be run up on a shelving beach.

After hearing this good news I was eager to get away from the beach camp. The wind when blowing was favorable for the run along the coast. The weather had been fine for two days and a change might come at any hour. I told all hands that we would make a start early on the following morning. A newly killed seal provided a luxurious supper of steak and blubber, and then we slept comfortably till the dawn.

The morning of April 17 came fine and clear. The sea was smooth, but in the offing we could see a line of pack, which seemed to be approaching. We had noticed already pack and bergs being driven by the current to the east and then sometimes coming back with a rush to the west. The current ran as fast as five miles an hour, and it was a set of this kind that had delayed Wild on his return from the spit. The rise and fall of the tide was only about five feet at this time, but the moon was making for full and the tides were increasing. The appearance of ice emphasized the impor-tance of getting away promptly. It would be a serious matter to be prisoned on the beach by the pack. The boats were soon afloat in the shallows, and after a hurried breakfast all hands worked hard getting our gear and stores aboard. A mishap befell us when we were launching the boats. We were using oars as rollers, and three of these were broken, leaving us short for the journey that had still to be under-taken. The preparations took longer than I had expected; indeed, there seemed to be some reluctance on the part of several men to leave the barren safety of the little beach and venture once more on the ocean. But the move was impera-tive, and by 11 a.m. we were away, the *James Caird* leading.

Just as we rounded the small island occupied by the ringed penguins the "willywaw" swooped down from the 2000-ft. cliffs behind us, a herald of the southerly gale that was to spring up within half an hour.

Soon we were straining at the oars with the gale on our bows. Never had we found a more severe task. The wind shifted from the south to the southwest, and the shortage of oars became a serious matter. The *James Caird*, being the heaviest boat, had to keep a full complement of rowers, while the *Dudley Docker* and the *Stancomb Wills* went short and took turns using the odd oar. A big swell was thundering against the cliffs and at times we were almost driven on to the rocks by swirling green waters. We had to keep close inshore in order to avoid being embroiled in the raging sea, which was lashed snow white and quickened by the furious squalls into a living mass of sprays. After two hours of strenuous labor we were almost exhausted, but we were fortunate enough to find comparative shelter behind a point of rock. Overhead towered the sheer cliffs for hundreds of feet, the seabirds that fluttered from the crannies of the rock dwarfed by the height. The boats rose and fell in the big swell, but the sea was not breaking in our little haven, and we rested there while we ate our cold ration. Some of the men had to stand by the oars in order to pole the boats off the cliff face.

After half an hour's pause I gave the order to start again. The *Dudley Docker* was pulling with three oars, as the *Stancomb Wills* had the odd one, and she fell away to leeward in a particularly heavy squall. I anxiously watched her battling up against wind and sea. It would have been useless to take the *James Caird* back to the assistance of the *Dudley Docker* since we were hard pressed to make any progress ourselves in the heavier boat. The only thing was to go ahead and hope for the best. All hands were wet to the skin again and many men were feeling the cold severely. We forged on slowly and passed inside a great pillar of rock standing out to sea and towering to a height of about 2400 ft. A line of reef stretched between the shore and this pillar, and I thought as we approached that we would have to face the raging sea outside; but a break in the white surf revealed a gap in the reef and we labored through, with the wind driving clouds of spray on our port beam. The *Stancomb Wills* followed safely. In the stinging spray I lost sight of the *Dudley Docker* altogether. It was obvious she would have to go outside the pillar as she was making so much leeway, but I could not see what happened to her and I dared not pause. It was a bad time. At last, about 5 p.m., the *James Caird* and the *Stancomb Wills* reached comparatively calm water and we saw Wild's beach just ahead of us. I looked back vainly for the *Dudley Docker*.

Rocks studded the shallow water round the spit and the sea surged amongst them. I ordered the *Stancomb Wills* to run on to the beach at the place that looked smoothest, and in a few moments the first boat was ashore, the men jumping out and holding her against the receding wave. Immediately I saw she was safe I ran the *James Caird* in. Some of us scrambled up the beach through the fringe of the surf and slipped the painter round a rock, so as to hold the boat against the backwash. Then we began to get the stores and gear out, working like men possessed, for the boats could not be pulled up till they had been emptied. The blubber stove was quickly alight and the cook began to prepare a hot drink. We were laboring at the boats when I noticed Rickenson turn white and stagger in the surf. I pulled him out of reach of the water and sent him up to the stove, which had been placed in the shelter of some rocks. McIlroy went to him and found that his heart had been temporarily unequal to the strain placed upon it. He was in a bad way and needed prompt medical attention. There are some men who will do more than their share of work and who will attempt more than they are physically able to accomplish. Rickenson was one of these eager souls. He was suffering, like many other members of the Expedition, from bad salt-water boils. Our wrists, arms, and legs were attacked. Apparently this infliction was due to constant soaking with sea water, the chafing of wet clothes, and exposure.

I was very anxious about the *Dudley Docker,* and my eyes as well as my thoughts were turned eastward as we carried the stores ashore; but within half an hour the missing boat appeared, laboring through the spume-white sea, and presently she reached the comparative calm of the bay. We watched her coming with that sense of relief that the mariner feels when he crosses the harbor bar. The tide was going out rapidly, and Worsley lightened the *Dudley Docker* by placing some cases on an outer rock, where they were retrieved subsequently. Then he beached his boat, and with many hands at work we soon had our belongings ashore and our three craft above highwater mark. The spit was by no means an ideal camping ground; it was rough, bleak, and inhospitable—just an acre or two of rock and shingle, with the sea foaming around it except where the snow slope, running up to a glacier, formed the landward boundary. But some of the larger rocks provided a measure of shelter from the wind, and as we clustered round the blubber stove, with the acrid smoke blowing into our faces, we were quite a cheerful company. After all, another stage of the homeward journey had been accomplished and we could afford to forget for an hour the problems of the future. Life was not so bad. We ate our evening meal while the snow drifted down from the surface of the glacier, and our chilled bodies grew warm. Then we dried a little tobacco at the stove and enjoyed our pipes before we crawled into our tents. The snow had made it impossible for us to find the tide line and we were uncertain how far the sea was going to encroach upon our beach. I pitched my tent on the seaward side of the camp so that I

might have early warning of danger, and, sure enough, about
2 a.m. a little wave forced its way under the tent cloth. This
was a practical demonstration that we had not gone far
enough back from the sea, but in the semidarkness it was
difficult to see where we could find safety. Perhaps it was
fortunate that experience had inured us to the unpleasantness of sudden forced changes of camp. We took down the
tents and re-pitched them close against the high rocks at
the seaward end of the spit, where large boulders made an
uncomfortable resting place. Snow was falling heavily.
Then all hands had to assist in pulling the boats farther up
the beach, and at this task we suffered a serious misfortune.
Two of our four bags of clothing had been placed under the
bilge of the *James Caird,* and before we realized the danger
a wave had lifted the boat and carried the two bags back into
the surf. We had no chance of recovering them. This accident did not complete the tale of the night's misfortunes.
The big eight-man tent was blown to pieces in the early
morning. Some of the men who had occupied it took refuge
in other tents, but several remained in their sleeping bags
under the fragments of cloth until it was time to turn out.

A southerly gale was blowing on the morning of April 18
and the drifting snow was covering everything. The outlook
was cheerless indeed, but much work had to be done and we
could not yield to the desire to remain in the sleeping bags.
Some sea elephants were lying about the beach above highwater mark, and we killed several of the younger ones for
their meat and blubber. The big tent could not be replaced,
and in order to provide shelter for the men we turned the
Dudley Docker upside down and wedged up the weather
side with boulders. We also lashed the painter and stern-
rope round the heaviest rocks we could find, so as to guard
against the danger of the boat being moved by the wind.
The two bags of clothing were bobbing about amid the brash
and glacier ice to the windward side of the spit, and it did

not seem possible to reach them. The gale continued all day, and the fine drift from the surface of the glacier was added to the big flakes of snow falling from the sky. I made a careful examination of the spit with the object of ascertaining its possibilities as a camping ground. Apparently some of the beach lay above highwater mark and the rocks that stood above the shingle gave a measure of shelter. It would be possible to mount the snow slope towards the glacier in fine weather, but I did not push my exploration in that direction during the gale. At the seaward end of the spit was the mass of rock already mentioned. A few thousand ringed penguins, with some gentoos, were on these rocks, and we had noted this fact with a great deal of satisfaction at the time of our landing. The ringed penguin is by no means the best of the penguins from the point of view of the hungry traveler, but it represents food. At 8 a.m. that morning I noticed the ringed penguins mustering in orderly fashion close to the water's edge, and thought that they were preparing for the daily fishing excursion; but presently it became apparent that some important move was on foot. They were going to migrate, and with their departure much valuable food would pass beyond our reach. Hurriedly we armed ourselves with pieces of sledgerunner and other improvised clubs, and started towards the rookery. We were too late. The leaders gave their squawk of command and the columns took to the sea in unbroken ranks. Following their leaders, the penguins dived through the surf and reappeared in the heaving water beyond. A very few of the weaker birds took fright and made their way back to the beach, where they fell victims later to our needs; but the main army went northwards and we saw them no more. We feared that the gentoo penguins might follow the example of their ringed cousins, but they stayed with us; apparently they had not the migratory habit. They were comparatively few in number, but from time to time they would come in from the sea and walk up our beach. The gentoo is the most strongly marked of all the smaller varieties of penguins as far as coloring is concerned, and it far surpasses the adelie in weight of legs and breast, the points that particularly appealed to us.

The deserted rookery was sure to be above highwater mark at all times, and we mounted the rocky ledge in search of a place to pitch our tents. The penguins knew better than to rest where the sea could reach them even when the highest tide was supported by the strongest gale. The disadvantages of a camp on the rookery were obvious. The smell was strong, to put it mildly, and was not likely to grow less pronounced when the warmth of our bodies thawed the surface. But our choice of places was not wide, and that afternoon we dug out a site for two tents in the debris of the rookery, leveling it off with snow and rocks. My tent, No. 1, was pitched close under the cliff, and there during my stay on Elephant Island I lived. Crean's tent was close by, and the other three tents, which had fairly clean snow under them, were some yards away. The fifth tent was a ramshackle affair. The material of the torn eight-man tent had been drawn over a rough framework of oars, and shelter of a kind provided for the men who occupied it.

The arrangement of our camp, the checking of our gear, the killing and skinning of seals and sea elephants occupied us during the day, and we took to our sleeping bags early. I and my companions in No. 1 tent were not destined to spend a pleasant night. The heat of our bodies soon melted the snow and refuse beneath us, and the floor of the tent became an evil-smelling yellow mud. The snow drifting from the cliff above us weighted the sides of the tent, and during the night a particularly stormy gust brought our little home down on top of us. We stayed underneath the snow-laden cloth till the morning, for it seemed a hopeless business to set about re-pitching the tent amid the storm that was raging in the darkness of the night.

The weather was still bad on the morning of April 19. Some of the men were showing signs of demoralization. They were disinclined to leave the tents when the hour came for turning out, and it was apparent they were thinking more of the discomforts of the moment than of the good fortune that had brought us to sound ground and comparative safety. The condition of the gloves and headgear shown me by some discouraged men illustrated the proverbial carelessness of the sailor. The articles had frozen stiff during the night, and the owners considered, it appeared, that this state of affairs provided them with a grievance, or at any rate gave them the right to grumble. They said they wanted dry clothes and that their health would not admit of their doing any work. Only by rather drastic methods were they induced to turn to. Frozen gloves and helmets undoubtedly are very uncomfortable, and the proper thing is to keep these articles thawed by placing them inside one's shirt during the night.

The southerly gale, bringing with it much snow, was so severe that as I went along the beach to kill a seal I was blown down by a gust. The cooking pots from No. 2 tent took a flying run into the sea at the same moment. A case of provisions which had been placed on them to keep them safe had been capsized by a squall. These pots, fortunately, were not essential, since nearly all our cooking was done over the blubber stove. The galley was set up by the rocks close to my tent, in a hole we had dug through the debris of the penguin rookery. Cases of stores gave some shelter from the wind and a spread sail kept some of the snow off the cook when he was at work. He had not much idle time. The amount of seal and sea elephant steak and blubber consumed by our hungry party was almost incredible. He did not lack assistance—the neighborhood of the blubber stove had attractions for every member of the party; but he earned everybody's gratitude by his unflagging energy in preparing meals that to us at least were savory and satisfying. Frankly, we needed all the comfort that the hot food could give us. The icy fingers of the gale searched every cranny of our beach and pushed relentlessly through our worn garments and tattered tents. The snow, drifting from the glacier and falling from the skies, swathed us and our gear and set traps for our stumbling feet. The rising sea beat against the rocks and shingle and tossed fragments of floe ice within a few feet of our boats. Once during the morning the sun shone through the racing clouds and we had a glimpse of blue sky; but the promise of fair weather was not redeemed. The consoling feature of the situation was that our camp was safe. We could endure the discomforts, and I felt that all hands would be benefited by the opportunity for rest and recuperation.

CHAPTER IX

THE BOAT JOURNEY

THE INCREASING SEA made it necessary for us to drag the boats farther up the beach. This was a task for all hands, and after much labor we got the boats into safe positions among the rocks and made fast the painters to big boulders. Then I discussed with Wild and Worsley the chances of reaching South Georgia before the winter locked the seas against us. Some effort had to be made to secure relief. Privation and exposure had left their mark on the party, and the health and mental condition of several men were causing me serious anxiety. Blackborrow's feet, which had been frostbitten during the boat journey, were in a bad way, and the two doctors feared that an operation would be necessary. They told me that the toes would have to be amputated unless animation could be restored within a short period. Then the food supply was a vital consideration. We had left ten cases of provisions in the crevice of the rocks at our first camping place on the island. An examination of our stores showed that we had full rations for the whole party for a period of five weeks. The rations could be spread over three months on a reduced allowance and probably would be supplemented by seals and sea elephants to some extent. I did not dare to count with full confidence on supplies of meat and blubber, for the animals seemed to have deserted the beach and the winter was near. Our stocks included three seals and two and a half skins (with blubber attached). We were mainly dependent on the blubber for fuel, and, after making a preliminary survey of the situation, I decided that the party must be limited to one hot meal a day.

A boat journey in search of relief was necessary and must

not be delayed. That conclusion was forced upon me. The nearest port where assistance could certainly be secured was Port Stanley, in the Falkland Islands, 540 miles away, but we could scarcely hope to beat up against the prevailing northwesterly wind in a frail and weakened boat with a small sail area. South Georgia was over 800 miles away, but lay in the area of the west winds, and I could count upon finding whalers at any of the whaling stations on the east coast. A boat party might make the voyage and be back with relief within a month, provided that the sea was clear of ice and the boat survive the great seas. It was not difficult to decide that South Georgia must be the objective, and I proceeded to plan ways and means. The hazards of a boat journey across 800 miles of stormy sub-Antarctic ocean were obvious, but I calculated that at worst the venture would add nothing to the risks of the men left on the island. There would be fewer mouths to feed during the winter and the boat would not require to take more than one month's provisions for six men, for if we did not make South Georgia in that time we were sure to go under. A consideration that had weight with me was that there was no chance at all of any search being made for us on Elephant Island.

The case required to be argued in some detail, since all hands knew that the perils of the proposed journey were extreme. The risk was justified solely by our urgent need of assistance. The ocean south of Cape Horn in the middle of May is known to be the most tempestuous storm-swept area of water in the world. The weather then is unsettled, the skies are dull and overcast, and the gales are almost unceasing. We had to face these conditions in a small and weather-beaten boat, already strained by the work of the months that had passed. Worsley and Wild realized that the attempt must be made, and they both asked to be allowed to accompany me on the voyage. I told Wild at once that he would have to stay behind. I relied upon him to hold the party together

while I was away and to make the best of his way to Deception Island with the men in the spring in the event of our
failure to bring help. Worsley I would take with me, for I
had a very high opinion of his accuracy and quickness as a
navigator, and especially in the snapping and working out
of positions in difficult circumstances—an opinion that was
only enhanced during the actual journey. Four other men
would be required, and I decided to call for volunteers, although, as a matter of fact, I pretty well knew which of the
people I would select. Crean I proposed to leave on the island as a right-hand man for Wild, but he begged so hard to
be allowed to come in the boat that, after consultation with
Wild, I promised to take him. I called the men together,
explained my plan, and asked for volunteers. Many came
forward at once. Some were not fit enough for the work that
would have to be done, and others would not have been
much use in the boat since they were not seasoned sailors,
though the experiences of recent months entitled them to
some consideration as seafaring men. McIlroy and Macklin
were both anxious to go but realized that their duty lay on
the island with the sick men. They suggested that I should
take Blackborrow in order that he might have shelter and
warmth as quickly as possible, but I had to veto this idea. It
would be hard enough for fit men to live in the boat. Indeed,
I did not see how a sick man, lying helpless in the bottom
of the boat, could possibly survive in the heavy weather we
were sure to encounter. I finally selected McNeish, McCarthy, and Vincent in addition to Worsley and Crean. The
crew seemed a strong one, and as I looked at the men I felt
confidence increasing.

The decision made, I walked through the blizzard with
Worsley and Wild to examine the *James Caird*. The 20-ft.
boat had never looked big; she appeared to have shrunk in
some mysterious way when I viewed her in the light of our
new undertaking. She was an ordinary ship's whaler, fairly

strong, but showing signs of the strains she had endured since the crushing of the *Endurance*. Where she was holed in leaving the pack was, fortunately, about the water line and easily patched. Standing beside her, we glanced at the fringe of the storm-swept, tumultuous sea that formed our path. Clearly, our voyage would be a big adventure. I called the carpenter and asked him if he could do anything to make the boat more seaworthy. He first inquired if he was to go with me, and seemed quite pleased when I said "Yes." He was over fifty years of age and not altogether fit, but he had a good knowledge of sailing boats and was very quick. McCarthy said that he could contrive some sort of covering for the *James Caird* if he might use the lids of the cases and the four sledge runners that we had lashed inside the boat for use in the event of a landing on Graham Island at Wilhelmina Bay. This bay, at one time the goal of our desire, had been left behind in the course of our drift, but we had retained the runners. The carpenter proposed to complete the covering with some of our canvas, and he set about making his plans at once.

Noon had passed and the gale was more severe than ever. We could not proceed with our preparations that day. The tents were suffering in the wind and the sea was rising. We made our way to the snow slope at the shoreward end of the spit, with the intention of digging a hole in the snow large enough to provide shelter for the party. I had an idea that Wild and his men might camp there during my absence, since it seemed impossible that the tents could hold together for many more days against the attacks of the wind; but an examination of the spot indicated that any hole we could dig probably would be filled quickly by the drift. At dark, about 5 p.m., we all turned in, after a supper consisting of a pannikin of hot milk, one of our precious biscuits, and a cold penguin leg each.

The gale was stronger than ever on the following morning

(April 20). No work could be done. Blizzard and snow, snow and blizzard, sudden lulls and fierce returns. During the lulls we could see on the far horizon to the northeast bergs of all shapes and sizes driving along before the gale, and the sinister appearance of the swift moving masses made us thankful indeed that, instead of battling with the storm amid the ice, we were required only to face the drift from the glaciers and the inland heights. The gusts might throw us off our feet, but at least we fell on solid ground and not on the rocking floes. Two seals came up on the beach that day, one of them within ten yards of my tent. So urgent was our need of food and blubber that I called all hands and organized a line of beaters instead of simply walking up to the seal and hitting it on the nose. We were prepared to fall upon this seal *en masse* if it attempted to escape. The kill was made with a pick handle, and in a few minutes five days' food and six days' fuel were stowed in a place of safety among the boulders above highwater mark. During this day the cook, who had worked well on the floe and throughout the boat journey, suddenly collapsed. I happened to be at the galley at the moment and saw him fall. I pulled him down the slope to his tent and pushed him into its shelter with orders to his tentmates to keep him in his sleeping bag until I allowed him to come out or the doctors said he was fit enough. Then I took out to replace the cook one of the men who had expressed a desire to lie down and die. The task of keeping the galley fire alight was both difficult and strenuous, and it took his thoughts away from the chances of immediate dissolution. In fact, I found him a little later gravely concerned over the drying of a naturally not overclean pair of socks which were hung up in close proximity to our evening milk. Occupation had brought his thoughts back to the ordinary cares of life.

There was a lull in the bad weather on April 21, and the carpenter started to collect material for the decking of the

James Caird. He fitted the mast of the *Stancomb Wills* fore and aft inside the *James Caird* as a hog-back and thus strengthened the keel with the object of preventing our boat "hogging"—that is, buckling in heavy seas. He had not sufficient wood to provide a deck, but by using the sledge runners and box lids he made a framework extending from the forecastle aft to a well. It was a patched-up affair, but it provided a base for a canvas covering. We had a bolt of canvas frozen stiff, and this material had to be cut and then thawed out over the blubber stove, foot by foot, in order that it might be sewn into the form of a cover. When it had been nailed and screwed into position it certainly gave an appearance of safety to the boat, though I had an uneasy feeling that it bore a strong likeness to stage scenery, which may look like a granite wall and is in fact nothing better than canvas and lath. As events proved, the covering served its purpose well. We certainly could not have lived through the voyage without it.

Another fierce gale was blowing on April 22, interfering with our preparations for the voyage. The cooker from No. 5 tent came adrift in a gust, and, although it was chased to the water's edge, it disappeared for good. Blackborrow's feet were giving him much pain, and McIlroy and Macklin thought it would be necessary for them to operate soon. They were under the impression then that they had no chloroform, but they found some subsequently in the medicine chest after we had left. Some cases of stores left on a rock off the spit on the day of our arrival were retrieved during this day. We were setting aside stores for the boat journey and choosing the essential equipment from the scanty stock at our disposal. Two ten-gallon casks had to be filled with water melted down from ice collected at the foot of the glacier. This was a rather slow business. The blubber stove was kept going all night, and the watchmen emptied the water into the casks from the pot in which the ice was melted. A

working party started to dig a hole in the snow slope about
forty feet above sea level with the object of providing a site
for a camp. They made fairly good progress at first, but the
snow drifted down unceasingly from the inland ice, and in
the end the party had to give up the project.

The weather was fine on April 23, and we hurried forward
our preparations. It was on this day I decided finally that the
crew for the *James Caird* should consist of Worsley, Crean,
McNeish, McCarthy, Vincent, and myself. A storm came on
about noon, with driving snow and heavy squalls. Occasionally the air would clear for a few minutes, and we could see
a line of pack ice, five miles out, driving across from west
to east. This sight increased my anxiety to get away quickly.
Winter was advancing, and soon the pack might close completely round the island and stay our departure for days or
even for weeks. I did not think that ice would remain around
Elephant Island continuously during the winter, since the
strong winds and fast currents would keep it in motion. We
had noticed ice and bergs going past at the rate of four or
five knots. A certain amount of ice was held up about the
end of our spit, but the sea was clear where the boat would
have to be launched.

Worsley, Wild, and I climbed to the summit of the seaward rocks and examined the ice from a better vantage point
than the beach offered. The belt of pack outside appeared to
be sufficiently broken for our purposes, and I decided that,
unless the conditions forbade it, we would make a start in
the *James Caird* on the following morning. Obviously the
pack might close at any time. This decision made, I spent
the rest of the day looking over the boat, gear, and stores,
and discussing plans with Worsley and Wild.

Our last night on the solid ground of Elephant Island was
cold and uncomfortable. We turned out at dawn and had
breakfast. Then we launched the *Stancomb Wills* and loaded
her with stores, gear, and ballast, which would be trans-

ferred to the *James Caird* when the heavier boat had been launched. The ballast consisted of bags made from blankets and filled with sand, making a total weight of about 1000 lb. In addition we had gathered a number of round boulders and about 250 lb. of ice, which would supplement our two casks of water.

The stores taken in the *James Caird*, which would last six men for one month, were as follows:

> 30 boxes of matches.
> 6½ gallons paraffin.
> 1 tin methylated spirit.
> 10 boxes of flamers.
> 1 box of blue lights.
> 2 Primus stoves with spare parts and prickers.
> 1 Nansen aluminum cooker.
> 6 sleeping bags.
> A few spare socks.
> A few candles and some blubber oil in an oil bag.

Food:
> 3 cases sledging rations = 300 rations.
> 2 cases nut food   = 200 ”
> 2 cases biscuits   = 600 biscuits.
> 1 case lump sugar.
> 30 packets of Trumilk.
> 1 tin of Bovril cubes.
> 1 tin of Cerebos salt.
> 36 gallons of water.
> 112 lb. of ice.

Instruments:
Sextant.	Sea anchor.
Binoculars.	Charts.
Prismatic compass.	Aneroid.

The swell was slight when the *Stancomb Wills* was launched and the boat got under way without any difficulty; but half an hour later, when we were pulling down the *James Caird,* the swell increased suddenly. Apparently the movement of the ice outside had made an opening and allowed the sea to run in without being blanketed by the line of pack. The swell made things difficult. Many of us got wet to the waist while dragging the boat out—a serious matter in that climate. When the *James Caird* was afloat in the surf she nearly capsized among the rocks before we could get her clear, and Vincent and the carpenter, who were on the deck, were thrown into the water. This was really bad luck, for the two men would have small chance of drying their clothes after we had got under way. Hurley, who had the eye of the professional photographer for "incidents," secured a picture of the upset, and I firmly believe that he would have liked the two unfortunate men to remain in the water until he could get a "snap" at close quarters; but we hauled them out immediately, regardless of his feelings.

The *James Caird* was soon clear of the breakers. We used all the available ropes as a long painter to prevent her drifting away to the northeast, and then the *Stancomb Wills* came alongside, transferred her load, and went back to the shore for more. As she was being beached this time the sea took her stern and half filled her with water. She had to be turned over and emptied before the return journey could be made. Every member of the crew of the *Stancomb Wills* was wet to the skin. The water casks were towed behind the *Stancomb Wills* on this second journey, and the swell, which was increasing rapidly, drove the boat on to the rocks, where one of the casks was slightly stove in. This accident proved later to be a serious one, since some sea water had entered the cask and the contents were now brackish.

By midday the *James Caird* was ready for the voyage. Vincent and the carpenter had secured some dry clothes by

exchange with members of the shore party (I heard afterwards that it was a full fortnight before the soaked garments
were finally dried), and the boat's crew was standing by
waiting for the order to cast off. A moderate westerly breeze
was blowing. I went ashore in the *Stancomb Wills* and had
a last word with Wild, who was remaining in full command,
with directions as to his course of action in the event of our
failure to bring relief, but I practically left the whole situation and scope of action and decision to his own judgment,
secure in the knowledge that he would act wisely. I told him
that I trusted the party to him and said good-bye to the men.
Then we pushed off for the last time, and within a few minutes I was aboard the *James Caird*. The crew of the *Stancomb Wills* shook hands with us as the boats bumped
together and offered us the last good wishes. Then, setting
our jib, we cut the painter and moved away to the northeast.
The men who were staying behind made a pathetic little
group on the beach, with the grim heights of the island behind them and the sea seething at their feet, but they waved
to us and gave three hearty cheers. There was hope in their
hearts and they trusted us to bring the help that they needed.

I had all sails set, and the *James Caird* quickly dipped the
beach and its line of dark figures. The westerly wind took
us rapidly to the line of pack, and as we entered it I stood
up with my arm around the mast, directing the steering, so
as to avoid the great lumps of ice that were flung about in
the heave of the sea. The pack thickened and we were forced
to turn almost due east, running before the wind towards a
gap I had seen in the morning from the high ground. I could
not see the gap now, but we had come out on its bearing
and I was prepared to find that it had been influenced by the
easterly drift. At four o'clock in the afternoon we found the
channel, much narrower than it had seemed in the morning
but still navigable. Dropping sail, we rowed through without
touching the ice anywhere, and by 5:30 p.m. we were clear

of the pack with open water before us. We passed one more
piece of ice in the darkness an hour later, but the pack lay
behind, and with a fair wind swelling the sails we steered
our little craft through the night, our hopes centered on our
distant goal. The swell was very heavy now, and when the
time came for our first evening meal we found great difficulty in keeping the Primus lamp alight and preventing the
hoosh splashing out of the pot. Three men were needed to
attend to the cooking, one man holding the lamp and two
men guarding the aluminum cooking pot, which had to be
lifted clear of the Primus whenever the movement of the
boat threatened to cause a disaster. Then the lamp had to be
protected from water, for sprays were coming over the bows
and our flimsy decking was by no means watertight. All
these operations were conducted in the confined space under
the decking, where the men lay or knelt and adjusted themselves as best they could to the angles of our cases and ballast. It was uncomfortable, but we found consolation in the
reflection that without the decking we could not have used
the cooker at all.

The tale of the next sixteen days is one of supreme strife
amid heaving waters. The sub-Antarctic Ocean lived up to
its evil winter reputation. I decided to run north for at least
two days while the wind held and so get into warmer
weather before turning to the east and laying a course for
South Georgia. We took two-hourly spells at the tiller. The
men who were not on watch crawled into the sodden sleeping bags and tried to forget their troubles for a period; but
there was no comfort in the boat. The bags and cases
seemed to be alive in the unfailing knack of presenting their
most uncomfortable angles to our rest-seeking bodies. A
man might imagine for a moment that he had found a position of ease, but always discovered quickly that some un-
yielding point was impinging on muscle or bone. The first
night aboard the boat was one of acute discomfort for us all,

and we were heartily glad when the dawn came and we could set about the preparation of a hot breakfast.

This record of the voyage to South Georgia is based upon scanty notes made day by day. The notes dealt usually with the bare facts of distances, positions, and weather, but our memories retained the incidents of the passing days in a period never to be forgotten. By running north for the first two days I hoped to get warmer weather and also to avoid lines of pack that might be extending beyond the main body. We needed all the advantage that we could obtain from the higher latitude for sailing on the great circle, but we had to be cautious regarding possible ice streams. Cramped in our narrow quarters and continually wet by the spray, we suffered severely from cold throughout the journey. We fought the seas and the winds and at the same time had a daily struggle to keep ourselves alive. At times we were in dire peril. Generally we were upheld by the knowledge that we were making progress towards the land where we would be, but there were days and nights when we lay hove to, drifting across the storm-whitened seas and watching, with eyes interested rather than apprehensive, the uprearing masses of water, flung to and fro by Nature in the pride of her strength. Deep seemed the valleys when we lay between the reeling seas. High were the hills when we perched momentarily on the tops of giant combers. Nearly always there were gales. So small was our boat and so great were the seas that often our sail flapped idly in the calm between the crests of two waves. Then we would climb the next slope and catch the full fury of the gale where the wool-like whiteness of the breaking water surged around us. We had our moments of laughter—rare, it is true, but hearty enough. Even when cracked lips and swollen mouths checked the outward and visible signs of amusement we could see a joke of the primitive kind. Man's sense of humor is always most easily stirred by the petty misfortunes of his neighbors, and I shall

never forget Worsley's efforts on one occasion to place the
hot aluminum stand on top of the Primus stove after it had
fallen off in an extra-heavy roll. With his frostbitten fingers
he picked it up, dropped it, picked it up again, and toyed
with it gingerly as though it were some fragile article of
lady's wear. We laughed, or rather gurgled with laughter.

The wind came up strong and worked into a gale from
the northwest on the third day out. We stood away to the
east. The increasing seas discovered the weaknesses of our
decking. The continuous blows shifted the box lids and
sledge runners so that the canvas sagged down and accumulated water. Then icy trickles, distinct from the driving
sprays, poured fore and aft into the boat. The nails that the
carpenter had extracted from cases at Elephant Island and
used to fasten down the battens were too short to make firm
the decking. We did what we could to secure it, but our
means were very limited, and the water continued to enter
the boat at a dozen points. Much baling was necessary, and
nothing that we could do prevented our gear from becoming
sodden. The searching runnels from the canvas were really
more unpleasant than the sudden definite douches of the
sprays. Lying under the thwarts during watches below, we
tried vainly to avoid them. There were no dry places in the
boat, and at last we simply covered our heads with our Burberrys and endured the all-pervading water. The baling was
work for the watch. Real rest we had none. The perpetual
motion of the boat made repose impossible; we were cold,
sore, and anxious. We moved on hands and knees in the
semidarkness of the day under the decking. The darkness
was complete by 6 p.m., and not until 7 a.m. of the following day could we see one another under the thwarts. We had
a few scraps of candle, and they were preserved carefully in
order that we might have light at mealtimes. There was one
fairly dry spot in the boat, under the solid original decking
at the bows, and we managed to protect some of our biscuit

from the salt water; but I do not think any of us got the taste of salt out of our mouths during the voyage.

The difficulty of movement in the boat would have had its humorous side if it had not involved us in so many aches and pains. We had to crawl under the thwarts in order to move along the boat, and our knees suffered considerably. When a watch turned out it was necessary for me to direct each man by name when and where to move, since if all hands had crawled about at the same time the result would have been dire confusion and many bruises. Then there was the trim of the boat to be considered. The order of the watch was four hours on and four hours off, three men to the watch. One man had the tiller ropes, the second man attended to the sail, and the third baled for all he was worth. Sometimes when the water in the boat had been reduced to reasonable proportions, our pump could be used. This pump, which Hurley had made from the Flinders bar case of our ship's standard compass, was quite effective, though its capacity was not large. The man who was attending the sail could pump into the big outer cooker, which was lifted and emptied overboard when filled. We had a device by which the water could go direct from the pump into the sea through a hole in the gunwale, but this hole had to be blocked at an early stage of the voyage, since we found that it admitted water when the boat rolled.

While a new watch was shivering in the wind and spray, the men who had been relieved groped hurriedly among the soaked sleeping bags and tried to steal a little of the warmth created by the last occupants; but it was not always possible for us to find even this comfort when we went off watch. The boulders that we had taken aboard for ballast had to be shifted continually in order to trim the boat and give access to the pump, which became choked with hairs from the moulting sleeping bags and finneskoe. The four reindeer-skin sleeping bags shed their hair freely owing to the contin-

uous wetting, and soon became quite bald in appearance.
The moving of the boulders was weary and painful work.
We came to know every one of the stones by sight and
touch, and I have vivid memories of their angular peculiari-
ties even today. They might have been of considerable interest as geological specimens to a scientific man under
happier conditions. As ballast they were useful. As weights
to be moved about in cramped quarters they were simply
appalling. They spared no portion of our poor bodies. Another of our troubles, worth mention here, was the chafing
of our legs by our wet clothes, which had not been changed
now for seven months. The insides of our thighs were
rubbed raw, and the one tube of Hazeline cream in our medicine chest did not go far in alleviating our pain, which was
increased by the bite of the salt water. We thought at the
time that we never slept. The fact was that we would doze
off uncomfortably, to be aroused quickly by some new ache
or another call to effort. My own share of the general unpleasantness was accentuated by a finely developed bout of
sciatica. I had become possessor of this originally on the
floe several months earlier.

Our meals were regular in spite of the gales. Attention to
this point was essential, since the conditions of the voyage
made increasing calls upon our vitality. Breakfast, at 8 a.m.,
consisted of a pannikin of hot hoosh made from Bovril
sledging ration, two biscuits, and some lumps of sugar.
Lunch came at 1 p.m., and comprised Bovril sledging ration,
eaten raw, and a pannikin of hot milk for each man. Tea, at
5 p.m., had the same menu. Then during the night we had a
hot drink, generally of milk. The meals were the bright beacons in those cold and stormy days. The glow of warmth
and comfort produced by the food and drink made optimists
of us all. We had two tins of Virol, which we were keeping
for an emergency; but, finding ourselves in need of an oil
lamp to eke out our supply of candles, we emptied one of

the tins in the manner that most appealed to us, and fitted it with a wick made by shredding a bit of canvas. When this lamp was filled with oil it gave a certain amount of light, though it was easily blown out, and was of great assistance to us at night. We were fairly well off as regarded fuel, since we had 6½ gallons of petroleum.

A severe southwesterly gale on the fourth day out forced us to heave to. I would have liked to have run before the wind, but the sea was very high and the *James Caird* was in danger of broaching to and swamping. The delay was vexatious, since up to that time we had been making sixty or seventy miles a day; good going with our limited sail area. We hove to under double-reefed mainsail and our little jigger, and waited for the gale to blow itself out. During that afternoon we saw bits of wreckage, the remains probably of some unfortunate vessel that had failed to weather the strong gales south of Cape Horn. The weather conditions did not improve, and on the fifth day out the gale was so fierce that we were compelled to take in the double-reefed mainsail and hoist our small jib instead. We put out a sea anchor to keep the *James Caird*'s head up to the sea. This anchor consisted of a triangular canvas bag fastened to the end of the painter and allowed to stream out from the bows. The boat was high enough to catch the wind, and, as she drifted to leeward, the drag of the anchor kept her head to windward. Thus our boat took most of the seas more or less end on. Even then the crests of the waves often would curl right over us and we shipped a great deal of water, which necessitated unceasing baling and pumping. Looking out abeam, we would see a hollow like a tunnel formed as the crest of a big wave toppled over on to the swelling body of water. A thousand times it appeared as though the *James Caird* must be engulfed; but the boat lived. The southwesterly gale had its birthplace above the Antarctic Continent, and its freezing breath lowered the temperature far towards zero. The sprays

froze upon the boat and gave bows, sides, and decking a
heavy coat of mail. This accumulation of ice reduced the
buoyancy of the boat, and to that extent was an added peril;
but it possessed a notable advantage from one point of view.
The water ceased to drop and trickle from the canvas, and
the spray came in solely at the well in the after part of the
boat. We could not allow the load of ice to grow beyond a
certain point, and in turns we crawled about the decking
forward, chipping and picking at it with the available tools.

When daylight came on the morning of the sixth day out
we saw and felt that the *James Caird* had lost her resiliency.
She was not rising to the oncoming seas. The weight of the
ice that had formed in her and upon her during the night
was having its effect, and she was becoming more like a log
than a boat. The situation called for immediate action. We
first broke away the spare oars, which were encased in ice
and frozen to the sides of the boat, and threw them overboard. We retained two oars for use when we got inshore.
Two of the fur sleeping bags went over the side; they were
thoroughly wet, weighing probably 40 lb. each, and they
had frozen stiff during the night. Three men constituted the
watch below, and when a man went down it was better to
turn into the wet bag just vacated by another man than to
thaw out a frozen bag with the heat of his unfortunate body.
We now had four bags, three in use and one for emergency
use in case a member of the party should break down permanently. The reduction of weight relieved the boat to some
extent, and vigorous chipping and scraping did more. We
had to be very careful not to put axe or knife through the
frozen canvas of the decking as we crawled over it, but gradually we got rid of a lot of ice. The *James Caird* lifted to
the endless waves as though she lived again.

About 11 a.m. the boat suddenly fell off into the trough
of the sea. The painter had parted and the sea anchor had
gone. This was serious. The *James Caird* went away to lee-

ward, and we had no chance at all of recovering the anchor and our valuable rope, which had been our only means of keeping the boat's head up to the seas without the risk of hoisting sail in a gale. Now we had to set the sail and trust to its holding. While the *James Caird* rolled heavily in the trough, we beat the frozen canvas until the bulk of the ice had cracked off it and then hoisted it. The frozen gear worked protestingly, but after a struggle our little craft came up to the wind again, and we breathed more freely. Skin frostbites were troubling us, and we had developed large blisters on our fingers and hands. I shall always carry the scar of one of these frostbites on my left hand, which became badly inflamed after the skin had burst and the cold had bitten deeply.

We held the boat up to the gale during that day, enduring as best we could discomforts that amounted to pain. The boat tossed interminably on the big waves under grey, threatening skies. Our thoughts did not embrace much more than the necessities of the hour. Every surge of the sea was an enemy to be watched and circumvented. We ate our scanty meals, treated our frostbites, and hoped for the improved conditions that the morrow might bring. Night fell early, and in the lagging hours of darkness we were cheered by a change for the better in the weather. The wind dropped, the snow squalls became less frequent, and the sea moderated. When the morning of the seventh day dawned there was not much wind. We shook the reef out of the sail and laid our course once more for South Georgia. The sun came out bright and clear, and presently Worsley got a snap for longitude. We hoped that the sky would remain clear until noon, so that we could get the latitude. We had been six days out without an observation, and our dead reckoning naturally was uncertain. The boat must have presented a strange appearance that morning. All hands basked in the sun. We hung our sleeping bags to the mast and spread our socks and other gear all over the deck. Some of the ice had melted off the *James Caird* in the early morning after the gale began to slacken, and dry patches were appearing in the decking. Porpoises came blowing round the boat, and Cape pigeons wheeled and swooped within a few feet of us. These little black-and-white birds have an air of friendliness that is not possessed by the great circling albatross. They had looked grey against the swaying sea during the storm as they darted about over our heads and uttered their plaintive cries. The albatrosses, of the black or sooty variety, had watched with hard, bright eyes, and seemed to have a quite impersonal interest in our struggle to keep afloat amid the battering seas. In addition to the Cape pigeons an occasional stormy petrel flashed overhead. Then there was a small bird, unknown to me, that appeared always to be in a fussy, bustling state, quite out of keeping with the surroundings. It irritated me. It had practically no tail, and it flitted about vaguely as though in search of the lost member. I used to find myself wishing it would find its tail and have done with the silly fluttering.

We reveled in the warmth of the sun that day. Life was not so bad, after all. We felt we were well on our way. Our gear was drying, and we could have a hot meal in comparative comfort. The swell was still heavy, but it was not breaking and the boat rode easily. At noon Worsley balanced himself on the gunwale and clung with one hand to the stay of the mainmast while he got a snap of the sun. The result was more than encouraging. We had done over 380 miles and were getting on for halfway to South Georgia. It looked as though we were going to get through.

The wind freshened to a good stiff breeze during the afternoon, and the *James Caird* made satisfactory progress. I had not realized until the sunlight came how small our boat really was. There was some influence in the light and warmth, some hint of happier days, that made us revive memories of other voyages, when we had stout decks beneath our feet, unlimited food at our command, and pleasant cabins for our ease. Now we clung to a battered little boat, "alone, alone, all, all alone, alone on a wide, wide sea." So low in the water were we that each succeeding swell cut off our view of the skyline. We were a tiny speck in the vast vista of the sea—the ocean that is open to all and merciful to none, that threatens even when it seems to yield, and that is pitiless always to weakness. For a moment the consciousness of the forces arrayed against us would be almost overwhelming. Then hope and confidence would rise again as our boat rose to a wave and tossed aside the crest in a sparkling shower like the play of prismatic colors at the foot of a waterfall. My double-barreled gun and some cartridges had been stowed aboard the boat as an emergency precaution against a shortage of food, but we were not disposed to destroy our little neighbors, the Cape pigeons, even for the sake of fresh meat. We might have shot an albatross, but the wandering king of the ocean aroused in us something of the feeling that inspired, too late, the Ancient Mariner. So the gun remained among the stores and sleeping bags in the narrow quarters beneath our leaking deck, and the birds followed us unmolested.

The eighth, ninth, and tenth days of the voyage had few features worthy of special note. The wind blew hard during those days, and the strain of navigating the boat was unceasing, but always we made some advance towards our goal. No bergs showed on our horizon, and we knew that we were clear of the ice fields. Each day brought its little round of troubles, but also compensation in the form of food and growing hope. We felt that we were going to succeed. The odds against us had been great, but we were winning through. We still suffered severely from the cold, for, though the temperature was rising, our vitality was declining owing to shortage of food, exposure, and the necessity of maintaining our cramped positions day and night. I found that it was now absolutely necessary to prepare hot milk for all hands during the night, in order to sustain life till dawn. This meant lighting the Primus lamp in the darkness and involved an increased drain on our small store of matches. It was the rule that one match must serve when the Primus was being lit. We had no lamp for the compass and during the early days of the voyage we would strike a match when the steersman wanted to see the course at night; but later the necessity for strict economy impressed itself upon us, and the practice of striking matches at night was stopped. We had one watertight tin of matches. I had stowed away in a pocket, in readiness for a sunny day, a lens from one of the telescopes, but this was of no use during the voyage. The sun seldom shone upon us. The glass of the compass got broken one night, and we contrived to mend it with adhesive tape from the medicine-chest. One of the memories that comes to me from those days is of Crean singing at the tiller. He always sang while he was steering, and nobody ever discovered what the song was. It was devoid of tune and as monotonous as the chanting of a Buddhist monk at his prayers; yet somehow it was cheerful. In moments of inspiration Crean would attempt "The Wearing of the Green."

On the tenth night Worsley could not straighten his body after his spell at the tiller. He was thoroughly cramped, and we had to drag him beneath the decking and massage him before he could unbend himself and get into a sleeping bag. A hard northwesterly gale came up on the eleventh day (May 5) and shifted to the southwest in the late afternoon. The sky was overcast and occasional snow squalls added to the discomfort produced by a tremendous cross-sea—the worst, I thought, that we had experienced. At midnight I was at the tiller and suddenly noticed a line of clear sky between the south and southwest. I called to the other men that the sky was clearing, and then a moment later I realized that what I had seen was not a rift in the clouds but the white crest of an enormous wave. During twenty-six years' experience of the ocean in all its moods I had not encountered a wave so gigantic. It was a mighty upheaval of the ocean, a thing quite apart from the big white-capped seas that had been our tireless enemies for many days. I shouted, "For God's sake, hold on! It's got us!" Then came a moment of suspense that seemed drawn out into hours. White surged the foam of the breaking sea around us. We felt our boat lifted and flung forward like a cork in breaking surf. We were in a seething chaos of tortured water; but somehow the boat lived through it, half full of water, sagging to the dead weight and shuddering under the blow. We baled with the energy of men fighting for life, flinging the water over the sides with every receptacle that came to our hands, and after ten minutes of uncertainty we felt the boat renew her life beneath us. She floated again and ceased to lurch drunkenly as though dazed by the attack of the sea. Earnestly we hoped that never again would we encounter such a wave.

The conditions in the boat, uncomfortable before, had been made worse by the deluge of water. All our gear was thoroughly wet again. Our cooking stove had been floating about in the bottom of the boat, and portions of our last hoosh seemed to have permeated everything. Not until 3 a.m., when we were all chilled almost to the limit of endurance, did we manage to get the stove alight and make ourselves hot drinks. The carpenter was suffering particularly, but he showed grit and spirit. Vincent had for the past week ceased to be an active member of the crew, and I could not easily account for his collapse. Physically he was one of the strongest men in the boat. He was a young man, he had served on North Sea trawlers, and he should have been able to bear hardships better than McCarthy, who, not so strong, was always happy.

The weather was better on the following day (May 6), and

we got a glimpse of the sun. Worsley's observation showed
that we were not more than a hundred miles from the northwest corner of South Georgia. Two more days with a favorable wind and we would sight the promised land. I hoped
that there would be no delay, for our supply of water was
running very low. The hot drink at night was essential, but
I decided that the daily allowance of water must be cut down
to half a pint per man. The lumps of ice we had taken aboard
had gone long ago. We were dependent upon the water we
had brought from Elephant Island, and our thirst was increased by the fact that we were now using the brackish
water in the breaker that had been slightly stove in in the
surf when the boat was being loaded. Some sea water had
entered at that time.

Thirst took possession of us. I dared not permit the allowance of water to be increased since an unfavorable wind
might drive us away from the island and lengthen our voyage by many days. Lack of water is always the most severe
privation that men can be condemned to endure, and we
found, as during our earlier boat voyage, that the salt water
in our clothing and the salt spray that lashed our faces made
our thirst grow quickly to a burning pain. I had to be very
firm in refusing to allow any one to anticipate the morrow's
allowance, which I was sometimes begged to do. We did the
necessary work duly and hoped for the land. I had altered
the course to the east so as to make sure of our striking the
island, which would have been impossible to regain if we
had run past the northern end. The course was laid on our
scrap of chart for a point some thirty miles down the coast.
That day and the following day passed for us in a sort of
nightmare. Our mouths were dry and our tongues were
swollen. The wind was still strong and the heavy sea forced
us to nagivate carefully, but any thought of our peril from
the waves was buried beneath the consciousness of our raging thirst. The bright moments were those when we each

Endurance cutting through open pack ice. (ROYAL GEOGRAPHICAL SOCIETY, LONDON)

The men take a stroll on a huge floe of consolidated pack ice, January 1915.

(ROYAL GEOGRAPHICAL SOCIETY, LONDON)

One of the many soccer games played by the crew.

(ROYAL GEOGRAPHICAL SOCIETY, LONDON)

The sled dogs being exercised on an ice floe, January 1915.
(ROYAL GEOGRAPHICAL SOCIETY, LONDON)

Full Speed Ahead. *Endurance* under full sail, attempting to break through a lead in the ice, January 24, 1915. (ROYAL GEOGRAPHICAL SOCIETY, LONDON)

Trying to cut a way for the ship through the ice to a lead 400 yards ahead, February 14, 1915.
(ROYAL GEOGRAPHICAL SOCIETY, LONDON)

Disaster was never far away when working on the thin ice. A crewmember is pulled to safety during the ice-cutting around *Endurance*.
(ROYAL GEOGRAPHICAL SOCIETY, LONDON)

Pylon Avenue. The rope served as a guide in bad weather when a man might have easily become lost in a whiteout.

(ROYAL GEOGRAPHICAL SOCIETY, LONDON)

Unusual and beautiful ice flowers were formed by a lead in the ice opening up and then rapidly freezing over.

(ROYAL GEOGRAPHICAL SOCIETY, LONDON)

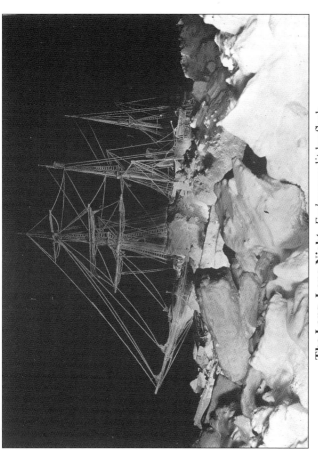

The Long, Long Night. *Endurance* lit by flash.
(ROYAL GEOGRAPHICAL SOCIETY, LONDON)

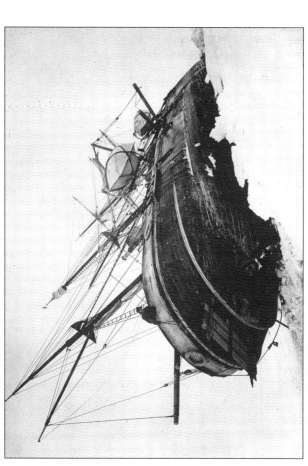

Endurance heeled over thirty degrees to port.
(Royal Geographical Society, London)

The End. *Endurance* was crushed by pressure ice.
(Royal Geographical Society, London)

Shackleton and Wild at Ocean Camp.
(ROYAL GEOGRAPHICAL SOCIETY, LONDON)

The *James Caird* is hauled on a sledge to Ocean Camp.
(ROYAL GEOGRAPHICAL SOCIETY, LONDON)

Shackleton, right, surveys Ocean Camp. The lookout atop the platform scans the horizon for cracks in the floe.

(ROYAL GEOGRAPHICAL SOCIETY, LONDON)

At Patience Camp, photographer Frank Hurley (left) skins a penguin for fueling the blubber stove made from old oil drums. A rapidly aged Shackleton sits to the right.

(ROYAL GEOGRAPHICAL SOCIETY, LONDON)

The first landing ever made on Elephant Island, April 15, 1916.
(ROYAL GEOGRAPHICAL SOCIETY, LONDON)

The *James Caird* is pulled higher on the beach at Elephant Island. There was little shelter as the sheer rock walls practically jutted straight up out of the ocean.
(ROYAL GEOGRAPHICAL SOCIETY, LONDON)

Shackleton departs from Elephant Island in the *James Caird* to a hopeful farewell from the men left behind.

The Rescue. The crew, bags faithfully packed, awaits pickup by the *Yelcho*, the Chilean tugboat that finally made it through the ice on August 30, 1916.

(ROYAL GEOGRAPHICAL SOCIETY, LONDON)

The hut on Elephant Island—two overturned boats were home to twenty-two men for over four months.

(ROYAL GEOGRAPHICAL SOCIETY, LONDON)

received our one mug of hot milk during the long, bitter watches of the night. Things were bad for us in those days, but the end was coming. The morning of May 8 broke thick and stormy, with squalls from the northwest. We searched the waters ahead for a sign of land, and though we could see nothing more than had met our eyes for many days, we were cheered by a sense that the goal was near at hand. About ten o'clock that morning we passed a little bit of kelp, a glad signal of the proximity of land. An hour later we saw two shags sitting on a big mass of kelp, and knew then that we must be within ten or fifteen miles of the shore. These birds are as sure an indication of the proximity of land as a light-house is, for they never venture far to sea. We gazed ahead with increasing eagerness, and at 12:30 p.m., through a rift in the clouds, McCarthy caught a glimpse of the black cliffs of South Georgia, just fourteen days after our departure from Elephant Island. It was a glad moment. Thirst-ridden, chilled, and weak as we were, happiness irradiated us. The job was nearly done.

We stood in towards the shore to look for a landing place, and presently we could see the green tussock grass on the ledges above the surf-beaten rocks. Ahead of us and to the south, blind rollers showed the presence of uncharted reefs along the coast. Here and there the hungry rocks were close to the surface, and over them the great waves broke, swirling viciously and spouting thirty and forty feet into the air. The rocky coast appeared to descend sheer to the sea. Our need of water and rest was well nigh desperate, but to have attempted a landing at that time would have been suicidal. Night was drawing near, and the weather indications were not favorable. There was nothing for it but to haul off till the following morning, so we stood away on the starboard tack until we had made what appeared to be a safe offing. Then we hove to in the high westerly swell. The hours passed slowly as we waited the dawn, which would herald,

we fondly hoped, the last stage of our journey. Our thirst
was a torment and we could scarcely touch our food; the
cold seemed to strike right through our weakened bodies. At
5 a.m. the wind shifted to the northwest and quickly increased to one of the worst hurricanes any of us had ever
experienced. A great cross-sea was running, and the wind
simply shrieked as it tore the tops off the waves and converted the whole seascape into a haze of driving spray.
Down into valleys, up to tossing heights, straining until her
seams opened, swung our little boat, brave still but laboring
heavily. We knew that the wind and set of the sea was driving us ashore, but we could do nothing. The dawn showed
us a storm-torn ocean, and the morning passed without
bringing us a sight of the land; but at 1 p.m., through a rift
in the flying mists, we got a glimpse of the huge crags of
the island and realized that our position had become desperate. We were on a dead lee shore, and we could gauge our
approach to the unseen cliffs by the roar of the breakers
against the sheer walls of rock. I ordered the double-reefed
mainsail to be set in the hope that we might claw off, and
this attempt increased the strain upon the boat. The *James
Caird* was bumping heavily, and the water was pouring in
everywhere. Our thirst was forgotten in the realization of
our imminent danger, as we baled unceasingly, and adjusted
our weights from time to time; occasional glimpses showed
that the shore was nearer. I knew that Annewkow Island lay
to the south of us, but our small and badly marked chart
showed uncertain reefs in the passage between the island
and the mainland, and I dared not trust it, though as a last
resort we could try to lie under the lee of the island. The
afternoon wore away as we edged down the coast, with the
thunder of the breakers in our ears. The approach of evening
found us still some distance from Annewkow Island, and,
dimly in the twilight, we could see a snow-capped mountain
looming above us. The chance of surviving the night, with

the driving gale and the implacable sea forcing us on to the lee shore, seemed small. I think most of us had a feeling that the end was very near. Just after 6 p.m., in the dark, as the boat was in the yeasty backwash from the seas flung from this ironbound coast, then, just when things looked their worst, they changed for the best. I have marveled often at the thin line that divides success from failure and the sudden turn that leads from apparently certain disaster to comparative safety. The wind suddenly shifted, and we were free once more to make an offing. Almost as soon as the gale eased, the pin that locked the mast to the thwart fell out. It must have been on the point of doing this throughout the hurricane; and if it had gone nothing could have saved us; the mast would have snapped like a carrot. Our backstays had carried away once before when iced up and were not too strongly fastened now. We were thankful indeed for the mercy that had held that pin in its place throughout the hurricane.

We stood off shore again, tired almost to the point of apathy. Our water had long been finished. The last was about a pint of hairy liquid, which we strained through a bit of gauze from the medicine chest. The pangs of thirst attacked us with redoubled intensity, and I felt that we must make a landing on the following day at almost any hazard. The night wore on. We were very tired. We longed for day. When at last the dawn came on the morning of May 10 there was practically no wind, but a high cross-sea was running. We made slow progress towards the shore. About 8 a.m. the wind backed to the northwest and threatened another blow. We had sighted in the meantime a big indentation which I thought must be King Haakon Bay, and I decided that we must land there. We set the bows of the boat towards the bay and ran before the freshening gale. Soon we had angry reefs on either side. Great glaciers came down to the sea and offered no landing place. The sea spouted on the reefs and thundered against the shore. About noon we sighted a line of jagged reef, like blackened teeth, that seemed to bar the entrance to the bay. Inside, comparatively smooth water stretched eight or nine miles to the head of the bay. A gap in the reef appeared, and we made for it. But the fates had' another rebuff for us. The wind shifted and blew from the east right out of the bay. We could see the way through the reef, but we could not approach it directly. That afternoon we bore up, tacking five times in the strong wind. The last tack enabled us to get through, and at last we were in the wide mouth of the bay. Dusk was approaching. A small cove, with a boulder-strewn beach guarded by a reef, made a break in the cliffs on the south side of the bay, and we turned in that direction. I stood in the bows directing the steering as we ran through the kelp and made the passage of the reef. The entrance was so narrow that we had to take in the oars, and the swell was piling itself right over the reef into the cove; but in a minute or two we were inside, and in the gathering darkness the *James Caird* ran in on a swell and touched the beach. I sprang ashore with the short painter and held on when the boat went out with the backward surge. When the *James Caird* came in again three of the men got ashore, and they held the painter while I climbed some rocks with another line. A slip on the wet rocks twenty feet up nearly closed my part of the story just at the moment when we were achieving safety. A jagged piece of rock held me and at the same time bruised me sorely. However, I made fast the line, and in a few minutes we were all safe on the beach, with the boat floating in the surging water just off the shore. We heard a gurgling sound that was sweet music in our ears, and, peering around, found a stream of fresh water almost at our feet. A moment later we were down on our knees drinking the pure, ice-cold water in long draughts that put new life into us. It was a splendid moment.

The next thing was to get the stores and ballast out of the boat, in order that we might secure her for the night. We carried the stores and gear above the highwater mark and threw out the bags of sand and the boulders that we knew so well. Then we attempted to pull the empty boat up the beach, and discovered by this effort how weak we had become. Our united strength was not sufficient to get the *James Caird* clear of the water. Time after time we pulled together, but without avail. I saw that it would be necessary to have food and rest before we beached the boat. We made fast a line to a heavy boulder and set a watch to fend the *James Caird* off the rocks of the beach. Then I sent Crean round to the left side of the cove, about thirty yards away, where I had noticed a little cave as we were running in. He could not see much in the darkness, but reported that the place certainly promised some shelter. We carried the sleeping bags round and found a mere hollow in the rock face, with a shingle floor sloping at a steep angle to the sea. There we prepared a hot meal, and when the food was finished I ordered the men to turn in. The time was now about 8 p.m., and I took the first watch beside the *James Caird,* which was still afloat in the tossing water just off the beach.

Fending the *James Caird* off the rocks in the darkness was awkward work. The boat would have bumped dangerously if allowed to ride in with the waves that drove into the cove. I found a flat rock for my feet, which were in a bad way owing to cold, wetness, and lack of exercise in the boat, and during the next few hours I labored to keep the *James Caird* clear of the beach. Occasionally I had to rush into the seething water. Then, as a wave receded, I let the boat out on the alpine rope so as to avoid a sudden jerk. The heavy painter had been lost when the sea anchor went adrift. The *James Caird* could be seen but dimly in the cove, where the high black cliffs made the darkness almost complete, and the strain upon one's attention was great. After several hours had passed I found that my desire for sleep was becoming irresistible, and at 1 a.m. I called Crean. I could hear him groaning as he stumbled over the sharp rocks on his way down the beach. While he was taking charge of the *James*

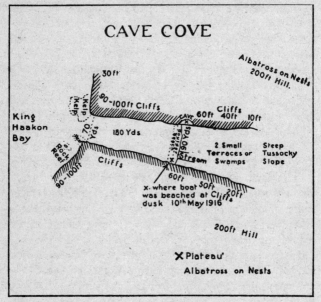

CAVE COVE

Albatross on Nests
200ft Hill.

30 ft

Kelp

90-100ft Cliffs

Cliffs
60ft 40ft 10ft

King
Haakon
Bay

180 Yds

Ave.

90 Yds

2 Small
Terraces or
Swamps

Steep
Tussocky
Slope

Rock
Reef

Cliffs

Stream

90-100

60ft
x. where boat 50ft
was beached at Cliffs 20ft
dusk 10th May 1916

200ft Hill

X Plateau'
Albatross on Nests

Caird she got adrift, and we had some anxious moments. Fortunately, she went across towards the cave and we secured her unharmed. The loss or destruction of the boat at this stage would have been a very serious matter, since we probably would have found it impossible to leave the cove except by sea. The cliffs and glaciers around offered no practicable path towards the head of the bay. I arranged for one-hour watches during the remainder of the night and then took Crean's place among the sleeping men and got some sleep before the dawn came.

The sea went down in the early hours of the morning

(May 11), and after sunrise we were able to set about getting the boat ashore, first bracing ourselves for the task with another meal. We were all weak still. We cut off the topsides and took out all the movable gear. Then we waited for Byron's "great ninth wave," and when it lifted the *James Caird* in we held her and, by dint of great exertion, worked her round broadside to the sea. Inch by inch we dragged her up until we reached the fringe of the tussock grass and knew that the boat was above highwater mark. The rise of the tide was about five feet, and at spring tide the water must have reached almost to the edge of the tussock grass. The completion of this job removed our immediate anxieties, and we were free to examine our surroundings and plan the next move. The day was bright and clear.

King Haakon Bay is an eight-mile sound penetrating the coast of South Georgia in an easterly direction. We had noticed that the northern and southern sides of the sound were formed by steep mountain ranges, their flanks furrowed by mighty glaciers, the outlets of the great ice sheet of the interior. It was obvious that these glaciers and the precipitous slopes of the mountains barred our way inland from the cove. We must sail to the head of the sound. Swirling clouds and mist wreaths had obscured our view of the sound when we were entering, but glimpses of snow slopes had given us hope that an overland journey could be begun from that point. A few patches of very rough, tussocky land, dotted with little tarns, lay between the glaciers along the foot of the mountains, which were heavily scarred with scree slopes. Several magnificent peaks and crags gazed out across their snowy domains to the sparkling waters of the sound.

Our cove lay a little inside the southern headland of King Haakon Bay. A narrow break in the cliffs, which were about a hundred feet high at this point, formed the entrance to the cove. The cliffs continued inside the cove on each side and

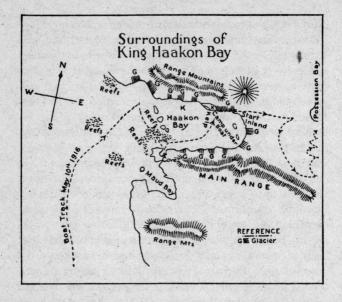

merged into a hill which descended at a steep slope to the boulder beach. The slope, which carried tussock grass, was not continuous. It eased at two points into little peaty swamp terraces dotted with frozen pools and drained by two small streams. Our cave was a recess in the cliff on the lefthand end of the beach. The rocky face of the cliff was undercut at this point, and the shingle thrown up by the waves formed a steep slope, which we reduced to about one in six by scraping the stones away from the inside. Later we strewed the rough floor with the dead, nearly dry underleaves of the tussock grass, so as to form a slightly soft bed for our sleeping bags. Water had trickled down the face of the cliff and formed long icicles, which hung down in front of the cave to the length of about fifteen feet. These icicles provided shelter, and when we had spread our sails below them, with the assistance of oars, we had quarters that, in the circumstances, had to be regarded as reasonably comfortable. The camp at least was dry, and we moved our gear there with confidence. We built a fireplace and arranged our sleeping bags and blankets around it. The cave was about 8 ft. deep and 12 ft. wide at the entrance.

While the camp was being arranged Crean and I climbed the tussock slope behind the beach and reached the top of a headland overlooking the sound. There we found the nests of albatrosses, and, much to our delight, the nests contained young birds. The fledglings were fat and lusty, and we had no hesitation about deciding that they were destined to die at an early age. Our most pressing anxiety at this stage was a shortage of fuel for the cooker. We had rations for ten more days, and we knew now that we could get birds for food; but if we were to have hot meals we must secure fuel. The store of petroleum carried in the boat was running very low, and it seemed necessary to keep some quantity for use on the over-land journey that lay ahead of us. A sea elephant or a seal would have provided fuel as well as food, but we could see none in the neighborhood. During the morning we started a fire in the cave with wood from the topsides of the boat, and though the dense smoke from the damp sticks inflamed our tired eyes, the warmth and the prospect of hot food were ample compensation. Crean was cook that day, and I suggested to him that he should wear his goggles, which he happened to have brought with him. The goggles helped him a great deal as he bent over the fire and tended the stew. And what a stew it was! The young albatrosses weighed about fourteen pounds each fresh killed, and we estimated that they weighed at least six pounds each when cleaned and dressed for the pot. Four birds went into the pot for six men, with a Bovril ration for thickening. The flesh was white and succulent, and the bones, not fully formed, almost melted in our mouths. That was a memorable meal. When we had eaten our fill, we dried our tobacco in the embers of the fire and smoked

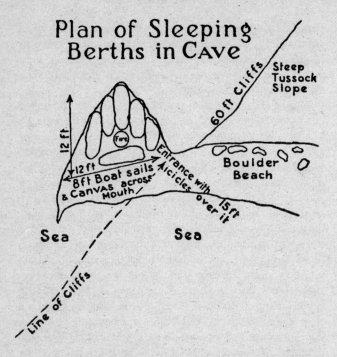

Plan of Sleeping
Berths in Cᴀᴠᴇ

contentedly. We made an attempt to dry our clothes, which
were soaked with salt water, but did not meet with much success. We could not afford to have a fire except for cooking
purposes until blubber or driftwood had come our way.

The final stage of the journey had still to be attempted. I
realized that the condition of the party generally, and particularly of McNeish and Vincent, would prevent us putting to
sea again except under pressure of dire necessity. Our boat,
moreover, had been weakened by the cutting away of the
topsides, and I doubted if we could weather the island. We
were still 150 miles away from Stromness whaling station
by sea. The alternative was to attempt the crossing of the
island. If we could not get over, then we must try to secure

enough food and fuel to keep us alive through the winter, but this possibility was scarcely thinkable. Over on Elephant Island twenty-two men were waiting for the relief that we alone could secure for them. Their plight was worse than ours. We must push on somehow. Several days must elapse before our strength would be sufficiently recovered to allow us to row or sail the last nine miles up to the head of the bay. In the meantime we could make what preparations were possible and dry our clothes by taking advantage of every scrap of heat from the fires we lit for the cooking of our meals. We turned in early that night, and I remember that I dreamed of the great wave and aroused my companions with a shout of warning as I saw with half-awakened eyes the towering cliff on the opposite side of the cove.

Shortly before midnight a gale sprang up suddenly from the northeast with rain and sleet showers. It brought quantities of glacier ice into the cove, and by 2 a.m. (May 12) our little harbor was filled with ice, which surged to and fro in the swell and pushed its way on to the beach. We had solid rock beneath our feet and could watch without anxiety. When daylight came rain was falling heavily, and the temperature was the highest we had experienced for many months. The icicles overhanging our cave were melting down in streams and we had to move smartly when passing in and out lest we should be struck by falling lumps. A fragment weighing fifteen or twenty pounds crashed down while we were having breakfast. We found that a big hole had been burned in the bottom of Worsley's reindeer sleeping bag during the night. Worsley had been awakened by a burning sensation in his feet, and had asked the men near him if his bag was all right; they looked and could see nothing wrong. We were all superficially frostbitten about the feet, and this condition caused the extremities to burn painfully, while at the same time sensation was lost in the skin. Worsley thought that the uncomfortable heat of his feet was due to

the frostbites, and he stayed in his bag and presently went
to sleep again. He discovered when he turned out in the
morning that the tussock grass which we had laid on the
floor of the cave had smouldered outwards from the fire and
had actually burned a large hole in the bag beneath his feet.
Fortunately, his feet were not harmed.

Our party spent a quiet day, attending to clothing and
gear, checking stores, eating and resting. Some more of the
young albatrosses made a noble end in our pot. The birds
were nesting on a small plateau above the righthand end of
our beach. We had previously discovered that when we were
landing from the boat on the night of May 10 we had lost
the rudder. The *James Caird* had been bumping heavily
astern as we were scrambling ashore, and evidently the rudder was then knocked off. A careful search of the beach and
the rocks within our reach failed to reveal the missing article. This was a serious loss, even if the voyage to the head
of the sound could be made in good weather. At dusk the
ice in the cove was rearing and crashing on the beach. It had
forced up a ridge of stones close to where the *James Caird*
lay at the edge of the tussock grass. Some pieces of ice were
driven right up to the canvas wall at the front of our cave.
Fragments lodged within two feet of Vincent, who had the
lowest sleeping place, and within four feet of our fire. Crean
and McCarthy had brought down six more of the young
albatrosses in the afternoon, so we were well supplied with
fresh food. The air temperature that night probably was not
lower than 38° or 40° Fahr., and we were rendered uncomfortable in our cramped sleeping quarters by the unaccustomed warmth. Our feelings towards our neighbors
underwent a change. When the temperature was below 20°
Fahr. we could not get too close to one another—every man
wanted to cuddle against his neighbor; but let the temperature rise a few degrees and the warmth of another man's
body ceased to be a blessing. The ice and the waves had a
voice of menace that night, but I heard it only in my dreams.

The bay was still filled with ice on the morning of Saturday, May 13, but the tide took it all away in the afternoon. Then a strange thing happened. The rudder, with all the broad Atlantic to sail in and the coasts of two continents to search for a resting place, came bobbing back into our cove. With anxious eyes we watched it as it advanced, receded again, and then advanced once more under the capricious influence of wind and wave. Nearer and nearer it came as we waited on the shore, oars in hand, and at last we were able to seize it. Surely a remarkable salvage! The day was bright and clear; our clothes were drying and our strength was returning. Running water made a musical sound down the tussock slope and among the boulders. We carried our blankets up the hill and tried to dry them in the breeze 300 ft. above sea level. In the afternoon we began to prepare the *James Caird* for the journey to the head of King Haakon Bay. A noon observation on this day gave our latitude as 54° 10′ 47″ S., but according to the German chart the position should have been 54° 12′ S. Probably Worsley's observation was the more accurate. We were able to keep the fire alight until we went to sleep that night, for while climbing the rocks above the cove I had seen at the foot of a cliff a broken spar, which had been thrown up by the waves. We could reach this spar by climbing down the cliff, and with a reserve supply of fuel thus in sight we could afford to burn the fragments of the *James Caird*'s topsides more freely.

During the morning of this day (May 13) Worsley and I tramped across the hills in a northeasterly direction with the object of getting a view of the sound and possibly gathering some information that would be useful to us in the next stage of our journey. It was exhausting work, but after covering about 2½ miles in two hours, we were able to look east, up the bay. We could not see very much of the country that we would have to cross in order to reach the whaling station on the other side of the island. We had passed several brooks and frozen tarns, and at a point where we had to take to the beach on the shore of the sound we found some wreckage—an 18-ft. pine spar (probably part of a ship's topmast), several pieces of timber, and a little model of a ship's hull, evidently a child's top. We wondered what tragedy that pitiful little plaything indicated. We encountered also some gentoo penguins and a young sea elephant, which Worsley killed.

When we got back to the cave at 3 p.m., tired, hungry, but rather pleased with ourselves, we found a splendid meal of stewed albatross chicken waiting for us. We had carried a quantity of blubber and the sea elephant's liver in our blouses, and we produced our treasures as a surprise for the men. Rough climbing on the way back to camp had nearly persuaded us to throw the stuff away, but we had held on (regardless of the condition of our already sorely tried clothing), and had our reward at the camp. The long bay had been a magnificent sight, even to eyes that had dwelt on grandeur long enough and were hungry for the simple, familiar things of everyday life. Its green-blue waters were being beaten to fury by the northwesterly gale. The mountains, "stern peaks that dared the stars," peered through the mists, and between them huge glaciers poured down from the great ice slopes and fields that lay behind. We counted twelve glaciers and heard every few minutes the reverberating roar caused by masses of ice calving from the parent streams.

On May 14 we made our preparations for an early start on the following day if the weather held fair. We expected to be able to pick up the remains of the sea elephant on our way up the sound. All hands were recovering from the chafing caused by our wet clothes during the boat journey. The insides of our legs had suffered severely, and for some time after landing in the cove we found movement extremely uncomfortable. We paid our last visit to the nests of the albatrosses, which were situated on a little undulating plateau above the cave amid tussocks, snow patches, and little frozen tarns. Each nest consisted of a mound over a foot high of tussock grass, roots, and a little earth. The albatross lays one egg and very rarely two. The chicks, which are hatched in January, are fed on the nest by the parent birds for almost seven months before they take to the sea and fend for themselves. Up to four months of age the chicks are beautiful white masses of downy fluff, but when we arrived on the scene their plumage was almost complete. Very often one of the parent birds was on guard near the nest. We did not enjoy attacking these birds, but our hunger knew no law. They tasted so very good and assisted our recuperation to such an extent that each time we killed one of them we felt a little less remorseful.

May 15 was a great day. We made our hoosh at 7:30 a.m. Then we loaded up the boat and gave her a flying launch down the steep beach into the surf. Heavy rain had fallen in the night and a gusty northwesterly wind was now blowing, with misty showers. The *James Caird* headed to the sea as if anxious to face the battle of the waves once more. We passed through the narrow mouth of the cove with the ugly rocks and waving kelp close on either side, turned to the east, and sailed merrily up the bay as the sun broke through the mists and made the tossing waters sparkle around us. We were a curious-looking party on that bright morning, but we were feeling happy. We even broke into song, and, but for our Robinson Crusoe appearance, a casual observer might have taken us for a picnic party sailing in a Norwegian fiord or one of the beautiful sounds of the west coast of New Zealand. The wind blew fresh and strong, and a small sea broke on the coast as we advanced. The surf was sufficient to have endangered the boat if we had attempted to land where the carcass of the sea elephant was lying, so we decided to go on to the head of the bay without risking anything, particularly as we were likely to find sea elephants on the upper beaches. The big creatures have a habit of seeking peaceful quarters protected from the waves. We had hopes, too, of finding penguins. Our expectation as far as the sea elephants were concerned was not at fault. We heard the roar of the bulls as we neared the head of the bay, and soon afterwards saw the great unwieldy forms of the beasts lying on a shelving beach towards the bay head. We rounded a high, glacier-worn bluff on the north side, and at 12:30 p.m. we ran the boat ashore on a low beach of sand and pebbles, with tussock growing above highwater mark. There were hundreds of sea elephants lying about, and our anxieties with regard to food disappeared. Meat and blubber enough to feed our party for years was in sight. Our landing place was about a mile and a half west of the northeast corner of the bay. Just east of us was a glacier snout ending on the beach but giving a passage towards the head of the bay, except at high water or when a very heavy surf was running. A cold, drizzling rain had begun to fall, and we provided ourselves with shelter as quickly as possible. We hauled the *James Caird* up above highwater mark and turned her over just to the lee or east side of the bluff. The spot was separated from the mountainside by a low morainic bank, rising twenty or thirty feet above sea level. Soon we had converted the boat into a very comfortable cabin *à la* Peggotty, turfing it round with tussocks, which we dug up with knives. One side of the *James Caird* rested on stones so as to afford a low entrance, and when we had finished she looked as though she had grown there. McCarthy entered into this work with great spirit. A sea elephant provided us with fuel and meat, and that evening found a well-fed and fairly contented party at rest in Peggotty Camp.

Our camp, as I have said, lay on the north side of King Haakon Bay near the head. Our path towards the whaling stations led round the seaward end of the snouted glacier on the east side of the camp and up a snow slope that appeared to lead to a pass in the great Allardyce Range, which runs northwest and southeast and forms the main backbone of South Georgia. The range dipped opposite the bay into a well-defined pass from east to west. An ice sheet covered most of the interior, filling the valleys and disguising the configuration of the land, which, indeed, showed only in big rocky ridges, peaks, and nunataks. When we looked up the pass from Peggotty Camp the country to the left appeared to offer two easy paths through to the opposite coast, but we knew that the island was uninhabited at that point (Possession Bay). We had to turn our attention farther east, and it was impossible from the camp to learn much of the conditions that would confront us on the overland journey. I planned to climb to the pass and then be guided by the configuration of the country in the selection of a route eastward to Stromness Bay, where the whaling stations were established in the minor bays, Leith, Husvik, and Stromness. A range of mountains with precipitous slopes, forbidding peaks, and large glaciers lay immediately to the south of King Haakon Bay and seemed to form a continuation of the main range. Between this secondary range and the pass above our camp a great snow upland sloped up to the inland ice sheet and reached a rocky ridge that stretched athwart our path and seemed to bar the way. This ridge was a right-angled offshoot from the main ridge. Its chief features were four rocky peaks with spaces between that looked from a distance as though they might prove to be passes.

The weather was bad on Tuesday, May 16, and we stayed under the boat nearly all day. The quarters were cramped but gave full protection from the weather, and we regarded our little cabin with a great deal of satisfaction. Abundant meals of sea-elephant steak and liver increased our contentment. McNeish reported during the day that he had seen rats feeding on the scraps, but this interesting statement was not verified. One would not expect to find rats at such a spot, but there was a bare possibility that they had landed from a wreck and managed to survive the very rigorous conditions.

A fresh west-southwesterly breeze was blowing on the following morning (Wednesday, May 17), with misty squalls, sleet, and rain. I took Worsley with me on a pioneer journey to the west with the object of examining the country to be traversed at the beginning of the overland journey. We went round the seaward end of the snouted glacier, and after tramping about a mile over stony ground and snow-coated debris, we crossed some big ridges of scree and moraines. We found that there was good going for a sledge as far as the northeast corner of the bay, but did not get much information regarding the conditions farther on owing to the view becoming obscured by a snow squall. We waited a quarter of an hour for the weather to clear but were forced to turn back without having seen more of the country. I had satisfied myself, however, that we could reach a good snow slope leading apparently to the inland ice. Worsley reckoned from the chart that the distance from our camp to Husvik, on an east magnetic course, was seventeen geographical miles, but we could not expect to follow a direct line. The carpenter started making a sledge for use on the overland journey. The materials at his disposal were limited in quantity and scarcely suitable in quality.

We overhauled our gear on Thursday, May 18, and hauled our sledge to the lower edge of the snouted glacier. The vehicle proved heavy and cumbrous. We had to lift it empty over bare patches of rock along the shore, and I realized that it would be too heavy for three men to manage amid the snow plains, glaciers, and peaks of the interior. Worsley and Crean were coming with me, and after consultation we decided to leave the sleeping bags behind us and make the journey in very light marching order. We would take three days' provisions for each man in the form of sledging ration and biscuit. The food was to be packed in three socks, so that each member of the party could carry his own supply. Then we were to take the Primus lamp filled with oil, the small cooker, the carpenter's adze (for use as an ice axe), and the alpine rope, which made a total length of fifty feet when knotted. We might have to lower ourselves down steep slopes or cross crevassed glaciers. The filled lamp would provide six hot meals, which would consist of sledging ration boiled up with biscuit. There were two boxes of matches left, one full and the other partially used. We left the full box with the men at the camp and took the second box, which contained forty-eight matches. I was unfortunate as regarded footgear, since I had given away my heavy Burberry boots on the floe, and had now a comparatively light pair in poor condition. The carpenter assisted me by putting several screws in the sole of each boot with the object of providing a grip on the ice. The screws came out of the *James Caird*.

We turned in early that night, but sleep did not come to me. My mind was busy with the task of the following day. The weather was clear and the outlook for an early start in the morning was good. We were going to leave a weak party behind us in the camp. Vincent was still in the same condition, and he could not march. McNeish was pretty well broken up. The two men were not capable of managing for themselves and McCarthy must stay to look after them. He might have a difficult task if we failed to reach the whaling station. The distance to Husvik, according to the chart, was no more than seventeen geographical miles in a direct line, but we had very scanty knowledge of the conditions of the interior. No man had ever penetrated a mile from the coast of South Georgia at any point, and the whalers I knew regarded the country as inaccessible. During that day, while we were walking to the snouted glacier, we had seen three wild duck flying towards the head of the bay from the eastward. I hoped that the presence of these birds indicated tussock land and not snow fields and glaciers in the interior, but the hope was not a very bright one.

We turned out at 2 a.m. on the Friday morning and had

our hoosh ready an hour later. The full moon was shining in a practically cloudless sky, its rays reflected gloriously from the pinnacles and crevassed ice of the adjacent glaciers. The huge peaks of the mountains stood in bold relief against the sky and threw dark shadows on the waters of the sound. There was no need for delay, and we made a start as soon as we had eaten our meal. McNeish walked about 200 yds. with us; he could do no more. Then we said good-bye and he turned back to the camp. The first task was to get round the edge of the snouted glacier, which had points like fingers projecting towards the sea. The waves were reaching the points of these fingers, and we had to rush from one across to another when the waters receded. We soon reached the east side of the glacier and noticed its great activity at this point. Changes had occurred within the preceding twenty-four hours. Some huge pieces had broken off, and the masses of mud and stone that were being driven before the advancing ice showed movement. The glacier was like a gigantic plough driving irresistibly towards the sea.

Lying on the beach beyond the glacier was wreckage that told of many ill-fated ships. We noticed stanchions of teak-wood, liberally carved, that must have come from ships of the older type; ironbound timbers with the iron almost rusted through; battered barrels and all the usual debris of the ocean. We had difficulties and anxieties of our own, but as we passed that graveyard of the sea we thought of the many tragedies written in the wave-worn fragments of lost vessels. We did not pause, and soon we were ascending a snow slope, heading due east on the last lap of our long trail.

The snow surface was disappointing. Two days before we had been able to move rapidly on hard, packed snow; now we sank over our ankles at each step and progress was slow. After two hours' steady climbing we were 2500 ft. above sea level. The weather continued fine and calm, and as the ridges drew nearer and the western coast of the island spread out below, the bright moonlight showed us that the interior was broken tremendously. High peaks, impassable cliffs, steep snow slopes, and sharply descending glaciers were prominent features in all directions, with stretches of snow plain overlaying the ice sheet of the interior. The slope we were ascending mounted to a ridge and our course lay direct to the top. The moon, which proved a good friend during this journey, threw a long shadow at one point and told us that the surface was broken in our path. Warned in time, we avoided a huge hole capable of swallowing an army. The bay was now about three miles away, and the continued roaring of a big glacier at the head of the bay came to our ears. This glacier, which we had noticed during the stay at Peggotty Camp, seemed to be calving almost continuously.

I had hoped to get a view of the country ahead of us from the top of the slope, but as the surface became more level beneath our feet, a thick fog drifted down. The moon became obscured and produced a diffused light that was more trying than darkness, since it illuminated the fog without guiding our steps. We roped ourselves together as a precaution against holes, crevasses, and precipices, and I broke trail through the soft snow. With almost the full length of the rope between myself and the last man we were able to steer an approximately straight course, since, if I veered to the right or the left when marching into the blank wall of the fog, the last man on the rope could shout a direction. So, like a ship with its "port," "starboard," "steady," we tramped through the fog for the next two hours.

Then, as daylight came, the fog thinned and lifted, and from an elevation of about 3000 ft. we looked down on what seemed to be a huge frozen lake with its farther shores still obscured by the fog. We halted there to eat a bit of biscuit while we discussed whether we would go down and cross the flat surface of the lake, or keep on the ridge we had already reached. I decided to go down, since the lake lay on our course. After an hour of comparatively easy travel through the snow we noticed the thin beginnings of crevasses. Soon they were increasing in size and showing fractures, indicating that we were traveling on a glacier. As the daylight brightened the fog dissipated; the lake could be seen more clearly, but still we could not discover its east shore. A little later the fog lifted completely, and then we saw that our lake stretched to the horizon, and realized suddenly that we were looking down upon the open sea on the east coast of the island. The slight pulsation at the shore showed that the sea was not even frozen; it was the bad light that had deceived us. Evidently we were at the top of Possession Bay, and the island at that point could not be more than five miles across from the head of King Haakon Bay. Our rough chart was inaccurate. There was nothing for it but to start up the glacier again. That was about seven o'clock in the morning, and by nine o'clock we had more than recovered our lost ground. We regained the ridge and then struck southeast, for the chart showed that two more bays indented the coast before Stromness. It was comforting to realize that we would have the eastern water in sight during our journey, although we could see there was no way around the shoreline owing to steep cliffs and glaciers. Men lived in houses lit by electric light on the east coast. News of the outside world waited us there, and, above all, the east coast meant for us the means of rescuing the twenty-two men we had left on Elephant Island.

CHAPTER X

ACROSS SOUTH GEORGIA

THE SUN ROSE in the sky with every appearance of a fine day, and we grew warmer as we toiled through the soft snow. Ahead of us lay the ridges and spurs of a range of mountains, the transverse range that we had noticed from the bay. We were traveling over a gently rising plateau, and at the end of an hour we found ourselves growing uncomfortably hot. Years before, on an earlier expedition, I had declared that I would never again growl at the heat of the sun, and my resolution had been strengthened during the boat journey. I called it to mind as the sun beat fiercely on the blinding white snow slope. After passing an area of crevasses we paused for our first meal. We dug a hole in the snow about three feet deep with the adze and put the Primus into it. There was no wind at the moment, but a gust might come suddenly. A hot hoosh was soon eaten and we plodded on towards a sharp ridge between two of the peaks already mentioned. By 11 a.m. we were almost at the crest. The slope had become precipitous and it was necessary to cut steps as we advanced. The adze proved an excellent instrument for this purpose, a blow sufficing to provide a foothold. Anxiously but hopefully I cut the last few steps and stood upon the razorback, while the other men held the rope and waited for my news. The outlook was disappointing. I looked down a sheer precipice to a chaos of crumpled ice 1500 ft. below. There was no way down for us. The country to the east was a great snow upland, sloping upwards for a distance of seven or eight miles to a height of over 4000 ft. To the north it fell away steeply in glaciers into the bays, and to the south it was broken by huge outfalls from the inland ice sheet. Our path lay between the glaciers and the outfalls, but first we had to descend from the ridge on which we stood.

Cutting steps with the adze, we moved in a lateral direction round the base of a dolomite, which blocked our view to the north. The same precipice confronted us. Away to the northeast there appeared to be a snow slope that might give a path to the lower country, and so we retraced our steps down the long slope that had taken us three hours to climb. We were at the bottom in an hour. We were now feeling the strain of the unaccustomed marching. We had done little walking since January and our muscles were out of tune. Skirting the base of the mountain above us, we came to a gigantic bergschrund, a mile and a half long and 1000 ft. deep. This tremendous gully, cut in the snow and ice by the fierce winds blowing round the mountain, was semicircular in form, and it ended in a gentle incline. We passed through it, under the towering precipice of ice, and at the far end we had another meal and a short rest. This was at 12:30 p.m. Half a pot of steaming Bovril ration warmed us up, and when we marched again ice inclines at angles of 45 degrees did not look quite as formidable as before.

Once more we started for the crest. After another weary climb we reached the top. The snow lay thinly on blue ice at the ridge, and we had to cut steps over the last fifty yards. The same precipice lay below, and my eyes searched vainly for a way down. The hot sun had loosened the snow, which was now in a treacherous condition, and we had to pick our way carefully. Looking back, we could see that a fog was rolling up behind us and meeting in the valleys a fog that was coming up from the east. The creeping grey clouds were a plain warning that we must get down to lower levels before becoming enveloped.

The ridge was studded with peaks, which prevented us getting a clear view either to the right or to the left. The situation in this respect seemed no better at other points within our reach, and I had to decide that our course lay back the way we had come. The afternoon was wearing on and the fog was rolling up ominously from the west. It was of the utmost importance for us to get down into the next valley before dark. We were now up 4500 ft. and the night temperature at that elevation would be very low. We had no tent and no sleeping bags, and our clothes had endured much rough usage and had weathered many storms during the last ten months. In the distance, down the valley below us, we could see tussock grass close to the shore, and if we could get down it might be possible to dig out a hole in one of the lower snowbanks, line it with dry grass, and make ourselves fairly comfortable for the night. Back we went, and after a detour we reached the top of another ridge in the fading light. After a glance over the top I turned to the anxious faces of the two men behind me and said, "Come on, boys." Within a minute they stood beside me on the ice ridge. The surface fell away at a sharp incline in front of us, but it merged into a snow slope. We could not see the bottom clearly owing to mist and bad light, and the possibility of the slope ending in a sheer fall occurred to us; but the fog that was creeping up behind allowed no time for hesitation. We descended slowly at first, cutting steps in the hard snow; then the surface became softer, indicating that the gradient was less severe. There could be no turning back now, so we unroped and slid in the fashion of youthful days. When we stopped on a snow bank at the foot of the slope we found that we had descended at least 900 ft. in two or three minutes. We looked back and saw the grey fingers of the fog appearing on the ridge, as though reaching after the intruders into untrodden wilds. But we had escaped.

The country to the east was an ascending snow upland dividing the glaciers of the north coast from the outfalls of the south. We had seen from the top that our course lay between two huge masses of crevasses, and we thought that the road ahead lay clear. This belief and the increasing cold made us abandon the idea of camping. We had another meal at 6 p.m. A little breeze made cooking difficult in spite of the shelter provided for the cooker by a hole. Crean was the cook, and Worsley and I lay on the snow to windward of the lamp so as to break the wind with our bodies. The meal over, we started up the long, gentle ascent. Night was upon us, and for an hour we plodded along in almost complete darkness, watching warily for signs of crevasses. Then about 8 p.m. a glow which we had seen behind the jagged peaks resolved itself into the full moon, which rose ahead of us and made a silver pathway for our feet. Along that pathway in the wake of the moon we advanced in safety, with the shadows cast by the edges of crevasses showing black on either side of us. Onwards and upwards through soft snow we marched, resting now and then on hard patches which had revealed themselves by glittering ahead of us in the white light. By midnight we were again at an elevation of about 4000 ft. Still we were following the light, for as the moon swung round towards the northeast our path curved in that direction. The friendly moon seemed to pilot our weary feet. We could have had no better guide. If in bright daylight we had made that march we would have followed the course that was traced for us that night.

Midnight found us approaching the edge of a great snow field, pierced by isolated nunataks which cast long shadows like black rivers across the white expanse. A gentle slope to the northeast lured our all-too-willing feet in that direction. We thought that at the base of the slope lay Stromness Bay. After we had descended about 300 ft. a thin wind began to attack us. We had now been on the march for over twenty hours, only halting for our occasional meals. Wisps of cloud drove over the high peaks to the southward, warning us that wind and snow were likely to come. After 1 a.m. we cut a pit in the snow, piled up loose snow around it, and started the Primus again. The hot food gave us another renewal of energy. Worsley and Crean sang their old songs when the Primus was going merrily. Laughter was in our hearts, though not on our parched and cracked lips.

We were up and away again within half an hour, still downward to the coast. We felt almost sure now that we were above Stromness Bay. A dark object down at the foot of the slope looked like Mutton Island, which lies off Husvik. I suppose our desires were giving wings to our fancies, for we pointed out joyfully various landmarks revealed by the now vagrant light of the moon, whose friendly face was cloud-swept. Our high hopes were soon shattered. Crevasses warned us that we were on another glacier, and soon we looked down almost to the seaward edge of the great riven ice mass. I knew there was no glacier in Stromness and realized that this must be Fortuna Glacier. The disappointment was severe. Back we turned and tramped up the glacier again, not directly tracing our steps but working at a tangent to the southeast. We were very tired.

At 5 a.m. we were at the foot of the rocky spurs of the range. We were tired, and the wind that blew down from the heights was chilling us. We decided to get down under the lee of a rock for a rest. We put our sticks and the adze on the snow, sat down on them as close to one another as possible, and put our arms round each other. The wind was bringing a little drift with it and the white dust lay on our clothes. I thought that we might be able to keep warm and have half an hour's rest this way. Within a minute my two companions were fast asleep. I realized that it would be disastrous if we all slumbered together, for sleep under such conditions merges into death. After five minutes I shook them into consciousness again, told them that they had slept for half an hour, and gave the word for a fresh start. We were so stiff that for the first two or three hundred yards we marched with our knees bent. A jagged line of peaks with a gap like a

broken tooth confronted us. This was the ridge that runs in a
southerly direction from Fortuna Bay, and our course eastward to Stromness lay across it. A very steep slope led up to
the ridge and an icy wind burst through the gap.

We went through the gap at 6 a.m. with anxious hearts as
well as weary bodies. If the farther slope had proved impassable our situation would have been almost desperate;
but the worst was turning to the best for us. The twisted,
wave-like rock formations of Husvik Harbor appeared right
ahead in the opening of dawn. Without a word we shook
hands with one another. To our minds the journey was over,
though as a matter of fact twelve miles of difficult country
had still to be traversed. A gentle snow slope descended at
our feet towards a valley that separated our ridge from the
hills immediately behind Husvik, and as we stood gazing
Worsley said solemnly, "Boss, it looks too good to be true!"
Down we went, to be checked presently by the sight of water
2500 ft. below. We could see the little wave ripples on the
black beach, penguins strutting to and fro, and dark objects
that looked like seals lolling lazily on the sand. This was an
eastern arm of Fortuna Bay, separated by the ridge from the
arm we had seen below us during the night. The slope we
were traversing appeared to end in a precipice above this
beach. But our revived spirits were not to be damped by
difficulties on the last stage of the journey, and we camped
cheerfully for breakfast. While Worsley and Crean were digging a hole for the lamp and starting the cooker I climbed a
ridge above us, cutting steps with the adze, in order to secure an extended view of the country below. At 6:30 a.m. I
thought I heard the sound of a steam whistle. I dared not be
certain, but I knew that the men at the whaling station would
be called from their beds about that time. Descending to the
camp I told the others, and in intense excitement we
watched the chronometer for seven o'clock, when the whalers would be summoned to work. Right to the minute the

steam whistle came to us, borne clearly on the wind across the intervening miles of rock and snow. Never had any one of us heard sweeter music. It was the first sound created by outside human agency that had come to our ears since we left Stromness Bay in December 1914. That whistle told us that men were living near, that ships were ready, and that within a few hours we should be on our way back to Elephant Island to the rescue of the men waiting there under the watch and ward of Wild. It was a moment hard to describe. Pain and ache, boat journeys, marches, hunger and fatigue seemed to belong to the limbo of forgotten things, and there remained only the perfect contentment that comes of work accomplished.

My examination of the country from a higher point had not provided definite information, and after descending I put the situation before Worsley and Crean. Our obvious course lay down a snow slope in the direction of Husvik. "Boys," I said, "this snow slope seems to end in a precipice, but perhaps there is no precipice. If we don't go down we shall have to make a detour of at least five miles before we reach level going. What shall it be?" They both replied at once. "Try the slope." So we started away again downwards. We abandoned the Primus lamp, now empty, at the breakfast camp and carried with us one ration and a biscuit each. The deepest snow we had yet encountered clogged our feet, but we plodded downward, and after descending about 500 ft., reducing our altitude to 2000 ft. above sea level, we thought we saw the way clear ahead. A steep gradient of blue ice was the next obstacle. Worsley and Crean got a firm footing in a hole excavated with the adze and then lowered me as I cut steps until the full 50 ft. of our alpine rope was out. Then I made a hole big enough for the three of us, and the other two men came down the steps. My end of the rope was anchored to the adze and I had settled myself in the hole braced for a strain in case they slipped. When we all stood

in the second hole I went down again to make more steps,
and in this laborious fashion we spent two hours descending
about 500 ft. Half way down we had to strike away diago-
nally to the left, for we noticed that the fragments of ice
loosened by the adze were taking a leap into space at the
bottom of the slope. Eventually we got off the steep ice,
very gratefully, at a point where some rocks protruded, and
we could see then that there was a perilous precipice directly
below the point where we had started to cut steps. A slide
down a slippery slope, with the adze and our cooker going
ahead, completed this descent, and incidentally did considerable damage to our much-tried trousers.

When we picked ourselves up at the bottom we were not
more than 1500 ft. above the sea. The slope was comparatively easy. Water was running beneath the snow, making
"pockets" between the rocks that protruded above the white
surface. The shells of snow over these pockets were traps
for our feet; but we scrambled down, and presently came to
patches of tussock. A few minutes later we reached the
sandy beach. The tracks of some animals were to be seen,
and we were puzzled until I remembered that reindeer,
brought from Norway, had been placed on the island and
now ranged along the lower land of the eastern coast. We
did not pause to investigate. Our minds were set upon reaching the haunts of man, and at our best speed we went along
the beach to another rising ridge of tussock. Here we saw
the first evidence of the proximity of man, whose work, as
is so often the case, was one of destruction. A recently killed
seal was lying there, and presently we saw several other bodies bearing the marks of bullet wounds. I learned that men
from the whaling station at Stromness sometimes go round
to Fortuna Bay by boat to shoot seals.

Noon found us well up the slope on the other side of the
bay working east-southeast, and half an hour later we were
on a flat plateau, with one more ridge to cross before we

descended into Husvik. I was leading the way over this plateau when I suddenly found myself up to my knees in water
and quickly sinking deeper through the snow crust. I flung
myself down and called to the others to do the same, so as
to distribute our weight on the treacherous surface. We were
on top of a small lake, snow-covered. After lying still for a
few moments, we got to our feet and walked delicately, like
Agag, for 200 yds., until a rise in the surface showed us that
we were clear of the lake.

At 1:30 p.m. we climbed round a final ridge and saw a
little steamer, a whaling boat, entering the bay 2500 ft.
below. A few moments later, as he hurried forward, the masts
of a sailing ship lying at a wharf came in sight. Minute figures moving to and fro about the boats caught our gaze, and
then we saw the sheds and factory of Stromness whaling station. We paused and shook hands, a form of mutual congratulation that had seemed necessary on four other occasions in
the course of the expedition. The first time was when we
landed on Elephant Island, the second when we reached
South Georgia, and the third when we reached the ridge and
saw the snow slope stretching below on the first day of the
overland journey, then when we saw Husvik rocks.

Cautiously we started down the slope that led to warmth
and comfort. The last lap of the journey proved extraordinarily difficult. Vainly we searched for a safe, or a reasonably safe, way down from the steep ice-clad mountainside.
The sole possible pathway seemed to be a channel cut by
water running from the upland. Down through icy water we
followed the course of this stream. We were wet to the waist,
shivering, cold, and tired. Presently our ears detected an un-
welcome sound that might have been musical under other
conditions. It was the splashing of a waterfall, and we were
at the wrong end. When we reached the top of this fall we
peered over cautiously and discovered that there was a drop
of 25 or 30 ft., with impassable ice cliffs on both sides. To

go up again was scarcely thinkable in our utterly wearied condition. The way down was through the waterfall itself. We made fast one end of our rope to a boulder with some difficulty, due to the fact that the rocks had been worn smooth by the running water. Then Worsley and I lowered Crean, who was the heaviest man. He disappeared altogether in the falling water and came out gasping at the bottom. I went next, sliding down the rope, and Worsley, who was the lightest and most nimble member of the party, came last. At the bottom of the fall we were able to stand again on dry land. The rope could not be recovered. We had flung down the adze from the top of the fall and also the logbook and the cooker wrapped in one of our blouses. That was all, except our wet clothes, that we brought out of the Antarctic, which we had entered a year and a half before with well-found ship, full equipment, and high hopes. That was all of tangible things; but in memories we were rich. We had pierced the veneer of outside things. We had "suffered, starved, and triumphed, groveled down yet grasped at glory, grown bigger in the bigness of the whole." We had seen God in his splendors, heard the text that Nature renders. We had reached the naked soul of man.

Shivering with cold, yet with hearts light and happy, we set off towards the whaling station, now not more than a mile and a half distant. The difficulties of the journey lay behind us. We tried to straighten ourselves up a bit, for the thought that there might be women at the station made us painfully conscious of our uncivilized appearance. Our beards were long and our hair was matted. We were un-washed and the garments that we had worn for nearly a year without a change were tattered and stained. Three more un-pleasant-looking ruffians could hardly have been imagined. Worsley produced several safety pins from some corner of his garments and effected some temporary repairs that really emphasized his general disrepair. Down we hurried, and when quite close to the station we met two small boys ten or twelve years of age. I asked these lads where the manager's house was situated. They did not answer. They gave us one look—a comprehensive look that did not need to be repeated. Then they ran from us as fast as their legs would carry them. We reached the outskirts of the station and passed through the "digesting-house," which was dark inside. Emerging at the other end, we met an old man, who started as if he had seen the Devil himself and gave us no time to ask any question. He hurried away. This greeting was not friendly. Then we came to the wharf, where the man in charge stuck to his station. I asked him if Mr. Sorlle (the manager) was in the house.

"Yes," he said as he stared at us.

"We would like to see him," said I.

"Who are you?" he asked.

"We have lost our ship and come over the island," I replied.

"You have come over the island?" he said in a tone of entire disbelief.

The man went towards the manager's house and we followed him. I learned afterwards that he said to Mr. Sorlle: "There are three funny-looking men outside, who say they have come over the island and they know you. I have left them outside." A very necessary precaution from his point of view.

Mr. Sorlle came out to the door and said. "Well?"

"Don't you know me?" I said.

"I know your voice," he replied doubtfully. "You're the mate of the *Daisy*."

"My name is Shackleton," I said.

Immediately, he put out his hand and said, "Come in. Come in."

"Tell me, when was the war over?" I asked.

"The war is not over," he answered. "Millions are being killed. Europe is mad. The world is mad."

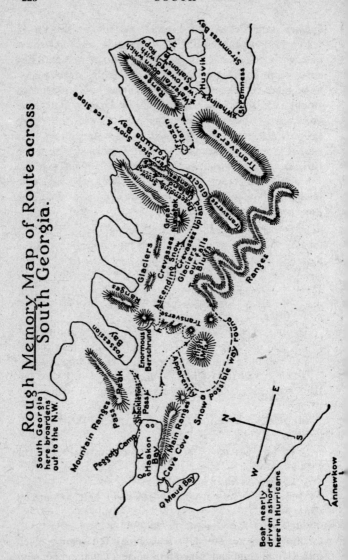

Rough Memory Map of Route across South Georgia.

Mr. Sorlle's hospitality had no bounds. He would scarcely let us wait to remove our freezing boots before he took us into his house and gave us seats in a warm and comfortable room. We were in no condition to sit in anybody's house until we had washed and got into clean clothes, but the kindness of the station manager was proof even against the unpleasantness of being in a room with us. He gave us coffee and cakes in the Norwegian fashion, and then showed us upstairs to the bathroom, where we shed our rags and scrubbed ourselves luxuriously.

Mr. Sorlle's kindness did not end with his personal care for the three wayfarers who had come to his door. While we were washing he gave orders for one of the whaling vessels to be prepared at once in order that it might leave that night for the other side of the island and pick up the three men there. The whalers knew King Haakon Bay, though they never worked on that side of the island. Soon we were clean again. Then we put on delightful new clothes supplied from the station stores and got rid of our superfluous hair. Within an hour or two we had ceased to be savages and had become civilized men again. Then came a splendid meal, while Mr. Sorlle told us of the arrangements he had made and we discussed plans for the rescue of the main party on Elephant Island.

I arranged that Worsley should go with the relief ship to show the exact spot where the carpenter and his two companions were camped, while I started to prepare for the relief of the party on Elephant Island. The whaling vessel that was going round to King Haakon Bay was expected back on the Monday morning, and was to call at Grytviken Harbor, the port from which we had sailed in December 1914, in order that the magistrate resident there might be informed of the fate of the *Endurance*. It was possible that letters were awaiting us there. Worsley went aboard the whaler at ten o'clock that night and turned in. The next day the relief ship

entered King Haakon Bay and he reached Peggotty Camp
in a boat. The three men were delighted beyond measure to
know that we had made the crossing in safety and that their
wait under the upturned *James Caird* was ended. Curiously
enough, they did not recognize Worsley, who had left them
a hairy, dirty ruffian and had returned his spruce and shaven
self. They thought he was one of the whalers. When one of
them asked why no member of the party had come round
with the relief, Worsley said, "What do you mean?" "We
thought the Boss or one of the others would come round,"
they explained. "What's the matter with you?" said Worsley. Then it suddenly dawned upon them that they were
talking to the man who had been their close companion for
a year and a half. Within a few minutes the whalers had
moved our bits of gear into their boat. They towed off the
James Caird and hoisted her to the deck of their ship. Then
they started on the return voyage. Just at dusk on Monday
afternoon they entered Stromness Bay, where the men of
the whaling station mustered on the beach to receive the
rescued party and to examine with professional interest the
boat we had navigated across 800 miles of the stormy ocean
they knew so well.

When I look back at those days I have no doubt that Providence guided us, not only across those snow fields, but
across the storm-white sea that separated Elephant Island
from our landing place on South Georgia. I know that during that long and racking march of thirty-six hours over the
unnamed mountains and glaciers of South Georgia it
seemed to me often that we were four, not three. I said nothing to my companions on the point, but afterwards Worsley
said to me, "Boss, I had a curious feeling on the march that
there was another person with us." Crean confessed to the
same idea. One feels "the dearth of human words, the
roughness of mortal speech" in trying to describe things
intangible, but a record of our journeys would be incomplete
without a reference to a subject very near to our hearts.

CHAPTER XI

THE RESCUE

OUR FIRST NIGHT at the whaling station was blissful. Crean and I shared a beautiful room in Mr. Sorlle's house, with electric light and two beds, warm and soft. We were so comfortable that we were unable to sleep. Late at night a steward brought us tea, bread and butter and cakes, and we lay in bed reveling in the luxury of it all. Outside a dense snowstorm, which started two hours after our arrival and lasted until the following day, was swirling and driving about the mountain slopes. We were thankful indeed that we had made a place of safety, for it would have gone hard with us if we had been out on the mountains that night. Deep snow lay everywhere when we got up the following morning.

After breakfast Mr. Sorlle took us round to Husvik in a motor launch. We were listening avidly to his account of the war and of all that had happened while we were out of the world of men. We were like men arisen from the dead to a world gone mad. Our minds accustomed themselves gradually to the tales of nations in arms, of deathless courage and unimagined slaughter, of a world conflict that had grown beyond all conceptions, of vast red battlefields in grimmest contrast with the frigid whiteness we had left behind us. The reader may not realize quite how difficult it was for us to envisage nearly two years of the most stupendous war of history. The locking of the armies in the trenches, the sinking of the *Lusitania,* the murder of Nurse Cavell, the use of poison gas and liquid fire, the submarine warfare, the Gallipoli campaign, the hundred other incidents of the war, almost stunned us at first, and then our minds began to compass the train of events and develop a perspective. I suppose our experience was unique. No other civilized men could have been as blankly ignorant of world-shaking happenings as we were when we reached Stromness Whaling Station.

I heard the first rumor of the *Aurora*'s misadventures in the Ross Sea from Mr. Sorlle. Our host could tell me very little. He had been informed that the *Aurora* had broken away from winter quarters in McMurdo Sound and reached New Zealand after a long drift, and that there was no news of the shore party. His information was indefinite as to details, and I had to wait until I reached the Falkland Islands some time later before getting a definite report concerning the *Aurora*. The rumor that had reached South Georgia, however, made it more than ever important that I should bring out the rest of the Weddell Sea party quickly, so as to free myself for whatever effort was required on the Ross Sea side.

When we reached Husvik that Sunday morning we were warmly greeted by the magistrate (Mr. Bernsten), whom I knew of old, and the other members of the little community. Moored in the harbor was one of the largest of the whalers, the *Southern Sky*, owned by an English company but now laid up for the winter. I had no means of getting into communication with the owners without dangerous delay, and on my accepting all responsibility Mr. Bernsten made arrangements for me to take this ship down to Elephant Island. I wrote out an agreement with Lloyd's for the insurance of the ship. Captain Thom, an old friend of the Expedition, happened to be in Husvik with his ship, the *Orwell,* loading oil for use in Britain's munition works, and he at once volunteered to come with us in any capacity. I asked him to come as captain of the *Southern Sky.* There was no difficulty about getting a crew. The whalers were eager to assist in the rescue of men in distress. They started work that Sunday to prepare and stow the ship. Parts of the engines were ashore, but willing hands made light labor. I purchased from the station stores all the stores and equipment required, including special comforts for the men we hoped to rescue, and by Tuesday morning the *Southern Sky* was ready to sail. I feel it is my duty as well as my pleasure to thank here the Norwegian whalers of South Georgia for the sympathetic hands they stretched out to us in our need. Among memories of kindness received in many lands sundered by the seas, the recollection of the hospitality and help given to me in South Georgia ranks high. There is a brotherhood of the sea. The men who go down to the sea in ships, serving and suffering, fighting their endless battle against the caprice of wind and ocean, bring into their own horizons the perils and troubles of their brother sailormen.

The *Southern Sky* was ready on Tuesday morning, and at nine o'clock we steamed out of the bay, while the whistles of the whaling station sounded a friendly farewell. We had forgathered aboard Captain Thom's ship on the Monday night with several whaling captains who were bringing up their sons to their own profession. They were "old stagers" with faces lined and seamed by the storms of half a century, and they were even more interested in the story of our voyage from Elephant Island than the younger generation was. They congratulated us on having accomplished a remarkable boat journey. I do not wish to belittle our success with the pride that apes humility. Under Providence we had overcome great difficulties and dangers, and it was pleasant to tell the tale to men who knew those sullen and treacherous southern seas.

McCarthy, McNeish, and Vincent had been landed on the Monday afternoon. They were already showing some signs of increasing strength under a regime of warm quarters and abundant food. The carpenter looked woefully thin after he had emerged from a bath. He must have worn a lot of clothes when he landed from the boat, and I did not realize how he had wasted till I saw him washed and changed. He was a man over fifty years of age, and the strain had told upon him more than upon the rest of us. The rescue came just in time for him.

The early part of the voyage down to Elephant Island in
the *Southern Sky* was uneventful. At noon on Tuesday, May
23, we were at sea and steaming at ten knots on a southwesterly course. We made good progress, but the temperature fell
very low, and the signs gave me some cause for anxiety as
to the probability of encountering ice. On the third night out
the sea seemed to grow silent. I looked over the side and saw
a thin film of ice. The sea was freezing around us and the ice
gradually grew thicker, reducing our speed to about five
knots. Then lumps of old pack began to appear among the
new ice. I realized that an advance through pack ice was out
of the question. The *Southern Sky* was a steel-built steamer,
and her structure, while strong to resist the waves, would not
endure the blows of masses of ice. So I took the ship north,
and at daylight on Friday we got clear of the pancake ice.
We skirted westward, awaiting favorable conditions. The
morning of the 28th was dull and overcast, with little wind.
Again the ship's head was turned to the southwest, but at 3
p.m. a definite line of pack showed up on the horizon. We
were about 70 miles from Elephant Island, but there was no
possibility of taking the steamer through the ice that barred
the way. Northwest again we turned. We were directly north
of the island on the following day, and I made another move
south. Heavy pack formed an impenetrable barrier.

To admit failure at this stage was hard, but the facts had
to be faced. The *Southern Sky* could not enter ice of even
moderate thickness. The season was late, and we could not
be sure that the ice would open for many months, though
my opinion was that the pack would not become fast in that
quarter even in the winter, owing to the strong winds and
currents. The *Southern Sky* could carry coal for ten days
only, and we had been out six days. We were 500 miles
from the Falkland Islands and about 600 miles from South
Georgia. So I determined that, since we could not wait about
for an opening, I would proceed to the Falklands, get a more

suitable vessel either locally or from England, and make a
second attempt to reach Elephant Island from that point.

We encountered very bad weather on the way up, but in
the early afternoon of May 31 we arrived at Port Stanley,
where the cable provided a link with the outer world. The
harbormaster came out to meet us, and after we had dropped
anchor I went ashore and met the Governor, Mr. Douglas
Young. He offered me his assistance at once. He telephoned
to Mr. Harding, the manager of the Falkland Islands station,
and I learned, to my keen regret, that no ship of the type
required was available at the islands. That evening I cabled
to London a message to His Majesty the King, the first account of the loss of the *Endurance* and the subsequent adventures of the Expedition. The next day I received the
following message from the King:

"Rejoice to hear of your safe arrival in the Falkland
Islands and trust your comrades on Elephant Island may
soon be rescued.

GEORGE R.I."

The events of the days that followed our arrival at the
Falkland Islands I will not attempt to describe in detail. My
mind was bent upon the rescue of the party on Elephant
Island at the earliest possible moment. Winter was advancing, and I was fully conscious that the lives of some of my
comrades might be the price of unnecessary delay. A pro-
posal had been made to send a relief ship from England, but
she could not reach the southern seas for many weeks. In
the meantime I got into communication with the Governments of the South American Republics by wireless and
cable and asked if they had any suitable ship I could use for
a rescue. I wanted a wooden ship capable of pushing into
loose ice, with fair speed and a reasonable coal capacity.
Messages of congratulation and goodwill were reaching me

from all parts of the world, and the kindness of hundreds of friends in many lands was a very real comfort in a time of anxiety and stress.

The British Admiralty informed me that no suitable vessel was available in England and that no relief could be expected before October. I replied that October would be too late. Then the British Minister in Montevideo telegraphed me regarding a trawler named *Instituto de Pesca No. 1*, belonging to the Uruguayan Government. She was a stout little vessel, and the Government had generously offered to equip her with coal, provisions, clothing, etc., and send her across to the Falkland Islands for me to take down to Elephant Island. I accepted this offer gladly, and the trawler was in Port Stanley on June 10. We started south at once.

The weather was bad but the trawler made good progress, steaming steadily at about six knots, and in the bright, clear dawn of the third day we sighted the peaks of Elephant Island. Hope ran high; but our ancient enemy the pack was lying in wait, and within twenty minutes of the island the trawler was stopped by an impenetrable barrier of ice. The pack lay in the form of a crescent, with a horn to the west of the ship stretching north. Steaming northeast, we reached another horn and saw that the pack, heavy and dense, then trended away to the east. We made an attempt to push into the ice, but it was so heavy that the trawler was held up at once and began to grind in the small thick floes, so we cautiously backed out. The propeller, going slowly, was not damaged, though any moment I feared we might strip the blades. The island lay on our starboard quarter, but there was no possibility of approaching it. The Uruguayan engineer reported to me that he had three days' coal left, and I had to give the order to turn back. A screen of fog hid the lower slopes of the island, and the men watching from the camp on the beach could not have seen the ship. Northward we steamed again, with the engines knocking badly, and after encountering a new gale, made Port Stanley with the bunkers nearly empty and the engines almost broken down. H.M.S. *Glasgow* was in the port, and the British sailors gave us a hearty welcome as we steamed in.

The Uruguayan Government offered to send the trawler to Punta Arenas and have her dry-docked there and made ready for another effort. One of the troubles on the voyage was that according to estimate the trawler could do ten knots on six tons of coal a day, which would have given us a good margin to allow for lying off the ice; but in reality, owing to the fact that she had not been in dock for a year, she only developed a speed of six knots on a consumption of ten tons a day. Time was precious and these preparations would have taken too long. I thanked the Government then for its very generous offer, and I want to say now that the kindness of the Uruguayans at this time earned my warmest gratitude. I ought to mention also the assistance given me by Lieut. Ryan, a Naval Reserve officer who navigated the trawler to the Falklands and came south on the attempt at relief. The *Instituto de Pesca* went off to Montevideo and I looked around for another ship.

A British mailboat, the *Orita,* called at Port Stanley opportunely, and I boarded her with Worsley and Crean and crossed to Punta Arenas in the Magellan Straits. The reception we received there was heartening. The members of the British Association of Megallanes took us to their hearts. Mr. Allan McDonald was especially prominent in his untiring efforts to assist in the rescue of our twenty-two companions on Elephant Island. He worked day and night, and it was mainly due to him that within three days they had raised a sum of £1500 amongst themselves, chartered the schooner *Emma* and equipped her for our use. She was a forty-year-old oak schooner, strong and seaworthy, with an auxiliary oil engine.

Out of the complement of ten men all told who were manning the ship, there were eight different nationalities; but they were all good fellows and understood perfectly what was wanted. The Chilean Government lent us a small steamer, the *Yelcho,* to tow us part of the way. She could not touch ice though, as she was built of steel. However, on July 12 we passed her our tow rope and proceeded on our way. In bad weather we anchored next day, and although the wind increased to a gale I could delay no longer, so we hove up anchor in the early morning of the 14th. The strain on the tow rope was too great. With the crack of a gun the rope broke. Next day the gale continued, and I will quote from the log of the *Emma,* which Worsley kept as navigating officer. "9 a.m.—Fresh, increasing gale; very rough, lumpy sea. 10 a.m.—Tow rope parted. 12 noon. Similar weather. 1 p.m.—Tow rope parted again. Set foresail and forestay-sail and steered southeast by south. 3 p.m.—*Yelcho* hailed us and said that the ship's bilges were full of water (so were our decks) and they were short of coal. Sir Ernest told them that they could return to harbor. After this the *Yelcho* steamed into San Sebastian Bay." After three days of continuous bad weather we were left alone to attempt once more to rescue the twenty-two men on Elephant Island, for whom by this time I entertained very grave fears.

At dawn of Friday, July 21, we were within a hundred miles of the island, and we encountered the ice in the half-light. I waited for the full day and then tried to push through. The little craft was tossing in the heavy swell, and before she had been in the pack for ten minutes she came down on a cake of ice and broke the bobstay. Then the water inlet of the motor choked with ice. The schooner was tossing like a cork in the swell, and I saw after a few bumps that she was actually lighter than the fragments of ice around her. Progress under such conditions was out of the question. I worked the schooner out of the pack and stood to the east. I ran her through a line of pack towards the south that night, but was forced to turn to the northeast, for the ice trended in that direction as far as I could see. We hove to for the night, which was now sixteen hours long. The winter was well advanced and the weather conditions were thoroughly bad. The ice to the southward was moving north rapidly. The motor engine had broken down and we were entirely dependent on the sails. We managed to make a little southing during the next day, but noon found us 108 miles from the island. That night we lay off the ice in a gale, hove to, and morning found the schooner iced up. The ropes, cased in frozen spray, were as thick as a man's arm, and if the wind had increased much we would have had to cut away the sails, since there was no possibility of lowering them. Some members of the scratch crew were played out by the cold and the violent tossing. The schooner was about seventy feet long, and she responded to the motions of the storm-racked sea in a manner that might have disconcerted the most seasoned sailors.

I took the schooner south at every chance, but always the line of ice blocked the way. The engineer, who happened to be an American, did things to the engines occasionally, but he could not keep them running, and the persistent south winds were dead ahead. It was hard to turn back a third time, but I realized we could not reach the island under those conditions, and we must turn north in order to clear the ship of heavy masses of ice. So we set a northerly course, and after a tempestuous passage reached Port Stanley once more. This was the third reverse, but I did not abandon my belief that the ice would not remain fast around Elephant Island during the winter, whatever the armchair experts at home might say.

We reached Port Stanley in the schooner on August 8, and I learned there that the ship *Discovery* was to leave England at once and would be at the Falkland Islands about the middle of September. My good friend the Governor said I could settle down at Port Stanley and take things quietly

for a few weeks. The street of that port is about a mile and
a half long. It has the slaughterhouse at one end and the
graveyard at the other. The chief distraction is to walk from
the slaughterhouse to the graveyard. For a change one may
walk from the graveyard to the slaughterhouse. Ellaline Ter-
riss was born at Port Stanley—a fact not forgotten by the
residents, but she had not lived there much since. I could
not content myself to wait for six or seven weeks, knowing
that six hundred miles away my comrades were in dire need.
I asked the Chilean Government to send the *Yelcho,* the
steamer that had towed us before, to take the schooner
across to Punta Arenas, and they consented promptly, as
they had done to every other request of mine. So in a northwest gale we went across, narrowly escaping disaster on the
way, and reached Punta Arenas on August 14.

There was no suitable ship to be obtained. The weather
was showing some signs of improvement, and I begged the
Chilean Government to let me have the *Yelcho* for a last
attempt to reach the island. She was a small steel-built
steamer, quite unsuitable for work in the pack, but I promised that I would not touch the ice. The Government was
willing to give me another chance, and on August 25 I
started south on the fourth attempt at relief. This time Providence favored us. The little steamer made a quick run down
in comparatively fine weather, and I found as we neared
Elephant Island that the ice was open. A southerly gale had
sent it northward temporarily, and the *Yelcho* had her chance
to slip through. We approached the island in a thick fog. I
did not dare to wait for this to clear, and at 10 a.m. on August 30 we passed some stranded bergs. Then we saw the
sea breaking on a reef, and I knew that we were just outside
the island. It was an anxious moment, for we had still to
locate the camp and the pack could not be trusted to allow
time for a prolonged search in thick weather; but presently
the fog lifted and revealed the cliffs and glaciers of Elephant

Island. I proceeded to the east, and at 11:40 a.m. Worsley's keen eyes detected the camp, almost invisible under its covering of snow. The men ashore saw us at the same time, and we saw tiny black figures hurry to the beach and wave signals to us. We were about a mile and a half away from the camp. I turned the *Yelcho* in, and within half an hour reached the beach with Crean and some of the Chilean sailors. I saw a little figure on a surf-beaten rock and recognized Wild. As I came nearer I called out, "Are you all well?" and he answered, "We are all well, boss," and then I heard three cheers. As I drew close to the rock I flung packets of cigarettes ashore; they fell on them like hungry tigers, for well I knew that for months tobacco was dreamed of and talked of. Some of the hands were in a rather bad way, but Wild had held the party together and kept hope alive in their hearts. There was no time then to exchange news or congratulations. I did not even go up the beach to see the camp, which Wild assured me had been much improved. A heavy sea was running and a change of wind might bring the ice back at any time. I hurried the party aboard with all possible speed, taking also the records of the Expedition and essential portions of equipment. Everybody was aboard the *Yelcho* within an hour, and we steamed north at the little steamer's best speed. The ice was open still, and nothing worse than an expanse of stormy ocean separated us from the South American coast.

During the run up to Punta Arenas I heard Wild's story, and blessed again the cheerfulness and resource that had served the party so well during four and a half months of privation. The twenty-two men on Elephant Island were just at the end of their resources when the *Yelcho* reached them. Wild had husbanded the scanty stock of food as far as possible and had fought off the devils of despondency and despair on that little sand-spit, where the party had a precarious foothold between the grim ice fields and the

treacherous, ice-strewn sea. The pack had opened occasionally, but much of the time the way to the north had been
barred. The *Yelcho* had arrived at the right moment. Two
days earlier she could not have reached the island, and a few
hours later the pack may have been impenetrable again.
Wild had reckoned that help would come in August, and
every morning he had packed his kit, in cheerful anticipation that proved infectious, as I have no doubt it was meant
to be. One of the party to whom I had said "Well, you all
were packed up ready," replied, "You see, boss, Wild never
gave up hope, and whenever the sea was at all clear of ice
he rolled up his sleeping bag and said to all hands, 'Roll up
your sleeping bags, boys; the boss may come today' "; and
so it came to pass that we suddenly came out of the fog,
and, from a black outlook, in an hour all were in safety
homeward bound. The food was eked out with seal and penguin meat, limpets, and seaweed. Seals had been scarce, but
the supply of penguins had held out fairly well during the
first three months. The men were down to the last Bovril
ration, the only form of hot drink they had, and had scarcely
four days' food in hand at the time of the rescue. The camp
was in constant danger of being buried by the snow, which
drifted heavily from the heights behind, and the men moved
the accumulations with what implements they could provide. There was danger that the camp would become completely invisible from the sea, so that a rescue party might
look for it in vain.

"It had been arranged that a gun should be fired from the
relief ship when she got near the island," said Wild. "Many
times when the glaciers were 'calving,' and chunks fell off
with a report like a gun, we thought that it was the real
thing, and after a time we got to distrust these signals. As a
matter of fact, we saw the *Yelcho* before we heard any gun.
It was an occasion one will not easily forget. We were just
assembling for lunch to the call of 'Lunch O!' and I was

serving out the soup, which was particularly good that day, consisting of boiled seal's backbone, limpets, and seaweed, when there was another hail from Marston of 'Ship O!' Some of the men thought it was 'Lunch O!' over again, but when there was another yell from Marston lunch had no further attractions. The ship was about a mile and a half away and steaming past us. A smoke signal was the agreed sign from the shore, and, catching up somebody's coat that was lying about, I struck a pick into a tin of kerosene kept for the purpose, poured it over the coat, and set it alight. It flared instead of smoking; but that didn't matter, for you had already recognized the spot where you had left us and the *Yelcho* was turning in."

We encountered bad weather on the way back to Punta Arenas, and the little *Yelcho* labored heavily; but she had light hearts aboard. We entered the Straits of Magellan on September 3 and reached Rio Secco at 8 a.m. I went ashore, found a telephone, and told the Governor and my friends at Punta Arenas that the men were safe. Two hours later we were at Punta Arenas, where we were given a welcome none of us is likely to forget. The Chilean people were no less enthusiastic than the British residents. The police had been instructed to spread the news that the *Yelcho* was coming with the rescued men, and lest the message should fail to reach some people, the fire alarm had been rung. The whole populace appeared to be in the streets. It was a great reception, and with the strain of long, anxious months lifted at last, we were in a mood to enjoy it.

The next few weeks were crowded ones, but I will not attempt here to record their history in detail. I received congratulations and messages of friendship and good cheer from all over the world, and my heart went out to the good people who had remembered my men and myself in the press of terrible events on the battlefields. The Chilean Government placed the *Yelcho* at my disposal to take the men up to Valparaiso and Santiago. We reached Valparaiso on September 27. Everything that could swim in the way of a boat was out to meet us, the crews of Chilean warships were lined up, and at least thirty thousand thronged the streets. I lectured in Santiago on the following evening for the British Red Cross and a Chilean naval charity. The Chilean flag and the Union Jack were draped together, the band played the Chilean national anthem, "God Save the King," and the "Marseillaise," and the Chilean Minister for Foreign Affairs spoke from the platform and pinned an Order on my coat. I saw the President and thanked him for the help that he had given a British expedition. His Government had spent £4000 on coal alone. In reply he recalled the part that British sailors had taken in the making of the Chilean Navy.

The Chilean Railway Department provided a special train to take us across the Andes, and I proceeded to Montevideo in order to thank personally the President and Government of Uruguay for the help they had given generously in the earlier relief voyages. We were entertained royally at various spots *en route*. We went also to Buenos Aires on a brief call. Then we crossed the Andes again. I had made arrangements by this time for the men and the staff to go to England. All hands were keen to take their places in the Empire's fighting forces. My own immediate task was the relief of the marooned Ross Sea party, for news had come to me of the *Aurora*'s long drift in the Ross Sea and of her return in a damaged condition to New Zealand. Worsley was to come with me. We hurried northwards via Panama, steamship and train companies giving us everywhere the most cordial and generous assistance, and caught at San Francisco a steamer that would get us to New Zealand at the end of November. I had been informed that the New Zealand Government was making arrangements for the relief of the Ross Sea party, but my information was incomplete, and I was very anxious to be on the spot myself as quickly as possible.

CHAPTER XII

ELEPHANT ISLAND

THE TWENTY-TWO MEN who had been left behind on Elephant Island were under the command of Wild, in whom I had absolute confidence, and the account of their experiences during the long four and a half months' wait while I was trying to get help to them, I have secured from their various diaries, supplemented by details which I obtained in conversation on the voyage back to civilization.

The first consideration, which was even more important than that of food, was to provide shelter. The semi-starvation during the drift on the ice floe, added to the exposure in the boats, and the inclemencies of the weather encountered after our landing on Elephant Island, had left its mark on a good many of them. Rickenson, who bore up gamely to the last, collapsed from heart failure. Blackborrow and Hudson could not move. All were frostbitten in varying degrees; and their clothes, which had been worn continuously for six months, were much the worse for wear. The blizzard which sprang up the day that we landed at Cape Wild lasted for a fortnight, often blowing at the rate of seventy to ninety miles an hour, and occasionally reaching even higher figures. The tents which had lasted so well and endured so much were torn to ribbons, with the exception of the square tent occupied by Hurley, James, and Hudson. Sleeping bags and clothes were wringing wet, and the physical discomforts were tending to produce acute mental depression. The two remaining boats had been turned upside down with one gunwale resting on the snow, and the other raised about two feet on rocks and cases, and under these the sailors and some of the scientists, with the two invalids, Rickenson and Blackborrow, found head cover at least. Shelter from the weather and warmth to dry their clothes was imperative, so Wild hastened the excavation of the ice cave in the slope which had been started before I left.

The high temperature, however, caused a continuous stream of water to drip from the roof and sides of the ice cave, and as with twenty-two men living in it the temperature would be practically always above freezing, there would have been no hope of dry quarters for them there. Under the direction of Wild they, therefore, collected some big flat stones, having in many cases to dig down under the snow which was covering the beach, and with these they erected two substantial walls four feet high and nineteen feet apart.

"We are all ridiculously weak, and this part of the work was exceedingly laborious and took us more than twice as long as it would have done had we been in normal health. Stones that we could easily have lifted at other times we found quite beyond our capacity, and it needed two or three of us to carry some that would otherwise have been one man's load. Our difficulties were added to by the fact that most of the more suitable stones lay at the farthest end of the spit, some one hundred and fifty yards away. Our weakness is best compared with that which one experiences on getting up from a long illness; one 'feels' well, but physically enervated.

"The site chosen for the hut was the spot where the stove had been originally erected on the night of our arrival. It lay between two large boulders, which, if they would not actually form the walls of the hut, would at least provide a valuable protection from the wind. Further protection was provided to the north by a hill called Penguin Hill, at the end of the spit. As soon as the walls were completed and squared off, the two boats were laid upside down on them side by side. The exact adjustment of the boats took some time, but was of paramount importance if our structure was

to be the permanent affair that we hoped it would be. Once
in place they were securely chocked up and lashed down to
the rocks. The few pieces of wood that we had were laid
across from keel to keel, and over this the material of one
of the torn tents was spread and secured with guys to the
rocks. The walls were ingeniously contrived and fixed up
by Marston. First he cut the now useless tents into suitable
lengths; then he cut the legs of a pair of seaboots into narrow strips, and using these in much the same way that the
leather binding is put round the edge of upholstered chairs,
he nailed the tent cloth all round the insides of the outer
gunwales of the two boats in such a way that it hung down
like a valance to the ground, where it was secured with spars
and oars. A couple of overlapping blankets made the door,
superseded later by a sack-mouth door cut from one of the
tents. This consisted of a sort of tube of canvas sewn on to
the tent cloth, through which the men crawled in or out,
tying it up as one would the mouth of a sack as soon as the
man had passed through. It is certainly the most convenient
and efficient door for these conditions that has ever been
invented.

"Whilst the side walls of the hut were being fixed, others
proceeded to fill the interstices between the stones of the
end walls with snow. As this was very powdery and would
not bind well, we eventually had to supplement it with the
only spare blanket and an overcoat. All this work was very
hard on our frostbitten fingers, and materials were very limited.

"At last all was completed and we were invited to bring
in our sodden bags, which had been lying out in the drizzling rain for several hours; for the tents and boats that had
previously sheltered them had all been requisitioned to form
our new residence.

"We took our places under Wild's direction. There was
no squabbling for best places, but it was noticeable that

there was something in the nature of a rush for the billets up on the thwarts of the boats.

"Rickenson, who was still very weak and ill, but very cheery, obtained a place in the boat directly above the stove, and the sailors having lived under the *Stancomb Wills* for a few days while she was upside down on the beach, tacitly claimed it as their own, and flocked up on to its thwarts as one man. There was one 'upstair' billet left in this boat, which Wild offered to Hussey and Lees simultaneously, saying that the first man that got his bag up could have the billet. Whilst Lees was calculating the pros and cons Hussey got his bag, and had it up just as Lees had determined that the pros had it. There were now four men up on the thwarts of the *Dudley Docker,* and the five sailors and Hussey on those of the *Stancomb Wills,* the remainder disposing themselves on the floor."

The floor was at first covered with snow and ice, frozen in amongst the pebbles. This was cleared out, and the remainder of the tents spread out over the stones. Within the shelter of these cramped but comparatively palatial quarters cheerfulness once more reigned amongst the party. The blizzard, however, soon discovered the flaws in the architecture of their hut, and the fine drift-snow forced its way through the crevices between the stones forming the end walls. Jaeger sleeping bags and coats were spread over the outside of these walls, packed over with snow and securely frozen up, effectively keeping out this drift.

At first all the cooking was done outside under the lee of some rocks, further protection being provided by a wall of provision cases. There were two blubber stoves made from old oil drums, and one day, when the blizzard was unusually severe, an attempt was made to cook the meals inside the hut. There being no means of escape for the pungent blubber smoke, the inmates had rather a bad time, some being affected with a form of smoke blindness similar to snow blindness, very painful and requiring medical attention.

A chimney was soon fitted, made by Kerr out of the tin lining on one of the biscuit cases, and passed through a close-fitting tin grummet sewn into the canvas of the roof just between the keels of the two boats, and the smoke nuisance was soon a thing of the past. Later on, another old oil drum was made to surround this chimney, so that two pots could be cooked at once on the one stove. Those whose billets were near the stove suffered from the effects of the local thaw caused by its heat, but they were repaid by being able to warm up portions of steak and hooshes left over from previous meals, and even to warm up those of the less fortunate ones, for a consideration. This consisted generally of part of the hoosh or one or two pieces of sugar.

The cook and his assistant, which latter job was taken by each man in turn, were called about 7 a.m., and breakfast was generally ready by about 10 a.m.

Provision cases were then arranged in a wide circle round the stove, and those who were fortunate enough to be next to it could dry their gear. So that all should benefit equally by this, a sort of "General Post" was carried out, each man occupying his place at mealtimes for one day only, moving up one the succeeding day. In this way eventually every man managed to dry his clothes, and life began to assume a much brighter aspect.

The great trouble in the hut was the absence of light. The canvas walls were covered with blubber soot, and with the snowdrifts accumulating round the hut its inhabitants were living in a state of perpetual night. Lamps were fashioned out of sardine tins, with bits of surgical bandage for wicks; but as the oil consisted of seal oil rendered down from the blubber, the remaining fibrous tissue being issued very sparingly at lunch, by the by, and being considered a great delicacy, they were more a means of conserving the scanty store of matches than of serving as illuminants.

Wild was the first to overcome this difficulty by sewing

into the canvas wall the glass lid of a chronometer box.
Later on three other windows were added, the material in
this case being some celluloid panels from a photograph
case of mine which I had left behind in a bag. This enabled
the occupants of the floor billets who were near enough to
read and sew, which relieved the monotony of the situation
considerably.

"Our reading material consisted at this time of two books
of poetry, one book of 'Nordenskjöld's Expedition,' one or
two torn volumes of the 'Encyclopedia Britannica,' and a
penny cookery book, owned by Marston. Our clothes,
though never presentable, as they bore the scars of nearly
ten months of rough usage, had to be continually patched to
keep them together at all."

As the floor of the hut had been raised by the addition of
loads of clean pebbles, from which most of the snow had
been removed, during the cold weather it was kept comparatively dry. When, however, the temperature rose to just
above freezing point, as occasionally happened, the hut became the drainage pool of all the surrounding hills. Wild
was the first to notice it by remarking one morning that his
sleeping bag was practically afloat. Other men examined
theirs with a like result, so baling operations commenced
forthwith. Stones were removed from the floor and a large
hole dug, and in its gloomy depths the water could be seen
rapidly rising. Using a saucepan for a baler, they baled out
over 100 gallons of dirty water. The next day 150 gallons
were removed, the men taking it in turns to bale at intervals
during the night; 160 more gallons were baled out during
the next twenty-four hours, till one man rather pathetically
remarked in his diary, "This is what nice, mild, high temperatures mean to us: no wonder we prefer the cold." Eventually, by removing a portion of one wall a long channel was
dug nearly down to the sea, completely solving the problem.
Additional precautions were taken by digging away the

snow which surrounded the hut after each blizzard, sometimes entirely obscuring it.

A huge glacier across the bay behind the hut nearly put
an end to the party. Enormous blocks of ice weighing many
tons would break off and fall into the sea, the disturbance
thus caused giving rise to great waves. One day Marston was
outside the hut digging up the frozen seal for lunch with a
pick, when a noise "like an artillery barrage" startled him.
Looking up he saw that one of these tremendous waves, over
thirty feet high, was advancing rapidly across the bay,
threatening to sweep hut and inhabitants into the sea. A
hastily shouted warning brought the men tumbling out, but
fortunately the loose ice which filled the bay damped the
wave down so much that, though it flowed right under the
hut, nothing was carried away. It was a narrow escape
though, as had they been washed into the sea nothing could
have saved them.

Although they themselves gradually became accustomed
to the darkness and the dirt, some entries in their diaries
show that occasionally they could realize the conditions
under which they were living.

"The hut grows more grimy every day. Everything is a
sooty black. We have arrived at the limit where further in-
crements from the smoking stove, blubber lamps, and cooking gear are unnoticed. It is at least comforting to feel that
we can become no filthier. Our shingle floor will scarcely
bear examination by strong light without causing even us to
shudder and express our disapprobation at its state. Oil
mixed with reindeer hair, bits of meat, sennegrass, and penguin feathers form a conglomeration which cements the
stones together. From time to time we have a spring clean-
ing, but a fresh supply of flooring material is not always
available, as all the shingle is frozen up and buried by deep
rifts. Such is our Home Sweet Home."

"All joints are aching through being compelled to lie on
the hard, rubbly floor which forms our bedsteads."

Again, later on, one writes: "Now that Wild's window allows a shaft of light to enter our hut, one can begin to 'see' things inside. Previously one relied upon one's sense of touch, assisted by the remarks from those whose faces were inadvertently trodden on, to guide one to the door. Looking down in the semidarkness to the far end, one observes two very small smoky flames that dimly illuminate a row of five, endeavoring to make time pass by reading or argument. These are Macklin, Kerr, Wordie, Hudson, and Blackborrow—the last two being invalids.

"The center of the huts is filled with the cases which do duty for the cook's bed, the meat and blubber boxes, and a mummified-looking object, which is Lees in his sleeping bag. The near end of the floor space is taken up with the stove, with Wild and McIlroy on one side, and Hurley and James on the other. Marston occupies a hammock most of the night—and day—which is slung across the entrance. As he is large and the entrance very small, he invariably gets bumped by those passing in and out. His vocabulary at such times is interesting.

"In the attic, formed by the two upturned boats, live ten unkempt and careless lodgers, who drop boots, mitts, and other articles of apparel on to the men below. Reindeer hairs rain down incessantly day and night, with every movement that they make in their moulting bags. These, with penguin feathers and a little grit from the floor, occasionally savor the hooshes. Thank heavens man is an adaptable brute! If we dwell sufficiently long in this hut, we are likely to alter our method of walking, for our ceiling, which is but four feet six inches high at its highest part, compels us to walk bent double or on all fours.

"Our doorway—Cheetham is just crawling in now, bringing a shower of snow with him—was originally a tent entrance. When one wishes to go out, one unties the cord securing the door, and crawls or wriggles out, at the same time exclaiming 'Thank goodness I'm in the open air!' This should suffice to describe the atmosphere inside the hut, only pleasant when charged with the overpowering yet appetizing smell of burning penguin steaks.

"From all parts there dangles an odd collection of blubbery garments, hung up to dry, through which one crawls, much as a chicken in an incubator. Our walls of tent canvas admit as much light as might be expected from a closed Venetian blind. It is astonishing how we have grown accustomed to inconveniences, and tolerate, at least, habits which a little time back were regarded with repugnance. We have no forks, but each man has a sheath-knife and a spoon, the latter in many cases having been fashioned from a piece of box lid. The knife serves many purposes. With it we kill, skin, and cut up seals and penguins, cut blubber into strips for the fire, very carefully scrape the snow off our hut walls, and then after a perfunctory rub with an oily penguin skin, use it at meals. We are as regardless of our grime and dirt as is the Eskimo. We have been unable to wash since we left the ship, nearly ten months ago. For one thing we have no soap or towels, only bare necessities being brought with us; and, again, had we possesed these articles, our supply of fuel would only permit us to melt enough ice for drinking purposes. Had one man washed, half a dozen others would have had to go without a drink all day. One cannot suck ice to relieve the thirst, as at these low temperatures it cracks the lips and blisters the tongue. Still, we are all very cheerful."

During the whole of their stay on Elephant Island the weather was described by Wild as "simply appalling." Stranded as they were on a narrow, sandy beach surrounded by high mountains, they saw little of the scanty sunshine during the brief intervals of clear sky. On most days the air was full of snowdrift blown from the adjacent heights. Elephant Island being practically on the outside edge of the

pack, the winds which passed over the relatively warm
ocean before reaching it clothed it in a "constant pall of fog
and snow."

On April 25, the day after I left for South Georgia, the
island was beset by heavy pack ice, with snow and a wet
mist. Next day was calmer, but on the 27th, to quote one of
the diaries, they experienced "the most wretched weather
conceivable. Raining all night and day, and blowing hard.
Wet to the skin." The following day brought heavy fog and
sleet, and a continuance of the blizzard. April ended with a
terrific windstorm which nearly destroyed the hut. The one
remaining tent had to be dismantled, the pole taken down,
and the inhabitants had to lie flat all night under the icy
canvas. This lasted well into May, and a typical May day is
described as follows: "A day of terrific winds, threatening
to dislodge our shelter. The wind is a succession of hurricane gusts that sweep down the glacier immediately south-
southwest of us. Each gust heralds its approach by a low
rumbling which increases to a thunderous roar. Snow,
stones, and gravel are flying about, and any gear left un-
weighted by very heavy stones is carried away to sea."

Heavy bales of sennegrass, and boxes of cooking gear,
were lifted bodily in the air and carried away out of sight.
Once the wind carried off the floor cloth of a tent which six
men were holding on to and shaking the snow off. These
gusts often came with alarming suddenness, and without
any warning. Hussey was outside in the blizzard digging up
the day's meat, which had frozen to the ground, when a gust
caught him and drove him down the spit towards the sea.
Fortunately, when he reached the softer sand and shingle
below highwater mark, he managed to stick his pick into
the ground and hold on with both hands till the squall had
passed.

On one or two rare occasions they had fine, calm, clear
days. The glow of the dying sun on the mountains and gla-

ciers filled even the most materialistic of them with wonder and admiration. These days were sometimes succeeded by calm, clear nights, when, but for the cold, they would have stayed out on the sandy beach all night.

About the middle of May a terrific blizzard sprang up, blowing from sixty to ninety miles an hour, and Wild entertained grave fears for their hut. One curious feature noted in this blizzard was the fact that huge ice sheets as big as windowpanes, and about a quarter of an inch thick, were being hurled about by the wind, making it as dangerous to walk about outside as if one were in an avalanche of splintered glass. Still, these winds from the south and southwest, though invariably accompanied by snow and low temperatures, were welcome in that they drove the pack-ice away from the immediate vicinity of the island, and so gave rise on each occasion to hopes of relief. Northeast winds, on the other hand, by filling the bays with ice and bringing thick misty weather, made it impossible to hope for any ship to approach them.

Towards the end of May a period of dead calm set in, with ice closely packed all around the island. This gave place to northeast winds and mist, and at the beginning of June came another southwest blizzard, with cold driving snow. "The blizzard increased to terrific gusts during the night, causing us much anxiety for the safety of our hut. There was little sleep, all being apprehensive of the canvas roof ripping off, and the boats being blown out to sea."

Thus it continued, alternating between southwest blizzards, when they were all confined to the hut, and northeast winds, bringing cold, damp, misty weather.

On June 25 a severe storm from northwest was recorded, accompanied by strong winds and heavy seas, which encroached upon their little sandy beach up to within four yards of their hut.

Towards the end of July and the beginning of August they

had a few fine, calm, clear days. Occasional glimpses of the sun, with high temperatures, were experienced, after south-west winds had blown all the ice away, and the party, their spirits cheered by Wild's unfailing optimism, again began to look eagerly for the rescue ship.

The first three attempts at their rescue unfortunately coincided with the times when the island was beset with ice, and though on the second occasion we approached close enough to fire a gun, in the hope that they would hear the sound and know that we were safe and well, yet so accustomed were they to the noise made by the calving of the adjacent glacier that either they did not hear or the sound passed unnoticed. On August 16 pack was observed on the horizon, and next day the bay was filled with loose ice, which soon consolidated. Soon afterwards huge old floes and many bergs drifted in. "The pack appears as dense as we have ever seen it. No open water is visible, and 'ice-blink' girdles the horizon. The weather is wretched—a stagnant calm of air and ocean alike, the latter obscured by dense pack through which no swell can penetrate, and a wet mist hangs like a pall over land and sea. The silence is oppressive. There is nothing to do but to stay in one's sleeping bag, or else wander in the soft snow and become thoroughly wet." Fifteen inches of snow fell in the next twenty-four hours, making over two feet between August 18 and 21. A slight swell next day from the northeast ground up the pack-ice, but this soon subsided, and the pack became consolidated once more. On August 27 a strong west-southwest wind sprang up and drove all this ice out of the bay, and except for some stranded bergs left a clear ice-free sea through which we finally made our way from Punta Arenas to Elephant Island.

As soon as I had left the island to get help for the rest of the Expedition, Wild set all hands to collect as many seals and penguins as possible, in case their stay was longer than was at first anticipated. A sudden rise in temperature caused a whole lot to go bad and become unfit for food, so while a fair reserve was kept in hand too much was not accumulated.

At first the meals, consisting mostly of seal meat with one hot drink per day, were cooked on a stove in the open. The snow and wind, besides making it very unpleasant for the cook, filled all the cooking pots with sand and grit, so during the winter the cooking was done inside the hut.

A little Cerebos salt had been saved, and this was issued out at the rate of three-quarters of an ounce per man per week. Some of the packets containing the salt had broken, so that all did not get the full ration. On the other hand, one man dropped his week's ration on the floor of the hut, amongst the stones and dirt. It was quickly collected, and he found to his delight that he had enough now to last him for three weeks. Of course it was not *all* salt. The hot drink consisted at first of milk made from milk powder up to about one-quarter of its proper strength. This was later on diluted still more, and sometimes replaced by a drink made from a pea soup-like packing from the Bovril sledging rations. For midwinter's day celebrations, a mixture of one teaspoonful of methylated spirit in a pint of hot water, flavored with a little ginger and sugar, served to remind some of cocktails and *Veuve Cliquot.*

At breakfast each had a piece of seal or half a penguin breast. Luncheon consisted of one biscuit on three days a week, nut-food on Thursday, bits of blubber, from which most of the oil had been extracted for the lamps, on two days a week, and nothing on the remaining day. On this day breakfast consisted of a half-strength sledging ration. Supper was almost invariably seal and penguin, cut up very finely and fried with a little seal blubber.

There were occasionally very welcome variations from this menu. Some paddies—a little white bird not unlike a pigeon—were snared with a loop of string, and fried, with

one water-sodden biscuit, for lunch. Enough barley and peas
for one meal all round of each had been saved, and when
this was issued it was a day of great celebration. Sometimes,
by general consent, the luncheon biscuit would be saved,
and, with the next serving of biscuit, was crushed in a canvas bag into a powder and boiled with a little sugar, making
a very satisfying pudding. When blubber was fairly plentiful
there was always a saucepan of cold water, made from melting down the pieces of ice which had broken off from the
glacier, fallen into the sea, and been washed ashore, for
them to quench their thirst in. As the experience of Arctic
explorers tended to show that sea water produced a form of
dysentery, Wild was rather diffident about using it. Penguin
carcasses boiled in one part of sea water to four of fresh
were a great success though, and no ill effects were felt by
anybody.

The ringed penguins migrated north the day after we
landed at Cape Wild, and though every effort was made to
secure as large a stock of meat and blubber as possible, by
the end of the month the supply was so low that only one
hot meal a day could be served. Twice the usual number of
penguin steaks were cooked at breakfast, and the ones intended for supper were kept hot in the pots by wrapping up
in coats, etc. "Clark put our saucepanful in his sleeping bag
today to keep it hot, and it really was a great success in spite
of the extra helping of reindeer hairs that it contained. In
this way we can make ten penguin skins do for one day."

Some who were fortunate enough to catch penguins with
fairly large undigested fish in their gullets used to warm
these up in tins hung on bits of wire round the stove.

"All the meat intended for hooshes is cut up inside the
hut, as it is too cold outside. As the boards which we use
for the purpose are also used for cutting up tobacco, when
we still have it, a definite flavor is sometimes imparted to
the hoosh, which, if anything, improves it."

Their diet was now practically all meat, and not too much of that, and all the diaries bear witness to their craving for carbohydrates, such as flour, oatmeal, etc. One man longingly speaks of the cabbages which grow on Kerguelen Island. By June 18 there were only nine hundred lumps of sugar left, i.e. just over forty pieces each. Even my readers know what shortage of sugar means at this very date, but from a different cause. Under these circumstances it is not surprising that all their thoughts and conversation should turn to food, past and future banquets, and second helpings that had been once refused.

A census was taken, each man being asked to state just what he would like to eat at that moment if he were allowed to have anything that he wanted. All, with but one exception, desired a suet pudding of some sort—the "duff" beloved of sailors. Macklin asked for many returns of scrambled eggs on hot buttered toast. Several voted for "a prodigious Devonshire dumpling," while Wild wished for "any old dumpling so long as it was a large one." The craving for carbohydrates, such as flour and sugar, and for fats was very real. Marston had with him a small penny cookery book. From this he would read out one recipe each night, so as to make them last. This would be discussed very seriously, and alterations and improvements suggested, and then they would turn into their bags to dream of wonderful meals that they could never reach. The following conversation was recorded in one diary:

"WILD: 'Do you like doughnuts?'

"MCILROY: 'Rather!'

"WILD: 'Very easily made, too. I like them cold with a little jam.'

"MCILROY: 'Not bad; but how about a huge omelette?'

"WILD: 'Fine!' (with a deep sigh).

"Overhead, two of the sailors are discussing some extraordinary mixture of hash, applesauce, beer, and cheese.

Marston is in his hammock reading from his penny cookery book. Further down, some one eulogizes Scotch shortbread. Several of the sailors are talking of spotted dog, sea pie, and Lockhart's with great feeling. Someone mentions nut food, whereat the conversation becomes general, and we all decide to buy one pound's worth of it as soon as we get to civilization, and retire to a country house to eat it undisturbed. At present we really mean it, too!"

Midwinter's day, the great Polar festival, was duly observed. A "magnificent breakfast" of sledging ration hoosh, full strength and well boiled to thicken it, with hot milk was served. Luncheon consisted of a wonderful pudding, invented by Wild, made of powdered biscuit boiled with twelve pieces of mouldy nut food. Supper was a very finely cut seal hoosh flavored with sugar.

After supper they had a concert, accompanied by Hussey on his "indispensable banjo." This banjo was the last thing to be saved off the ship before she sank, and I took it with us as a mental tonic. It was carried all the way through with us, and landed on Elephant Island practically unharmed, and did much to keep the men cheerful. Nearly every Saturday night such a concert was held, when each one sang a song about some other member of the party. If that other one objected to some of the remarks, a worse one was written for the next week.

The cook, who had carried on so well and for so long, was given a rest on August 9, and each man took it in turns to be cook for one week. As the cook and his "mate" had the privilege of scraping out the saucepans, there was some anxiety to secure the job, especially amongst those with the larger appetites. "The last of the methylated spirit was drunk on August 12, and from then onwards the King's health, 'sweethearts and wives,' and 'the Boss and crew of the *Caird*,' were drunk in hot water and ginger every Saturday night."

The penguins and seals which had migrated north at the beginning of winter had not yet returned, or else the ice foot, which surrounded the spit to a thickness of six feet, prevented them from coming ashore, so that food was getting short. Old seal bones, that had been used once for a meal and then thrown away, were dug up and stewed down with sea water. Penguin carcasses were treated likewise. Limpets were gathered from the pools disclosed between the rocks below high tide, after the pack-ice had been driven away. It was a cold job gathering these little shellfish, as for each one the whole hand and arm had to be plunged into the icy water, and many score of these small creatures had to be collected to make anything of a meal. Seaweed boiled in sea water was used to eke out the rapidly diminishing stock of seal and penguin meat. This did not agree with some of the party. Though it was acknowledged to be very tasty it only served to increase their appetite—a serious thing when there was nothing to satisfy it with! One man remarked in his diary: "We had a sumptuous meal today—nearly five ounces of solid food each."

It is largely due to Wild, and to his energy, initiative, and resource, that the whole party kept cheerful all along, and, indeed, came out alive and so well. Assisted by the two surgeons, Drs. McIlroy and Macklin, he had ever a watchful eye for the health of each one. His cheery optimism never failed, even when food was very short and the prospect of relief seemed remote. Each one in his diary speaks with admiration of him. I think without doubt that all the party who were stranded on Elephant Island owe their lives to him. The demons of depression could find no foothold when he was around; and, not content with merely "telling," he was "doing" as much as, and very often more than, the rest. He showed wonderful capabilities of leadership and more than justified the absolute confidence that I placed in him. Hussey, with his cheeriness and his banjo, was another vital factor in chasing away any tendency to downheartedness.

Once they were settled in their hut, the health of the party was quite good. Of course, they were all a bit weak, some were lightheaded, all were frostbitten, and others, later, had attacks of heart failure. Blackborrow, whose toes were so badly frostbitten in the boats, had to have all five amputated while on the island. With insufficient instruments and no proper means of sterilizing them, the operation, carried out as it was in a dark, grimy hut, with only a blubber stove to keep up the temperature and with an outside temperature well below freezing, speaks volumes for the skill and initiative of the surgeons. I am glad to be able to say that the operation was very successful, and after a little treatment ashore, very kindly given by the Chilean doctors at Punta Arenas, he has now completely recovered and walks with only a slight limp. Hudson, who developed bronchitis and hip disease, was practically well again when the party was rescued. All trace of the severe frostbites suffered in the boat journey had disappeared, though traces of recent superficial ones remained on some. All were naturally weak when rescued, owing to having been on such scanty rations for so long, but all were alive and very cheerful, thanks to Frank Wild.

August 30, 1916, is described in their diaries as a "day of wonders." Food was very short, only two days' seal and penguin meat being left, and no prospect of any more arriving. The whole party had been collecting limpets and seaweed to eat with the stewed seal bones. Lunch was being served by Wild, Hurley and Marston waiting outside to take a last long look at the direction from which they expected the ship to arrive. From a fortnight after I had left, Wild would roll up his sleeping bag each day with the remark, "Get your things ready, boys, the Boss may come today." And sure enough, one day the mist opened and revealed the ship for which they had been waiting and longing and hoping for over four months. "Marston was the first to notice it,

and immediately yelled out 'Ship O!' The inmates of the
hut mistook it for a call of 'Lunch O!' so took no notice at
first. Soon, however, we heard him pattering along the snow
as fast as he could run, and in a gasping, anxious voice,
hoarse with excitement, he shouted, 'Wild, there's a ship!
Hadn't we better light a flare?' We all made one dive for our
narrow door. Those who could not get through tore down
the canvas walls in their hurry and excitement. The hoosh
pot with our precious limpets and seaweed was kicked over
in the rush. There, just rounding the island which had previously hidden her from our sight, we saw a little ship flying
the Chilean flag.

"We tried to cheer, but excitement had gripped our vocal
cords. Macklin had made a rush for the flagstaff, previously
placed in the most conspicuous position on the ice slope.
The running gear would not work, and the flag was frozen
into a solid, compact mass; so he tied his jersey to the top
of the pole for a signal.

"Wild put a pick through our last remaining tin of petrol,
and soaking coats, mitts, and socks with it, carried them to
the top of Penguin Hill at the end of our spit, and soon they
were ablaze.

"Meanwhile most of us had gathered on the foreshore
watching with anxious eyes for any signs that the ship had
seen us, or for any answering signals. As we stood and
gazed she seemed to turn away as if she had not seen us.
Again and again we cheered, though our feeble cries could
certainly not have carried so far. Suddenly she stopped, a
boat was lowered, and we could recognize Sir Ernest's figure as he climbed down the ladder. Simultaneously we burst
into a cheer, and then one said to the other, 'Thank God, the
Boss is safe.' For I think that his safety was of more concern
to us than was our own.

"Soon the boat approached near enough for the Boss,
who was standing up in the bows, to shout to Wild, 'Are

you all well?' To which he replied, 'All safe, all well,' and
we could see a smile light up the Boss's face as he said,
'Thank God!'

"Before he could land he threw ashore handsful of cigarettes and tobacco; and these the smokers, who for two
months had been trying to find solace in such substitutes as
seaweed, finely chopped pipe bowls, seal meat, and sennegrass, grasped greedily.

"Blackborrow, who could not walk, had been carried to
a high rock and propped up in his sleeping bag, so that he
could view the wonderful scene.

"Soon we were tumbling into the boat, and the Chilean
sailors, laughing up at us, seemed as pleased at our rescue
as we were. Twice more the boat returned, and within an
hour of our first having sighted the boat we were heading
northwards to the outer world from which we had had no
news since October 1914, over twenty-two months before.
We are like men awakened from a long sleep. We are trying
to acquire suddenly the perspective which the rest of the
world has acquired gradually through two years of war.
There are many events which have happened of which we
shall never know.

"Our first meal, owing to our weakness and the atrophied
state of our stomachs, proved disastrous to a good many.
They soon recovered though. Our beds were just shake-
downs on cushions and settees, though the officer on watch
very generously gave up his bunk to two of us. I think we
got very little sleep that night. It was just heavenly to lie and
listen to the throb of the engines, instead of to the crack of
the breaking floe, the beat of the surf on the ice-strewn
shore, or the howling of the blizzard.

"We intend to keep August 30 as a festival for the rest of
our lives."

You readers can imagine my feelings as I stood in the
little cabin watching my rescued comrades feeding.

CHAPTER XIII

THE ROSS SEA PARTY

I NOW TURN to the fortunes and misfortunes of the Ross Sea
Party and the *Aurora*. In spite of extraordinary difficulties
occasioned by the breaking out of the *Aurora* from her winter quarters before sufficient stores and equipment had been
landed, Captain Æneas Mackintosh and the party under his
command achieved the object of this side of the Expedition.
For the depot that was the main object of the Expedition was
laid in the spot that I had indicated, and if the transcontinental party had been fortunate enough to have crossed they
would have found the assistance, in the shape of stores, that
would have been vital to the success of their undertaking.
Owing to the dearth of stores, clothing, and sledging equipment, the depot party was forced to travel more slowly and
with greater difficulty than would have otherwise been the
case. The result was that in making this journey the greatest
qualities of endurance, self sacrifice, and patience were
called for, and the call was not in vain, as you reading the
following pages will realize. It is more than regrettable that
after having gone through those many months of hardship
and toil, Mackintosh and Hayward should have been lost.
Spencer-Smith during those long days, dragged by his comrades on the sledge, suffering but never complaining, became an example to all men. Mackintosh and Hayward
owed their lives on that journey to the unremitting care and
strenuous endeavors of Joyce, Wild, and Richards, who, also
scurvy-stricken but fitter than their comrades, dragged them
through the deep snow and blizzards on the sledges. I think
that no more remarkable story of human endeavor has been
revealed than the tale of that long march which I have col-

lated from various diaries. Unfortunately, the diary of the leader of this side of the Expedition was lost with him. The outstanding feature of the Ross Sea side was the journey made by these six men. The earlier journeys for the first year did not produce any sign of the qualities of leadership among the others. Mackintosh was fortunate for the long journey in that he had these three men with him: Ernest Wild, Richards, and Joyce.

Before proceeding with the adventures of this party I want to make clear in these pages how much I appreciate the assistance I received both in Australia and New Zealand, especially in the latter dominion. And among the many friends there it is not invidious on my part to lay special stress on the name of Leonard Tripp, who has been my mentor, counsellor, and friend for many years, and who, when the Expedition was in precarious and difficult circumstances, devoted his energy, thought, and gave his whole time and advice to the best interests of our cause. I also must thank Edward Saunders, who for the second time has greatly helped me in preparing an Expedition record for publication.

To the Dominion Government I tender my warmest thanks. To the people of New Zealand, and especially to those many friends—too numerous to mention here—who helped us when our fortunes were at a low ebb, I wish to say that their kindness in an evergreen memory to me. If ever a man had cause to be grateful for assistance in dark days, I am he.

The *Aurora,* under the command of Captain Æneas Mackintosh, sailed from Hobart for the Ross Sea on December 24, 1914. The ship had refitted in Sydney, where the State and Federal Governments had given generous assistance, and would be able, if necessary, to spend two years in the Antarctic. My instructions to Captain Mackintosh, in brief, were to proceed to the Ross Sea, make a base at some convenient point in or near McMurdo Sound, land stores and equipment, and lay depots on the Great Ice Barrier in the direction of the Beardmore Glacier for the use of the party that I expected to bring overland from the Weddell Sea coast. This program would involve some heavy sledging, but the ground to be covered was familiar, and I had not anticipated that the work would present any great difficulties. The *Aurora* carried materials for a hut, full equipment for landing and sledging parties, stores and clothing of all the kinds required, and an ample supply of sledges. There were also dog teams and one of the motor tractors. I had told Captain Mackintosh that it was possible the transcontinental journey would be attempted in the 1914–15 season in the event of the landing on the Weddell Sea coast proving unexpectedly easy, and it would be his duty, therefore, to lay out depots to the south immediately after his arrival at his base. I had directed him to place a depot of food and fuel oil at lat. 80° S. in 1914–15, with horns and flags as guides to a sledging party approaching from the direction of the Pole. He would place depots farther south in the 1915–16 season.

The *Aurora* had an uneventful voyage southwards. She anchored off the sealing huts at Macquarie Island on Christmas Day, December 25. The wireless station erected by Sir Douglas Mawson's Australian Antarctic Expedition could be seen on a hill to the northwest with the Expedition's hut at the base of the hill. This hut was still occupied by a meterological staff, and later in the day the meterologist, Mr. Tulloch, came off to the ship and had dinner aboard. The *Aurora* had some stores for the Macquarie Island party, and these were sent ashore during succeeding days in the boats. The landing place was a rough, kelp-guarded beach, where lay the remains of the New Zealand barque *Clyde*. Macquarie Island anchorages are treacherous, and several ships engaged in the sealing and whaling trade have left their

bones on the rocky shores, where bask great herds of seals
and sea elephants. The *Aurora* sailed from the island on
December 31, and three days later they sighted the first iceberg, a tabular berg rising 250 ft. above the sea. This was in
lat. 62° 40′ S., long. 169° 58′ E. The next day, in lat. 64°
27′ 38″ S., the *Aurora* passed through the first belt of pack
ice. At 9 a.m. on January 7, Mount Sabine, a mighty peak
of the Admiralty Range, South Victoria Land, was sighted
seventy-five miles distant.

In had been proposed that a party of three men should
travel to Cape Crozier from winter quarters during the winter months in order to secure emperor penguins' eggs. The
ship was to call at Cape Crozier, land provisions, and erect
a small hut of fibro concrete sheets for the use of this party.
The ship was off the Cape on the afternoon of January 9,
and a boat put off with Stenhouse, Cope, Joyce, Ninnis,
Mauger, and Aitken to search for a landing place. "We
steered in towards the Barrier," wrote Stenhouse, "and
found an opening leading into a large bight which jutted
back to eastward into the Barrier. We endeavored without
success to scale the steep ice foot under the cliffs, and then
proceeded up the bay. Pulling along the edge of perpendicular ice, we turned into a bay in the ice cliff and came to a
cul-de-sac, at the head of which was a grotto. At the head of
the grotto and on a ledge of snow were perched some adelie
penguins. The beautiful green and blue tints in the ice coloring made a picture as unreal as a stage setting. Coming back
along the edge of the bight towards the land, we caught and
killed one penguin, much to the surprise of another, which
ducked into a niche in the ice and, after much squawking,
was extracted with a boat hook and captured. We returned
to our original landing, and were fortunate in our time, for
no sooner had we cleared the ledge where Ninnis had been
hanging in his endeavor to catch the penguin than the barrier
calved and a piece weighing hundreds of tons toppled over
into the sea.

"Since we left the ship a mist had blown up from the south, and when we arrived back at the entrance to the bay the ship could be but dimly seen. We found a slope on the ice foot, and Joyce and I managed, by cutting steps, to climb up to a ledge of debris between the cliffs and the ice, which we thought might lead to the vicinity of the emperor penguin rookery. I sent the boat back to the ship to tell the captain of our failure to find a spot where we could depot the hut and stores, and then, with Joyce, set out to walk along the narrow land between the cliffs and the ice to the southward in hopes of finding the rookery. We walked for about a mile along the foot of the cliffs, over undulating paths, sometimes crawling carefully down a gully and then over rocks and debris which had fallen from the steep cliffs which towered above us, but we saw no signs of a rookery or any place where a rookery could be. Close to the cliffs and separated from them by the path on which we traveled, the Barrier in its movement towards the sea had broken and showed signs of pressure. Seeing a turn in the cliffs ahead, which we thought might lead to better prospects, we trudged on, and were rewarded by a sight which Joyce admitted as being the grandest he had ever witnessed. The Barrier had come into contact with the cliffs and, from where we viewed it, it looked as if icebergs had fallen into a tremendous cavern and lay jumbled together in wild disorder. Looking down into that wonderful picture one realized a little the 'eternalness' of things.

"We had not long to wait, and, much as we wished to go ahead, had to turn back. I went into a small crevasse; no damage. Arriving back at the place where we left the boat we found it had not returned, so sat down under an overhang and smoked and enjoyed the sense of loneliness. Soon the boat appeared out of the mist, and the crew had much news for us. After we left the ship the captain maneuvered her in order to get close to the Barrier, but, unfortunately, the en-

gines were loath to be reversed when required to go astern
and the ship hit the Barrier end on. The Barrier here is about
twenty feet high, and her jib boom took the weight and
snapped at the cap. When I returned Thompson was busy
getting the broken boom and gear aboard. Luckily the cap
was not broken and no damage was done aloft, but it was
rather a bad introduction to the Antarctic. There is no place
to land the Cape Crozier hut and stores, so we must build a
hut in the winter here, which will mean so much extra sledging from winter quarters. Bad start, good finish! Joyce and
I went aloft to the crow's nest, but could see no opening in
the Barrier to eastward where a ship might enter and get
farther south."

Mackintosh proceeded into McMurdo Sound. Heavy pack
delayed the ship for three days, and it was not until January
16 that she reached a point off Cape Evans, where he landed
ten tons of coal and ninety-eight cases of oil. During succeeding days Captain Mackintosh worked the *Aurora* southward, and by January 24 he was within nine miles of Hut
Point. There he made the ship fast to sea ice, then breaking
up rapidly, and proceeded to arrange sledging parties. It was
his intention to direct the laying of the depots himself and
to leave his first officer, Lieut. J. R. Stenhouse, in command
of the *Aurora,* with instructions to select a base and land a
party.

The first objective was Hut Point, where stands the hut
erected by the *Discovery* expedition in 1902. An advance
party, consisting of Joyce (in charge), Jack, and Gaze, with
dogs and fully loaded sledges, left the ship on January 24;
Mackintosh, with Wild and Smith, followed the next day;
and a supporting party, consisting of Cope (in charge), Stevens, Ninnis, Haywood, Hooke, and Richards, left the ship
on January 30. The first two parties had dog teams. The
third party took with it the motor tractor, which does not
appear to have given the good service that I had hoped to

get from it. These parties had a strenuous time during the weeks that followed. The men, fresh from shipboard, were not in the best of training, and the same was true of the dogs. It was unfortunate that the dogs had to be worked so early after their arrival in the Antarctic. They were in poor condition and they had not learned to work together as teams. The result was the loss of many of the dogs, and this proved a serious matter in the following season. Captain Mackintosh's record of the sledging in the early months of 1915 is fairly full. It will not be necessary here to follow the fortunes of the various parties in detail, for although the men were facing difficulties and dangers, they were on well traveled ground, which has been made familiar to most readers by the histories of earlier Expeditions.

Captain Mackintosh and his party left the *Aurora* on the evening of January 25. They had nine dogs and one heavily loaded sledge, and started off briskly to the accompaniment of a cheer from their shipmates. The dogs were so eager for exercise after their prolonged confinement aboard the ship that they dashed forward at their best speed, and it was necessary for one man to sit upon the sledge in order to moderate the pace. Mackintosh had hoped to get to Hut Point that night, but luck was against him. The weather broke after he had traveled about five miles, and snow, which completely obscured all landmarks, sent him into camp on the sea ice. The weather was still thick on the following morning, and the party, making a start after breakfast, missed its way. "We shaped a course where I imagined Hut Point to be," wrote Captain Mackintosh in his diary, "but when the sledge meter showed thirteen miles fifty yards, which is four miles in excess of the distance from the ship to Hut Point, I decided to halt again. The surface was changing considerably and the land was still obscured. We have been traveling over a thick snow surface, in which we sink deeply, and the dogs are not too cheerful about it." They started again at

noon on January 27, when the weather had cleared sufficiently to reveal the land, and reached Hut Point at 4 p.m.
The sledge meter showed that the total distance traveled had
been over seventeen miles. Mackintosh found in the hut a
note from Joyce, who had been there on the 25th, and who
reported that one of his dogs had been killed in a fight with
its companions. The hut contained some stores left there
by earlier Expeditions. The party stayed there for the night.
Mackintosh left a note for Stenhouse directing him to place
provisions in the hut in case the sledging parties did not
return in time to be taken off by the ship. Early next morning Joyce reached the hut. He had encountered bad ice and
had come back to consult with Mackintosh regarding the
route to be followed. Mackintosh directed him to steer out
towards Black Island in crossing the head of the Sound beyond Hut Point.

Mackintosh left Hut Point on January 28. He had taken
some additional stores, and he mentions that the sledge now
weighed 1200 lb. This was a heavy load, but the dogs were
pulling well and he thought it practicable. He encountered
difficulty almost at once after descending the slope from the
point to the sea ice, for the sledge stuck in soft snow and
the party had to lighten the load and relay until they reached
a better surface. They were having trouble with the dogs,
which did not pull cheerfully, and the total distance covered
in the day was under four miles. The weather was warm
and the snow consequently was soft. Mackintosh had decided that it would be best to travel at night. A fall of
snow held up the party throughout the following day, and
they did not get away from their camp until shortly before
midnight. "The surface was abominably soft," wrote Mackintosh. "We harnessed ourselves on to the sledge and with
the dogs made a start, but we had a struggle to get off. We
had not gone very far when in deeper snow we stopped
dead. Try as we would, no movement could be produced.

Reluctantly we unloaded and began the tedious task of re-laying. The work, in spite of the lighter load on the sledge, proved terrific for ourselves and for the dogs. We struggled for four hours, and then set camp to await the evening, when the sun would not be so fierce and the surface might be better. I must say I feel somewhat despondent, as we are not getting on as well as I expected, or do we find it as easy as one would gather from reading."

The two parties met again that day. Joyce also had been compelled to relay his load, and all hands labored strenu-ously and advanced slowly. They reached the edge of the Barrier on the night of January 30 and climbed an easy slope to the Barrier surface, about thirty feet above the sea ice. The dogs were showing signs of fatigue, and when Mackin-tosh camped at 6:30 a.m. on January 31, he reckoned that the distance covered in twelve and a half hours had been about two and a half miles. The men had killed a seal at the edge of the sea ice and placed the meat on a cairn for future use. One dog, having refused to pull, had been left behind with a good feed of meat, and Mackintosh hoped the animal would follow. The experiences of the party during the days that followed can be indicated by some extracts from Mack-intosh's diary.

"*Sunday, January* 31.—Started off this afternoon at 3 p.m. Surface too dreadful for words. We sink into snow at times up to our knees, the dogs struggling out of it panting and making great efforts. I think the soft snow must be ac-counted for by a phenomenally fine summer without much wind. After proceeding about 1000 yds. I spotted some poles on our starboard side. We shaped course for these and found Captain Scott's Safety Camp. We unloaded a relay here and went back with empty sledge for the second relay. It took us four hours to do just this short distance. It is exas-perating. After we had got the second load up we had lunch. Then we dug round the poles, while snow fell, and after getting down about three feet we came across, first, a bag of oats, lower down two cases of dog biscuit—one with a complete week's ration, the other with seal meat. A good find. About forty paces away we found a venesta lid sticking out of the snow. Smith scraped round this with his ice axe and presently discovered one of the motor sledges Captain Scott used. Everything was just as it had been left, the petrol-tank partly filled and apparently undeteriorated. We marked the spot with a pole. The snow clearing, we proceeded with a relay. We got only half a mile, still struggling in deep snow, and then went back for the second load. We can still see the cairn erected at the Barrier edge and a black spot which we take to be the dog.

"*February* 1.—We turned out at 7:30 p.m., and after a meal broke camp. We made a relay of two and a half miles. The sledge meter stopped during this relay. Perhaps that is the cause of our mileage not showing. We covered seven and a half miles in order to bring the load two and a half miles. After lunch we decided, as the surface was getting better, to make a shot at traveling with the whole load. It was a back-breaking job. Wild led the team, while Smith and I pulled in harness. The great trouble is to get the sledge started after the many unavoidable stops. We managed to cover one mile. This even is better than relaying. We then camped—the dogs being entirely done up, poor brutes.

"*February* 2.—We were awakened this afternoon, while in our bags, by hearing Joyce's dogs barking. They have done well and have caught us up. Joyce's voice was heard presently, asking us the time. He is managing the full load. We issued a challenge to race him to the Bluff, which he accepted. When we turned out at 6:30 p.m. his camp was seen about three miles ahead. About 8 p.m., after our hoosh, we made a start, and reached Joyce's camp at 1 a.m. The dogs have been pulling well, seeing the camp ahead, but when we arrived off it they were not inclined to go on. After a little persuasion and struggle we got off, but not for long. This starting business is terrible work. We have to shake the sledge and its big load while we shout to the dogs to start. If they do not pull together it is useless. When we get the sledge going we are on tenter hooks lest it stop again on the next soft slope, and this often occurs. Sledging is real hard work; but we are getting along."

The surface was better on February 2, and the party covered six miles without relaying. They camped in soft snow, and when they started the next day they were two hours relaying over one hundred and fifty yards. Then they got into Joyce's track and found the going better. Mackintosh overtook Joyce on the morning of February 4 and went ahead, his party breaking trail during the next march. They covered ten miles on the night of the 4th. One dog had "chucked his hand in" on the march, and Mackintosh mentions that he intended to increase the dogs' allowance of food. The surface was harder, and during the night of February 5 Mackintosh covered eleven miles twenty-five yards, but he finished with two dogs on the sledge. Joyce was traveling by day, so that the parties passed one another daily on the march.

A blizzard came from the south on February 10 and the parties were confined to their tents for over twenty-four hours. The weather moderated on the morning of the next day, and at 11 a.m. Mackintosh camped beside Joyce and proceeded to rearrange the parties. One of his dogs had died on the 9th, and several others had ceased to be worth much for pulling. He had decided to take the best dogs from the two teams and continue the march with Joyce and Wild, while Smith, Jack, and Gaze went back to Hut Point with the remaining dogs. This involved the adjustment of sledge loads in order that the proper supplies might be available for the depots. He had eight dogs and Smith had five. A depot of oil and fuel was laid at this point and marked by a cairn with a bamboo pole rising ten feet above it. The change made the better progress. Smith turned back at once, and the other party went ahead fairly rapidly, the dogs being able to haul the sledge without much assistance from the men. The party built a cairn of snow after each hour's traveling to serve as guides to the depot and as marks for the return journey. Another blizzard held the men up on February 13, and they had an uncomfortable time in their sleeping bags owing to low temperature.

During succeeding days the party plodded forward. They were able to cover from five to twelve miles a day, according to the surface and weather. They built the cairns regularly and checked their route by taking bearings of the mountains to the west. They were able to cover from five to twelve miles a day, the dogs pulling fairly well. They reached lat. 80° S. on the afternoon of February 20. Mackintosh had hoped to find a depot laid in that neighborhood by Captain Scott, but no trace of it was seen. The surface had been very rough during the afternoon, and for that reason the depot to be laid there was named Rocky Mountain Depot. The stores were to be placed on a substantial cairn, and smaller cairns were to be built at right angles to the depot as a guide to the overland party. "As soon as breakfast was over," wrote Mackintosh the next day, "Joyce and Wild went off with a light sledge and the dogs to lay out the cairns and place flags to the eastward, building them at every mile. The outer cairn had a large flag and a note indicating the position of the dept. I remained behind to get angles and fix our position with the theodolite. The temperature was very low this morning, and handling the theodolite was not too warm a job for the fingers. My whiskers froze to the metal while I was taking a sight. After five hours the others arrived back. They had covered ten miles, five miles out and five miles back. During the afternoon we finished the cairn, which we have built to a height of eight feet. It is a solid square erection which ought to stand a good deal of weathering, and on top we have placed a bamboo pole with a flag, making the total height twenty-five feet. Building the cairn was a fine warming job, but the ice on our whiskers often took some ten minutes thawing out. Tomorrow we hope to lay out the cairns to the westward, and then to shape our course for the Bluff."

The weather became bad again during the night. A blizzard kept the men in their sleeping bags on February 21, and it was not until the afternoon of the 23rd that Mackintosh and Joyce made an attempt to lay out the cairns to the west. They found that two of the dogs had died during the storm, leaving seven dogs to haul the sledge. They marked a mile and half to the westward and built a cairn, but the weather was very thick and they did not think it wise to proceed farther. They could not see more than a hundred yards and the tent was soon out of sight. They returned to the camp, and stayed there until the morning of February 24, when they started the return march with snow still falling. "We did get off from our camp," says Mackintosh, "but had only proceeded about four hundred yards when the fog came on so thick that we could scarcely see a yard ahead, so we had to pitch the tent again, and are now sitting inside hoping the weather will clear. We are going back with only ten day's provisions, so it means pushing on for all we are worth. These stoppages are truly annoying. The poor dogs are feeling hungry; they eat their harness or any straps that may be about. We can give them nothing beyond their allowance of three biscuits each as we are on bare rations ourselves; but I feel sure they require more than one pound a day. That is what they are getting now. . . . After lunch we found it a little clearer, but a very bad light. We decided to push on. It is weird traveling in this light. There is no contrast or outline; the sky and the surface are one, and we cannot discern undulations, which we encounter with disastrous results. We picked up the first of our outward cairns. This was most fortunate. After passing a second cairn everything became blotted out, and so we were forced to camp, after covering 4 miles 703 yds. The dogs are feeling the pangs of hunger and devouring everything they see. They will eat anything except rope. If we had not wasted those three days we might have been able to give them a good feed at the Bluff depot, but now that is impossible. It is snowing hard."

The experiences of the next few days were unhappy. Another blizzard brought heavy snow and held the party up throughout the 25th and 26th. "Outside is a scene of chaos. The snow, whirling along with the wind, obliterates everything. The dogs are completely buried, and only a mound with a ski sticking up indicates where the sledge is. We long to be off, but the howl of the wind shows how impossible it is. The sleeping bags are damp and sticky, so are our clothes. Fortunately, the temperature is fairly high and they do not freeze. One of the dogs gave a bark and Joyce went to investigate. He found that Major, feeling hungry, had dragged his way to Joyce's ski and eaten off the leather binding. Another dog has eaten all his harness, canvas, rope, leather, brass, and rivets. I am afraid the dogs will not pull through; they all look thin and these blizzards do not improve matters. . . . We have a week's provisions and one hundred and sixty miles to travel. It appears that we will have to get another week's provisions from the depot, but don't wish it. Will see what luck tomorrow. Of course, at Bluff we can replenish."

"We are now reduced to one meal in the twenty-four hours," wrote Mackintosh a day later. "This going without food keeps us colder. It is a rotten, miserable time. It is bad enough having this wait, but we have also the wretched thought of having to use the provisions already depoted, for which we have had all this hard struggle." The weather cleared on the 27th, and in the afternoon Mackintosh and Joyce went back to the depot, while Wild remained behind to build a cairn and attempt to dry the sleeping bags in the sun. The stores left at the depot had been two and a quarter tins of biscuit (42 lb. to the tin), rations for three men for three weeks in bags, each intended to last one week, and three tins of oil. Mackintosh took one of the weekly bags from the depot and returned to the camp. The party resumed the homeward journey the next morning, and with a sail on the sledge to take advantage of the southerly breeze, covered nine miles and a half during the day. But the dogs had reached almost the limit of their endurance; three of them fell out, unable to work longer, while on the march. That evening, for the first time since leaving the *Aurora,* the men saw the sun dip to the horizon in the south, a reminder that the Antarctic summer was nearing its close.

The remaining four dogs collapsed on March 2. "After lunch we went off fairly well for half an hour. Then Nigger commenced to wobble about, his legs eventually giving under him. We took him out of his harness and let him travel along with us, but he has given us all he can, and now can only lay down. After Nigger, my friend Pompey collapsed. The drift, I think, accounts a good deal for this. Pompey has been splendid of late, pulling steadily and well. Then Scotty, the last dog but one, gave up. They are all lying down in our tracks. They have a painless death, for they curl up in the snow and fall into a sleep from which they will never wake. We are left with one dog, Pinkey. He has not been one of the pullers, but he is not despised. We can afford to give him plenty of biscuit. We must nurse him and see if we cannot return with one dog at least. We are now pulling ourselves, with the sail (the floor-cloth of the tent) set and Pinkey giving a hand. At one stage a terrific gust came along and capsized the sledge. The sail was blown off the sledge, out of its guys, and we prepared to camp, but the wind fell again to a moderate breeze, so we repaired the sledge and proceeded.

"It is blowing hard this evening, cold too. Another wonderful sunset. Golden colors illuminate the sky. The moon
casts beautiful rays in combination with the more vivid ones
from the dipping sun. If all was as beautiful as the scene we
could consider ourselves in some paradise, but it is dark and
cold in the tent and I shiver in a frozen sleeping bag. The
inside fur is a mass of ice, congealed from my breath. One
creeps into the bag, toggles up with half-frozen fingers, and
hears the crackling of the ice. Presently drops of thawing
ice are falling on one's head. Then comes a fit of shivers.
You rub yourself and turn over to warm the side of the bag
which has been uppermost. A puddle of water forms under
the body. After about two hours you may doze off, but I
always wake with the feeling that I have not slept a wink."

The party made only three and a half miles on March 3.
They were finding the sledge exceedingly heavy to pull, and
Mackintosh decided to remove the outer runners and scrape
the bottom. These runners should have been taken off before
the party started, and the lower runners polished smooth. He
also left behind all spare gear, including dog harness, in
order to reduce weight, and found the lighter sledge easier to
pull. The temperature that night was $-28°$ Fahr., the lowest
recorded during the journey up to that time. "We are struggling along at a mile an hour," wrote Mackintosh on the
5th. "It is a very hard pull, the surface being very sticky.
Pinkey still accompanies us. We hope we can get him in. He
is getting all he wants to eat. So he ought." The conditions
of travel changed the next day. A southerly wind made possible the use of the sail, and the trouble was to prevent the
sledge bounding ahead over rough sastrugi and capsizing.
The handling of ropes and the sail caused many frostbites,
and occasionally the men were dragged along the surface by
the sledge. The remaining dog collapsed during the afternoon and had to be left behind. Mackintosh did not feel that
he could afford to reduce the pace. The sledge meter had

got out of order, so the distance covered in the day was not
recorded. The wind increased during the night, and by the
morning of the 7th was blowing with blizzard force. The
party did not move again until the morning of the 8th. They
were still finding the sledge very heavy and were disap-
pointed at their slow progress, their marches being six to
eight miles a day. On the 10th they got the Bluff Peak in
line with Mount Discovery. My instructions had been that
the Bluff depot should be laid on this line, and as the depot
had been placed north of the line on the outward journey,
owing to thick weather making it impossible to pick up the
landmarks, Mackintosh intended now to move the stores to
the proper place. He sighted the depot flag about four miles
away, and after pitching camp at the new depot site, he went
across with Joyce and Wild and found the stores as he had
left them.

"We loaded the sledge with the stores, placed the large
mark flag on the sledge, and proceeded back to our tent,
which was now out of sight. Indeed it was not wise to come
out as we did without tent or bag. We had taken the chance,
as the weather had promised fine. As we proceeded it grew
darker and darker, and eventually we were traveling by only
the light of stars, the sun having dipped. After four and a
half hours we sighted the little green tent. It was hard pulling
the last two hours and very weird traveling in the dark. We
have put in a good day, having had fourteen hours' solid
marching. We are now sitting in here enjoying a very excellent thick hoosh. A light has been improvised out of an old
tin with methylated spirit."

The party spent the next day in their sleeping bags, while
a blizzard raged outside. The weather was fine again on
March 12, and they built a cairn for the depot. The stores
placed on this cairn comprised a six weeks' supply of biscuit
and three weeks' full ration for three men, and three tins
of oil. Early in the afternoon the men resumed their march

northwards and made three miles before camping. "Our bags are getting into a bad state," wrote Mackintosh, "as it is some time now since we have had an opportunity of drying them. We use our bodies for drying socks and such like clothing, which we place inside our jerseys and produce when required. Wild carries a regular wardrobe in this position, and it is amusing to see him searching round the back of his clothes for a pair of socks. Getting away in the mornings is our bitterest time. The putting on of the finneskoe is a nightmare, for they are always frozen stiff, and we have a great struggle to force our feet into them. The icy sennegrass round one's fingers is another punishment that causes much pain. We are miserable until we are actually on the move, then warmth returns with the work. Our conversation now is principally conjecture as to what can have happened to the other parties. We have various ideas."

Saturday, March 13, was another day spent in the sleeping bags. A blizzard was raging and everything was obscured. The men saved food by taking only one meal during the day, and they felt the effect of the short rations in lowered vitality. Both Joyce and Wild had toes frostbitten while in their bags and found difficulty in getting the circulation restored. Wild suffered particularly in this way and his feet were very sore. The weather cleared a little the next morning, but the drift began again before the party could break camp, and another day had to be spent in the frozen bags.

The march was resumed on March 15. "About 11 p.m. last night the temperature commenced to get lower and the gale also diminished. The lower temperature caused the bags, which were moist, to freeze hard. We had no sleep and spent the night twisting and turning. The morning brought sunshine and pleasure, for the hot hoosh warmed our bodies and gave a glow that was most comforting. The sun was out, the weather fine and clear but cold. At 8:30 a.m. we made a start. We take a long time putting on our finneskoe, although we get up earlier to allow for this. This morning we were over four hours getting away. We had a fine surface this morning for marching, but we did not make much headway. We did the usual four miles before lunch. The temperature was −23° Fahr. A mirage made the sastrugi appear to be dancing like some ice goblins. Joyce calls them 'dancing jimmies.' After lunch we traveled well, but the distance for the day was only 7 miles 400 yds. We are blaming our sledge meter for the slow rate of progress. It is extraordinary that on the days when we consider we are making good speed we do no more than on days when we have a tussle."

"*March* 15.—The air temperature this morning was −35° Fahr. Last night was one of the worst I have ever experienced. To cap everything, I developed toothache, presumably as a result of frostbitten cheek. I was in positive agony. I groaned and moaned, got the medicine chest, but could find nothing there to stop the pain. Joyce, who had wakened up, suggested methylated spirit, so I damped some cotton wool, then placed it in the tooth, with the result that I burnt the inside of my mouth. All this time my fingers, being exposed (it must have been at least 50° below zero), were continually having to be brought back. After putting on the methylated spirit I went back to the bag, which, of course, was frozen stiff. I wriggled and moaned till morning brought relief by enabling me to turn out. Joyce and Wild both had a bad night, their feet giving them trouble. My feet do not affect me so much as theirs. The skin has peeled off the inside of my mouth, exposing a raw sore, as the result of the methylated spirit. My tooth is better though. We have had to reduce our daily ration. Frostbites are frequent in consequence. The surface became very rough in the afternoon, and the light, too, was bad owing to cumulus clouds being massed over the sun. We are continually falling, for we are unable to distinguish the high and low parts of the sastrugi surface. We are traveling on our ski. We camped at

6 p.m. after traveling 6 miles 100 yds. I am writing this sitting up in the bag. This is the first occasion I have been able to do this for some time, for usually the cold has penetrated through everything should one have the bag open. The temperature is a little higher tonight, but still it is −21° Fahr. (53° of frost). Our matches, among other things, are running short, and we have given up using any except for lighting the Primus."

The party found the light bad again the next day. After stumbling on ski among the sastrugi for two hours, the men discarded the ski and made better progress; but they still had many falls, owing to the impossibility of distinguishing slopes and irregularities in the grey, shadowless surface of the snow. They made over nine and a half miles that day, and managed to cover ten miles on the following day, March 18, one of the best marches of the journey. "I look forward to seeing the ship. All of us bear marks of our tramp. Wild takes first place. His nose is a picture for *Punch* to be jealous of; his ears, too, are sore, and one big toe is a black sore. Joyce has a good nose and many minor sores. My jaw is swollen from the frostbite I got on the cheek, and I also have a bit of a nose. . . . We have discarded the ski, which we hitherto used, and travel in the finneskoe. This makes the sledge go better but it is not so comfortable traveling as on ski. We encountered a very high, rough sastrugi surface, most remarkably high, and had a cold breeze in our faces during the march. Our beards and moustaches are masses of ice. I will take care I am clean-shaven next time I come out. The frozen moustache makes the lobes of the nose freeze more easily than they would if there was no ice alongside them. . . . I ask myself why on earth one comes to these parts of the earth. Here we are, frostbitten in the day, frozen at night. What a life!" The temperature at 1 p.m. that day was −23° Fahr., i.e. 55° of frost.

The men camped abreast of "Corner Camp," where they

had been on February 1, on the evening of March 19. The next day, after being delayed for some hours by bad weather, they turned towards Castle Rock and proceeded across the disturbed area where the Barrier impinges upon the land. Joyce put his foot through the snow covering of a fairly large crevasse, and the course had to be changed to avoid this danger. The march for the day was only 2 miles 900 yds. Mackintosh felt that the pace was too slow, but was unable to quicken it owing to the bad surfaces. The food had been cut down to close upon half rations, and at this reduced rate the supply still in hand would be finished in two days. The party covered 7 miles 570 yds. on the 21st, and the hoosh that night was "no thicker than tea." "The first thought this morning was that we must do a good march," wrote Mackintosh on March 22. "Once we can get to Safety Camp (at the junction of the Barrier with the sea ice) we are right. Of course we can as a last resort abandon the sledge and take a run into Hut Point, about twenty-two miles away. . . . We have managed quite a respectable fore-noon march. The surface was hard, so we took full advantage of it. With our low food the cold is penetrating. We had lunch at 1 p.m., and then had left over one meal at full rations and a small quantity of biscuits. The temperature at lunchtime was −6° Fahr. Erebus is emitting large volumes of smoke, traveling in a southeasterly direction, and a red glare is also discernible. After lunch we again accomplished a good march, the wind favoring us for two hours. We are anxiously looking out for Safety Camp." The distance for the day was 8 miles 1525 yds.

"*March* 23, 1915.—No sooner had we camped last night than a blizzard with drift came on and has continued ever since. This morning finds us prisoners. The drift is lashing into the sides of the tent and everything outside is obscured. This weather is rather alarming, for if it continues we are in a bad way. We have just made a meal of cocoa mixed with biscuit crumbs. This has warmed us up a little, but on empty stomachs the cold is penetrating."

The weather cleared in the afternoon, but too late for the men to move that day. They made a start at 7 a.m. on the 24th after a meal of cocoa and biscuit crumbs. "We have some biscuit crumbs in the bag and that is all. Our start was made under most bitter circumstances, all of us being attacked by frostbites. It was an effort to bare hands for an instant. After much rubbing and 'bringing back' of extremities we started. Wild is a mass of bites, and we are all in a bad way. We plugged on, but warmth would not come into our bodies. We had been pulling about two hours when Joyce's smart eyes picked up a flag. We shoved on for all we were worth, and as we got closer, sure enough, the cases of provisions loomed up. Then what feeds we promised to give ourselves. It was not long before we were putting our gastronomic capabilities to the test. Pemmican was brought down from the depot, with oatmeal to thicken it, as well as sugar. While Wild was getting the Primus lighted he called out to us that he believed his ear had gone. This was the last piece of his face left whole—nose, cheeks, and neck all having bites. I went into the tent and had a look. The ear was a pale green. I quickly put the palm of my hand to it and brought it round. Then his fingers went, and to stop this and bring back the circulation he put them over the lighted Primus, a terrible thing to do. As a result he was in agony. His ear was brought round all right, and soon the hot hoosh sent warmth tingling through us. We felt like new beings. We simply ate till we were full, mug after mug. After we had been well satisfied, we replaced the cases we had pulled down from the depot and proceeded towards the Gap. Just before leaving Joyce discovered a note left by Spencer-Smith and Richards. This told us that both the other parties had returned to the Hut and apparently all was well. So that is good. When we got to the Barrier edge we found the ice

cliff on to the newly formed sea ice not safe enough to bear
us, so we had to make a detour along the Barrier edge and,
if the sea ice was not negotiable, find a way up by Castle
Rock. At 7 p.m., not having found any suitable place to descend to the sea ice, we camped. Tonight we have the Primus
going and warming our frozen selves. I hope to make Hut
Point tomorrow."

Mackintosh and his companions broke camp on the morning of March 25, with the thermometer recording 55° of
frost, and, after another futile search for a way down the ice
cliff to the sea ice, they proceeded towards Castle Rock.
While in this course they picked up sledge tracks, and, following these, they found a route down to the sea ice. Mackintosh decided to depot the sledge on top of a well-marked
undulation and proceeded without gear. A short time later
the three men, after a scramble over the cliffs of Hut Point,
reached the door of the hut. "We shouted. No sound. Shouted
again, and presently a dark object appeared. This turned out
to be Cope, who was by himself. The other members of the
party had gone out to fetch the gear off their sledge, which
they also had left. Cope had been laid up, so did not go with
them. We soon were telling each other's adventures, and we
heard then how the ship had called here on March 11 and
picked up Spencer-Smith, Richards, Ninnis, Hooke, and
Gaze, the present members here being Cope, Hayward,
and Jack. A meal was soon prepared. We found here even
a blubber fire, luxurious, but what a state of dirt and
grease! However, warmth and food are at present our principal objects. While we were having our meal Jack and Hayward appeared. . . . Late in the evening we turned into dry
bags. As there are only three bags here, we take it in turns to
use them. Our party have the privilege. . . . I got a letter here
from Stenhouse giving a summary of his doings since we
left him. The ship's party also have not had a rosy time."

Mackintosh learned here that Spencer-Smith, Jack, and

Gaze, who had turned back on February 10, had reached
Hut Point without difficulty. The third party, headed by
Cope, had also been out on the Barrier but had not done
much. This party had attempted to use the motor tractor, but
had failed to get effective service from the machine and had
not proceeded far afield. The motor was now lying at Hut
Point. Spencer-Smith's party and Cope's party had both returned to Hut Point before the end of February.

The six men now at Hut Point were cut off from the winter quarters of the Expedition at Cape Evans by the open
water of McMurdo Sound. Mackintosh naturally was anxious to make the crossing and get in touch with the ship and
the other members of the shore party; but he could not make
a move until the sea ice became firm, and, as events occurred, he did not reach Cape Evans until the beginning of
June. He went out with Cope and Hayward on March 29 to
get his sledge and brought it as far as Pram Point, on the
south side of Hut Point. He had to leave the sledge there
owing to the condition of the sea ice. He and his companions lived an uneventful life under primitive conditions at
the hut. The weather was bad, and though the temperatures
recorded were low, the young sea ice continually broke
away. The blubber stove in use at the hut seemed to have
produced soot and grease in the usual large quantities, and
the men and their clothing suffered accordingly. The whites
of their eyes contrasted vividly with the dense blackness of
their skins. Wild and Joyce had a great deal of trouble with
their frostbites. Joyce had both feet blistered, his knees were
swollen, and his hands also were blistered. Jack devised
some blubber lamps, which produced an uncertain light and
much additional smoke. Mackintosh records that the members of the party were contented enough but "unspeakably
dirty," and he writes longingly of baths and clean clothing.
The store of seal blubber ran low early in April, and all
hands kept a sharp lookout for seals. On April 15 several

seals were seen and killed. The operations of killing and skinning made worse the greasy and blackened clothes of the men. It is to be regretted that though there was a good deal of literature available, especially on this particular district, the leaders of the various parties had not taken advantage of it and so supplemented their knowledge. Joyce and Mackintosh of course had had previous Antarctic experience: but it was open to all to have carefully studied the detailed instructions published in the books of the three last Expeditions in this quarter.

CHAPTER XIV

WINTERING IN McMURDO SOUND

THE *Aurora,* after picking up six men at Hut Point on March 11, had gone back to Cape Evans. The position chosen for the winter quarters of the *Aurora* was at Cape Evans, immediately off the hut erected by Captain Scott on his last Expedition. The ship on March 14 lay about forty yards off shore, bows seaward. Two anchors had been taken ashore and embedded in heavy stone rubble, and to these anchors were attached six steel hawsers. The hawsers held the stern, while the bow was secured by the ordinary ship's anchors. Later, when the new ice had formed round the *Aurora,* the cable was dragged ashore over the smooth surface and made fast. The final moorings thus were six hawsers and one cable astern, made fast to the shore anchors, and two anchors with about seventy fathoms of cable out forward. On March 23 Mr. Stenhouse landed a party consisting of Stevens, Spencer-Smith, Gaze, and Richards in order that they might carry out routine observations ashore. These four men took up their quarters in Captain Scott's hut. They had been instructed to kill seals for meat and blubber. The landing of stores, gear, and coal did not proceed at all rapidly, it being assumed that the ship would remain at her moorings throughout the winter. Some tons of coal were taken ashore during April, but most of it stayed on the beach, and much of it was lost later when the sea ice went out. This shore party was in the charge of Stevens, and his report, handed to me much later, gives a succinct account of what occurred, from the point of view of the men at the hut.

"CAPE EVANS, ROSS ISLAND, *July 30, 1915.*

"On the 23rd March, 1915, a party consisting of Spencer-Smith, Richards, and Gaze was landed at Cape Evans Hut in my charge. Spencer-Smith received independent instructions to devote his time exclusively to photography. I was verbally instructed that the main duty of the party was to obtain a supply of seals for food and fuel. Scientific work was also to be carried on.

"Meteorological instruments were at once installed, and experiments were instituted on copper electrical thermometers in order to supplement our meager supply of instruments and enable observations of earth, ice, and sea temperatures to be made. Other experimental work was carried on, and the whole of the time of the scientific members of the party was occupied. All seals seen were secured. On one or two occasions the members of the shore party were summoned to work on board ship.

"In general the weather was unsettled, blizzards occurring frequently and interrupting communication with the ship across the ice. Only small, indispensable supplies of stores and no clothes were issued to the party on shore. Only part of the scientific equipment was able to be transferred to the shore, and the necessity to obtain that prevented some members of the party landing all their personal gear.

"The ship was moored stern on to the shore, at first well over one hundred yards from it. There were two anchors out ahead and the vessel was made fast to two others sunk in the ground ashore by seven wires. The strain on the wires was kept constant by tightening up from time to time such as became s'ack, and easing cables forward, and in this way the ship was brought much closer inshore. A cable was now run out to the south anchor ashore, passed on board through a fairlead under the port end of the bridge, and made fast to bollards forward. Subsequent strain due to ice and wind pressure on the ship broke three of the wires. Though I be-

lieve it was considered on board that the ship was secure,
there was still considerable anxiety felt. The anchors had
held badly before, and the power of the ice pressure on the
ship was uncomfortably obvious.

"Since the ship had been moored the bay had frequently
frozen over, and the ice had as frequently gone out on account of blizzards. The ice does not always go out before
the wind has passed its maximum. It depends on the state
of tides and currents; for the sea ice has been seen more
than once to go out bodily when a blizzard had almost completely calmed down.

"On the 6th May the ice was in and people passed freely
between the shore and the ship. At 11 p.m. the wind was
south, backing to southeast, and blew at forty miles per
hour. The ship was still in her place. At 3 a.m. on the 7th
the wind had not increased to any extent, but ice and ship
had gone. As she was not seen to go we are unable to say
whether the vessel was damaged. The shore end of the cable
was bent twice sharply, and the wires were loose. On the
afternoon of the 7th the weather cleared somewhat, but
nothing was seen of the ship. The blizzard only lasted some
twelve hours. Next day the wind became northerly, but on
the 10th there was blowing the fiercest blizzard we have so
far experienced from the southeast. Nothing has since been
seen or heard of the ship, though a lookout was kept.

"Immediately the ship went as accurate an inventory as
possible of all stores ashore was made, and the rate of consumption of foodstuffs so regulated that they would last ten
men for not less than one hundred weeks. Coal had already
been used with the utmost economy. Little could be done
to cut down the consumption, but the transference to the
neighborhood of the hut of such of the coal landed previously by the ship as was not lost was pushed on. Meat also
was found to be very short; it was obvious that neither it
nor coal could be made to last two years, but an evidently
necessary step in the ensuing summer would be the ensuring

of an adequate supply of meat and blubber, for obtaining which the winter presented little opportunity. Meat and coal were, therefore, used with this consideration in mind, as required but as carefully as possible.

"A. STEVENS."

The men ashore did not at once abandon hope of the ship returning before the Sound froze firmly. New ice formed on the sea whenever the weather was calm, and it had been broken up and taken out many times by the blizzards. During the next few days eager eyes looked seaward through the dim twilight of noon, but the sea was covered with a dense black mist and nothing was visible. A northerly wind sprang up on May 8 and continued for a few hours, but it brought no sign of the ship, and when on May 10 the most violent blizzard yet experienced by the party commended, hope grew slender. The gale continued for three days, the wind attaining a velocity of seventy miles an hour. The snow drift was very thick and the temperature fell to $-20°$ Fahr. The shore party took a gloomy view of the ship's chances of safety among the ice floes of the Ross Sea under such conditions.

Stevens and his companions made a careful survey of their position and realized that they had serious difficulties to face. No general provisions and no clothing of the kind required for sledging had been landed from the ship. Much of the sledging gear was also aboard. Fortunately, the hut contained both food and clothing, left there by Captain Scott's Expedition. The men killed as many seals as possible and stored the meat and blubber. June 2 brought a welcome addition to the party in the form of the men who had been forced to remain at Hut Point until the sea ice became firm. Mackintosh and those with him had incurred some risk in making the crossing, since open water had been seen on their route by the Cape Evans party only a short time before. There were now ten men at Cape Evans—namely, Mackintosh, Spencer-Smith, Joyce, Wild, Cope, Stevens, Hayward,

Gaze, Jack, and Richards. The winter had closed down upon
the Antarctic and the party would not be able to make any
move before the beginning of September. In the meantime
they overhauled the available stores and gear, made plans
for the work of the forthcoming spring and summer, and
lived the severe but not altogether unhappy life of the polar
explorer in winter quarters. Mackintosh, writing on June 5,
surveyed his position:

"The decision of Stenhouse to make this bay the wintering
place of the ship was not reached without much thought and
consideration of all eventualities. Stenhouse had already tried
the Glacier Tongue and other places, but at each of them the
ship had been in an exposed and dangerous position. When
this bay was tried the ship withstood several severe blizzards,
in which the ice remained in on several occasions. When the
ice did go out the moorings held. The ship was moored bows
north. She had both anchors down forward and two anchors
buried astern, to which the stern moorings were attached with
seven lengths of wire. Taking all this into account, it was
quite a fair judgment on his part to assume that the ship
would be secure here. The blizzard that took the ship and the
ice out of the bay was by no means as severe as others she
had weathered. The accident proves again the uncertainty of
conditions in these regions. I only pray and trust that the ship
and those aboard are safe. I am sure they will have a thrilling
story to tell when we see them."

The *Aurora* could have found safe winter quarters farther
up McMurdo Sound, towards Hut Point, but would have run
the risk of being frozen in over the following summer, and
I had given instructions to Mackintosh before he went south
that this danger must be avoided.

"Meanwhile we are making all preparations here for a prolonged stay. The shortage of clothing is our principal hardship. The members of the party from Hut Point have the
clothes we wore when we left the ship on January 25. We
have been without a wash all that time, and I cannot imagine

a dirtier set of people. We have been attempting to get a wash ever since we came back, but owing to the blow during the last two days no opportunity has offered. All is working smoothly here, and every one is taking the situation very philosophically. Stevens is in charge of the scientific staff and is now the senior officer ashore. Joyce is in charge of the equipment and has undertaken to improvise clothes out of what canvas can be found here. Wild is working with Joyce. He is a cheerful, willing soul. Nothing ever worries or upsets him, and he is ever singing or making some joke or performing some amusing prank. Richards has taken over the keeping of the meteorological log. He is a young Australian, a hard, conscientious worker, and I look forward to good results from his endeavors. Jack, another young Australian, is his assistant. Hayward is the handy man, being responsible for the supply of blubber. Gaze, another Australian, is working in conjunction with Hayward. Spencer-Smith, the *padre,* is in charge of photography, and, of course, assists in the general routine work. Cope is the medical officer.

"The routine here is as follows: Four of us, myself, Stevens, Richards, and Spencer-Smith, have breakfast at 7 a.m. The others are called at 9 a.m., and their breakfast is served. Then the table is cleared, the floor is swept, and the ordinary work of the day is commenced. At 1 p.m. we have what we call a 'counter lunch,' that is, cold food and cocoa. We work from 2 p.m. till 5 p.m. After 5 p.m. people can do what they like. Dinner is at 7. The men play games, read, write up diaries. We turn in early, since we have to economize fuel and light. Night watches are kept by the scientific men, who have the privilege of turning in during the day. The day after my arrival here I gave an outline of our situation and explained the necessity for economy in the use of fuel, light, and stores, in view of the possibility that we may have to stay here for two years. . . . We are not going to commence work for the sledging operations until we know more definitely the fate of the *Aurora.* I dare not think any disaster has occurred."

During the remaining days of June the men washed and mended clothes, killed seals, made minor excursions in the neighborhood of the hut, and discussed plans for the future. They had six dogs, two being bitches without experience of sledging. One of these bitches had given birth to a litter of pups, but she proved a poor mother and the young ones died. The animals had plenty of seal meat and were tended carefully.

Mackintosh called a meeting of all hands on June 26 for the discussion of the plans he had made for the depot-laying expedition to be undertaken during the following spring and summer. "I gave an outline of the position and invited discussion from the members. Several points were brought up. I had suggested that one of our party should remain behind for the purpose of keeping the meteorological records and laying in a supply of meat and blubber. This man would be able to hand my instructions to the ship and pilot a party to the Bluff. It had been arranged that Richards should do this. Several objected on the ground that the whole complement would be necessary, and, after the matter had been put to the vote, it was agreed that we should delay the decision until the parties had some practical work and we had seen how they fared. The shortage of clothing was discussed, and Joyce and Wild have agreed to do their best in this matter. October sledging (on the Barrier) was mentioned as being too early, but is to be given a trial. These were the most important points brought up, and it was mutually and unanimously agreed that we could do no more. . . . I know we are doing our best."

The party was anxious to visit Cape Royds, north of Cape Evans, but at the end of June open water remained right across the Sound and a crossing was impossible. At Cape Royds is the hut used by the Shackleton Expedition of 1907–1909, and the stores and supplies it contains might have proved very useful. Joyce and Wild make finneskoe (fur boots) from spare sleeping bags. Mackintosh mentions that the necessity of economizing clothing and footgear prevented the men taking as much exercise as they would otherwise have done. A fair supply of canvas and leather had been found in the hut, and some men tried their hands at making shoes. Many seals had been killed and brought in, and the supply of meat and blubber was ample for present needs.

During July Mackintosh made several trips northwards on the sea ice, but found always that he could not get far. A crack stretched roughly from Inaccessible Island to the Barne Glacier, and the ice beyond looked weak and loose. The improving light told of the returning sun. Richards and Jack were weighing out stores in readiness for the sledging expeditions. Mackintosh, from the hill behind the hut, saw open water stretching westward from Inaccessible Island on August 1, and noted that probably McMurdo Sound was never completely frozen over. A week later the extent of the open water appeared to have increased, and the men began to despair of getting to Cape Royds. Blizzards were frequent and persistent. A few useful articles were found in the neighborhood of the hut as the light improved, including some discarded socks and underwear, left by members of the Scott Expedition, and a case of candied peel, which was used for cakes. A small fire broke out in the hut on August 12. The acetylene-gas lighting plant installed in the hut by Captain Scott had been rigged, and one day it developed a leak. A member of the party searched for the leak with a lighted candle, and the explosion that resulted fired some woodwork. Fortunately the outbreak was extinguished quickly. The loss of the hut at this stage would have been a tragic incident.

Mackintosh and Stevens paid a visit to Cape Royds on August 13. They had decided to attempt the journey over the Barne Glacier, and after crossing a crevassed area they got to the slopes of Cape Barne and thence down to the sea ice. They found this ice to be newly formed, but sufficiently strong for their purpose, and soon reached the Cape Royds hut. "The outer door of the hut we found to be off," wrote Mackintosh. "A little snow had drifted into the porch, but

with a shovel, which we found outside, this was soon
cleared away. We then entered, and in the center of the hut
found a pile of snow and ice, which had come through the
open ventilator in the roof of the hut. We soon closed this.
Stevens prepared a meal while I cleared the ice and snow
away from the middle of the hut. After our meal we commenced taking an inventory of the stores inside. Tobacco
was our first thought. Of this we found one tin of Navy Cut
and a box of cigars. Soap, too, which now ensures us a wash
and clean clothes when we get back. We then began to look
round for a sleeping bag. No bags were here, however, but
on the improvised beds of cases we found two mattresses,
an old canvas screen, and two blankets. We took it in turns
to turn in. Stevens started first, while I kept the fire going.
No coal or blubber was here, so we had to use wood, which,
while keeping the person alongside it warm, did not raise
the temperature of the hut over freezing point. Over the
stove in a conspicuous place we found a notice left by
Scott's party that parties using the hut should leave the
dishes clean."

Mackintosh and Stevens stayed at the Cape Royds hut
over the next day and made a thorough examination of the
stores there. They found outside the hut a pile of cases containing meats, flour, dried vegetables, and sundries, at least
a year's supply for a party of six. They found no new clothing, but made a collection of worn garments, which could
be mended and made serviceable. Carrying loads of their
spoils, they set out for Cape Evans on the morning of August 15 across the sea ice. Very weak ice barred the way and
they had to travel round the coast. They got back to Cape
Evans in two hours. During their absence Wild and Gaze
had climbed Inaccessible Island, Gaze having an ear badly
frostbitten on the journey. The tobacco was divided among
the members of the party. A blizzard was raging the next
day, and Mackintosh congratulated himself on having chosen the time for his trip fortunately.

The record of the remaining part of August is not eventful. All hands were making preparations for the sledging, and were rejoicing in the increasing daylight. The party tried the special sledging ration prepared under my own direction, and "all agreed it was excellent both in bulk and taste." Three emperor penguins, the first seen since the landing, were caught on August 19. By that time the returning sun was touching with gold the peaks of the Western Mountains and throwing into bold relief the massive form of Erebus. The volcano was emitting a great deal of smoke, and the glow of its internal fires showed occasionally against the smoke-clouds above the crater. Stevens, Spencer-Smith, and Cope went to Cape Royds on the 20th, and were still there when the sun made its first appearance over Erebus on the 26th. Preceding days had been cloudy, and the sun, although above the horizon, had not been visible. "The morning broke clear and fine," wrote Mackintosh. "Over Erebus the sun's rays peeped through the massed cumulus and produced the most gorgeous cloud effects. The light made us all blink and at the same time caused the greatest exuberance of spirits. We felt like men released from prison. I stood outside the hut and looked at the truly wonderful scenery all round. The West Mountains were superb in their wild grandeur. The whole outline of peaks, some eighty or ninety miles distant, showed up, stencilled in delicate contrast to the skyline. The immense ice slopes shone white as alabaster against dark shadows. The sky to the west over the mountains was clear, except for low-lying banks at the foot of the slopes round about Mount Discovery. To the south hard streaks of stratus lay heaped up to 30 degrees above the horizon. . . . Then Erebus commenced to emit volumes of smoke, which rose hundreds of feet and trailed away in a northwesterly direction. The southern slopes of Erebus were enveloped in a mass of cloud." The party from Cape Royds returned that afternoon, and there was disappointment at their report that no more tobacco had been found.

The sledging of stores to Hut Point, in preparation for
the depot-laying journeys on the Barrier, was to begin on
September 1. Mackintosh, before that date, had discussed
plans fully with the members of his party. He considered
that sufficient sledging provisions were available at Cape
Evans, the supply landed from the ship being supplemented
by the stores left by the Scott Expedition of 1912–13 and
the Shackleton Expedition of 1907–09. The supply of clothing and tents was more difficult. Garments brought from the
ship could be supplemented by old clothing found at Hut
Point and Cape Evans. The Burberry windproof outer garments were old and in poor order for the start of a season's
sledging. Old sleeping bags had been cut up to make finneskoe (fur boots) and mend other sleeping bags. Three
tents were available, one sound one landed from the *Aurora,*
and two old ones left by Captain Scott. Mackintosh had
enough sledges, but the experience of the first journey with
the dogs had been unfortunate, and there were now only
four useful dogs left. They did not make a full team and
would have to be used merely as an auxiliary to man-
haulage.

The scheme adopted by Mackintosh, after discussion with
the members of his party, was that nine men, divided into
three parties of three each, should undertake the sledging.
One man would be left at Cape Evans to continue the meteorological observations during the summer. The motor tractor, which had been left at Hut Point, was to be brought to
Cape Evans and, if possible, put into working order. Mackintosh estimated that the provisions required for the consumption of the depot parties, and for the depots to be
placed southward to the foot of the Beardmore Glacier,
would amount to 4000 lb. The first depot was to be placed
off Minna Bluff, and from there southward a depot was to
be placed on each degree of latitude. The final depot would
be made at the foot of the Beardmore Glacier. The initial

task would be the haulage of stores from Cape Evans to Hut Point, a distance of 13 miles. All the sledging stores had to be taken across, and Mackintosh proposed to place additional supplies there in case a party, returning late from the Barrier, had to spend winter months at Hut Point.

The first party, consisting of Mackintosh, Richards, and Spencer-Smith, left Cape Evans on September 1 with 600 lb. of stores on one sledge, and had an uneventful journey to Hut Point. They pitched a tent halfway across the bay, on the sea ice, and left it there for the use of the various parties during the month. At Hut Point they cleared the snow from the motor tractor and made some preliminary efforts to get it into working order. They returned to Cape Evans on the 3rd. The second trip to Hut Point was made by a party of nine, with three sledges. Two sledges, man hauled, were loaded with 1278 lb. of stores, and a smaller sledge, drawn by the dogs, carried the sleeping bags. This party encountered a stiff southerly breeze, with low temperature, and, as the men were still in rather soft condition, they suffered much from frostbites. Joyce and Gaze both had their heels badly blistered. Mackintosh's face suffered, and other men had fingers and ears "bitten." When they returned Gaze had to travel on a sledge, since he could not set foot to the ground. They tried to haul the motor to Cape Evans on this occasion, but left it for another time after covering a mile or so. The motor was not working and was heavy to pull.

Eight men made the third journey to Hut Point, Gaze and Jack remaining behind. They took 660 lb. of oil and 630 lb. of stores. From Hut Point the next day (September 14) the party proceeded with loaded sledges to Safety Camp, on the edge of the Barrier. This camp would be the starting point for the march over the Barrier to the Minna Bluff depot. They left the two sledges, with 660 lbs. of oil and 500 lb. of oatmeal, sugar, and sundries, at Safety Camp and returned to Hut Point. The dogs shared the work on this journey. The

next day Mackintosh and his companions took the motor to
Cape Evans, hauling it with its grip wheels mounted on a
sledge. After a pause due to bad weather, a party of eight
men took another load to Hut Point on September 24, and
on to Safety Camp the next day. They got back to Cape
Evans on the 26th. Richards meanwhile had overhauled the
motor and given it some trial runs on the sea ice. But he
reported that the machine was not working satisfactorily,
and Mackintosh decided not to persevere with it.

"Everybody is up to his eyes in work," runs the last entry
in the journal left by Mackintosh at Cape Evans. "All gear
is being overhauled, and personal clothing is having the last
stitches. We have been improvising shoes to replace the
finneskoe, of which we are badly short. Wild has made an
excellent shoe out of an old horse rug he found here, and
this is being copied by other men. I have made myself a pair
of mits out of an old sleeping bag. Last night I had a bath,
the second since being here. . . . I close this journal today
(September 30) and am packing it with my papers here. Tomorrow we start for Hut Point. Nine of us are going on the
sledge party for laying depots—namely, Stevens, Spencer-
Smith, Joyce, Wild, Cope, Hayward, Jack, Richards, and
myself. Gaze, who is still suffering from bad feet, is remaining behind and will probably be relieved by Stevens after
our first trip. With us we take three months' provisions to
leave at Hut Point. I continue this journal in another book,
which I keep with me."

The nine men reached Hut Point on October 1. They took
the last loads with them. Three sledges and three tents were
to be taken on to the Barrier, and the parties were as follows:
No. 1: Mackintosh, Spencer-Smith, and Wild; No. 2: Joyce,
Cope, and Richards; No. 3: Jack, Hayward, and Gaze. On
October 3 and 4 some stores left at Half-Way Camp were
brought in, and other stores were moved on to Safety Camp.
Bad weather delayed the start of the depot-laying expedition
from Hut Point until October 9.

CHAPTER XV

LAYING THE DEPOTS

MACKINTOSH'S ACCOUNT of the depot-laying journeys undertaken by his parties in the summer of 1915–16 unfortunately is not available. The leader of the parties kept a diary, but he had the book with him when he was lost on the sea ice in the following winter. The narrative of the journeys has been compiled from the notes kept by Joyce, Richards, and other members of the parties, and I may say here that it is a record of dogged endeavor in the face of great difficulties and serious dangers. It is always easy to be wise after the event, and one may realize now that the use of the dogs, untrained and soft from shipboard inactivity, on the comparatively short journey undertaken immediately after the landing in 1915 was a mistake. The result was the loss of nearly all the dogs before the longer and more important journeys of 1915–16 were undertaken. The men were sledging almost continuously during a period of six months; they suffered from frostbite, scurvy, snow blindness, and the utter weariness of overtaxed bodies. But they placed the depots in the required positions, and if the Weddell Sea party had been able to make the crossing of the Antarctic continent, the stores and fuel would have been waiting for us where we expected to find them.

The position on October 9 was that the nine men at Hut Point had with them the stores required for the depots and for their own maintenance throughout the summer. The remaining dogs were at Cape Evans with Gaze, who had a sore heel and had been replaced temporarily by Stevens in the sledging party. A small quantity of stores had been conveyed already to Safety Camp on the edge of the Barrier

beyond Hut Point. Mackintosh intended to form a large
depot off Minna Bluff, seventy miles out from Hut Point.
This would necessitate several trips with heavy loads. Then
he would use the Bluff depot as a base for the journey to
Mount Hope, at the foot of the Beardmore Glacier, where
the final depot was to be laid.

The party left Hut Point on the morning of October 9,
the nine men hauling on one rope and trailing three loaded
sledges. They reached Safety Camp in the early afternoon,
and, after repacking the sledges with a load of about 2000
lb., they began the journey over the Barrier. The pulling
proved exceedingly heavy, and they camped at the end of
half a mile. It was decided next day to separate the sledges,
three men to haul each sledge. Mackintosh hoped that better
progress could be made in this way. The distance for the
day was only four miles, and the next day's journey was no
better. Joyce mentions that he had never done harder pulling, the surface being soft, and the load amounting to 220
lb. per man. The new arrangement was not a success, owing
to differences in hauling capacity and inequalities in the
loading of the sledges; and on the morning of the 12th,
Mackintosh, after consultation, decided to push forward
with Wild and Spencer-Smith, hauling one sledge and a relatively light load, and leave Joyce and the remaining five
men to bring two sledges and the rest of the stores at their
best pace. This arrangement was maintained on the later
journeys. The temperatures were falling below − 30° Fahr.
at some hours, and, as the men perspired freely while hauling their heavy loads in the sun, they suffered a great deal
of discomfort in the damp and freezing clothes at night.
Joyce cut down his load on the 13th by depoting some rations and spare clothing, and made better progress. He was
building snow cairns as guideposts for use on the return
journey. He mentions passing some large crevasses during
succeeding days. Persistent head winds with occasional drift

made the conditions unpleasant and caused many frostbites. When the surface was hard, and the pulling comparatively easy, the men slipped and fell continually, "looking much like classical dancers."

On the 20th a northerly wind made possible the use of a sail, and Joyce's party made rapid progress. Jack sighted a bamboo pole during the afternoon, and Joyce found that it marked a depot he had laid for my own "Farthest South" party in 1908. He dug down in the hope of finding some stores, but the depot had been cleared. The party reached the Bluff depot on the evening of the 21st and found that Mackintosh had been there on the 19th. Mackintosh had left 178 lb. of provisions, and Joyce left one sledge and 273 lb. of stores. The most interesting incident of the return journey was the discovery of a note left by Mr. Cherry Garrard for Captain Scott on March 19, 1912, only a few days before the latter perished at his camp farther south. An upturned sledge at this point was found to mark a depot of dog biscuit and motor oil, laid by one of Captain Scott's parties. Joyce reached Safety Camp on the afternoon of the 27th, and, after dumping all spare gear, pushed on to Hut Point in a blizzard. The sledges nearly went over a big drop at the edge of the Barrier, and a few moments later Stevens dropped down a crevasse to the length of his harness. "Had a tough job getting him up, as we had no alpine rope and had to use harness," wrote Joyce. "Got over all right and had a very hard pull against wind and snow, my face getting frostbitten as I had to keep looking up to steer. We arrived at the hut about 7:30 p.m. after a very hard struggle. We found the Captain and his party there. They had been in for three days. Gaze was also there with the dogs. We soon had a good feed and forgot our hard day's work."

Mackintosh decided to make use of the dogs on the second journey to the Bluff depot. He thought that with the aid of the dogs heavier loads might be hauled. This plan in-

volved the dispatch of a party to Cape Evans to get dog
pemmican. Mackintosh himself, with Wild and Spencer-
Smith, started south again on October 29. Their sledge overturned on the slope down to the sea ice, and the rim of their
tent spread was broken. The damage did not appear serious,
and the party soon disappeared round Cape Armitage. Joyce
remained in charge at Hut Point, with instructions to get dog
food from Cape Evans and make a start south as soon as
possible. He sent Stevens, Hayward, and Cope to Cape
Evans the next day, and busied himself with the repair of
sledging gear. Cope, Hayward, and Gaze arrived back from
Cape Evans on November 1, Stevens having stayed at the
base. A blizzard delayed the start southward, and the party
did not get away until November 5. The men pulled in harness with the four dogs, and, as the surface was soft and the
loads on the two sledges were heavy, the advance was slow.
The party covered 5 miles 700 yards on the 6th, 4 miles 300
yards on the 7th, and 8 miles 1800 yards on the 9th, with
the aid of a light northerly wind. They passed on the 9th a
huge bergstrom, with a drop of about 70 feet from the flat
surface of the Barrier. Joyce thought that a big crevasse had
caved in. "We took some photographs," wrote Joyce. "It is
a really extraordinary fall-in of ice, with cliffs of blue ice
about 70 feet high, and heavily crevassed, with overhanging
snow curtains. One could easily walk over the edge coming
from the north in thick weather." Another bergstrom, with
crevassed ice around it, was encountered on the 11th. Joyce
reached the Bluff depot on the evening of the 14th and
found that he could leave 624 lb. of provisions. Mackintosh
had been there several days earlier and had left 188 lb. of
stores.

Joyce made Hut Point again on November 20 after an
adventurous day. The surface was good in the morning and
he pushed forward rapidly. About 10:30 a.m. the party encountered heavy pressure ice with crevasses, and had many

narrow escapes. "After lunch we came on four crevasses quite suddenly. Jack fell through. We could not alter course, or else we should have been steering among them, so galloped right across. We were going so fast that the dogs that went through were jerked out. It came on very thick at 2 p.m. Every bit of land was obscured, and it was hard to steer. Decided to make for Hut Point, and arrived at 6:30 p.m., after doing twenty-two miles, a very good performance. I had a bad attack of snow blindness and had to use cocaine. Hayward also had a bad time. I was laid up and had to keep my eyes bandaged for three days. Hayward, too." The two men were about again on November 24, and the party started south on its third journey to the Bluff on the 25th. Mackintosh was some distance ahead, but the two parties met on the 28th and had some discussion as to plans. Mackintosh was proceeding to the Bluff depot with the intention of taking a load of stores to the depot placed on lat. 80° S. in the first season's sledging. Joyce, after depositing his third load at the Bluff, would return to Hut Point for a fourth and last load, and the parties would then join forces for the journey southward to Mount Hope.

Joyce left 729 lb. at the Bluff depot on December 2, reached Hut Point on December 7, and, after allowing dogs and men a good rest, he moved southward again on December 13. This proved to be the worst journey the party had made. The men had much trouble with crevasses, and they were held up by blizzards on December 16, 18, 19, 22, 23, 26, and 27. They spent Christmas Day struggling through soft snow against an icy wind and drift. The party reached the Bluff depot on December 28, and found that Mackintosh, who had been much delayed by the bad weather, had gone south two days earlier on his way to the 80° S. depot. He had not made much progress and his camp was in sight. He had left instructions for Joyce to follow him. The Bluff depot was now well stocked. Between 2800 and 2900 lb. of provisions had been dragged to the depot for the use of parties working to the south of this point. This quantity was in addition to stores placed there earlier in the year.

Joyce left the Bluff depot on December 29, and the parties were together two days later. Mackintosh handed Joyce instructions to proceed with his party to lat. 81° S., and place a depot there. He was then to send three men back to Hut Point and proceed to lat. 82° S., where he would lay another depot. Then if provisions permitted he would push south as far as lat. 83°. Mackintosh himself was reinforcing the depot at lat. 80° S. and would then carry on southward. Apparently his instructions to Joyce were intended to guard against the contingency of the parties failing to meet. The dogs were hauling well, and though their number was small they were of very great assistance. The parties were now ninety days out from Cape Evans, and "all hands were feeling fit."

The next incident of importance was the appearance of a defect in one of the two Primus lamps used by Joyce's party. The lamps had all seen service with one or other of Captain Scott's parties, and they had not been in first class condition when the sledging commenced. The threatened failure of a lamp was a matter of grave moment, since a party could not travel without the means of melting snow and preparing hot food. If Joyce took a faulty lamp past the 80° S. depot, his whole party might have to turn back at lat. 81° S., and this would imperil the success of the season's sledging. He decided, therefore, to send three men back from the 80° S. depot, which he reached on January 6, 1916. Cope, Gaze, and Jack were the men to return. They took the defective Primus and a light load, and by dint of hard traveling, without the aid of dogs, they reached Cape Evans on January 16.

Joyce, Richards, and Hayward went forward with a load of 1280 lb., comprising twelve weeks' sledging rations, dog food and depot supplies, in addition to the sledging gear.

They built cairns at short intervals as guides to the depots. Joyce was feeding the dogs well and giving them a hot hoosh every third night. "It is worth it for the wonderful amount of work they are doing. If we can keep them to 82° S. I can honestly say it is through their work we have got through." On January 8 Mackintosh joined Joyce, and from that point the parties, six men strong, went forward together. They marched in thick weather during January 10, 11, and 12, keeping the course by means of cairns, with a scrap of black cloth on top of each one. It was possible, by keeping the cairns in line behind the sledges and building new ones as old ones disappeared, to march on an approximately straight line. On the evening of the 12th they reached lat. 81° S., and built a large cairn for the depot. The stores left here were three weeks' rations for the ordinary sledging unit of three men. This quantity would provide five days' rations for twelve men, half for the use of the overland party, and half for the depot party on its return journey.

The party moved southwards again on January 13 in bad weather. "After a little consultation we decided to get under way," wrote Joyce. "Although the weather is thick, and snow is falling, it is worth while to make the effort. A little patience with the direction and the cairns, even if one has to put them up 200 yds. apart, enables us to advance, and it seems that this weather will never break. We have cut up an old pair of trousers belonging to Richards to place on the sides of the cairns, so as to make them more prominent. It was really surprising to find how we got on in spite of the snow and the pie crust surface. We did 5 miles 75 yds. before lunch. The dogs are doing splendidly. I really don't know how we should manage if it were not for them. . . . The distance for the day was 10 miles 720 yds., a splendid performance considering surface and weather."

The weather cleared on the 14th; and the men were able to get bearings from the mountains to the westward. They

advanced fairly rapidly during succeeding days, the daily
distances being from ten to twelve miles, and reached lat.
82° S. on the morning of January 18. The depot here, like
the depot at 81° S., contained five days' provisions for
twelve men. Mackintosh was having trouble with the Primus
lamp in his tent, and this made it inadvisable to divide the
party again. It was decided, therefore, that all should proceed, and that the next and last depot should be placed on
the base of Mount Hope, at the foot of the Beardmore Glacier, in lat. 83° 30′ S. The party proceeded at once and advanced five miles beyond the depot before camping on the
evening of the 18th.

The sledge loads were now comparatively light, and on
the 19th the party covered 13 miles 700 yds. A new trouble
was developing, for Spencer-Smith was suffering from
swollen and painful legs, and was unable to do much pulling. Joyce wrote on the 21st that Smith was worse, and that
Mackintosh was showing signs of exhaustion. A mountain
that he believed to be Mount Hope could be seen right
ahead, over thirty miles away. Spencer-Smith, who had
struggled forward gamely and made no unnecessary com-
plaints, started with the party the next morning and kept
going until shortly before noon. Then he reported his inability to proceed, and Mackintosh called a halt. Spencer-Smith
suggested that he should be left with provisions and a tent
while the other members of the party pushed on to Mount
Hope, and pluckily assured Mackintosh that the rest would
put him right and that he would be ready to march when
they returned. The party agreed, after a brief consultation,
to adopt this plan. Mackintosh felt that the depot must be
laid, and that delay would be dangerous. Spencer-Smith was
left with a tent, one sledge, and provisions, and told to expect the returning party in about a week. The tent was made
as comfortable as possible inside, and food was placed
within the sick man's reach. Spencer-Smith bade his com-

panions a cheery good-bye after lunch, and the party was six or seven miles away before evening. Five men had to squeeze into one tent that night, but with a minus temperature they did not object to being crowded.

On January 23 a thick fog obscured all landmarks, and as bearings of the mountains were now necessary the party had to camp at 11 a.m., after traveling only four miles. The thick weather continued over the 24th, and the men did not move again until the morning of the 25th. They did 17¾ miles that day, and camped at 6 p.m. on the edge of "the biggest ice pressure" Joyce had ever seen. They were steering in towards the mountains and were encountering the tremendous congestion created by the flow of the Beardmore Glacier into the barrier ice.

"We decided to keep the camp up," ran Joyce's account of the work done on January 26. "Skipper, Richards, and myself roped ourselves together, I taking the lead, to try and find a course through this pressure. We came across very wide crevasses, went down several, came on top of a very high ridge, and such a scene! Imagine thousands of tons of ice churned up to a depth of about 300 ft. We took a couple of photographs, then carried on to the east. At last we found a passage through, and carried on through smaller crevasses to Mount Hope, or we hoped it was the mountain by that name. We can see a great glacier ahead which we take for the Beardmore, which this mountain is on, but the position on the chart seems wrong. [It was not.—*E.H.S.*] We nearly arrived at the ice foot when Richards saw something to the right, which turned out to be two of Captain Scott's sledges, upright, but three-quarters buried in snow. Then we knew for certain this was the place we had struggled to get to. So we climbed the glacier on the slope and went up about one and a quarter miles, and saw the great Beardmore Glacier stretching to the south. It is about twenty-five miles wide—a most wonderful sight. Then we returned to our camp, which

we found to be six miles away. We left at 8 a.m. and arrived
back at 3 p.m., a good morning's work. We then had lunch.
About 4 p.m. we got under way and proceeded with the two
sledges and camped about 7 o'clock. Wild, Hayward, and
myself then took the depot up the Glacier, a fortnight's provisions. We left it lashed to a broken sledge, and put up a
large flag. I took two photographs of it. We did not arrive
back until 10:30 p.m. It was rather a heavy pull up. I was
very pleased to see our work completed at last. . . . Turned
in 12 o'clock. The distance done during day 22 miles."

The party remained in camp until 3:30 p.m. on the 27th,
owing to a blizzard with heavy snow. Then they made a
start in clearer weather and got through the crevassed area
before camping at 7 p.m. Joyce was suffering from snow
blindness. They were now homeward bound, with 365 miles
to go. They covered 16½ miles on the 28th, with Joyce absolutely blind and hanging to the harness for guidance, "but
still pulling his whack." They reached Spencer-Smith's
camp the next afternoon and found him in his sleeping bag,
quite unable to walk. Joyce's diary of this date contains a
rather gloomy reference to the outlook, since he guessed
that Mackintosh also would be unable to make the homeward march. "The dogs are still keeping fit," he added. "If
they will only last to 80° S. we shall then have enough food
to take them in, and then if the ship is in I guarantee they
will live in comfort the remainder of their lives."

No march could be made on the 30th, since a blizzard
was raging. The party made 8 miles on the 31st, with Spencer-Smith on one of the sledges in his sleeping bag. The
sufferer was quite helpless, and had to be lifted and carried
about, but his courage did not fail him. His words were
cheerful even when his physical suffering and weakness
were most pronounced. The distance for February 1 was 13
miles. The next morning the party abandoned one sledge in
order to lighten the load, and proceeded with a single

sledge, Spencer-Smith lying on top of the stores and gear. The distance for the day was 15½ miles. They picked up the 82° S. depot on February 3, and took one week's provisions, leaving two weeks' rations for the overland party. Joyce, Wild, Richards, and Hayward were feeling fit, Mackintosh was lame and weak; Spencer-Smith's condition was alarming. The party was being helped by strong southerly winds, and the distances covered were decidedly good. The sledge meter recorded 15 miles 1700 yds. on February 4, 17 miles 1400 yds. on the 5th, 18 miles 1200 yds. on the 6th, and 13 miles 1000 yds. on the 7th, when the 81° S. depot was picked up at 10:30 a.m., and one week's stores taken, two weeks' rations being left.

The march to the next depot, at 80° S., was uneventful. The party made good marches in spite of bad surfaces and thick weather, and reached the depot late in the afternoon of February 12. The supply of stores at this depot was ample, and the men took a fortnight's rations (calculated on a three-man basis), leaving nearly four weeks' rations. Spencer-Smith seemed a little better, and all hands were cheered by the rapid advance. February 14, 15, and 16 were bad days, the soft surface allowing the men to sink to their knees at times. The dogs had a rough time, and the daily distances fell to about eight miles. Mackintosh's weakness was increasing. Then on the 18th, when the party was within twelve miles of the Bluff depot, a furious blizzard made traveling impossible. This blizzard raged for five days. Rations were reduced on the second day, and the party went on half rations the third day.

"Still blizzarding," wrote Joyce on the 20th. "Things are serious, what with our patient and provisions running short. Dog provisions are nearly out, and we have to halve their rations. We are now on one cup of hoosh among the three of us, with one biscuit and six lumps of sugar. The most serious of calamities is that our oil is running out. We have plenty of tea, but no fuel to cook it with." The men in Mack-intosh's tent were in no better plight. Mackintosh himself was in a bad way. He was uncertain about his ability to resume the march, but was determined to try.

"Still blizzarding," wrote Joyce again on the 21st. "We are lying in pools of water made by our bodies through stay-ing in the same place for such a long time. I don't know what we shall do if this does not ease. It has been blowing continuously without a lull. The food for today was one cup of pemmican amongst three of us, one biscuit each, and two cups of tea among the three." The kerosene was exhausted, but Richards improvised a lamp by pouring some spirit (in-tended for priming the oil lamp) into a mug, lighting it, and holding another mug over it. It took half an hour to heat a mug of melted snow in this way. "Same old thing, no ceas-ing of this blizzard," was Joyce's note twenty-four hours later. "Hardly any food left except tea and sugar. Richards, Hayward, and I, after a long talk, decided to get under way tomorrow in any case, or else we shall be sharing the fate of Captain Scott and his party. The other tent seems to be very quiet, but now and again we hear a burst of song from Wild, so they are in the land of the living. We gave the dogs the last of their food tonight, so we shall have to push, as a great deal depends on them." Further quotations from Joyce's diary tell their own story.

"*February* 23, *Wednesday.*—About 11 o'clock saw a break in the clouds and the sun showing. Decided to have the meal we kept for getting under way. Sang out to the Skipper's party that we should shift as soon as we had a meal. I asked Wild, and found they had a bag of oatmeal, some Bovril cubes, one bag of chocolate, and eighteen bis-cuits, so they are much better off than we are. After we had our meal we started to dig out our sledge, which we found right under. It took us two hours, and one would hardly credit how weak we were. Two digs of the shovel and we were out of breath. This was caused through our lying up on practically no food. After getting sledge out we took it around to the Skipper's tent on account of the heavy sastrugi, which was very high. Got under way about 2:20. Had to stop very often on account of sail, etc. About 3:20 the Skipper, who had tied himself to the rear of the sledge, found it impossible to proceed. So after a consultation with Wild and party, decided to pitch their tent, leaving Wild to look after the Skipper and Spencer-Smith, and make the best of our way to the depot, which is anything up to twelve miles away. So we made them comfortable and left them about 3:40. I told Wild I should leave as much as possible and get back 26th or 27th, weather permitting, but just as we left them it came on to snow pretty hard, sun going in, and we found even with the four dogs we could not make more than one-half to three-quarters of a mile an hour. The surface is so bad that sometimes you go in up to your waist; still in spite of all this we carried on until 6:35. Camped in a howling blizzard. I found my left foot badly frostbitten. Now after this march we came into our banquet—one cup of tea and half a biscuit. Turned in at 9 o'clock. Situation does not look very cheerful. This is really the worst surface I have ever come across in all my journeys here."

Mackintosh had stayed on his feet as long as was humanly possible. The records of the outward journey show clearly that he was really unfit to continue beyond the 82° S. depot, and other members of the party would have liked him to have stayed with Spencer-Smith at lat. 83° S. But the responsibility for the work to be done was primarily his, and he would not give in. He had been suffering for several weeks from what he cheerfully called "a sprained leg," owing to scurvy. He marched for half an hour on the 23rd before breaking down, but had to be supported partly by Richards. Spencer-Smith was sinking. Wild, who stayed in charge of the two invalids, was in fairly good condition.

Joyce, Richards, and Hayward had difficulty in reaching the depot with a nearly empty sledge. An attempt to make their journey with two helpless men might have involved the loss of the whole party.

"*February* 24, *Thursday.*—Up at 4:30; had one cup of tea, half biscuit; under way after 7. Weather, snowing and blowing like yesterday. Richards, laying the cairns, had great trouble in getting the compass within 10° on account of wind. During the forenoon had to stop every quarter of an hour on account of our breath. Every time the sledge struck a drift she stuck in (although only 200 lb.), and in spite of three men and four dogs we could only shift her with the 1—2—3 haul. I wonder if this weather will ever clear up. Camped in an exhausted condition about 12:10. Lunch, half cup of weak tea and quarter biscuit, which took over half an hour to make. Richards and Hayward went out of tent to prepare for getting under way, but the force of wind and snow drove them back. The force of wind is about seventy to eighty miles per hour. We decided to get the sleeping bags in, which took some considerable time. The worst of camping is the poor dogs and our weak condition, which means we have to get out of our wet sleeping bags and have another half cup of tea without working for it. With scrapings from dog tank it is a very scanty meal. This is the second day the dogs have been without food, and if we cannot soon pick up depot and save the dogs it will be almost impossible to drag our two invalids back the one hundred miles which we have to go. The wind carried on with unabating fury until 7 o'clock, and then came a lull. We at once turned out, but found it snowing so thickly that it was impossible to proceed on account of our weakness. No chance must we miss. Turned in again. Wind sprang up again with heavy drift 8:30. In spite of everything my tent-mates are very cheerful and look on the bright side of every-thing. After a talk we decided to wait and turned in. It is really wonderful what dreams we have, especially of food. Trusting in Providence for fine weather tomorrow.

"*February 25, Friday.*—Turned out 4:45. Richards prepared our usual banquet, half cup of tea, quarter biscuit, which we relished. Under way at 7, carried on, halting every ten minutes or quarter of an hour. Weather, snowing and blowing same as yesterday. We are in a very weak state, but we cannot give in. We often talk about poor Captain Scott and the blizzard that finished him and party. If we had stayed in our tent another day I don't think we should have got under way at all, and we would have shared the same fate. But if the worst comes we have made up our minds to carry on and die in harness. If any one were to see us on trek they would be surprised: three men staggering on with four dogs, very weak; practically empty sledge with fair wind and just crawling along; our clothes are all worn out, finneskoe and sleeping bags torn. Tent is our worst point, all torn in front, and we are afraid to camp on account of it, as it is too cold to mend it. We camped for our grand lunch at noon. After five hours' struggling I think we did about three miles. After lunch sat in our tent talking over the situation. Decided to get under way again as soon as there is any clearance. Snowing and blowing, force about fifty or sixty miles an hour.

"*February 26, Saturday.*—Richards went out 1:10 a.m. and found it clearing a bit, so we got under way as soon as possible, which was 2:10 a.m. About 2:35 Richards sighted depot, which seemed to be right on top of us. I suppose we camped no more than three-quarters of a mile from it. The dogs sighted it, which seemed to electrify them. They had new life and started to run, but we were so weak that we could not go more than 200 yds. and then spell. I think another day would have seen us off. Arrived at depot 3:25; found it in a dilapidated condition, cases all about the place. I don't suppose there has ever been a weaker party arrive at

any depot, either north or south. After a hard struggle got
our tent up and made camp. Then gave the dogs a good feed
of pemmican. If ever dogs saved the lives of any one they
have saved ours. Let us hope they will continue in good
health, so that we can get out to our comrades. I started on
our cooking. Not one of us had any appetite, although we
were in the land of plenty, as we call this depot; plenty of
biscuit, etc., but we could not eat. I think it is the reaction,
not only in arriving here, but also finding no news of the
ship, which was arranged before we left. We all think there
has been a calamity there. Let us hope for the best. We decided to have rolled oats and milk for a start, which went
down very well, and then a cup of tea. How cheery the Primus sounds. It seems like coming out of a thick London fog
into a drawing room. After a consultation we decided to
have a meal of pemmican in four hours, and so on, until our
weakness was gone. *Later.*—Still the same weather. We
shall get under way and make a forced march back as soon
as possible. I think we shall get stronger traveling and feeding well. *Later.*—Weather will not permit us to travel yet.
Mended our torn tent with food bags. This took four hours.
Feeding the dogs every four hours, and Richards and Hayward built up depot. It is really surprising to find it takes
two men to lift a 50-lb case; it only shows our weakness.
Weather still the same; force of wind at times about seventy
to ninety miles an hour; really surprising how this can keep
on so long.

"*February* 27, *Sunday.*—Wind continued with fury the
whole night. Expecting every minute to have the tent blown
off us. Up 5 o'clock; found it so thick one could not get out
of the tent. We are still very weak, but think we can do the
twelve miles to our comrades in one long march. If only it
would clear up for just one day we would not mind. This is
the longest continuous blizzard I have ever been in. We have
not had a traveling day for eleven days, and the amount of

snow that has fallen is astonishing. *Later.*—Had a meal 10:30 and decided to get under way in spite of the wind and snow. Under way 12 o'clock. We have three weeks' food on sledge, about 160 lb., and one week's dog food, 50 lb. The whole weight, all told, about 600 lb., and also taking an extra sledge to bring back Captain Mackintosh. To our surprise we could not shift the sledges. After half an hour we got about ten yards. We turned the sledge up and scraped runners; it went a little better after. I am afraid our weakness is much more than we think. Hayward is in rather a bad way about his knees, which are giving him trouble and are very painful; we will give him a good massage when we camp. The dogs have lost all heart in pulling; they seem to think that going south again is no good to them; they seem to just jog along, and one cannot do more. I don't suppose our pace is more than one-half or three-quarters of a mile per hour. The surface is rotten, snow up to one's knees, and what with wind and drift a very bad outlook. Lunched about 4:30. Carried on until 11:20, when we camped. It was very dark making our dinner, but soon got through the process. Then Richards spent an hour or so in rubbing Hayward with methylated spirits, which did him a world of good. If he were to break up now I should not know what to do. Turned in about 1:30. It is now calm, but overcast with light falling snow.

"*February* 28, *Monday.*—Up at 6 o'clock; can just see a little skyline. Under way at 9 o'clock. The reason of delay, had to mend finneskoe, which are in a very dilapidated condition. I got my feet badly frostbitten yesterday. About 11 o'clock came on to snow, everything overcast. We ought to reach our poor boys in three or four hours, but Fate wills otherwise, as it came on again to blizzard force about 11:45. Camped at noon. I think the party must be within a very short distance, but we cannot go on as we might pass them, and as we have not got any position to go on except compass. *Later.*—Kept on blizzarding all afternoon and night.

"*February* 29, *Tuesday.*—Up at 5 o'clock; still very thick.
It cleared up a little to the south about 8 o'clock, when Richards sighted something black to the north of us, but could
not see properly what it was. After looking round sighted
camp to the south, so we got under way as soon as possible.
Got up to the camp about 12:45, when Wild came out to
meet us. We gave him a cheer, as we fully expected to find
all down. He said he had taken a little exercise every day;
they had not any food left. The Skipper then came out of
the tent, very weak and as much as he could do to walk. He
said, 'I want to thank you for saving our lives.' I told Wild
to go and give them a feed and not to eat too much at first
in case of reaction, as I am going to get under way as soon
as they have had a feed. So we had lunch, and the Skipper
went ahead to get some exercise, and after an hour's digging
out got everything ready for leaving. When we lifted Smith
we found he was in a great hole which he had melted
through. This party had been in one camp for twelve days.
We got under way and picked the Skipper up; he had fallen
down, too weak to walk. We put him on the sledge we had
brought out, and we camped about 8 o'clock. I think we did
about three miles—rather good with two men on the sledges
and Hayward in a very bad way. I don't think there has been
a party, either north or south, in such straits, three men
down and three of us very weak; but the dogs seem to have
new life since we turned north. I think they realize they are
homeward bound. I am glad we kept them, even when we
were starving. I knew they would have to come in at the
finish. We have now to look forward to southerly winds for
help, which I think we shall get at this time of year. Let us
hope the temperature will keep up, as our sleeping bags are
wet through and worn out, and all our clothes full of holes,
and finneskoe in a dilapidated condition; in fact, one would
not be out on a cold day in civilization with the rotten
clothes we have on. Turned in 11 o'clock, wet through, but

in a better frame of mind. Hope to try and reach the depot tomorrow, even if we have to march overtime.

"*March* 1, *Wednesday.*—Turned out usual time; a good south wind, but, worse luck, heavy drift. Set sail; put the Skipper on rear sledge. The temperature has gone down and it is very cold. Bluff in sight. We are making good progress, doing a good mileage before lunch. After lunch a little stronger wind. Hayward still hanging on to sledge; Skipper fell off twice. Reached depot 5:45. When camping found we had dropped our tent poles, so Richards went back a little way and spotted them through the binoculars about half a mile off, and brought them back. Hayward and I were very cold by that time, the drift very bad. Moral: See everything properly secured. We soon had our tent up, cooked our dinner in the dark, and turned in about 10 o'clock.

"*March* 2, *Thursday.*—Up as usual. Strong southwest wind with heavy drift. Took two weeks' provisions from the depot. I think that will last us through, as there is another depot about fifty miles north from here; I am taking the outside course on account of the crevasses, and one cannot take too many chances with two men on sledges and one crippled. Under way about 10 o'clock; lunched noon in a heavy drift; took an hour to get the tents up, etc., the wind being so heavy. Found sledges buried under snow after lunch, took some time to get under way. Wind and drift very heavy; set half sail on the first sledge and under way about 3:30. The going is perfect, sometimes sledges overtaking us. Carried on until 8 o'clock, doing an excellent journey for the day; distance about eleven or twelve miles. Gives one a bit of heart to carry on like this; only hope we can do this all the day. Had to cook our meals in the dark, but still we did not mind. Turned in about 11 o'clock, pleased with ourselves, although we were wet through with snow, as it got through all the holes in our clothes, and the sleeping bags are worse than awful.

"*March* 3, *Friday*.—Up the usual time. It has been blowing a raging blizzard all night. Found to our disgust utterly
impossible to carry on. Another few hours of agony in these
rotten bags. *Later*.—Blizzard much heavier. Amused myself
mending finneskoe and Burberrys, mits and socks. Had the
Primus while this operation was in force. Hoping for a fine
day tomorrow.

"*March* 4, *Saturday*.—Up 5:20. Still blizzarding, but
have decided to get under way as we will have to try and
travel through everything, as Hayward is getting worse, and
one doesn't know who is the next. No mistake it is scurvy,
and the only possible cure is fresh food. I sincerely hope the
ship is in; if not we shall get over the hills by Castle Rock,
which is rather difficult and will delay another couple of
days. Smith is still cheerful; he has hardly moved for weeks
and he has to have everything done for him. Got under way
9:35. It took some two hours to dig out dogs and sledges, as
they were completely buried. It is the same every morning
now. Set sail, going along pretty fair. Hayward gets on
sledge now and again. Lunched as usual; sledges got buried
again at lunchtime. It takes some time to camp now, and in
this drift it is awful. In the afternoon wind eased a bit and
drift went down. Found it very hard pulling with the third
man on sledge, as Hayward has been on all the afternoon.
Wind veered two points to south, so we had a fair wind. An
hour before we camped Erebus and Terror showing up, a
welcome sight. Only hope wind will continue. Drift is worst
thing to contend with as it gets into our clothes, which are
wet through now. Camped 8 o'clock. Cooked in the dark,
and turned in in our wet sleeping bags about 10 o'clock.
Distance about eight or nine miles.

"*March* 5, *Sunday*.—Turned out 6:15. Overslept a little;
very tired after yesterday. Sun shining brightly and no wind.
It seemed strange last night, no flapping of tent in one's
ears. About 8:30 came on to drift again. Under way 9:20,

both sails set. Sledge going hard, especially in soft places. If Hayward had not broken down we should not feel the weight so much. Lunch 12:45. Under way at 3. Wind and drift very heavy. A good job it is blowing some, or else we should have to relay. All land obscured. Distance about ten or eleven miles, a very good performance. Camped 7:10 in the dark. Patients not in the best of trim. I hope to get in, bar accidents, in four days.

"*March* 6, *Monday.*—Under way 9:20. Picked up thirty-two-mile depot 11 o'clock. Going with a fair wind in the forenoon, which eased somewhat after lunch and so caused very heavy work in pulling. It seems to me we shall have to depot some one if the wind eases at all. Distance during day about eight miles.

"*March* 7, *Tuesday.*—Under way 9 o'clock. Although we turn out at 5 it seems a long time to get under way. There is double as much work to do now with our invalids. This is the calmest day we have had for weeks. The sun is shining and all land in sight. It is very hard going. Had a little breeze about 11 o'clock, set sail, but work still very, very heavy. Hayward and Skipper going on ahead with sticks, very slow pace, but it will buck them up and do them good. If one could only get some fresh food! About 11 o'clock decided to camp and overhaul sledges and depot all gear except what is actually required. Under way again at 2, but surface being so sticky did not make any difference. After a consultation the Skipper decided to stay behind in a tent with three weeks' provisions, whilst we pushed on with Smith and Hayward. It seems hard, only about thirty miles away, and yet cannot get any assistance. Our gear is absolutely rotten, no sleep last night, shivering all night in wet bags. I wonder what will be the outcome of it all after our struggle. Trust in Providence. Distance about three and a half miles.

"*March* 8, *Wednesday.*—Under way 9:20. Wished the Skipper good-bye; took Smith and Hayward on. Had a fair

wind, going pretty good. Hope to arrive in Hut Point in four
days. Lunched at No. 2 depot. Distance about four and a
half miles. Under way as usual after lunch; head wind, going
very heavy. Carried on until 6:30. Distance about eight or
nine miles.

"*March* 9, *Thursday.*—Had a very bad night, cold intense. Temperature down to −29° all night. At 4 a.m. Spencer-Smith called out that he was feeling queer. Wild spoke
to him. Then at 5:45 Richards suddenly said, 'I think he has
gone.' Poor Smith, for forty days in pain he had been
dragged on the sledge, but never grumbled or complained.
He had a strenuous time in his wet bag, and the jolting of
the sledge on a very weak heart was not too good for him.
Sometimes when we lifted him on the sledge he would
nearly faint, but during the whole time he never complained.
Wild looked after him from the start. We buried him in his
bag at 9 o'clock at the following position: Ereb. 184°—Obs.
Hill 149°. We made a cross of bamboos, and built a mound
and cairn, with particulars. After that got under way with
Hayward on sledge. Found going very hard, as we had a
northerly wind in our faces, with a temperature Below 20°.
What with frostbites, etc., we are all suffering. Even the
dogs seem like giving in; they do not seem to take any interest in their work. We have been out much too long, and
nothing to cheer us up but a cold, cheerless hut. We did
about two and a half miles in the forenoon, Hayward tod-
dling ahead every time we had a spell. During lunch the
wind veered to the south with drift, just right to set sail. We
carried on with Hayward on sledge and camped in the dark
about 8 o'clock. Turned in at 10, weary, worn, and sad. Hoping to reach depot tomorrow.

"*March* 10, *Friday.*—Turned out as usual. Beam wind,
going pretty fair, very cold. Came into very soft snow about
3; arrived at Safety Camp 5 o'clock. Got to edge of Ice
Barrier; found passage over in a bay full of seals. Dogs got

very excited; had a job to keep them away. By the glasses it looked clear right to Cape Armitage which is four and a half miles away. Arrived there 8 o'clock, very dark and bad light. Found open water. Turned to climb slopes against a strong northeasterly breeze with drift. Found a place about a mile away, but we were so done up that it took until 11:30 to get gear up. This slope was about 150 yds. up, and every three paces we had to stop and get breath. Eventually camped and turned in aboaut 2 o'clock. I think this is the worst day I ever spent. What with the disappointment of not getting round the Point, and the long day and the thought of getting Hayward over the slopes, it is not very entertaining for sleep.

"*March* 11, *Saturday.*—Up at 7 o'clock; took binoculars and went over the slope to look around the Cape. To my surprise found the open water and pack at the Cape only extended for about a mile. Came down and gave the boys the good news. I think it would take another two hard days to get over the hills, and we are too weak to do much of that, as I am afraid of another collapsing. Richards and Wild climbed up to look at the back of the bay and found the ice secure. Got under way 10:30, went round the Cape and found ice; very slushy, but continued on. No turning now; got into hard ice shortly after, eventually arriving at Hut Point about 3 o'clock. It seems strange after our adventures to arrive back at the old hut. This place has been standing since we built it in 1901, and has been the starting point of a few expeditions since. When we were coming down the bay I could fancy the *Discovery* there when Scott arrived from his Farthest South in 1902, the ship decorated rainbow fashion, and Lieutenant Armitage giving out the news that Captain Scott had got to 82°.17′ S. We went wild that day. But now our homecoming is quite different. Hut half-full of snow through a window being left open and drift getting in; but we soon got it shipshape and Hayward in. I had the fire

going and plenty of vegetables on, as there was a fair supply
of dried vegetables. Then after we had a feed, Richards and
Wild went down the by and killed a couple of seals. I gave
a good menu of seal meat at night, and we turned in about
11 o'clock, full—too full in fact. As there is no news here
of the ship, and we cannot see her, we surmise she has gone
down with all hands. I cannot see there is any chance of her
being afloat or she would be here. I don't know how the
Skipper will take it.

"*March* 12, *Sunday*.—Heard groans proceeding from the
sleeping bags all night; all hands suffering from overeating.
Hayward not very well. Turned out 8 o'clock. Good breakfast—porridge, seal, vegetables, and coffee; more like a
banquet to us. After breakfast Richards and Wild killed a
couple of seals whilst I made the hut a bit comfy. Hayward
can hardly move. All of us in a very bad state, but we must
keep up exercise. My ankles and knees badly swollen, gums
prominent. Wild, very black around joints, and gums very
black. Richard about the best off. After digging hut out I
prepared food which I think will keep the scurvy down. The
dogs have lost their lassitude and are quite frisky, except
Oscar, who is suffering from overfeeding. After a strenuous
day's work turned in 10 o'clock.

"*Marach* 13, *Monday*.—Turned out 7 o'clock. Carried on
much the same as yesterday, bringing in seal blubber and
meat. Preparing for departure tomorrow; hope every one
will be all right. Made new dog harness and prepared
sledges. In afternoon cooked sufficient seal meat for our
journey out and back, and same for dogs. Turned in 10
o'clock, feeling much better.

"*March* 14, *Tuesday*.—A beautiful day. Under way after
lunch. One would think, looking at our party, that we were
the most ragged lot one could meet in a day's march; all our
clothes past mending, our faces black as minstrels'—a sort
of crowd one would run away from. Going pretty good. As

soon as we rounded Cape Armitage a dead head wind with a temperature of − 18° Fahr., so we are not in for a pleasant time. Arrived at Safety Camp 6 o'clock, turned in 8:30, after getting everything ready.

"*March* 15, *Wednesday*.—Under way as usual. Nice calm day. Had a very cold night, temperature going down to − 30° Fahr. Going along at a rattling good rate; in spite of our swollen limbs we did about fifteen miles. Very cold when we camped; temperature − 29° Fahr. Turned in 9 o'clock.

"*March* 16, *Thursday*.—Up before the sun, 4:45 a.m. Had a very cold night, not much sleep. Under way early. Going good. Passed Smith's grave 10:45 a.m. and had lunch at depot. Saw Skipper's camp just after, and looking through glass found him outside tent, much to the joy of all hands, as we expected him to be down. Picked him up 4:15 p.m. Broke the news of Smith's death and no ship. I gave him the date of the 17th to look out for our returning, so he had a surprise. We struck his camp and went north for about a mile and camped. We gave the Skipper a banquet of seal, vegetables, and black currant jam, the feed of his life. He seems in a bad way. I hope to get him in in three days, and I think fresh food will improve him. We turned in 8 o'clock. Distance done during day sixteen miles.

"*March* 17, *Friday*.—Up at 5 o'clock. Under way 8 a.m. Skipper feeling much better after feeding him up. Lunched a few yards past Smith's grave. Had a good afternoon, going fair. Distance about sixteen miles. Very cold night, temperature − 30° Fahr. What with wet bags and clothes, rotten.

"*March* 18, *Saturday*.—Turned out 5 o'clock. Had rather a cold night. Temperature − 29° Fahr. Surface very good. The Skipper walked for a little way, which did him good. Arrived at Safety Camp 4:10 p.m. To our delight found the sea ice in the same condition and arrived at Hut Point at 7 o'clock. Found Hayward still about same. Set to, made a good dinner, and all hands seem in the best of spirits. Now we have arrived and got the party in, it remains to themselves to get better. Plenty of exercise and fresh food ought to do miracles. We have been out 160 days, and done a distance of 1561 miles, a good record. I think the irony of fate was poor Smith going under a day before we got in. I think we shall all soon be well. Turned in 10:30 p.m. Before turning in Skipper shook us by the hand with great emotion, thanking us for saving his life."

Richards, summarizing the work of the parties, says that the journeys made between September 1 and March 18, a period of 160 days, totalled 1561 miles. The main journey, from Hut Point to Mount Hope and return, was 830 miles. "The equipment," he adds, "was old at the commencement of the season, and this told severely at the later stages of the journey. Three Primus lamps gave out on the journeys, and the old tent brought back by one of the last parties showed rents several feet in length. This hampered the traveling in the long blizzards. Finneskoe were also in pieces at the end, and time had frequently to be lost through repairs to clothing becoming imperative. This account would not be complete without some mention of the unselfish service rendered by Wild to his two ill tentmates. From the time he remained behind at the long blizzard till the death of Spencer-Smith he had two helpless men to attend to, and despite his own condition he was ever ready, night or day, to minister to their wants. This, in a temperature of −30° Fahr. at times, was no light task.

"Without the aid of four faithful friends, Oscar, Con, Gunner, and Towser, the party could never have arrived back. These dogs from November 5 accompanied the sledging parties, and, although the pace was often very slow, they adapted themselves well to it. Their endurance was fine. For three whole days at one time they had not a scrap of food, and this after a period on short rations. Though they were

feeble towards the end of the trip, their condition usually
was good, and those who returned with them will ever remember the remarkable service they rendered.

"The first indication of anything wrong with the general
health of the party occurred at about lat. 82° 30′ S., when
Spencer-Smith complaind of stiffness in the legs and discol-
oration. He attributed this to holes in his windproof clothing. At lat. 83° S., when he gave way, it was thought that the
rest would do him good. About the end of January Captain
Mackintosh showed very serious signs of lameness. At this
time his party had been absent from Hut Point, and consequently from fresh food, about three months.

"On the journey back Spencer-Smith gradually became
weaker, and for some time before the end was in a very
weak condition indeed. Captain Mackintosh, by great efforts, managed to keep his feet until the long blizzard was
encountered. Here it was that Hayward was first found to be
affected with the scurvy, his knees being stiff. In his case
the disease took him off his feet very suddenly, apparently
causing the muscles of his legs to contract till they could be
straightened hardly more than a right angle. He had slight
touches in the joints of the arms. In the cases of Joyce, Wild,
and Richards, joints became stiff and black in the rear, but
general weakness was the worst symptom experienced. Captain Mackintosh's legs looked the worst in the party."

The five men who were now at Hut Point found quickly
that some of the winter months must be spent there. They
had no news of the ship, and were justified in assuming that
she had not returned to the Sound, since if she had some
message would have been awaiting them at Hut Point, if not
farther south. The sea ice had broken and gone north within
a mile of the point, and the party must wait until the new
ice became firm as far as Cape Evans. Plenty of seal meat
was available, as well as dried vegetables, and the fresh food
improved the condition of the patients very rapidly. Rich-

ards massaged the swollen joints and found that this treatment helped a good deal. Before the end of March Mackintosh and Hayward, the worst sufferers, were able to take exercise. By the second week of April Mackintosh was free of pain, though the backs of his legs were still discolored.

A tally of the stores at the hut showed that on a reasonable allowance the supply would last till the middle of June. Richards and Wild killed many seals, so that there was no scarcity of meat and blubber. A few penguins were also secured. The sole means of cooking food and heating the hut was an improvised stove of brick, covered with two sheets of iron. This had been used by the former Expedition. The stove emitted dense smoke and often made the hut very uncomfortable, while at the same time it covered the men and all their gear with clinging and penetrating soot. Cleanliness was out of the question, and this increased the desire of the men to get across to Cape Evans. During April the sea froze in calm weather, but winds took the ice out again. On April 23 Joyce walked four miles to the north, partly on young ice two inches thick, and he thought then that the party might be able to reach Cape Evans within a few days. But a prolonged blizzard took the ice out right up to the Point, so that the open water extended at the end of April right up to the foot of Vinie's Hill. Then came a spell of calm weather, and during the first week of May the sea ice formed rapidly. The men made several short trips over it to the north. The sun had disappeared below the horizon in the middle of April, and would not appear again for over four months.

The disaster that followed is described by both Richards and Joyce. "And now a most regrettable incident occurred," wrote Richards. "On the morning of May 8, before breakfast, Captain Mackintosh asked Joyce what he thought of his going to Cape Evans with Hayward. Captain Mackintosh considered the ice quite safe, and the fine morning no doubt tempted him to exchange the quarters at the hut for the greater comfort and better food at Cape Evans." (Mackintosh naturally would be anxious to know if the men at Cape Evans were well and had any news of the ship.) "He was strongly urged at the time not to take the risk, as it was pointed out that the ice, although firm, was very young, and that a blizzard was almost sure to take part of it out to sea."

However, at about 1 p.m., with the weather apparently changing for the worse, Mackintosh and Hayward left, after promising to turn back if the weather grew worse. The last sight the watching party on the hill gained of them was when they were about a mile away, close to the shore, but apparently making straight for Cape Evans. At 3 p.m. a moderate blizzard was raging, which later increased in fury, and the party in the hut had many misgivings for the safety of the absent men.

On May 10, the first day possible, the three men left behind walked over new ice to the north to try and discover some trace as to the fate of the others. The footmarks were seen clearly enough raised up on the ice, and the track was followed for about two miles in a direction leading to Cape Evans. Here they ended abruptly, and in the dim light a wide stretch of water, very lightly covered with ice, was seen as far as the eye could reach. It was at once evident that part of the ice over which they had traveled had gone out to sea.

The whole party had intended, if the weather had held good, to have attempted the passage across with the full moon about May 16. On the date on which Mackintosh and Hayward left it was impossible that a sledge should travel the distance over the sea ice owing to the sticky nature of the surface. Hence their decision to go alone and leave the others to follow with the sledge and equipment when the surface should improve. That they had actually been lost was learned only on July 15, on which date the party from Hut Point arrived at Cape Evans.

The entry in Joyce's diary shows that he had very strong forebodings of disaster when Mackintosh and Hayward left. He warned them not to go, as the ice was thin and the weather was uncertain. Mackintosh seems to have believed that he and Hayward, traveling light, could get across to Cape Evans quickly before the weather broke, and if the blizzard had come two or three hours later they probably would have been safe. The two men carried no sleeping bags and only a small meal of chocolate and seal meat.

The weather during June was persistently bad. No move had been possible on May 16, the sea ice being out, and Joyce decided to wait until the next full moon. When this came the weather was boisterous, and so it was not until the full moon of July that the journey to Cape Evans was made. During June and July seals got very scarce, and the supply of blubber ran short. Meals consisted of little but seal meat and porridge. The small stock of salt was exhausted, but the men procured two and a half pounds by boiling down snow taken from the bottom layer next to the sea ice. The dogs recovered condition rapidly and did some hunting on their own account among the seals.

The party started for Cape Evans on July 15. They had expected to take advantage of the full moon, but by a strange chance they had chosen the period of an eclipse, and the moon was shadowed most of the time they were crossing the sea ice. The ice was firm, and the three men reached Cape Evans without difficulty. They found Stevens, Cope, Gaze, and Jack at the Cape Evans Hut, and learned that nothing had been seen of Captain Mackintosh and Hayward. The conclusion that these men had perished was accepted reluctantly. The party at the base consisted now of Stevens, Cope, Joyce, Richards, Gaze, Wild, and Jack.

The men settled down now to wait for relief. When opportunity offered Joyce led search parties to look for the bodies or any trace of the missing men, and he subsequently handed me the following report:

"I beg to report that the following steps were taken to try and discover the bodies of Captain Mackintosh and Mr. Hayward. After our party's return to the hut at Cape Evans, July 15, 1916, it was learned that Captain Mackintosh and Mr. Hayward had not arrived; and, being aware of the conditions under which they were last seen, all the members of the wintering party were absolutely convinced that these two men were totally lost and dead—that they could not have lived for more than a few hours at the outside in the blizzard that they had encountered, they being entirely unprovided with equipment of any sort.

"There was the barest chance that after the return of the sun some trace of their bodies might be found, so during the spring—that is, August and September 1916—and in the summer—December and January 1916–17—the following searches were carried out:

"(1) Wild and I thoroughly searched Inaccessible Island at the end of August 1916.

"(2) Various parties in September searched along the shore to the vicinity of Turks' Head.

"(3) In company with Messrs. Wild and Gaze I started from Hut Point, December 31, 1916, at 8 a.m., and a course was steered inshore as close as possible to the cliffs in order to search for any possible means of ascent. At a distance of half a mile from Hut Point we passed a snow slope which I had already ascended in June 1916; three and a half miles farther on was another snow slope which ended in Blue Ice Glacier slope, which we found impossible to climb, snow slope being formed by heavy winter snowfall. These were the only two places accessible. Distance on this day, 10 miles 1710 yds. covered. On January 1 search was continued round the south side of Glacier Tongue from the base towards the seaward end. There was much heavy pressure; it was impossible to reach the summit owing to the wide crack. Distance covered 4 miles 100 yds. On January 2 thick weather caused party to lay up. On 3rd, glacier was further examined, and several slopes formed by snow led to top of glacier, but crevasses between slope and the tongue prevented crossing. The party then proceeded round the Tongue to Tent Island, which was also searched, a complete tour of the island being made. It was decided to make for Cape Evans, as thick weather was approaching. We arrived at 8 p.m. Distance 8 miles 490 yds.

> "I remain, etc.,
>
> "ERNEST E. JOYCE.

"*To* Sir ERNEST SHACKLETON, C.V.O.,
    "*Commander,* I.T.A.E."

In September Richards was forced to lay up at the hut owing to a strained heart, due presumably to stress of work on the sledging journeys. Early in October a party consisting of Joyce, Gaze, and Wild spent several days at Cape Royds, where they skinned specimens. They sledged stores back to Cape Evans in case it should be found necessary to remain there over another winter. In September, Joyce, Gaze, and Wild went out to Spencer-Smith's grave with a wooden cross, which they erected firmly. Relief arrived on January 10, 1917, but it is necessary now to turn back to the events of May 1915, when the *Aurora* was driven from her moorings off Cape Evans.

CHAPTER XVI

THE *AURORA*'S DRIFT

AFTER MACKINTOSH LEFT the *Aurora* on January 25, 1915, Stenhouse kept the ship with difficulty off Tent Island. The ice anchors would not hold, owing to the continual breaking away of the pack, and he found it necessary much of the time to steam slow ahead against the floes. The third sledging party, under Cope, left the ship on the afternoon of the 31st, with the motor tractor towing two sledges, and disappeared towards Hut Point. Cope's party returned to the ship on February 2 and left again on February 5, after a delay caused by the loose condition of the ice. Two days later, after more trouble with drifting floes, Stenhouse proceeded to Cape Evans, where he took a line of soundings for the winter quarters. During the next month the *Aurora* occupied various positions in the neighborhood of Cape Evans. No secure moorings were available. The ship had to keep clear of threatening floes, dodge "growlers" and drifting bergs, and find shelter from the blizzards. A sudden shift of wind on February 24, when the ship was sheltering in the lee of Glacier Tongue, caused her to be jammed hard against the low ice off the glacier, but no damage was done. Early in March Stenhouse sent moorings ashore at Cape Evans, and on March 11 he proceeded to Hut Point, where he dropped anchor in Discovery Bay. Here he landed stores, amounting to about two months' full rations for twelve men, and embarked Spencer-Smith, Stevens, Hook, Richards, Ninnis, and Gaze, with two dogs. He returned to Cape Evans that evening.

"We had a bad time when we were 'sculling' about the Sound, first endeavoring to make Hut Point to land provi-

sions, and then looking for winter quarters in the neighborhood of Glacier Tongue," wrote Stenhouse afterwards. "The
ice kept breaking away in small floes, and we were apparently no nearer to anywhere than when the sledges left; we
were frustrated in every move. The ship broke away from
the fast ice in blizzards, and then we went dodging about
the Sound from the Ross Island side to the western pack,
avoiding and clearing floes and growlers in heavy drift when
we could see nothing, our compasses unreliable and the ship
short-handed. In that homeless time I kept watch and watch
with the second officer, and was hard pressed to know what
to do. Was ever ship in such predicament? To the northward
of Cape Royds was taboo, as also was the coast south of
Glacier Tongue. In a small stretch of icebound coast we had
to find winter quarters. The ice lingered on, and all this time
we could find nowhere to drop anchor, but had to keep
steam handy for emergencies. Once I tried the North Bay of
Cape Evans, as it apparently was the only ice-free spot. I
called all hands, and making up a boat's crew with one of
the firemen sent the whaler away with the second officer in
charge to sound. No sooner had the boat left ship than the
wind freshened from the northward, and large bergs and
growlers, setting into the bay, made the place untenable.
The anchorage I eventually selected seemed the best available—and here we are drifting, with all plans upset, when
we ought to be lying in winter quarters."

A heavy gale came up on March 12, and the *Aurora,* then
moored off Cape Evans, dragged her anchor and drifted out
of the bay. She went northward past Cape Barne and Cape
Royds in a driving mist, with a heavy storm sea running.
This gale was a particularly heavy one. The ship and gear
were covered with ice, owing to the freezing of spray, and
Stenhouse had anxious hours amid the heavy, ice-encum-
bered waters before the gale moderated. The young ice,
which was continually forming in the very low temperature,

helped to reduce the sea as soon as the gale moderated, and the *Aurora* got back to Cape Evans on the evening of the 13th. Ice was forming in the bay, and on the morning of the 14th Stenhouse took the ship into position for winter moorings. He got three steel hawsers out and made fast to the shore anchors. These hawsers were hove tight, and the *Aurora* rested then, with her stern to the shore, in seven fathoms. Two more wires were taken ashore the next day. Young ice was forming around the ship, and under the influence of wind and tide this ice began early to put severe strains upon the moorings. Stenhouse had the fires drawn and the boiler blown on the 20th, and the engineer reported at that time that the bunkers contained still 118 tons of coal.

The ice broke away between Cape Evans and Cape Barne on the 23rd, and pressure around the ship shattered the bay ice and placed heavy strains on the stern moorings. The young ice, about four inches thick, went out eventually and left a lead along the shore. The ship had set in towards the shore, owing to the pressure, and the stern was now in four-and-a-half fathoms. Stenhouse tightened the moorings and ran out an extra wire to the shore anchor. The nature of the ice movements is illustrated by a few extracts from the log:

"*March* 27, 5 p.m.—Ice broke away from shore and started to go out. 8 p.m.—Light southerly airs; fine; ice setting out to northwest; heavy pressure of ice on starboard side and great strain on moorings. 10 p.m.—Ice clear of ship.

"*March* 28.—New ice forming over bay. 3 a.m.—Ice which went out last watch set in towards bay. 5 a.m.—Ice coming in and overriding newly formed bay ice; heavy pressure on port side of ship; wires frozen into ice. 8 a.m.—Calm and fine; new ice setting out of bay. 5 p.m.—New ice formed since morning cleared from bay except area on port side of ship and stretching abeam and ahead for about 200 yds., which is held by bights of wire; new ice forming.

"*March* 29, 1:30 p.m.—New ice going out. 2 p.m.—
Hands on floe on port quarter clearing wires; stern in three
fathoms; hauled wires tight, bring stern more to eastward
and in four fathoms; hove in about one fathom of starboard
cable, which had dragged during recent pressure.

"*April* 10, 1:30 p.m.—Ice breaking from shore under influence of southeast wind. Two starboard quarter wires parted; all bights of stern wires frozen in ice; chain taking
weight. 2 p.m.—Ice opened, leaving ice in bay in line from
Cape to landward of glacier. 8 p.m.—Fresh wind; ship holding ice in bay; ice in Sound wind-driven to northwest.

"*April* 17, 1 a.m.—Pressure increased and wind shifted
to northwest. Ice continued to override and press into shore
until 5 o'clock; during this time pressure into bay was very
heavy; movement of ice in straits causing noise like heavy
surf. Ship took ground gently at rudder post during pressure;
bottom under stern shallows very quickly. 10 p.m.—Ice
moving out of bay to westward; heavy strain on after-moorings and cables, which are cutting the floe."

Stenhouse continued to nurse his moorings against the
onslaughts of the ice during the rest of April and the early
days of May. The break away from the shore came suddenly
and unexpectedly on the evening of May 6:

"*May* 6, 1915.—Fine morning with light breezes from
east-southeast. . . . 3:30 p.m.—Ice nearly finished. Sent
hands ashore for sledge-load. 4 p.m.—Wind freshening
with blizzardly appearance of sky. 8 p.m.—. . . Heavy strain
on after-moorings. 9:45 p.m.—The ice parted from the
shore; all moorings parted. Most fascinating to listen to
waves and chain breaking. In the thick haze I saw the ice
astern breaking up and the shore receding. I called all hands
and clapped relieving tackles (4-in. Manila luff tackles) on
to the cables on the fore part of the windlass. The bos'n had
rushed along with his hurricane lamp, and shouted, 'She's
away wi' it!' He is a good fellow and very conscientious. I

ordered steam on main engines, and the engine room staff, with Hooke and Ninnis, turned to. Grady, fireman, was laid up with a broken rib. As the ship, in the solid floe, set to the northwest, the cables rattled and tore at the hawse-pipes; luckily the anchors, lying as they were on a strip-sloping bottom, came away easily, without damage to windlass or hawse-pipes. Slowly as we disappeared into Sound, the light in the hut died away. At 11:30 p.m. the ice around us started to break up, the floes playing tattoo on the ship's sides. We were out in the Sound and catching the full force of the wind. The moon broke through the clouds after midnight and showed us the pack, stretching continuously to northward, and about one mile to the south. As the pack from the southward came up and closed in on the ship, the swell lessened and the banging of floes alongside eased a little.

"*May* 7, 8 a.m.—Wind east-southeast. Moderate gale with thick drift. The ice around ship is packing up and forming ridges about two feet high. The ship is lying with head to the eastward, Cape Bird showing to northeast. When steam is raised I have hopes of getting back to the fast ice near the Glacier Tongue. Since we have been in winter quarters the ice has formed and, held by the islands and land at Cape Evans, has remained north of the Tongue. If we can return we should be able now to moor to the fast ice. The engineers are having great difficulty with the sea connections, which are frozen. The main bow-down cock, from which the boiler is 'run up,' has been tapped and a screw plug put into it to allow of a hot iron rod being inserted to thaw out the ice between the cock and the ship's side— about two feet of hard ice. 4:30 p.m.—The hot iron has been successful. Donolly (second engineer) had the pleasure of stopping the first spurt of water through the pipe; he got it in the eye. Fires were lit in furnaces, and water commenced to blow in the boiler—the first blow in our defense against the terrific forces of Nature in the Antarctic. 8 p.m.—The gale has freshened, accompanied by thick drift."

The *Aurora* drifted helplessly throughout May 7. On the morning of May 8 the weather cleared a little and the Western Mountains became indistinctly visible. Cape Bird could also be seen. The ship was moving northwards with the ice. The daylight was no more than a short twilight of about two hours' duration. The boiler was being filled with ice, which had to be lifted aboard, broken up, passed through a small porthole to a man inside, and then carried to the manhole on top of the boiler. Stenhouse had the wireless aerial rigged during the afternoon, and at 5 p.m. was informed that the watering of the boiler was complete. The wind freshened to a moderate southerly gale, with thick drift, in the night, and this gale continued during the following day, the 9th. The engineer reported at noon that he had 40 lb. pressure in the boiler and was commencing the thawing of the auxiliary sea connection pump by means of a steam pipe.

"Cape Bird is the only land visible, bearing northeast true about eight miles distant," wrote Stenhouse on the afternoon of the 9th. "So this is the end of our attempt to winter in McMurdo Sound. Hard luck after four months' buffeting, for the last seven weeks of which we nursed our moorings. Our present situation calls for increasing vigilance. It is five weeks to the middle of winter. There is no sun, the light is little and uncertain, and we may expect many blizzards. We have no immediate water supply, as only a small quantity of fresh ice was aboard when we broke drift.

"The *Aurora* is fast in the pack and drifting God knows where. Well, there are prospects of a most interesting winter drift. We are all in good health, except Grady, whose rib is mending rapidly; we have good spirits and we will get through. But what of the poor beggars at Cape Evans, and the Southern Party? It is a dismal prospect for them. There are sufficient provisions at Cape Evans, Hut Point, and, I suppose, Cape Royds, but we have the remaining Burberrys, clothing, etc., for next year's sledging still on board. I see

little prospect of getting back to Cape Evans or anywhere in
the Sound. We are short of coal and held firmly in the ice. I
hope she drifts quickly to the northeast. Then we can endeavor to push through the pack and make for New Zealand,
coal and return to the Barrier eastward of Cape Crozier. This
could be done, I think, in the early spring, September. We
must get back to aid the depot-laying next season."

A violent blizzard raged on May 10 and 11. "I never remember such wind force," said Stenhouse. "It was difficult
to get along the deck." The weather moderated on the 12th,
and a survey of the ship's position was possible. "We are
lying in a field of ice with our anchors and seventy-five fathoms of cable on each hanging at the bows. The after-moorings were frozen into the ice astern of us at Cape Evans.
Previous to the date of our leaving our winter berth four
small wires had parted. When we broke away the chain two
of the heavy (4-in.) wires parted close to shore; the other
wire went at the butts. The chain and two wires are still fast
in the ice and will have to be dug out. This morning we
cleared the ice around the cables, but had to abandon the
heaving-in, as the steam froze in the return pipes from
the windlass exhaust, and the joints had to be broken and
the pipe thawed out. Hooke was 'listening in' from 8:30
p.m. to 12:30 a.m. for the Macquarie Island wireless station
(1340 miles away) or the Bluff (New Zealand) station (180
miles away), but had no luck."

The anchors were hove in by dint of much effort on the
13th and 14th, ice forming on the cable as it was hoisted
through a hole cut in the floe. Both anchors had broken, so
the *Aurora* had now one small kedge anchor left aboard.
The ship's position on May 14 was approximately forty-five
miles north, thirty-four west of Cape Evans. "In one week
we have drifted forty-five miles (geographical). Most of this
distance was covered during the first two days of the drift.
We appear to be nearly stationary. What movement there is

in the ice seems to be to the northwest towards the ice-bound coast. Hands who were after penguins yesterday reported much noise in the ice about one mile from the ship. I hope the floe around the ship is large enough to take its own pressure. We cannot expect much pressure from the south, as McMurdo Sound should soon be frozen over and the ice holding. Northeast winds would drive the pack in from the Ross Sea. I hope for the best. Plans for future development are ready, but probably will be checkmated again. . . . I took the anchors aboard. They are of further use as separate anchors, but they ornament the forecastle head, so we put them in their places. . . . The supply of fresh water is a problem. The engineer turned steam from the boiler into the main water tank (starboard) through a pipe leading from the main winch pipe to the tank top. The steam condenses before reaching the tank. I hope freezing does not burst the tank. A large tabular iceberg, calved from the Barrier, is silhouetted against the twilight glow in the sky about ten miles away. The sight of millions of tons of fresh ice is most tantalizing. It would be a week's journey to the berg and back over pack and pressure, and probably we could bring enough ice to last two days."

The record of the early months of the *Aurora*'s long drift in the Ross Sea is not eventful. The galley condenser was rigged, but the supply of fresh water remained a problem. The men collected fresh-fallen snow when possible and hoped to get within reach of fresh ice. Hooke and Ninnis worked hard at the wireless plant with the object of getting into touch with Macquarie Island, and possibly sending news of the ship's movements to Cape Evans. They got the wireless motor running and made many adjustments of the instruments and aerials, but their efforts were not successful. Emperor penguins approached the ship occasionally, and the birds were captured whenever possible for the fresh meat they afforded. The *Aurora* was quite helpless in the grip of the ice, and after the engine room bilges had been thawed and pumped out the boilers were blown down. The pressure had been raised to sixty pounds, but there was no chance of moving the ship, and the supply of coal was limited. The story of the *Aurora*'s drift during long months can be told briefly by means of extracts from Stenhouse's log:

"*May* 21.—Early this morning there appeared to be movements in the ice. The grating and grinding noise makes one feel the unimportance of man in circumstances like ours. Twilight towards noon showed several narrow, open leads about two cables from ship and in all directions. Unable to get bearing, but imagine that there is little or no alteration in ship's position, as ship's head is same, and Western Mountains appear the same. . . . Hope all is well at Cape Evans and that the other parties have returned safely. Wish we could relieve their anxiety.

"*May* 22.—Obtained good bearings of Beaufort Island, Cape Ross, and Dunlop Island, which put the ship in a position eighteen miles south 75° east (true) from Cape Ross. Since the 14th, when reliable bearings were last obtained, we have drifted northwest by north seven miles.

"*May* 24.—Blizzard from south-southeast continued until 9 p.m., when it moderated, and at 11:45 p.m. wind shifted to northwest, light, with snow. Quite a lot of havoc has been caused during this blow, and the ship has made much northing. In the morning the crack south of the ship opened to about three feet. At 2 p.m. felt heavy shock and the ship heeled to port about 70°. Found ice had cracked from port gangway to northwest, and parted from ship from gangway along to stern. Crack extended from stern to southeast. 7:35 p.m.—Ice cracked from port fore chains, in line parallel to previous crack. The ice broke again between the cracks and drifted to northwest for about ten yards. The ice to southward then commenced to break up, causing heavy strain on ship, and setting apparently north in large broken fields.

Ship badly jammed in. 9:15 p.m.—Ice closed in again around ship. Two heavy wind squalls with a short interval between followed by cessation of wind. We are in a laby-rinth of large rectangular floes (some with their points press-ing heavily against ship) and high-pressure ridges.

"*May* 25.—In middle watch felt pressure occasionally. Twilight showed a scene of chaos all around; one floe about three feet in thickness had upended, driven under ship on port quarter. As far as can be seen there are heavy blocks of ice screwed up on end, and the scene is like a graveyard. I think swell must have come up under ice from seaward (northeast), McMurdo Sound, and broken the ice, which af-terwards started to move under the influence of the blizzard. Hardly think swell came from the Sound, as the cracks were wending from northwest to southeast, and also as the Sound should be getting icebound by now. If swell came from northeast then there is open water not far away. I should like to know. I believe the Ross Sea is rarely entirely ice-cov-ered. Have bright moonlight now, which accentuates every-thing—the beauty and loneliness of our surroundings, and uselessness of ourselves, while in this prison: so near to Cape Evans and yet we might as well be anywhere as here. Have made our sledging-ration scales, and crew are busy making harness and getting sledging equipment ready for emergencies. Temperature—30° Fahr.

"*May* 26.—If the ship is nipped in the ice, the ship's com-pany (eighteen hands) will take to four sledges with one month's rations and make for nearest land. Six men and one sledge will endeavor to make Cape Evans via the western land, Butler Point, Hut Point, etc. The remaining twelve will come along with all possible speed, but no forced marches, killing and depoting penguins and seals for emergency re-treats. If the ship remains here and makes no further drift to the north, towards latter end of July light will be making. The sun returns August 23. The sea ice should be fairly safe, and a party of three, with one month's rations, will proceed to Cape Evans. If the ice sets north and takes the ship clear of land, we will proceed to New Zealand, bunker, get extra officer and four volunteers, provisions, etc., push south with all speed to the Barrier, put party on to the Barrier, about two miles east of Cape Crozier, and land all necessary stores and requirements. The ship will stand off until able to reach Cape Evans. If necessary, party will depot all stores possible at Corner Camp and go on to Cape Evans. If worst has happened my party will lay out the depot at the Beardmore for Shackleton. If the ship is released from the ice after September we must endeavor to reach Cape Evans before going north to bunker. We have not enough coal to hang about the Sound for many days.

"*May* 28.—By the position obtained by meridian altitude of stars and bearing of Mount Melbourne, we have drifted thirty-six miles northeast from last bearings taken on 23rd inst. The most of this must have been during the blizzard of the 24th. Mount Melbourne is one hundred and eleven miles due north of us, and there is some doubt in my mind as to whether the peak which we can see is this mountain. There may be a mirage. . . . In the evening had the soccer out on the ice by the light of a beautiful moon. The exercise and break from routine are a splendid tonic. Ice noises sent all hands on board.

"*June* 1.—Thick, hazy weather. In the afternoon a black streak appeared in the ice about a cable's length to the westward and stretching north and south. 8 p.m.—The black line widened and showed long lane of open water. Apparently we are fast in a floe which has broken from the main field. With thick weather we are uncertain of our position and drift. It will be interesting to find out what this crack in the ice signifies. I am convinced that there is open water, not far distant, in the Ross Sea. . . . Tonight Hooke is trying to call up Cape Evans. If the people at the hut have rigged the

set which was left there, they will hear 'All well' from the
Aurora. I hope they have. [The messages were not received.]

"*June* 8.—Made our latitude 75° 59′ S. by altitude of
Sirius. This is a very monotonous life, but all hands appear
to be happy and contented. Find that we are not too well off
for meals and will have to cut rations a little. Grady is taking
exercise now and should soon be well again. He seems very
anxious to get to work again, and is a good man. No wireless calls tonight, as there is a temporary breakdown—
condenser jar broken. There is a very faint display of aurora
in northern sky. It comes and goes almost imperceptibly, a
most fascinating sight. The temperature is −20° Fahr.; 52°
of frost is much too cold to allow one to stand for long.

"*June* 11.—Walked over to a very high pressure ridge
about a quarter of a mile north-northwest of the ship. In the
dim light walking over the ice is far from being monotonous, as it is almost impossible to see obstacles, such as
small, snowed-up ridges, which makes us wary and cautious. A dip in the sea would be the grand finale, but there
is little risk of this as the water freezes as soon as a lane
opens in the ice. The pressure ridge is about fifteen to
twenty feet high for several hundred feet, and the ice all
about it is bent up in a most extraordinary manner. At 9
p.m. Hooke called Cape Evans, 'All well—*Aurora,*' etc.; 10
p.m., weather reports for 8 p.m. sent to Wellington, New
Zealand, and Melbourne, via Macquarie Island. [The dispatch of messages from the *Aurora* was continued, but it
was learned afterwards that none of them had been received
by any station.]

"*June* 13.—The temperature in the chartroom ranges
from zero to a little above freezing point. This is a very
disturbing factor in rates of the chronometers (five in number, 3 G.M.T. and 2 Sid. T.), which are kept in cases in a
padded box, each case covered by a piece of blanket, and
the box covered by a heavy coat. In any enclosed place

where people pass their time, the niches and places where
no heat penetrates are covered with frozen breath. There
will be a big thaw out when the temperature rise.

"*June* 14.—Mount Melbourne is bearing north 14° west
(true). Our approximate position is forty miles east-northeast of Nordenskjöld Ice Tongue. At 9 p.m. Hooke called
Cape Evans and sent weather reports to Wellington and Melbourne via Macquarie Island. Hooke and Ninnis on several
evenings at about 11 o'clock have heard what happened to
be faint messages, but unreadable. He sent word to Macquarie Island of this in hopes that they would hear and increase the power.

"*June* 20.—During this last blow with its accompanying
drift snow there has been much leakage of current from the
aerial during the sending of reports. This is apparently due
to induction caused by the snow accumulating on the insula-
tors aloft, and thus rendering them useless, and probably to
increased inductive force of the current in a body of snow
drift. Hooke appears to be somewhat downhearted over it,
and, after discussing the matter, gave me a written report on
the nonsuccess (up to the present time) of his endeavors to
establish communication. He thinks that the proximity of
the Magnetic Pole and Aurora Australis might affect things.
The radiation is good and sufficient for normal conditions.
His suggestion to lead the down lead wires out to the ahead
and astern would increase scope, but I cannot countenance
it owing to unsettled state of ice and our too lofty poles.

"*June* 21.—Blowing gale from southwest throughout
day, but for short spell of westerly breeze about 5 p.m. Light
drift at frequent intervals, very hazy, and consequently no
land in sight during short twilight. Very hard up for mitts
and clothing. What little we have on board I have put to
one side for the people at the hut. Have given Thompson
instructions to turn crew to making pair mitts and helmet
out of Jaeger fleece for all hands forward. With strict econ-

omy we should make things spin out; cannot help worrying over our people at the hut. Although worrying does no good, one cannot do otherwise in this present impotent state. 11 p.m.—Wind howling and whistling through rigging. Outside, in glare of moon, flying drift and expanse of ice field. Desolation!

"*June* 22.—Today the sun has reached the limit of his northern declination and now he will start to come south. Observed this day as holiday, and in the evening had hands aft to drink to the health of the King and the Expedition. All hands are happy, but miss the others at Cape Evans. I pray to God we may soon be clear of this prison and in a position to help them. We can live now for sunlight and activity.

"*July* 1.—The 1st of July! Thank God. The days pass quickly. Through all my waking hours one long thought of the people at Cape Evans, but one must appear to be happy and take interest in the small happenings of shipboard.

"*July* 3.—Rather hazy with very little light. Moderate west-northwest to southwest winds until noon, when wind veered to south and freshened. No apparent change in ship's position; the berg is on the same bearing (1 point on the port quarter) and apparently the same distance off. Mount Melbourne was hidden behind a bank of clouds. This is our only landmark now, as Franklin Island is towered in perpetual gloom. Although we have had the berg in sight during all the time of our drift from the entrance to McMurdo Sound, we have not yet seen it in a favorable light, and, were it not for its movement, we might mistake it for a tabular island. It will be interesting to view our companion in the returning light—unless we are too close to it!

"*July* 5.—Dull grey day (during twilight) with light, variable, westerly breezes. All around hangs a heavy curtain of haze, and, although very light snow is falling, overhead is black and clear with stars shining. As soon as the faint noon light fades away the heavy low haze intensifies the darkness and makes one thankful that one has a good firm 'berth' in the ice. I don't care to contemplate the scene if the ice should break up at the present time.

"*July* 6.—Last night I thought I saw open water in the shape of a long black lane to the southward of the ship and extending in an easterly and westerly direction, but owing to the haze and light snow I could not be sure; this morning the lane was distinctly visible and appeared to be two or three hundred yards wide and two miles long. . . . At 6 p.m. loud pressure noises would be heard from the direction of the open lane and continued throughout the night. Shortly after 8 o'clock the grinding and hissing spread to our starboard bow (west-southwest), and the vibration caused by the pressure could be felt intermittently on board the ship. . . . The incessant grinding and grating of the ice to the southward, with seething noises, as of water rushing under ths ship's bottom, and ominous sounds, kept me on the *qui vive* all night, and the prospect of a breakup of the ice would have wracked my nerves had I not had them numbed by previous experiences.

"*July* 9.—At noon the sky to the northward had cleared sufficiently to allow of seeing Mount Melbourne, which appears now as a low peak to the northwest. Ship's position is twenty-eight miles north-northeast of Franklin Island. On the port bow and ahead of the ship there are some enormous pressure ridges; they seem to be the results of the recent and present ice movements. Pressure heard from the southward all day.

"*July* 13.—At 5 p.m. very heavy pressure was heard on the port beam and bow (south) and very close to the ship. This occurred again at irregular intervals. Quite close to the ship the ice could be seen bending upwards, and occasional jars were felt on board. I am inclined to think that we have set into a cul-de-sac and that we will now experience the full force of pressure from the south. We have prepared for the worst and can only hope for the best—a release from the ice with a seaworthy vessel under us.

"*July* 18.—This has been a day of events. About 8 a.m. the horizon to the north became clear and, as the light grew, the more westerly land showed up. This is the first clear day that we have had since the 9th of the month, and we have set a considerable distance to the northeast in the meantime. By meridian altitudes of stars and bearings of the land, which proved to be Coulman Islands, Mount Murchison, and Mount Melbourne, our position shows seventy-eight miles (geographical) northeast by north of Franklin Island. During the last three days we have drifted forty miles (geographical), so there has been ample reason for all the grinding and growling of pressure lately. The ship endured some several squeezes this day.

"*July* 20.—Shortly before breakfast the raucous voice of the emperor penguin was heard, and afterwards two were seen some distance from the ship. . . . The nearest mainland (in vicinity of Cape Washington) is ninety miles distant, as also is Coulman Island. Franklin Island is eighty miles southeast by south, and the pack is in motion. This is the emperor's hatching season, and here we meet them out in the cheerless desert of ice. . . . 10:45 p.m.—Heavy pressure around ship. Lanes opened and ship worked astern about twenty feet. The wires in the ice took the strain (lashings at mizen chains carried away) and carried away fair-lead bollard on port side of forecastle head.

"*July* 21, 1 a.m.—Lanes opened to about 40 ft. wide. Ship in open pool about 100 ft. wide. Heavy pressure in vicinity of ship. Called all hands and cut wires at the forecastle head. [These wires had remained frozen in the ice after the ship broke away from her moorings, and they had served a useful purpose at some times by checking ice movements close to the ship.] 2 a.m.—Ship swung athwart lane as the ice opened, and the floes on the port side pressed her stern round. 11:30 a.m.—Pack of killer whales came up in the lane around the ship. Some broke soft ice (about one inch thick) and pushed their heads through, rising to five or six feet perpendicularly out of the water. They were apparently having a look round. It is strange to see killers in this immense field of ice; open water must be near, I think. 5:15 p.m.—New ice of lanes cracked and opened. Floes on port side pushed stern on to ice (of floe); floes then closed in and nipped the ship fore and aft. the rudder was bent over to starboard and smashed. The solid oak and iron went like matchwood. 8 p.m.—Moderate south-southwest gale with drift. Much straining of timbers with pressure. 10 p.m.— Extra hard nip fore and aft; ship visibly hogged. Heavy pressure.

"*July* 22.—Ship in bad position in newly frozen lane, with bow and stern jammed against havy floes; heavy strain with much creaking and groaning. 8 a.m.—Called all hands to stations for sledges, and made final preparations for abandoning ship. Allotted special duties to several hands to facilitate quickness in getting clear should ship be crushed. Am afraid the ship's back will be broken if the pressure continues, but cannot relieve her. 2 p.m.—Ship lying easier. Poured sulphuric acid on the ice astern in hopes of rotting crack and relieving pressure on stern post, but unsuccessfully. Very heavy pressure on and around ship (taking strain fore and aft and on starboard quarter). Ship jumping and straining and listing badly. 10 p.m.—Ship has crushed her way into new ice on starboard side and slewed aslant lane with stern post clear of land ice. 12 p.m.—Ship is in safer position; lanes opening in every direction.

"*July* 23.—Caught glimpse of Coulman Island through haze. Position of ship south 14° east (true), eighty miles off Coulman Island. Pressure continued intermittently throughout the day and night, with occasional very heavy squeezes to the ship which made timbers crack and groan. The ship's stern is now in a more or less soft bed, formed of recently frozen ice of about one foot in thickness. I thank God that we have been spared through this fearful nightmare. I shall never forget the concertina motions of the ship during yesterday's and Wednesday's fore and aft nips.

"*July* 23.—Caught glimpse of Coulman Island through haze. Position of ship south 14° east (true), eighty miles off Coulman Island. Pressure continued intermittently throughout the day and night, with occasional very heavy squeezes to the ship which made timbers crack and groan. The ship's stern is now in a more or less soft bed, formed of recently frozen ice of about one foot in thickness. I thank God that we have been spared through this fearful nightmare. I shall never forget the concertina motions of the ship during yesterday's and Wednesday's fore and aft nips.

"*July* 24.—Compared with previous days this is a quiet one. The lanes have been opening and closing, and occasionally the ship gets a nasty squeeze against the solid floe on our starboard quarter. The more lanes that open the better, as they form 'springs' (when covered with thin ice, which makes to a thickness of three or four inches in a few hours) between the solid and heavier floes and fields. Surely we have been guided by the hands of Providence to have come in heavy grinding pack for over two hundred miles (geographical), skirting the icebound western shore, around and to the north of Franklin Island, and now into what appears a clear path to the open sea! In view of our precarious position and the lives of men in jeopardy, I sent this evening an aerogram to H.M. King George asking for a relief ship. I hope the wireless gets through. I have sent this message after much consideration, and know that in the event of our nonarrival in New Zealand on the specified date (November 1) a relief ship will be sent to aid the Southern Party.

"*July* 25.—Very heavy pressure about the ship. During the early hours a large field on the port quarter came charging up, and on meeting our floe tossed up a ridge from ten to fifteen feet high. The blocks of ice as they broke off crumbled and piled over each other to the accompaniment of a thunderous roar. Throughout the day the pressure continued, the floes alternately opening and closing, and the ship creaking and groaning during the nips between floes.

"*August* 4.—For nine days we have had southerly winds, and the last four we have experienced howling blizzards. I am sick of the sound of the infernal wind. Din! din! din! and darkness. We should have seen the sun today, but a bank of cumulus effectually hid him, although the daylight is a neverending joy.

"*August* 6.—The wind moderated towards 6 a.m., and about breakfast time, with a clear atmosphere, the land from near Cape Cotter to Cape Adare was visible. What a day of delights! After four days of thick weather we find ourselves in sight of Cape Adare in a position about forty-five miles east of Possession Isles; in this time we have been set one hundred miles. Good going. Mount Sabine, the first land seen by us when coming south, lies away to the westward, forming the highest peak (10,000 ft.) of a majestic range of mountains covered in eternal snow. Due west we can see the Possession Islands, lying under the stupendous bluff of Cape Downshire, which shows large patches of black rock. The land slopes down to the northwest of Cape Downshire, and rises again into the high peninsula about Cape Adare. We felt excited this morning in anticipation of seeing the sun, which rose about nine-thirty (local time). It was a glorious, joyful sight. We drank to something, and with very light hearts gave cheers for the sun.

"*August* 9.—Donolly got to work on the rudder again. It is a long job cutting through the iron sheathing plates of the rudder, and not too safe at present, as the ice is treacherous. Hooke says that the conditions are normal now. I wish for his sake that he could get through. He is a good sportsman and keeps on trying, although, I am convinced, he has little hope with this inadequate aerial.

"*August* 10.—The ship's position is lat. 70° 40′ S., forty miles north 29° east of Cape Adare. The distance drifted from August 2 to 6 was one hundred miles, and from the 6th to the 10th eighty-eight miles.

"*August* 12.—By observation and bearings of land we are forty-five miles northeast of Cape Adare, in lat. 70° 42′ S. This position is a little to the eastward of the position on the 10th. The bearings as laid off on a small-scale chart of gnomonic projection are very inaccurate, and here we are handicapped, as our chronometers have lost all regularity. Donolly and Grady are having quite a job with the iron platings on the rudder, but should finish the cutting tomorrow. A jury rudder is nearly completed. This afternoon we mixed some concrete for the lower part, and had to use boiling water, as the water froze in the mixing. The carpenter had made a good job of the rudder, although he has had to construct it on the quarterdeck in low temperatures and exposed to biting blasts.

"*August* 16.—We are 'backing and filling' about forty miles northeast of Cape Adare. This is where we expected to have made much mileage. However, we cannot grumble and must be patient. There was much mirage to the northward, and from the crow's nest a distinct appearance of open water could be seen stretching from north-northwest to northeast.

"*August* 17.—A glorious day! Land is distinctly visible, and to the northward the black fringe of water sky over the horizon hangs continuously. Hooke heard Macquarie Island 'speaking' Hobart. The message heard was the finish of the weather reports. We have hopes now of news in the near future.

"*August* 23.—Saw the land in the vicinity of Cape North. To the south-southwest the white cliffs and peaks of the inland ranges were very distinct, and away in the distance to the southwest could be seen a low stretch of undulating land. At times Mount Sabine was visible through the gloom. The latitude is 69° 44½' S. We are fifty-eight miles north, forty miles east of Cape North.

"*August* 24.—We lifted the rudder out of the ice and placed it clear of the stern, athwart the fore-and-aft line of the ship. We had quite a job with it (weight, four and a half tons), using treble- and double-sheaved blocks purchase, but with the endless chain tackle from the engine room, and plenty of 'beef' and leverage, we dragged it clear. All the pintles are gone at the fore part of the rudder; it is a clean break and bears witness to the terrific force exerted on the ship during the nip. I am glad to see the rudder upon the ice and clear of the propeller. The blade itself (which is solid oak and sheathed on two sides and after part halfway down, with three-quarter-inch iron plating) is undamaged, save for the broken pintles; the twisted portion is in the rudder trunk.

"*August* 25, 11 p.m.—Hooke has just been in with the good tidings that he has heard Macquarie and the Bluff (New Zealand) sending their weather reports and exchanging signals. Can this mean that they have heard our recent signals and are trying to get us now? Our motor has been out of order.

"*August* 26.—The carpenter has finished the jury rudder and is now at work on the lower end of the rudder truck, where the rudder burst into the stern timbers. We are lucky in having this opportunity to repair these minor damages, which might prove serious in a seaway.

"*August* 31, 6:30 a.m.—Very loud pressure noises to the southeast. I went aloft after breakfast and had the pleasure of seeing many open lanes in all directions. The lanes of yesterday are frozen over, showing what little chance there is of a general and continued breakup of the ice until the temperature rises. Land was visible, but far too distant for even approximate bearings. The berg still hangs to the northwest of the ship. We seem to have pivoted outwards from the land. We cannot get out of this too quickly, and although every one has plenty of work, and is cheerful, the uselessness of the ship in her present position palls.

"*September* 5.—The mizen wireless mast came down in a raging blizzard today. In the forenoon I managed to crawl to windward on the top of the bridge house, and under the lee of the chart house watched the mast bending over with the wind and swaying like the branch of a tree, but after the aerial had stood throughout the winter I hardly thought the mast would carry away. Luckily, as it is dangerous to life to be on deck in this weather (food is brought from the galley in relays through blinding drift and over big heaps of snow), no one was about when the mast carried away.

"*September* 8.—This is dull, miserable weather. Blow, snow, and calm for an hour or two. Sometimes it blows in this neighborhood without snow and sometimes with—this seems to be the only difference. I have two patients now, Larkman and Mugridge. Larkman was frostbitten on the great and second toes of the left foot some time ago, and has so far taken little notice of them. Now they are causing him some alarm as gangrene has set in. Mugridge is suffering from an intermittent rash, with red, inflamed skin and large, short-lived blisters. I don't know what the deuce it is, but the nearest description to it in a 'Materia Medica,' etc., is *pemphigus,* so pemphigus it is, and he has been 'toniced' and massaged.

"*September* 9.—This is the first day for a long time that we have registered a minimum temperature above zero for the twenty-four hours. It is pleasant to think that from noon to noon throughout the night the temperature never fell below +4° (28° frost), and with the increase of daylight it makes one feel that summer really is approaching.

"*September* 13.—All around the northern horizon there

is the appearance of an open water sky, but around the ship the prospect is dreary. The sun rose at 6:30 a.m. and set at 5:25 p.m. Ship's time—eleven hours five minutes of sunlight and seventeen hours light. Three hours twilight morning and evening. The carpenter is dismantling the taffrail (to facilitate the landing and, if necessary, the boarding of the jury rudder) and will construct a temporary, removable rail.

"*September* 16.—There has been much mirage all around the horizon, and to the eastward through south to southwest heavy frost smoke has been rising. Over the northern horizon a low bank of white fog hangs as though over the sea. I do not like these continued low temperatures. I am beginning to have doubts as to our release until the sun starts to rot the ice.

"*September* 17.—This is the anniversary of our departure from London. There are only four of the original eleven on board—Larkman, Ninnis, Mauger, and I. Much has happened since Friday, September 18, 1914, and I can recall the scene as we passed down the Thames with submarines and cruisers, in commission and bent on business, crossing our course. I can also remember the regret at leaving it all and the consequent 'fedupness.'

"*September* 21.—The sun is making rapid progress south, and we have had today over seventeen hours' light and twelve hours' sunlight. Oh for a release! The monotony and worry of our helpless position is deadly. I suppose Shackleton and his party will have started depot laying now and will be full of hopes for the future. I wonder whether the *Endurance* wintered in the ice or went north. I cannot help thinking that if she wintered in the Weddell Sea she will be worse off than the *Aurora*. What a lot we have to look for in the next six months—news of Shackleton and the *Endurance,* the party at Cape Evans, and the war.

"*September* 22.—Lat. 69° 12′ S.; long. 165° 00′ E. Sturge Island (Balleny Group) is bearing north (true) ninety miles distant. Light northwest airs with clear, fine weather. Sighted Sturge Island in the morning, bearing due north of us and appearing like a faint low shadow on the horizon. It is good to get a good landmark for fixing positions again, and it is good to see that we are making northerly progress, however small. Since breaking away from Cape Evans we have drifted roughly seven hundred and five miles around islands and past formidable obstacles, a wonderful drift! It is good to think that it has not been in vain, and that the knowledge of the set and drift of the pack will be a valuable addition to the sum of human knowledge. The distance from Cape Evans to our present position is seven hundred and five miles (geographical).

"*September* 27.—The temperature in my room last night was round about zero, rather chilly, but warm enough under the blankets. Hooke has dismantled his wireless gear. He feels rather sick about not getting communication, although he does not show it.

"*September* 30.—Ninnis has been busy now for the past week on the construction of a new tractor. He is building the body and will assemble the motor in the fore 'tween decks, where it can be lashed securely when we are released from the ice. I can see leads of open water from the mast-head, but we are still held firmly. How long?

"*October* 7.—As time wears on the possibility of getting back to the Barrier to land a party deserves consideration; if we do not get clear until late in the season we will have to turn south first, although we have no anchors and little moorings, no rudder and a short supply of coal. To leave a party on the Barrier would make us very short-handed; still, it can be done, and anything is preferable to the delay in assisting the people at Cape Evans. At 5 a.m. a beautiful parhelion formed around the sun. The sight so impressed the bos'n that he roused me out to see it."

During the month of October the *Aurora* drifted uneventfully. Stenhouse mentions that there was often an appearance of open water on the northern and eastern horizon. But anxious eyes were strained in vain for indications that the day of the ship's release was near at hand. Hooke had the wireless plant running again and was trying daily to get into touch with Macquarie Island, now about eight hundred and fifty miles distant. The request for a relief ship was to be renewed if communication could be established, for by this time, if all had gone well with the *Endurance*, the overland party from the Weddell Sea would have been starting. There was considerable movement of the ice towards the end of the month, lanes opening and closing, but the floe, some acres in area, into which the *Aurora* was frozen, remained firm until the early days of November. The cracks appeared close to the ship, due apparently to heavy drift causing the floe to sink. The temperatures were higher now, under the influence of the sun, and the ice was softer. Thawing was causing discomfort in the quarters aboard. The position on November 12 was reckoned to be lat. 66° 49′ S., long. 155° 17′ 45″ E. Stenhouse made a sounding on November 17, in lat. 66° 40′ S., long. 154° 45′ E., and found bottom at 194 fathoms. The bottom sample was mud and a few small stones. The sounding line showed a fairly strong undercurrent to the northwest. "We panned out some of the mud," says Stenhouse, "and in the remaining grit found several specks of gold." Two days later the trend of the current was southeasterly. There was a pronounced thaw on the 22nd. The cabins were in a dripping state, and recently fallen snow was running off the ship in little streams. All hands were delighted, for the present discomfort offered promise of an early breakup of the pack.

"*November* 23.—At 3 a.m. Young Island, Balleny Group, was seen bearing north 54° east (true). The island, which showed up clearly on the horizon, under a heavy stratus-covered sky, appeared to be very far distant. By latitude at

noon we are in 66° 26′ S. As this is the charted latitude of
Peak Foreman, Young Island, the bearing does not agree.
Land was seen at 8 a.m. bearing south 60° west (true). This,
which would appear to be Cape Hudson, loomed up through
the mists in the form of a high, bold headland, with low
undulating land stretching away to the south-southeast and
to the westward of it. The appearance of this headland has
been foretold for the last two days, by masses of black fog,
but it seems strange that land so high should not have been
seen before, as there is little change in the atmospheric conditions.

"*November* 24.—Overcast and hazy during forenoon.
Cloudy, clear, and fine in afternoon and evening. Not a vestige of land can be seen, so Cape Hudson is really 'Cape
Flyaway.' This is most weird. All hands saw the headland to
the southwest, and some of us sketched it. Now (afternoon),
although the sky is beautifully clear to the southwest, nothing can be seen. We cannot have drifted far from yesterday's
position. No wonder Wilkes reported land. 9 p.m.—A low
fringe of land appears on the horizon bearing southwest, but
in no way resembles our Cape of yesterday. This afternoon
we took a cast of the lead through the crack 200 yds. west
of the ship, but found no bottom at 700 fathoms."

An interesting incident on November 26 was the discovery of an emperor penguin rookery. Ninnis and Kavenagh
took a long walk to the northwest, and found the deserted
rookery. The depressions in the ice, made by the birds, were
about eighteen inches long and contained a greyish residue.
The rookery was in a hollow surrounded by pressure ridges
six feet high. Apparently about twenty birds had been there.
No pieces of eggshell were seen, but the petrels and skuas
had been there in force and probably would have taken all
scraps of this kind. The floes were becoming soft and "rotten," and walking was increasingly difficult. Deep pools of
slush and water covered with thin snow made traps for the

men. Stenhouse thought that a stiff blizzard would break up
the pack. His anxiety was increasing with the advance of the
season, and his log is a record of deep yearning to be free
and active again. But the grip of the pack was inexorable.
The hands had plenty of work on the *Aurora*, which was
being made shipshape after the buffeting of the winter
storms. Seals and penguins were seen frequently, and the
supply of fresh meat was maintained. The jury rudder was
ready to be shipped when the ship was released, but in the
meantime it was not being exposed to the attacks of the ice.
"No appreciable change in our surroundings," was the note
for December 17. "Every day past now reduces our chance
of getting out in time to go north for rudder, anchors, and
coal. If we break out before January 15 we might get north
to New Zealand and down to Cape Evans again in time to
pick up the parties. After that date we can only attempt to
go south in our crippled state, and short of fuel. With only
nine days' coal on board we would have little chance of
working through any Ross Sea pack, or of getting south at
all if we encountered many blizzards. Still there is a sporting
chance and luck may be with us. . . . Shackleton may be past
the Pole now. I wish our wireless calls had got through."

Christmas Day, with its special dinner and mild festivi-
ties, came and passed, and still the ice remained firm. The
men were finding some interest in watching the moulting of
emperor penguins, who were stationed at various points in
the neighborhood of the ship. They had taken station to leeward of hummocks, and appeared to move only when the
wind changed or the snow around them had become foul.
They covered but a few yards on these journeys, and even
then stumbled in their weakness. One Emperor was brought
on board alive, and the crew were greatly amused to see the
bird balancing himself on heels and tail, with upturned toes,
the position adopted when the egg is resting on the feet during the incubation period. The threat of a stiff "blow"

aroused hopes of release several times, but the blizzard—
probably the first Antarctic blizzard that was ever longed
for—did not arrive. New Year's Day found Stenhouse and
other men just recovering from an attack of snow blindness,
contracted by making an excursion across the floes without
snow goggles.

At the end of the first week in January the ship was in lat.
65° 45′ S. The pack was well broken a mile from the ship,
and the ice was rolling fast. Under the bows and stern the
pools were growing and stretching away in long lanes to the
west. A seal came up to blow under the stern on the 6th,
proving that there was an opening in the sunken ice there.
Stenhouse was economizing in food. No breakfast was
served on the ship, and seal or penguin meat was used for
at least one of the two meals later in the day. All hands
were short of clothing, but Stenhouse was keeping intact the
sledging gear intended for the use of the shore party. Strong,
variable winds on the 9th raised hopes again, and on the
morning of the 10th the ice appeared to be well broken from
half a mile to a mile distant from the ship in all directions.
"It seems extraordinary that the ship should be held in an
almost unbroken floe of about a mile square, the more so as
this patch was completely screwed and broken during the
smash in July, and contains many faults. In almost any direction at a distance of half a mile from the ship there are
pressure ridges of eight-inch ice piled twenty feet high. It
was provident that although so near these ridges were escaped."

The middle of January was passed and the *Aurora* lay
still in the ice. The period of continuous day was drawing
towards its close, and there was an appreciable twilight at
midnight. A dark water-sky could be seen on the northern
horizon. The latitude on January 24 was 65° 39½′ S.
Towards the end of the month Stenhouse ordered a thorough
overhaul of the stores and general preparations for a move.

The supply of flour and butter was ample. Other stores were running low, and the crew lost no opportunity of capturing seals and penguins. Adelies were traveling to the east-south-east in considerable numbers, but they could not be taken unless they approached the ship closely, owing to the soft condition of the ice. The wireless plant, which had been idle during the months of daylight, had been rigged again, and Hooke resumed his calls to Macquarie Island on February 2. He listened in vain for any indication that he had been heard. The pack was showing much movement, but the large floe containing the ship remained firm.

The breakup of the floe came on February 12. Strong northeast to southeast winds put the ice in motion and brought a perceptible swell. The ship was making some water, a foretaste of a trouble to come, and all hands spent the day at the pumps, reducing the water from three feet eight and a half inches in the wall to twelve inches, in spite of frozen pipes and other difficulties. Work had just finished for the night when the ice broke astern and quickly split in all directions under the influence of the swell. The men managed to save some seal meat which had been cached in a drift near the gangway. They lost the flagstaff, which had been rigged as a wireless mast out on the floe, but drew in the aerial. The ship was floating now amid fragments of floe, and bumbing considerably in the swell. A fresh southerly wind blew during the night, and the ship started to forge ahead gradually without sail. At 8:30 a.m. on the 13th Stenhouse set the foresail and foretopmast staysail, and the *Aurora* moved northward slowly, being brought up occasionally by large floes. Navigation under such conditions, without steam and without a rudder, was exceedingly difficult, but Stenhouse wished if possible to save his small remaining stock of coal until he cleared the pack, so that a quick run might be made to McMurdo Sound. The jury rudder could not be rigged in the pack. The ship was making about three and a half feet of water in the twenty-four hours, a quantity easily kept in check by the pumps.

During the 14th the *Aurora* worked very slowly northward through heavy pack. Occasionally the yards were backed or an ice anchor put into a floe to help her out of difficult places, but much of the time she steered herself. The jury rudder boom was topped into position in the afternoon, but the rudder was not to be shipped until open pack or open water was reached. The ship was held up all day on the 15th in lat. 64° 38′ S. Heavy floes barred progress in every direction. Attempts were made to work the ship by trimming sails and warping with ice anchors, but she could not be maneuvered smartly enough to take advantage of leads that opened and closed. This state of affairs continued throughout the 16th. That night a heavy swell was rolling under the ice and the ship had a rough time. One pointed floe ten or twelve feet thick was steadily battering, with a three-feet send, against the starboard side, and fenders only partially deadened the shock. "It is no use butting against this pack with steam power," wrote Stenhouse. "We would use all our meager supply of coal in reaching the limit of the ice in sight, and then we would be in a hole, with neither ballast nor fuel. . . . But if this stagnation lasts another week we will have to raise steam and consume our coal in an endeavor to get into navigable waters. I am afraid our chances of getting south are very small now."

The pack remained close, and on the 21st a heavy swell made the situation dangerous. The ship bumped heavily that night and fenders were of little avail. With each "send" of the swell the ship would bang her bows on the floe ahead, then bounce back and smash into another floe across her stern post. This floe, about six feet thick and 100 ft. across, was eventually split and smashed by the impacts. The pack was jammed close on the 23rd, when the noon latitude was 64° 36½′ S. The next change was for the worse. The pack loosened on the night of the 25th, and a heavy northwest swell caused the ship to bump heavily. This state of affairs recurred at intervals in succeeding days. "The battering and ramming of the floes increased in the early hours [of February 29] until it seemed as if some sharp floe or jagged underfoot must go through the ship's hull. At 6 a.m. we converted a large coir spring into a fender, and slipped it under the port quarter, where a pressured floe with a twenty to thirty feet underfoot was threatening to knock the propeller and stern post off altogether. At 9 a.m., after pumping ship, the engineer reported a leak in the way of the propeller shaft aft near the stern post on the port side. The carpenter cut part of the lining and filled the space between the timbers with Stockholm tar, cement, and oakum. He could not get at the actual leak, but his makeshift made a little difference. I am anxious about the propeller. This pack is a dangerous place for a ship now; it seems miraculous that the old Barky still floats."

The ice opened out a little on March 1. It was imperative to get the ship out of her dangerous situation quickly, as winter was approaching, and Stenhouse therefore ordered steam to be raised. Next morning he had the spanker gaff rigged over the stern for use as a temporary rudder while in the heavy pack. Steam had been raised to working pressure at 5:15 p.m. on the 2nd, and the *Aurora* began to work ahead to the westward. Progress was very slow owing to heavy floes and deep underfoots, which necessitated frequent stoppages of the engines. Open water was in sight to the north and northwest the next morning, after a restless night spent among the rocking floes. But progress was very slow. The *Aurora* went to leeward under the influence of a west-south-west breeze, and steering by means of the yards and a warp anchor was a ticklish business. The ship came to a full stop among heavy floes before noon on the 3rd, and three hours later, after vain attempts to warp ahead by means of ice anchors, Stenhouse had the fires partially drawn (to save coal) and banked.

No advance was made on March 4 and 5. A moderate gale from the east-northeast closed the ice and set it in motion, and the *Aurora*, with banked fires, rolled and bumped heavily. Seventeen bergs were in sight, and one of them was working southwards into the pack and threatening to approach the ship. During the night the engines were turned repeatedly by the action of ice on the propeller blades. "All theories about the swell being nonexistent in the pack are false," wrote the anxious master. "Here we are with a suggestion only of open water-sky, and the ship rolling her scuppers under and sitting down bodily on the floes." The ice opened when the wind moderated, and on the afternoon of the 6th the *Aurora* moved northward again. "Without a rudder (no jury rudder can yet be used amongst these swirling, rolling floes) the ship requires a lot of attention. Her head must be pointed between floes by means of ice anchors and warps, or by mooring to a floe and steaming round it. We kept a fairly good course between two bergs to our northward and made about five miles northing before, darkness coming on, the men could no longer venture on the floes with safety to fix the anchors."

The next three days were full of anxiety. The *Aurora* was held by the ice, and subjected to severe buffeting, while two bergs approached from the north. On the morning of the 10th the nearest berg was within three cables of the ship. But the pack had opened and by 9:30 a.m. the ship was out of the danger zone and headed north-northeast. The pack continued to open during the afternoon, and the *Aurora* passed through wide stretches of small loose floes and brash. Progress was good until darkness made a stop necessary. The next morning the pack was denser. Stenhouse shipped a preventer jury rudder (the weighted spanker gaff), but could not get steerage way. Broad leads were sighted to the northwest in the afternoon, and the ship got within a quarter of a mile of the nearest lead before being held up by heavy pack. She again bumped severely during the night, and the watch stood by with fenders to ease the more dangerous blows.

Early next morning Stenhouse lowered a jury rudder, with steering pennants to drag through the water, and moved north to northwest through heavy pack. He made sixteen miles that day on an erratic course, and then spent an anxious night with the ship setting back into the pack and being pounded heavily. Attempts to work forward to an open lead on the morning of the 13th were unsuccessful. Early in the afternoon a little progress was made, with all hands standing by to fend off high ice, and at 4:50 p.m. the *Aurora* cleared the main pack. An hour was spent shipping the jury rudder under the counter, and then the ship moved slowly northward. There was pack still ahead, and the bergs and growlers were a constant menace in the hours of darkness. Some anxious work remained to be done, since bergs and scattered ice extended in all directions, but at 2 p.m. on March 14 the *Aurora* cleared the last belt of pack in lat. 62° 27·5′ S., long. 157° 32′ E. "We 'spliced the main brace,' " says Stenhouse, "and blew three blasts of farewell to the pack with the whistle."

The *Aurora* was not at the end of her troubles, but the voyage up to New Zealand need not be described in detail. Any attempt to reach McMurdo Sound was now out of the question. Stenhouse had a battered, rudderless ship, with only a few tons of coal left in the bunkers, and he struggled northward in heavy weather against persistent adverse winds and head seas. The jury rudder needed constant nursing, and the shortage of coal made it impossible to get the best service from the engines. There were times when the ship could make no progress and fell about helplessly in a confused swell or lay hove to amid mountainous seas. She was short-handed, and one or two of the men were creating additional difficulties. But Stenhouse displayed throughout fine seamanship and dogged perseverance. He accomplished successfully one of the most difficult voyages on record, in an ocean area notoriously stormy and treacherous. On March 23 he established wireless communication with Bluff Station, New Zealand, and the next day was in touch with Wellington and Hobart. The naval officer in New Zealand waters offered assistance, and eventually it was arranged that the Otago Harbour Board's tug *Plucky* should meet the *Aurora* outside Port Chalmers. There were still bad days to be endured. The jury rudder partially carried away and had to be unshipped in a heavy sea. Stenhouse carried on, and in the early morning of April 2 the *Aurora* picked up the tug and was taken in tow. She reached Port Chalmers the following morning, and was welcomed with the warm hospitality that New Zealand has always shown towards Antarctic explorers.

CHAPTER XVII

THE LAST RELIEF

WHEN I REACHED New Zealand at the beginning of December 1916 I found that the arrangements for the relief were complete. The New Zealand Government had taken the task in hand earlier in the year, before I had got into touch with the outside world. The British and Australian Governments were giving financial assistance. The *Aurora* had been repaired and refitted at Port Chalmers during the year at considerable cost, and had been provisioned and coaled for the voyage to McMurdo Sound. My old friend Captain John K. Davis, who was a member of my first Antarctic Expedition in 1907–1909, and who subsequently commanded Dr. Mawson's ship in the Australian Antarctic Expedition, had been placed in command of the *Aurora* by the Governments, and he had engaged officers, engineers, and crew. Captain Davis came to Wellington to see me on my arrival there, and I heard his account of the position. I had interviews also with the Minister for Marine, the late Dr. Robert McNab, a kindly and sympathetic Scotsman who took a deep personal interest in the Expedition. Stenhouse also was in Wellington, and I may say again here that his account of his voyage and drift in the *Aurora* filled me with admiration for his pluck, seamanship, and resourcefulness.

After discussing the situation fully with Dr. McNab, I agreed that the arrangements already made for the Relief Expedition should stand. Time was important and there were difficulties about making any change of plans or control at the last moment. After Captain Davis had been at work for some months the Government agreed to hand the *Aurora* over to me free of liability on her return to New

Zealand. It was decided, therefore, that Captain Davis
should take the ship down to McMurdo Sound, and that I
should go with him to take charge of any shore operations
that might be necessary. I "signed on" at a salary of 1s. a
month, and we sailed from Port Chalmers on December 20,
1916. A week later we sighted ice again. The *Aurora* made
a fairly quick passage through the pack and entered the open
water of the Ross Sea on January 7, 1917.

Captain Davis brought the *Aurora* alongside the ice edge
off Cape Royds on the morning of January 10, and I went
ashore with a party to look for some record in the hut
erected there by my Expedition in 1907. I found a letter
stating that the Ross Sea party was housed at Cape Evans,
and was on my way back to the ship when six men, with
dogs and sledge, were sighted coming from the direction of
Cape Evans. At 1 p.m. this party arrived on board, and we
learned that of the ten members of the Expedition left behind when the *Aurora* broke away on May 6, 1915, seven
had survived, namely, A. Stevens, E. Joyce, H. E. Wild, J. L.
Cope, R. W. Richards, A. K. Jack, I. O. Gaze. These seven
men were all well, though they showed traces of the ordeal
through which they had passed. They told us of the deaths
of Mackintosh, Spencer-Smith, and Hayward, and of their
own anxious wait for relief.

All that remained to be done was to make a final search
for the bodies of Mackintosh and Hayward. There was no
possibility of either man being alive. They had been without
equipment when the blizzard broke the ice they were crossing. It would have been impossible for them to have survived more than a few days, and eight months had now
elapsed without news of them. Joyce had already searched
south of Glacier Tongue. I considered that further search
should be made in two directions, the area north of Glacier
Tongue, and the old depot off Butler Point, and I made a
report to Captain Davis to this effect.

On January 12 the ship reached a point five and a half miles east of Butler Point. I took a party across rubbly and waterlogged ice to within thirty yards of the piedmont ice, but owing to high cliffs and loose slushy ice could not make a landing. The land ice had broken away at the point cut by the cross bearings of the depot, but was visible in the form of two large bergs grounded to the north of Cape Bernacchi. There was no sign of the depot or of any person having visited the vicinity. We returned to the ship and proceeded across the Sound to Cape Bernacchi.

The next day I took a party ashore with the object of searching the area of Glacier Tongue, including Razorback Island, for traces of the two missing men. We reached the Cape Evans Hut at 1:30 p.m., and Joyce and I left at 3 p.m. for the Razorbacks. We conducted a search round both islands, returning to the hut at 7 p.m. The search had been fruitless. On the 14th I started with Joyce to search the north side of Glacier Tongue, but the surface drift, with wind from southeast, decided me not to continue, as the ice was from moving rapidly at the end of Cape Evans, and the pool between the hut and Inaccessible Island was growing larger. The wind increased in the afternoon. The next day a southeast blizzard was blowing, with drift half up the islands. I considered it unsafe to sledge that day, especially as the ice was breaking away from the south side of Cape Evans into the pool. We spent the day putting the hut in order.

We got up at 3 a.m. on the 16th. The weather was fine and calm. I started at 4:20 with Joyce to the south at the greatest possible speed. We reached Glacier Tongue about one and a half miles from the seaward end. Wherever there were not precipitous cliffs there was an even snow slope to the top. From the top we searched with glasses; there was nothing to be seen but blue ice, crevassed, showing no protuberances. We came down and, half running, half walking, worked about three miles towards the root of the glacier; but

I could see there was not the slightest chance of finding any remains owing to the enormous snow drifts wherever the cliffs were accessible. The base of the steep cliffs had drifts ten to fifteen feet high. We arrived back at the hut at 9:40, and left almost immediately for the ship. I considered that all places likely to hold the bodies of Mackintosh and Hayward had now been searched. There was no doubt to my mind that they met their deaths on the breaking of the thin ice when the blizzard arose on May 8, 1916. During my absence from the hut Wild and Jack had erected a cross to the memory of the three men who had lost their lives in the service of the Expedition.

Captain Davis took the ship northward on January 17. The ice conditions were unfavorable and pack barred the way. We stood over to the western coast towards Dunlop Island and followed it to Granite Harbor. No mark or depot of any kind was seen. The *Aurora* reached the main pack, about sixty miles from Cape Adare, on January 22. The ice was closed ahead, and Davis went south in open water to wait for better conditions. A northwest gale on January 28 enabled the ship to pass between the pack and the land off Cape Adare, and we crossed the Antarctic Circle on the last day of the month. On February 4 Davis sent a formal report to the New Zealand Government by wireless, and on February 9 the *Aurora* was berthed at Wellington. We were welcomed like returned brothers by the New Zealand people.

CHAPTER XVIII

THE FINAL PHASE

THE FOREGOING CHAPTERS of this book represent the general narrative of our Expedition. That we failed in accomplishing the object we set out for was due, I venture to assert, not to any neglect or lack of organization, but to the overwhelming natural obstacles, especially the unprecedented severe summer conditions on the Weddell Sea side. But though the Expedition was a failure in one respect, I think it was successful in many others. A large amount of important scientific work was carried out. The meteorological observations in particular have an economic bearing. The hydrographical work in the Weddell Sea has done much to clear up the mystery of this, the least known of all the seas. I have appended a short scientific memorandum to this volume, but the more detailed scientific results must wait until a more suitable time arrives, when more stable conditions prevail. Then results will be worked out.

To the credit side of the Expedition one can safely say that the comradeship and resource of the members of the Expedition was worthy of the highest traditions of Polar service; and it was a privilege to me to have had under my command men who, through dark days and the stress and strain of continuous danger, kept up their spirits and carried out their work regardless of themselves and heedless of the limelight. The same energy and endurance that they showed in the Antarctic they brought to the greater war in the Old World. And having followed our fortunes in the South you may be interested to know that practically every member of the Expedition was employed in one or other branches of the active fighting forces during the war. Several are still abroad, and for this very reason it has been impossible for me to obtain certain details for this book.

Of the fifty-three men who returned out of the fifty-six who left for the South, three have since been killed and five wounded. Four decorations have been won, and several members of the Expedition have been mentioned in dispatches. McCarthy, the best and most efficient of the sailors, always cheerful under the most trying circumstances, and who for these very reasons I chose to accompany me on the boat journey to South Georgia, was killed at his gun in the Channel. Cheetham, the veteran of the Antarctic, who had been more often south of the Antarctic circle than any man, was drowned when the vessel he was serving in was torpedoed, a few weeks before the Armistice. Ernest Wild, Frank Wild's brother, was killed while mine-sweeping in the Mediterranean. Mauger, the carpenter on the *Aurora,* was badly wounded while serving with the New Zealand Infantry, so that he is unable to follow his trade again. He is now employed by the New Zealand Government. The two surgeons, Macklin and McIlroy, served in France and Italy, McIlroy being badly wounded at Ypres. Frank Wild, in view of his unique experience of ice and ice conditions, was at once sent to the North Russian front, where his zeal and ability won him the highest praise.

Macklin served first with the Yorks and later transferred as medical officer to the Tanks, where he did much good work. Going to the Italian front with his battalion, he won the Military Cross for bravery in tending wounded under fire.

James joined the Royal Engineers, Sound-Ranging Section, and after much front-line work was given charge of a Sound-Ranging School to teach other officers this latest and most scientific addition to the art of war.

Wordie went to France with the Royal Field Artillery and was badly wounded at Armentières.

Hussey was in France for eighteen months with the Royal Garrison Artillery, serving in every big battle from Dixmude to Saint-Quentin.

Worsley, known to his intimates as Depth-Charge Bill, owing to his success with that particular method of destroying German submarines, has the Distinguished Service Order and three submarines to his credit.

Stenhouse, who commanded the *Aurora* after Mackintosh landed, was with Worsley as his second in command when one of the German submarines was rammed and sunk, and received the D.S.C. for his share in the fight. He was afterwards given command of a Mystery Ship, and fought several actions with enemy submarines.

Clark served on a mine-sweeper. Greenstreet was employed with the barges on the Tigris. Rickenson was commissioned as Engineer-Lieutenant, R.N. Kerr returned to the Merchant Service as an engineer.

Most of the crew of the *Endurance* served on minesweepers.

Of the Ross Sea Party, Mackintosh, Hayward, and Spencer-Smith died for their country as surely as any who gave up their lives on the fields of France and Flanders. Hooke, the wireless operator, now navigates an airship.

Nearly all of the crew of the *Aurora* joined the New Zealand Field Forces and saw active service in one or other of the many theaters of war. Several have been wounded, but it has been impossible to obtain details.

On my return, after the rescue of the survivors of the Ross Sea Party, I offered my services to the Government, and was sent on a mission to South America. When this was concluded I was commissioned as Major and went to North Russia in charge of Arctic Equipment and Transport, having with me Worsley, Stenhouse, Hussey, Macklin, and Brocklehurst, who was to have come South with us, but who, as a regular officer, rejoined his unit on the outbreak of war. He has been wounded three times and was in the retreat from Mons. Worsley was sent across to the Archangel front, where he did excellent work, and the others served with me on the Murmansk front. The mobile columns there had exactly the same clothing, equipment, and sledging food as we had on the Expedition. No expense was spared to obtain the best of everything for them, and as a result not a single case of avoidable frostbite was reported.

Taking the Expedition as a unit, out of fifty-six men three died in the Antarctic, three were killed in action, and five have been wounded, so that our casualties have been fairly high.

Though some have gone there are enough left to rally round and form a nucleus for the next Expedition, when troublous times are over and scientific exploration can once more be legitimately undertaken.

SCIENTIFIC WORK

By J. M. WORDIE, M.A. (Cantab.), Lieut. R.F.A.

THE RESEARCH UNDERTAKEN by the Expedition was originally planned for a shore party working from a fixed base on land, but it was only in South Georgia that this condition of affairs was fully realized. On this island, where a full month was spent, the geologist made very extensive collections, and began the mapping of the country; the magnetician had some of his instruments in working order for a short while; and the meteorologist was able to cooperate with the Argentine observer stationed at Grytviken. It had been realized how important the meteorological observations were going to be to the Argentine Government, and they accordingly did all in their power to help, both before and at the end of the Expedition. The biologist devoted most of his time, meanwhile, to the whaling industry, there being no less than seven stations on the island; he also made collections of the neritic fauna, and, accompanied by the photographer, studied the bird life and the habits of the sea elephants along the east coast.

By the time the actual southern voyage commenced, each individual had his own particular line of work which he was prepared to follow out. The biologist at first confined himself to collecting the *plankton,* and a start was made in securing water samples for temperature and salinity. In this, from the beginning, he had the help of the geologist, who also gave instructions for the taking of a line of soundings under the charge of the ship's officers. This period of the southward voyage was a very busy time so far as the scientists were concerned, for, besides their own particular work, they took their full share of looking after the dogs and work-

ing the ship watch by watch. At the same time, moreover,
the biologist had to try and avoid being too lavish with his
preserving material at the expense of the shore station collections which were yet to make.

When it was finally known that the ship had no longer any
chance of getting free of the ice in the 1914–1915 season, a
radical change was made in the arrangements. The scientists
were freed, as far as possible, from ship's duties, and were
thus able to devote themselves almost entirely to their own
particular spheres. The meteorological investigations took
on a more definite shape; the instruments intended for the
land base were set up on board ship, including self-record-
ing barographs, thermometers, and a Dines anemometer,
with which very satisfactory results were got. The physicist
set up his quadrant electrometer after a good deal of trouble,
but throughout the winter had to struggle constantly with
rime forming on the parts of his apparatus exposed to the
outer air. Good runs were being thus continually spoilt. The
determination of the magnetic constants also took up a good
part of his time.

Besides collecting *plankton* the biologist was now able to
put down one or other of his dredges at more frequent intervals, always taking care, however, not to exhaust his store
of preserving material, which was limited. The taking of
water samples was established on a better system, so that
the series should be about equally spaced out over the ship's
course. The geologist suppressed all thought of rocks,
though occasionally they were met with in bottom samples;
his work became almost entirely oceanographical, and included a study of the sea ice, of the physiography of the sea
floor as shown by daily soundings, and of the bottom deposits; besides this he helped the biologist in the temperature
and salinity observations.

The work undertaken and accomplished by each member
was as wide as possible; but it was only in keeping with the

spirit of the times that more attention should be paid to work from which practical and economic results were likely to accrue. The meteorologist had always in view the effect of Antarctic climate on the other southern continents, the geologist looked on ice from a seaman's point of view, and the biologist not unwillingly put whales in the forefront of his program. The accounts which follow on these very practical points show how closely scientific work in the Antarctic is in touch with, and helps on the economic development of, the inhabited lands to the north.

SEA-ICE NOMENCLATURE
By J. M. Wordie, M.A. (Cantab.), Lieut. R.F.A.

During the voyage of the *Endurance* it was soon noticed that the terms being used to describe different forms of ice were not always in agreement with those given in Markham's and Mill's glossary in "The Antarctic Manual," 1901. It was the custom, of course, to follow implicitly the terminology used by those of the party whose experience of ice dated back to Captain Scott's first voyage, so that the terms used may be said to be common to all Antarctic voyages of the present century. The principal changes, therefore, in nomenclature must date from the last quarter of the nineteenth century, when there was no one to pass on the traditional usage from the last naval Arctic Expedition in 1875 to the *Discovery* Expedition of 1901. On the latter ship Markham's and Mill's glossary was, of course, used, but apparently not slavishly; founded, as far as sea ice went, on Scoresby's, made in 1820, it might well have been adopted in its entirety, for no writer could have carried more weight than Scoresby the younger, combining as he did more than ten years' whaling experience with high scientific attainments. Above all others he could be accepted both by practical seamen and also by students of ice forms.

That the old terms of Scoresby did not all survive the period of indifference to Polar work, in spite of Markham and Mill, is an indication either that their usefulness has ceased or that the original usage has changed once and for all. A restatement of terms is therefore now necessary. Where possible the actual phrases of Scoresby and of his successors, Markham and Mill, are still used. The principle adopted, however, is to give preference to the words actually used by the Polar seamen themselves.

The following authorities have been followed as closely as possible:

W. Scoresby, Jun., "An Account of the Arctic Regions," 1820, vol. i, pp. 225–233, 238–241.

C. R. Markham and H. R. Mill in "The Antarctic Manual," 1901, pp. xiv–xvi.

J. Payer, "New Lands within the Arctic Circle," 1876, vol. i, pp. 3–14.

W. S. Bruce, "Polar Exploration" in Home University Library, c. 1911, pp. 54–71.

Reference should also be made to the annual publication of the Danish Meteorological Institute showing the Arctic ice conditions of the previous summer. This is published in both Danish and English, so that the terms used there are bound to have a very wide acceptance; it is hoped, therefore, that they may be the means of preventing the Antarctic terminology following a different line of evolution; for but seldom is a seaman found nowadays who knows both Polar regions. On the Danish charts six different kinds of sea ice are marked—namely, unbroken polar ice; land floe; great ice fields; tight pack ice; open ice; bay ice and brash. With the exception of bay ice, which is more generally known as young ice, all these terms pass current in the Antarctic.

Slush or *Sludge.*   The initial stages in the freezing of sea water, when its consistency becomes gluey or soupy. The term is also used (but not commonly) for brash ice still further broken down.

Pancake ice.   Small circular floes with raised rims; due to the breakup in a gently ruffled sea of the newly formed ice into pieces which strike against each other, and so form turned-up edges.

Young Ice.   Applied to all unhummocked ice up to about a foot in thickness. Owing to the fibrous or platy structure, the floes crack easily, and where the ice is not over thick a ship under steam cuts a passage without much difficulty. Young ice may originate from the coalescence of "pancakes," where the water is slightly ruffled; or else be a sheet of "black ice," covered maybe with "ice flowers," formed by the freezing of a smooth sheet of sea water.

In the Arctic it has been the custom to call this form of ice "bay ice"; in the Antarctic, however, the latter term is wrongly used for land floes (fast ice, etc.), and has been so misapplied consistently for fifteen years. The term bay ice should possibly, therefore, be dropped altogether, especially since, even in the Arctic, its meaning is not altogether a rigid one, as it may denote, first, the gluey "slush," which forms when sea water freezes, and, secondly, the firm level sheet ultimately produced.

Land floes.   Heavy but not necessarily hummocked ice, with generally a deep snow covering, which has remained held up in the position of growth by the enclosing nature of some feature of the coast, or by grounded bergs throughout the summer season when most of the ice breaks out. Its thickness is, therefore, above the average. Has been called at various times "fast ice," "coast ice," "land ice," "bay ice" by Shackleton and David and the Charcot Expedition;

and possibly what Drygalski calls *Schelfeis* is not very different.

Floe.　An area of ice, level or hummocked, whose limits are within sight. Includes all sizes between brash on the one hand and fields on the other. "Light floes" are between one and two feet in thickness (anything thinner being "young ice"). Those exceeding two feet in thickness are termed "heavy floes," being generally hummocked, and in the Antarctic, at any rate, covered by fairly deep snow.

Field.　A sheet of ice of such extent that its limits cannot be seen from the masthead.

Hummocking.　Includes all the processes of pressure formation whereby level young ice becomes broken up and built up into

Hummocky Floes.　The most suitable term for what has also been called "old pack" and "screwed pack" by David, and *Scholleneis* by German writers. In contrast to young ice, the structure is no longer fibrous, but becomes spotted or bubbly, a certain percentage of salt drains away, and the ice becomes almost translucent.

The Pack is a term very often used in a wide sense to include any area of sea ice, no matter what form it takes or how disposed. The French term is *banquise de dérive.*

Pack ice.　A more restricted use than the above, to include hummocky floes or close areas of young ice and light floes. Pack ice is "close" or "tight" if the floes constituting it are in contact; "open" if, for the most part, they do not touch. In both cases it hinders, but does not necessarily check, navigation; the contrary holds for

Drift ice.　Loose open ice, where the area of water exceeds that of ice. Generally drift ice is within reach of the swell, and is a stage in the breaking down of pack ice, the size of the floes being much smaller than in the latter. (Scoresby's use of the term drift ice for pieces of ice intermediate in size between floes and brash has, however, quite died out.) The Antarctic or Arctic pack usually has a girdle or fringe of drift ice.

Brash. Small fragments and roundish nodules; the wreck of other kinds of ice.

Bergy Bits. Pieces, about the size of a cottage, of glacier ice or of hummocky pack washed clear of snow.

Growlers. Still smaller pieces of sea ice than the above, greenish in color, and barely showing above water level.

Crack. Any sort of fracture or rift in the sea ice covering.

Lead or *Lane.* Where a crack opens out to such a width as to be navigable. In the Antarctic it is customary to speak of these as leads, even when frozen over to constitute areas of young ice.

Pools. Any enclosed water areas in the pack, where length and breadth are about equal.

METEOROLOGY

By L. D. A. Hussey, B.S.c. (Lond.), Capt. R.G.A.

The meteorological results of the Expedition, when properly worked out and correlated with those from other stations in the southern hemisphere, will be extremely valuable, both for their bearing on the science of meteorology in general, and for their practical and economic applications.

South America is, perhaps, more intimately concerned than any other country, but Australia, New Zealand, and South Africa are all affected by the weather conditions of the Antarctic. Researches are now being carried on which tend to show that the meteorology of the two hemispheres is more interdependent than was hitherto believed, so that a meteorological disturbance in one part of the world makes its presence felt, more or less remotely perhaps, all over the world.

It is evident, therefore, that a complete knowledge of the weather conditions in any part of the world, which it is understood carries with it the ability to make correct forecasts, can never be obtained unless the weather conditions in every other part are known. This makes the need for purely scientific Polar Expeditions so imperative, since our present knowledge of Arctic and Antarctic meteorology is very meager, and to a certain extent unsystematic. What is wanted is a chain of observing stations well equipped with instruments and trained observers stretching across the Antarctic Continent. A series of exploring ships could supplement these observations with others made by them while cruising in the Antarctic Seas. It would pay to do this, even for the benefit accruing to farmers, sailors, and others who are so dependent on the weather.

As an instance of the value of a knowledge of Antarctic weather conditions, it may be mentioned that, as the result of observations and researches carried out at the South Orkneys—a group of sub-Antarctic islands at the entrance to the Weddell Sea—it has been found that a cold winter in that sea is a sure precursor of a drought over the maize- and cereal-bearing area of Argentina three and a half years later. To the farmers the value of this knowledge so far in advance is enormous, and since England has some three hundred million pounds sterling invested in Argentine interests, Antarctic Expeditions have proved, and will prove, their worth even from a purely commercial point of view.

I have given just this one instance to satisfy those who question the utility of Polar Expeditions, but many more could be cited.

As soon as it was apparent that no landing could be made, and that we should have to spend a winter in the ship drifting round with the pack, instruments were set up and observations taken just as if we had been ashore.

A meteorological screen or box was erected on a platform over the stern, right away from the living quarters, and in it were placed the maximum and minimum thermometers, the recording barograph, and thermograph—an instrument which writes every variation of the temperature and pressure on a sheet of paper on a revolving drum—and the standard thermometer, a very carefully manufactured thermometer, with all its errors determined and tabulated. The other thermometers were all checked from this one. On top of the screen a Robinson's anemometer was screwed. This consisted of an upright rod, to the top of which were pivoted four arms free to revolve in a plane at right angles to it. At the end of these arms hemispherical cups were screwed. These were caught by the wind, and the arms revolved at a speed varying with the force of the wind. The speed of the wind could be read off on a dial below the arms.

In addition there was an instrument called a Dines anemometer, which supplied interesting tracings of the force, duration, and direction of the wind. There was an added advantage in the fact that the drum on which these results were recorded was comfortably housed down below, so that one could sit in a comparatively warm room and follow all the varying phases of the blizzard which was raging without. The barometer used was of the Kew standard pattern. When the ship was crushed, all the monthly records were saved, but the detailed tracings, which had been packed up in the hold, were lost. Though interesting they were not really essential. Continuous observations were made during the long drift on the floe, and while on Elephant Island the temperature was taken at midday each day as long as the thermometers lasted. The mortality amongst these instruments, especially those which were tied to a string and swung around, was very high.

A few extracts from the observations taken during 1915—the series for that year being practically complete—

may be of interest. January was dull and overcast, only 7
percent of the observations recording a clear blue sky, 71
percent being completely overcast.

The percentage of clear sky increased steadily up till June
and July, these months showing respectively 42 percent and
45.7 percent. In August 40 percent of the observations were
clear sky, while September showed a sudden drop to 27 percent. October weather was much the same, and November
was practically overcast the whole time, clear sky showing
at only 8 percent of the observations. In December the sky
was completely overcast for nearly 90 percent of the time.

Temperatures on the whole were fairly high, though a
sudden unexpected drop in February, after a series of heavy
northeasterly gales, caused the ship to be frozen in, and effectually put an end to any hopes of landing that year. The
lowest temperature experienced was in July, when $-35°$
Fahr., i.e. 67° below freezing, was reached. Fortunately, as
the sea was one mass of consolidated pack, the air was dry,
and many days of fine bright sunshine occurred. Later on,
as the pack drifted northwards and broke up, wide lanes of
water were formed, causing fogs and mist and dull overcast
weather generally. In short, it may be said that in the Weddell Sea the best weather comes in winter. Unfortunately
during that season the sun also disappears, so that one cannot enjoy it as much as one would like.

As a rule, too, southerly winds brought fine clear weather,
with marked fall in the temperature, and those from the
north were accompanied by mist, fog, and overcast skies,
with comparatively high temperatures. In the Antarctic a
temperature of 30°, i.e. 2° *below* freezing, is considered unbearably hot.

The greatest difficulty that was experienced was due to
the accumulation of rime on the instruments. In low temperatures everything became covered with ice crystals, depos-
ited from the air, which eventually grew into huge blocks.

Sometimes these blocks became dislodged and fell, making it dangerous to walk along the decks. The rime collected on the thermometers, the glass bowl of the sunshine recorder, and the bearings of the anemometer, necessitating the frequent use of a brush to remove it, and sometimes effectively preventing the instruments from recording at all.

One of our worst blizzards occurred on August 1, 1915, which was, for the ship, the beginning of the end. It lasted for four days, with cloudy and overcast weather for the three following days, and from that time onwards we enjoyed very little sun.

The weather that we experienced on Elephant Island can only be described as appalling. Situated as we were at the mouth of a gully, down which a huge glacier was slowly moving, with the open sea in front and to the left, and towering, snow-covered mountains on our right, the air was hardly ever free from snow drift, and the winds increased to terrific violence through being forced over the glacier and through the narrow gully. Huge blocks of ice were hurled about like pebbles, and cases of clothing and cooking utensils were whisked out of our hands and carried away to sea. For the first fortnight after our landing there, the gale blew, at times, at over one hundred miles an hour. Fortunately it never again quite reached that intensity, but on several occasions violent squalls made us very fearful for the safety of our hut. The island was almost continuously covered with a pall of fog and snow, clear weather obtaining occasionally when pack ice surrounded us. Fortunately a series of southwesterly gales had blown all the ice away to the northeast two days before the rescue ship arrived, leaving a comparatively clear sea for her to approach the island.

Being one solitary moving station in the vast expanse of the Weddell Sea, with no knowledge of what was happening anywhere around us, forecasting was very difficult and at times impossible. Great assistance in this direction was af-

forded by copies of Mr. R. C. Mossmann's researches and
papers on Antarctic meteorology, which he kindly supplied
to us.

I have tried to make this very brief account of the meteorological side of the Expedition rather more "popular" than
scientific, since the publication and scientific discussion of
the observations will be carried out elsewhere; but if, while
showing the difficulties under which we had to work, it em-
phasizes the value of Antarctic Expeditions from a purely
utilitarian point of view, and the need for further continuous
research into the conditions obtaining in the immediate
neighborhood of the Pole, it will have achieved its object.

PHYSICS

By R. W. JAMES, M.A. (Cantab.), B.Sc. (Lond.),
Capt. R.E.

OWING TO THE continued drift of the ship with the ice, the
program of physical observations originally made out had
to be considerably modified. It had been intended to set up
recording magnetic instruments at the base, and to take a
continuous series of records throughout the whole period of
residence there, absolute measurements of the earth's hori-
zontal magnetic force, of the dip and declination being taken
at frequent intervals for purposes of calibration. With the
ice continually drifting, and the possibility of the floe cracking at any time, it proved impracticable to set up the recording instruments, and the magnetic observations were confined to a series of absolute measurements taken whenever
opportunity occurred. These measurements, owing to the
drift of the ship, extend over a considerable distance, and
give a chain of values along a line stretching roughly from

77° S. lat. to 69° S. lat. This is not the place to give the actual results; it is quite enough to state that, as might have been expected from the position of the magnetic pole, the values obtained correspond to a comparatively low magnetic latitude, the value of the dip ranging from 63° to 68°.

So far as possible, continuous records of the electric potential gradient in the atmosphere were taken, a form of quadrant electrometer with a boom and ink recording, made by the Cambridge Scientific Instrument Company, being employed. Here again, the somewhat peculiar conditions made work difficult, as the instrument was very susceptible to small changes of level, such as occurred from time to time owing to the pressure of the ice on the ship. An ionium collector, for which the radioactive material was kindly supplied by Mr. F. H. Glew, was used. The chief difficulty to contend with was the constant formation of thick deposits of rime, which either grew over the insulation and spoiled it, or covered up the collector so that it could no longer act. Nevertheless, a considerable number of good records were obtained, which have not yet been properly worked out.

Conditions during the Expedition were very favorable for observations on the physical properties and natural history of sea ice, and a considerable number of results were obtained, which are, however, discussed elsewhere, mention of them being made here since they really come under the heading of physics.

In addition to these main lines of work, many observations of a miscellaneous character were made, including those on the occurrence and nature of parhelia or "mock suns," which were very common, and generally finely developed, and observations of the auroral displays, which were few and rather poor owing to the comparatively low magnetic latitude. Since most of the observations made are of little value without a knowledge of the place where they were made, and since a very complete set of soundings were

also taken, the daily determination of the ship's position was
a matter of some importance. The drift of the ship throws
considerable light on at least one geographical problem, that
of the existence of Morrell Land. The remainder of this ap-
pendix will therefore be devoted to a discussion of the methods used to determine the position of the ship from day to
day.

The latitude and longitude were determined astronomi-
cally every day when the sun or stars were visible, the position thus determined serving as the fixed points between
which the position on days when the sky was overcast could
be interpreted by the process known as "dead reckoning,"
that is to say, by estimating the speed and course of the ship,
taking into account the various causes affecting it. The sky
was often overcast for several days at a stretch, and it was
worthwhile to take a certain amount of care in the matter.
Captain Worsley constructed an apparatus which gave a
good idea of the direction of drift at any time. This consisted
of an iron rod, which passed through an iron tube, frozen
vertically into the ice, into the water below. At the lower
end of the rod, in the water, was a vane. The rod being free
to turn, the vane took up the direction of the current, the
direction being shown by an indicator attached to the top of
the rod. The direction shown depended, of course, on the
drift of the ice relative to the water, and did not take into
account any actual current which may have been carrying
the ice with it, but the true current seems never to have been
large, and the direction of the vane probably gave fairly accurately the direction of the drift of the ice. No exact idea
of the rate of drift could be obtained from the apparatus,
although one could get an estimate of it by displacing the
vane from its position of rest and noticing how quickly it
returned to it, the speed of return being greater the more
rapid the drift. Another means of estimating the speed and
direction of the drift was from the trend of the wire when a

sounding was being taken. The rate and direction of drift appeared to depend almost entirely on the wind velocity and direction at the time. If any true current effect existed, it is not obvious from a rough comparison of the drift with the prevailing wind, but a closer investigation of the figures may show some outstanding effect due to current.* The drift was always to the left of the actual wind direction. This effect is due to the rotation of the earth, a corresponding deviation to the right of the wind direction being noted by Nansen during the drift of the *Fram*. A change in the direction of the wind was often preceded by some hours by a change in the reading of the drift vane. This is no doubt due to the ice to windward being set in motion, the resulting disturbance traveling through the ice more rapidly than the approaching wind.

For the astronomical observations either the sextant or a theodolite was used. The theodolite employed was a light 3″ Vernier instrument by Carey Porter, intended for sledging work. This instrument was fairly satisfactory, although possibly rigidity had been sacrificed to lightness to rather too great an extent. Another point which appears worth mentioning is the following: The foot screws were of brass, the tribrach, into which they fitted, was made of aluminum for the sake of lightness. The two metals have a different coefficient of expansion, and while the feet fitted the tribrach at ordinary temperatures, they were quite loose at temperatures in the region of 20° Fahr. below zero. In any instrument designed for use at low temperatures, care should be taken that parts which have to fit together are made of the same material.

For determining the position in drifting pack ice, the theodolite proved to be a more generally useful instrument than

*Cf. "Scientific Results of Norwegian North Polar Expedition, 1893–96," vol. iii, p. 357.

the sextant. The ice floes are quite steady in really thick pack ice, and the theodolite can be set up and leveled as well as on dry land. The observations, both for latitude and longitude, consist in measuring the altitude of the sun or of a star. The chief uncertainty in this measurement is that introduced by the refraction of light by the air. At very low temperatures the correction to be applied on this account is uncertain, and, if possible, observations should always be made in pairs with a north star and a south star for a latitude, and an east star and a west star for a longitude. The refraction error will then usually mean out. This error affects observations both with the theodolite and the sextant, but in the case of the sextant another cause of error occurs. In using the sextant, the angle between the heavenly body and the visible horizon is measured directly. Even in dense pack-ice, if the observations are taken from the deck of the ship or from a hummock or a low berg, the apparent horizon is usually sharp enough for the purpose. In very cold weather, however, and particularly if there are open leads and pools between the observer and the horizon, there is frequently a great deal of mirage, and the visible horizon may be miraged up several minutes. This will reduce the altitude observed, and corrections on this account are practically impossible to apply. This error may be counterbalanced to some extent by pairing observations as described above, but it by no means follows that the mirage effect will be the same in the two directions. Then again, during the summer months, no stars will be visible, and observations for latitude will have to depend on a single noon sight of the sun. If the sun is visible at midnight its altitude will be too low for accurate observations, and in any case atmospheric conditions will be quite different from those prevailing at noon. In the Antarctic, therefore, conditions are peculiarly difficult for getting really accurate observations, and it is necessary to reduce the probability of error in a single observation as much as possible. When possible, observations of the altitude of a star or of the sun should be taken with the theodolite, since the altitude is referred to the spirit level of the instrument, and is independent of any apparent horizon. During the drift of the *Endurance* both means of observation were generally employed. A comparison of the results showed an agreement between sextant and theodolite within the errors of the instrument if the temperature was above about 20° Fahr. At lower temperatures there were frequently discrepancies which could generally be attributed to the mirage effects described above.

As the *Endurance* was carried by the ice drift well to the west of the Weddell Sea, towards the position of the supposed Morrell Land, the accurate determination of longitude became a matter of moment in view of the controversy as to the existence of this land. During a long voyage latitude can always be determined with about the same accuracy, the accuracy merely depending on the closeness with which altitudes can be measured. In the case of longitude matters are rather different. The usual method employed consists in the determination of the local time by astronomical observations, and the comparison of this time with Greenwich time, as shown by the ship's chronometer, an accurate knowledge of the errors and rate of the chronometer being required. During the voyage of the *Endurance* about fifteen months elapsed during which no check on the chronometers could be obtained by the observation of known land, and had no other check been applied there would have been the probability of large errors in the longitudes. For the purpose of checking the chronometers a number of observations of occultations were observed during the winter of 1915. An occultation is really the eclipse of a star by the moon. A number of such eclipses occur monthly, and are tabulated in the "Nautical Almanac." From the data given there it is possible to compute the Greenwich time at which the phenomenon ought to occur for an observer situated at any place on the earth, provided his position is known within a few miles, which will always be the case. The time of disappearance of the star by the chronometer to be corrected is noted. The actual Greenwich time of the occurrence is calculated, and the error of the chronometer is thus determined. With ordinary care the chronometer error can be determined in this way to within a few seconds, which is accurate enough for purposes of navigation. The principal difficulties of this method lie in the fact that comparatively few occultations occur, and those which do occur are usually of stars of the fifth magnitude or lower. In the Antarctic, conditions for observing occultation are rather favorable during the winter, since fifth-magnitude stars can be seen with a small telescope at any time during the twenty-four hours if the sky is clear, and the moon is also often above the horizon for a large fraction of the time. In the summer, however, the method is quite impossible, since, for some months, stars are not to be seen. No chronometer check could be applied until June 1915. On June 24 a series of four occultations were observed, and the results of the observations showed an error in longitude of a whole degree. In July, August, and September further occultations were observed, and a fairly reliable rate was worked out for the chronometers and watches. After the crushing of the ship on October 27, 1915, no further occultations were observed, but the calculated rates for the watches were employed, and the longitude deduced, using these rates on March 23, 1916, was only about 10' of arc in error, judging by the observations of Joinville Land made on that day. It is thus fairly certain that no large error can have been made in the determination of the position of the *Endurance* at any time during the drift, and her course can be taken as known with greater certainty than is usually the case in a voyage of such length.

SOUTH ATLANTIC WHALES
AND WHALING

By ROBERT S. CLARK, M.A., B.Sc., Lieut. R.N.V.R.

MODERN WHALING METHODS were introduced into sub-Antarctic seas in 1904, and operations commenced in the following year at South Georgia. So successful was the initial
venture that several companies were floated, and the fishing
area was extended to the South Shetlands, the South Orkneys, and as far as 67° S. along the western coast of Graham
Land. This area lies within the Dependencies of the Falkland Islands, and is under the control of the British Government, and its geographical position offers exceptional
opportunities for the successful prosecution of the industry
by providing a sufficient number of safe anchorages and
widely separated islands, where shore stations have been established. The Dependencies of the Falkland Islands lie
roughly within latitude 50° and 65° S. and longitude 25° and
70° W., and include the Falkland Islands, South Georgia,
South Sandwich, South Orkney, and South Shetland Islands, and part of Graham Land.

The industry is prosperous, and the products always find a
ready market. In this sub-Antarctic area alone, the resulting
products more than doubled the world's supply. The total
value of the Falkland Island Dependencies in 1913
amounted to £1,252,432, in 1914 to £1,300,978, in 1915 to
£1,333,401, and in 1916 to £1,774,570. This has resulted
chiefly from the marketing of whale oil and the by-product
guano, and represents for each total a season's capture of
several thousand whales. In 1916 the number of whales captured in this area was 11,860, which included 6000 for
South Georgia alone. Whale oil, which is now the product
of most economic value in the whaling industry, is produced
in four grades (some companies adding a fifth). These are

Nos. 0, I, II, III, IV, which in 1913 sold at £24, £22, £20, and £18 respectively per ton, net weight, barrels included (there are six barrels to a ton). The 1919 prices have increased to

£72 10s. per ton (barrels included) less 2½ percent.
£68 per ton (barrels included) less 2½ percent.
£65 per ton (barrels included) less 2½ percent.
£63 per ton (barrels included) less 2½ percent.

Whale oil can be readily transformed into glycerine: it is used in the manufacture of soap, and quite recently, both in this country and in Norway, it has been refined by means of a simple hardening process into a highly palatable and nutritious margarine. Wartime conditions emphasized the importance of the whale oil, and fortunately the supply was fairly constant for the production of the enormous quantities of glycerine required by the country in the manufacture of explosives. In relation to the food supply it was no less important in saving the country from a "fat" famine when the country was confronted with the shortage of vegetable and other animal oils. The production of guano, bone meal, and flesh meal may pay off the running expenses of a whaling station, but their value lies, perhaps, more in their individual properties. Flesh meal makes up into cattle cake, which forms an excellent fattening food for cattle, while bone meal and guano are very effective fertilizers. Guano is the meat—generally the residue of distillation—which goes through a process of drying and disintegration, and is mixed with the crushed bone in the proportion of two parts flesh to one part bone. This is done chiefly at the shore stations, and to a less extent on floating factories, though so far on the latter it has not proved very profitable. Whale flesh, though slightly greasy perhaps and of strong flavor, is quite palatable, and at South Georgia it made a welcome addition to our bill of

fare—the flesh of the humpback being used. A large supply
of whale flesh was "shipped" as food for the dogs on the
journey South, and this was eaten ravenously. It is interesting to note also the successful rearing of pigs at South Georgia—chiefly, if not entirely, on the whale products. The
whalebone or baleen plates, which at one time formed the
most valuable article of the Arctic fishery, may here be regarded as of secondary importance. The baleen plates of the
southern right whale reach only a length of about 7 ft., and
have been valued at £750 per ton, but the number of these
whales captured is very small indeed. In the case of the
other whalebone whales, the baleen plates are much smaller
and of inferior quality—the baleen of the sei whale probably
excepted, and this only makes about £85 per ton. Sperm
whales have been taken at South Georgia and the South
Shetlands, but never in any quantity, being more numerous
in warmer seas. The products and their value are too well
known to be repeated.

The *Endurance* reached South Georgia on November 5,
1914, and anchored in King Edward Cove, Cumberland
Bay, off Grytviken, the shore station of the Argentina Pesca
Company. During the month's stay at the island a considerable amount of time was devoted to a study of the whales
and the whaling industry, in the intervals of the general routine of expedition work, and simultaneously with other stud-
ies on the general life of this interesting sub-Antarctic
island. Visits were made to six of the seven existing stations,
observations were made on the whales landed, and useful
insight was gathered as to the general working of the industry.

From South Georgia the track of the *Endurance* lay in a
direct line to the South Sandwich Group, between Saunders
and Candlemas Islands. Then southeasterly and southerly
courses were steered to the Coats' Land barrier, along which
we steamed for a few hundred miles until forced westward,

when we were unfortunately held up in about lat. 76° 34' S.
and long. 37° 30' W. on January 19, 1915, by enormous
masses of heavy pack-ice. The ship drifted to lat. 76° 59' S.,
long. 37° 47' W. on March 19, 1915, and then west and
north until crushed in lat. 69° 5' S. and long. 51° 30' W. on
October 26, 1915. We continued drifting gradually north,
afloat on ice floes, past Graham Land and Joinville Island,
and finally took to the boats on April 9, 1916, and reached
Elephant Island on April 15. The Falkland Island Dependencies were thus practically circumnavigated, and it may be
interesting to compare the records of whales seen in the region outside and to the south of this area with the records
and the percentage of each species captured in the intensive
fishing area.

The most productive part of the South Atlantic lies south
of latitude 50° S., where active operations extend to and
even beyond the Antarctic circle. It appears to be the general
rule in Antarctic waters that whales are more numerous the
closer the association with ice conditions, and there seems
to be reasonable grounds for supposing that this may ex-
plain the comparatively few whales sighted by Expeditions
which have explored the more northerly and more open
seas, while the whalers themselves have even asserted that
their poor seasons have nearly always coincided with the
absence of ice, or with poor ice conditions. At all events,
those Expeditions which have penetrated far south and well
into the pack-ice have, without exception, reported the presence of whales in large numbers, even in the farthest south
latitudes, so that our knowledge of the occurrence of whales
in the Antarctic has been largely derived from these Expeditions, whose main object was either the discovery of new
land or the Pole itself. The largest number of Antarctic Expeditions has concentrated on the two areas of the South
Atlantic and the Ross Sea, and the records of the occur-
rences of whales have, in consequence, been concentrated

in these two localities. In the intervening areas, however, Expeditions, notably the *Belgica* on the western side and the *Gauss* on the eastern side of the Antarctic continent, have reported whales in moderately large numbers, so that the stock is by no means confined to the two areas above mentioned.

The effective fishing area may be assumed to lie within a radius of a hundred miles from each shore station and floating factory anchorage, and a rough estimate of all the Falkland stations works out at 160,000 square miles. The total for the whole Falkland area is about 2,000,000 square miles, which is roughly less than a sixth of the total Antarctic sea area. The question then arises as to how far the "catch percentage" during the short fishing season affects the total stock, but so far one can only conjecture as to the actual results from a comparison of the numbers seen, chiefly by scientific and other Expeditions, in areas outside the intensive fishing area with the numbers and percentage of each species captured in the intensive fishing area. Sufficient evidence, however, seems to point quite definitely to one species—the humpback—being in danger of extermination, but the blue and fin whales—the other two species of rorquals which form the bulk of the captures—appear to be as frequent now as they have ever been.

The whales captured at the various whaling stations of the Falkland area are confined largely to three species—blue whale (*Balænoptera musculus*), fin whale (*Balænoptera physalus*), and humpback (*Megaptera nodosa*); sperm whales (*Physeter catodon*) and right whales (*Balæna glacialis*) being only occasional and rare captures, while the sei whale (*Balænoptera borealis*) appeared in the captures at South Georgia in 1913, and now forms a large percentage of the captures at the Falkland Islands. During the earlier years of whaling at South Georgia, and up to the fishing season 1910–11, humpbacks formed practically the total

catch. In 1912–13 the following were the percentages for
the three rorquals in the captures at South Georgia and
South Shetlands:

Humpback 38 percent, fin whale 36 percent, blue whale
20 percent. Of late years the percentages have altered considerably, blue whales and fin whales predominating, humpbacks decreasing rapidly. In 1915 the South Georgia
Whaling Company (Messrs. Salvesen, Leith) captured 1085
whales, consisting of 15 percent humpback, 25 percent fin
whales, 58 percent blue whales, and 2 right whales. In the
same year the captures of three companies at the South
Shetlands gave 1512 whales, and the percentages worked
out at 12 percent humpbacks, 42 percent fin whales, and
45 percent blue whales. In 1919 the Southern Whaling and
Sealing Company captured (at Stromness, South Georgia)
529 whales, of which 2 percent were humpbacks, 51 percent
fin whales, and 45 percent blue whales. These captures do
not represent the total catch, but are sufficiently reliable to
show how the species are affected. The reduction in numbers of the humpback is very noticeable, and even allowing
for the possible increase in size of gear for the capture of
the larger and more lucrative blue and fin whales, there is
sufficient evidence to warrant the fears that the humpback
stock is threatened with extinction.

In the immediate northern areas—in the region from latitude 50° S. northward to the equator, which is regarded as
next in importance quantitatively to the sub-Antarctic,
though nothing like being so productive, the captures are
useful for a comparative study in distribution. At Saldanha
Bay, Cape Colony, in 1912, 131 whales were captured and
the percentages were as follows: 36 percent humpback, 13
percent fin whale, 4 percent blue whale, 46 percent sei
whale; while nearer the equator, at Port Alexander, the total
capture was 322 whales, and the percentages gave 98 percent humpback, and only 2 captures each of fin and sei

whales. In 1914, at South Africa (chiefly Saldanha Bay and Durban), out of a total of 839 whales 60 percent were humpback, 25 percent fin whales, and 13 percent blue whales. In 1916, out of a total of 853 whales 10 percent were humpback, 13 percent fin whales, 6 percent blue whales, 68 percent sperm whales, and 1 percent sei whales. In Chilean waters, in 1916, a total of 327 whales gave 31 percent humpbacks, 24 percent fin whales, 26 percent blue whales, 12 percent sperm whales, and 5 right whales. There seems then to be a definite interrelation between the two areas. The same species of whales are captured, and the periods of capture alternate with perfect regularity, the fishing season occurring from the end of November to April in the sub-Antarctic and from May to November in the sub-tropics. A few of the companies, however, carry on operations to a limited extent at South Georgia and at the Falkland Islands during the southern winter, but the fishing is by no means a profitable undertaking, though proving the presence of whales in this area during the winter months.

The migrations of whales are influenced by two causes:

(1) The distribution of their food supply;
(2) The position of their breeding grounds.

In the Antarctic, during the summer months, there is present in the sea an abundance of plant and animal life, and whales which feed on the small *plankton* organisms are correspondingly numerous, but in winter this state of things is reversed, and whales are poorly represented or absent, at least in the higher latitudes. During the drift of the *Endurance* samples of *plankton* were taken almost daily during an Antarctic summer and winter. From December to March, a few minutes' haul of a tow net at the surface was sufficient to choke up the meshes with the plant and animal life, but this abundance of surface life broke off abruptly in April, and subsequent hauls contained very small organisms until the return of daylight and the opening up of the pack ice. The lower water strata, down to about 100 fathoms, were only a little more productive, and *Euphausiæ* were taken in the hauls—though sparingly. During the winter spent at Elephant Island, our total catch of gentoo penguins amounted to 1436 for the period April 15 to August 30, 1916. All these birds were cut up, the livers and hearts were extracted for food, and the skins were used as fuel. At the same time the stomachs were invariably examined, and a record kept of the contents. The largest proportion of these contained the small crustacean *Euphausia,* and this generally to the exclusion of other forms. Occasionally, however, small fish were recorded. The quantity of *Euphausiæ* present in most of the stomachs was enormous for the size of the birds. These penguins were migrating, and came ashore only when the bays were clear of ice, as there were several periods of fourteen consecutive days when the bays and the surrounding sea were covered over with a thick compact mass of ice floes, and then penguins were entirely absent. *Euphausiæ,* then, seem to be present in sufficient quantity in certain, if not in all, sub-Antarctic waters during the southern winter. We may assume then that the migration to the south, during the Antarctic summer, is definitely in search of food. Observations have proved the existence of a northern migration, and it seems highly improbable that this should also be in search of food, but rather for breeding purposes, and it seems that the whales select the more temperate regions for the bringing forth of their young. This view is strengthened by the statistical fetal records, which show that pairing takes place in the northern areas, that the fetus is carried by the mother during the southern migration to the Antarctic, and that the calves are born in the more congenial waters north of the sub-Antarctic area. We have still to prove, however, the pos-

sibility of a circumpolar migration, and we are quite in the
dark as to the number of whales that remain in sub-Antarctic
areas during the Southern winter.

The following is a rough classification of whales, with
special reference to those known to occur in the South Atlantic:

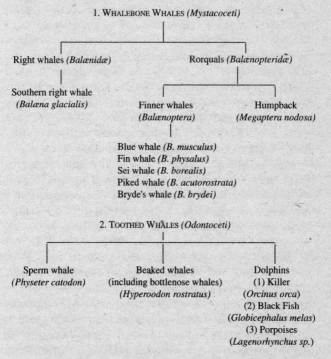

1. WHALEBONE WHALES *(Mystacoceti)*

Right whales *(Balænidæ)*

Southern right whale
(Balæna glacialis)

Rorquals *(Balænopteridæ)*

Finner whales
(Balænoptera)

Blue whale *(B. musculus)*
Fin whale *(B. physalus)*
Sei whale *(B. borealis)*
Piked whale *(B. acutorostrata)*
Bryde's whale *(B. brydei)*

Humpback
(Megaptera nodosa)

2. TOOTHED WHALES *(Odontoceti)*

Sperm whale
(Physeter catodon)

Beaked whales
(including bottlenose whales)
(Hyperoodon rostratus)

Dolphins
(1) Killer
(Orcinus orca)
(2) Black Fish
(Globicephalus melas)
(3) Porpoises
(Lagenorhynchus sp.)

The subdivision of whalebone whales is one of degree in
the size of the whalebone. These whales have enormously
muscular tongues, which press the water through the whalebone lamellae and thus, by a filtering process, retain the
small food organisms. The food of the whalebone whales is
largely the small crustacea which occur in the *plankton,*

though some whales (humpback, fin whales, and sei whales)
feed also on fish. The stomachs examined at South Georgia
during December 1914 belonged to the three species, humpbacks, fin whales, and blue whales, and all contained small
crustacea—*Euphausiæ,* with a mixture of *Amphipods.* The
toothed whales—sperms and bottlenoses—are known to
live on *squids,* and that there is an abundance of this type of
food in the Weddell Sea was proved by an examination of
penguin and sea stomachs. Emperor penguins (and hundreds of these were examined) were invariably found to contain *Cephalopod* "beaks," while large, partly digested
squids were often observed in Weddell seals. A dorsal fin is
present in the rorquals but absent in right whales. With other
characters, notably the size of the animal, it serves as a
ready mark of identification, but is occasionally confusing
owing to the variation in shape in some of the species.

With the exception of several schools of porpoises very
few whales were seen during the outward voyage. Not till
we approached the Falkland area did they appear in any
numbers. Four small schools of fin whales and a few humpbacks were sighted on October 28 and 29, 1914, in lat. 38°
01′ S., long. 55° 03′ W. and in lat. 40° 35′ S., long. 53° 11′
W., while *Globicephalus melas* was seen only once, in lat.
45° 17′ S., long. 48° 58′ W., on October 31, 1914. At South
Georgia the whales captured at the various stations in December 1914 were blue whales, fin whales, and humpbacks
(arranged respectively according to numbers captured).
During the fishing season 1914–15 (from December to
March) in the area covered—South Georgia to the South
Sandwich Islands and along Coats' Land to the head of the
Weddell Sea—the records of whales were by no means nu-
merous. Two records only could with certainty be assigned
to the humpback, and these were in the neighborhood of the
South Sandwich Islands. Pack-ice was entered in lat. 59° 55′
S., long. 18° 28′ W., and blue whales were recorded daily

until about 65° S. Between lat. 65° 43′ S., long. 17° 30′ W., on December 27, 1914, and lat. 69° 59′ S., long. 17° 31′ W., on January 3, 1915, no whales were seen. On January 4, however, in lat. 69° 59′ S., long. 17° 36′ W., two large sperm whales appeared close ahead of the ship in fairly open water, and were making westward. They remained sufficiently long on the surface to render their identification easy. Farther south, blue whales were only seen occasionally, and in fin whales could only be identified in one or two cases. Killers, however, were numerous, and the lesser piked whale was quite frequent. There was no doubt about the identity of this latter species as it often came close alongside the ship. From April to September (inclusive) the sea was frozen over (with the exception of local "leads"), and whales were found to be absent. In October whales again made their appearance, and from then onwards they were a daily occurrence. Identification of the species, however, was a difficult matter, for the *Endurance* was crushed and had sunk, and observations were only possible from the ice floe, or later on from the boats. The high vertical "spout" opening out into a dense spray was often visible, and denoted the presence of blue and fin whales. The lesser piked whale again appeared in the "leads" close to our "camp" floe, and was easily identified. An exceptional opportunity was presented to us on December 6, 1915, when a school of eight bottlenose whales (*Hyperoodon rostratus*) appeared in a small "pool" alongside "Ocean" Camp in lat. 67° 47′ S., long. 52° 18′ W. These ranged from about 20 ft. to a little over 30 ft. in length, and were of a uniform dark dun color—the large specimens having a dull yellow appearance. There were no white spots. At the edge of the pack ice during the first half of April 1916, about lat. 62° S. and long. 54° W. (entrance to Bransfield Strait), whales were exceedingly numerous, and these were chiefly fin whales, though a few seemed to be sei whales. It is interesting to note that the fishing season

1915–1916 was exceptionally productive—no less than 11,860 whales having been captured in the Falkland area alone.

The South Atlantic whaling industry, then, has reached a critical stage in development. It is now dependent on the captures of the large fin and blue whales, humpbacks having been rapidly reduced in numbers, so that the total stock appears to have been affected. With regard to the other species, the southern right whale has never been abundant in the captures, the sperm whale and the sei whale have shown a good deal of seasonal variation, though never numerous, and the bottlenose and lesser piked whale have so far not been hunted, except in the case of the latter for human food. The vigorous slaughter of whales both in the sub-Antarctic and in the sub-tropics, for the one area reacts on the other, calls for universal legislation to protect the whales from early commercial extinction, and the industry, which is of worldwide economic importance, from having to be abandoned. The British Government, with the control of the world's best fisheries, is thoroughly alive to the situation, and an Inter-departmental Committee, under the direction of the Colonial Office, is at present devising a workable scheme for suitable legislation for the protection of the whales and for the welfare of the industry.

THE EXPEDITION HUTS
AT McMURDO SOUND

By Sir E. H. Shackleton

The following notes are designed for the benefit of future explorers who may make McMurdo Sound a base for inland operations, and to clear any inaccuracies or ambiguities concerning the history, occupation, and state of these huts.

(1) The National Antarctic Expedition's Hut at Hut Point—the Head of McMurdo Sound

This hut was constructed by Captain Scott in 1902, by the Expedition sent out by the Royal Geographical Society, the Royal Society, the Government, and by private subscription. Captain Robert F. Scott was appointed to the command of the Expedition. I served as Third Lieutenant until February 1903, when I was invalided home through a broken blood vessel in the lungs, the direct result of scurvy contracted on the Southern journey. The *Discovery* hut was a large strong building, but was so draughty and cold in comparison with the ship, which was moored one hundred yards away, that it was, during the first year, never used for living quarters. Its sole use was as a storehouse, and a large supply of rough stores, such as flour, cocoa, coffee, biscuit, and tinned meat, was left there in the event of its being used as a place of retreat should any disaster overtake the ship. During the second year occasional parties camped inside the hut, but no bunks or permanent sleeping quarters were ever erected. The discomfort of the hut was a byword on the Expedition, but it formed an excellent depot and starting point for all parties proceeding to the south.

When the *Discovery* finally left McMurdo Sound, the hut was stripped of all gear, including the stove, but there was left behind a large depot of the stores mentioned above. I was not aware of this until I returned to McMurdo Sound in February 1908, when I sent Adams, Joyce, and Wild across to the hut while the *Nimrod* was lying off the ice.

On the return of the party they reported that the door had been burst open, evidently by a southerly blizzard, and was jammed by snow outside and in, so they made an entrance through one of the lee windows. They found the hut practically clear of snow, and the structure quite intact. I used the hut in the spring, i.e. September and October 1908, as a storehouse for the large amount of equipment, food, and oil that we were to take on the Southern journey. We built a sort of living room out of the cases of provisions, and swept out the debris. The Southern Party elected to sleep there before the start, but the supporting party slept outside in the tents, as they considered it warmer.

We still continued to use the lee window as means of ingress and egress to avoid continual shoveling away of the snow, which would be necessary as every southerly blizzard blocked up the main entrance. The various depot parties made use of the hut for replenishing their stores, which had been sledged from my own hut to Hut Point. On the night of March 3, 1909, I arrived with the Southern Party, with a sick man, having been absent on the march 128 days. Our position was bad, as the ship was north of us. We tried to burn the Magnetic Hut in the hope of attracting attention from the ship, but were not able to get it to light. We finally managed to light a flare of carbide, and the ship came down to us in a blizzard, and all were safely aboard at 1 a.m. on March 4, 1909. Before leaving the hut we jammed the window up with baulks of timber, to the best of our ability in the storm and darkness. The hut was used again by the Ross Sea Section of this last Expedition. The snow was cleared out and extra stores were placed in it. From reports I have received the *Discovery* Hut was in as good condition in 1917 as it was in 1902. The stores placed there in 1902 are intact. There are a few cases of extra provisions and oil in the hut, but no sleeping gear or accommodation, nor stoves, and it must not be looked upon as anything else than a shelter and a most useful *pied-à-terre* for the start of any Southern journey. No stores nor any equipment have been taken from it during either of my two Expeditions.

(2) CAPE ROYDS HUT

For several reasons, when I went into McMurdo Sound in 1908 in command of my own Expedition, known as the British Antarctic Expedition, after having failed to land on King Edward VII Land, I decided to build our hut at Cape Royds—a small promontory twenty-three miles north of Hut Point. Here the whole shore party lived in comfort through the winter of 1908. When spring came stores were sledged to Hut Point, so that should the sea ice break up early between these two places we might not be left in an awkward position. After the return of the Southern Party we went direct north to civilization, so I never visited my hut again. I had left, however, full instructions with Professor David as to the care of the hut, and before the whole Expedition left the hut was put in order. A letter was pinned in a conspicuous place inside, stating that there were sufficient provisions and equipment to last fifteen men for one year, indicating also the details of these provisions and the position of the coal store. The stove was in good condition, and the letter ended with an invitation for any succeeding party to make what use they required of stores and hut. The hut was then locked and the key nailed on the door in a conspicuous place. From the report of Captain Scott's last Expedition the hut was in good condition, and from a still later report from the Ross Sea side of this present Expedition the hut was still intact.

(3) CAPE EVANS HUT

This large and commodious hut was constructed by Captain Scott at Cape Evans on his last Expedition. The party lived in it in comfort, and it was left well supplied with stores in the way of food and oil and a certain amount of coal. Several of the scientific staff of this present Expedition were ashore in it, when the *Aurora,* which was to have been the permanent winter quarters, broke adrift in May 1915 and went north with the ice. The hut became the permanent living quarters for the ten marooned men, and thanks to the stores they were able to sustain life in comparative comfort, supplementing these stores from my hut at Cape Royds. In January 1917, after I had rescued the survivors, I had the hut put in order and locked up.

To sum up, there are three available huts in McMurdo Sound.

(*a*) The *Discovery* Hut, with a certain amount of rough stores, and only of use as a point of departure for the South.

(*b*) Cape Royds Hut, with a large amount of general stores but no clothing or equipment now.

(*c*) Cape Evans Hut, with a large amount of stores but no clothing or equipment and only a few sledges.

(4) DEPOTS SOUTH OF HUT POINT

In spite of the fact that several depots have been laid to the south of Hut Point on the Barrier, the last being at the Gap (the entrance to the Beardmore Glacier), no future Expedition should depend on them as the heavy snowfall obliterates them completely. There is no record of the depots of any Expedition being made use of by any subsequent Expedition. No party in any of my Expeditions has used any depot laid down by a previous Expedition.

INDEX